CRITICAL PEDAGOGY AND THE COVID-19 PANDEMIC

Also available from Bloomsbury

Education, Equality and Justice in the New Normal, edited by Inny Accioly
and Donaldo Macedo
Race, Politics, and Pandemic Pedagogy, Henry A. Giroux
*Postdigital Dialogues on Critical Pedagogy, Liberation Theology and Information
Technology*, Peter McLaren and Petar Jandrić
Critical Pedagogy for Healing, edited by Tricia M. Kress, Christopher Emdin
and Robert Lake
Transnational Feminist Politics, Education, and Social Justice,
edited by Silvia Edling and Sheila Macrine
Pedagogy of Hope, Paulo Freire
Pedagogy of the Heart, Paulo Freire
Pedagogy in Process, Paulo Freire
Education for Critical Consciousness, Paulo Freire

CRITICAL PEDAGOGY AND THE COVID-19 PANDEMIC

Keeping Communities Together in Times of Crisis

Edited by Fatma Mızıkacı and Eda Ata

BLOOMSBURY ACADEMIC
LONDON • NEW YORK • OXFORD • NEW DELHI • SYDNEY

BLOOMSBURY ACADEMIC
Bloomsbury Publishing Plc
50 Bedford Square, London, WC1B 3DP, UK
1385 Broadway, New York, NY 10018, USA
29 Earlsfort Terrace, Dublin 2, Ireland

BLOOMSBURY, BLOOMSBURY ACADEMIC and the Diana logo are trademarks
of Bloomsbury Publishing Plc

First published in Great Britain 2022

Cover design: Charlotte James
Cover artwork "screens" by Hazal Aksoydan (hazalaksoydan@gmail.com)

ISBN: HB: 978-1-3502-7488-4
       PB: 978-1-3502-7487-7
       ePDF: 978-1-3502-7489-1
       eBook: 978-1-3502-7490-7

Typeset by RefineCatch Limited, Bungay, Suffolk

To find out more about our authors and books visit www.bloomsbury.com
and sign up for our newsletters.

This book is dedicated to the centennial of the birth of Paulo Freire, to the victims of discrimination, to the victims of racism, who suffer from all types of antidemocratic and inhuman minds and their practices.

CONTENTS

Part I
NEW CULTURAL AND SOCIAL AGENDAS OF TOTALITARIAN REGIMES AND THEIR INFLUENCE ON EDUCATION IN THE TIME OF THE COVID-19 PANDEMIC

FIGURES

CONTRIBUTORS

Zeynep Alica is a teacher of English who has worked at different state schools for twenty years and is a PhD candidate in the Department of Adult Education and Lifelong Learning, Ankara University, Ankara, Turkey. Her research interests focus on transformative learning theory, social movement learning, feminist pedagogy and feminism as a social movement. She is writing her doctorate dissertation on transformative learning experiences of feminist activists. She co-edited a book with N. Samet Baykal and Ayhan Ural, titled, *Eleştirel Eğitim Seçkisi* (2014.)

Michael W. Apple is Professor of Curriculum and Instruction and Educational Policy Studies at the University of Wisconsin-Madison School of Education, Madison, Wisconsin, USA, where he has taught since 1970. Professor Apple is one of the foremost educational theorists in the world and a public intellectual, who is deeply committed to the empowerment and transformation of people through education. Michael specializes in understanding and analysing the relations between education and power. He has made major contributions to the fields of cultural politics, curriculum theory and research, and critical teaching. He has been a tireless advocate and activist-theorist for the development of democratic schools over four decades. He began teaching in elementary and secondary schools in New Jersey, where he grew up and served as president of the local teachers' union. He has spent his career working with educators, unions, dissident and disadvantaged groups throughout the world on democratizing educational policy and practice. Professor Apple's research centres on the limits and possibilities of critical educational policy and practice in a time of conservative restoration. He is the author and editor of many works, including: *Education and Power* (1995); *Ideology and Curriculum* (2004); *Can Education Change Society?* (2013); editor, *Global Crises, Social Justice, and Education* (2010); and co-editor with James A. Beane, *Democratic Schools* (2007). His books have been widely translated and published into many editions.

Eda Ata is Lecturer and currently pursuing a PhD in Lifelong Learning and Adult Education at the Faculty of Educational Sciences at Ankara University, Ankara, Turkey. She has been teaching, designing and coordinating English for Academic Purposes (EAP) courses at undergraduate level. Eda has a BA in Linguistics and an MSc in Adult Education. She has translated works by leading scholars from English to Turkish, including book chapters by Peter McLaren, *Essays on Critical Education* (2014); and Dave Hill, *Critical Education and Marxism* (2016). She has also published book reviews, interviews and poetry translation files in national literature magazines such as *Varlık* and *Hece*, along with several translations in the *Journal of Critical Pedagogy*. Eda recently wrote a short story in, *Hand to Hand: Transformative Activism Stories*, edited by Ebru Nihan Celkan, Sema Semih, Özge Ertem and Ayşe Gül Altınay (forthcoming). Eda is interested in volunteering for gender equality and is working on her thesis on ageing and activism.

Murat Ata is an English instructor at the Middle East Technical University, Northern Cyprus Campus, Mersin, Cyprus. He is also a PhD student in English Language Teaching at Eastern Mediterranean University, Gazimağusa, Cyprus. His research interests include educational technologies, machine translation, critical theory, global English and postcolonial theory. Murat co-wrote with Emre Debreli the article, 'Machine Translation in the Language Classroom: Turkish EFL Learners' and Instructors' Perceptions and Use', *IAFOR Journal of Education* (2021)

Ali Tansu Balcı is a PhD student at the Department of Lifelong Learning and Adult Education, Ankara University, Ankara, Turkey. His research interests are education policies, critical education and adult education. Ali's dissertation is titled, 'Social Transformation and Individual Empowerment in Agricultural Cooperatives as a Learning Environment'.

Antonia Darder is a distinguished international Freirian scholar. She is a public intellectual, educator, writer, activist and artist. Antonia holds the Leavey Presidential Endowed Chair of Ethics and Moral Leadership at Loyola Marymount University, Los Angeles, California, USA; is Distinguished Visiting Professor of Education at the University of Johannesburg, Johannesburg, South Africa; and Professor Emerita of Education Policy, Organization, and Leadership at the University of Illinois Urbana-Champaign, Champaign, Illinois, USA. She is an American Educational Research Association Fellow and recipient of the American Educational Research Association Scholars of Color Lifetime Contribution Award, as well as the Freire Social Justice Award and the Paulo Freire Legacy Award. Antonia has worked tirelessly for almost forty years to fiercely counter social and material inequalities in schools and communities. The author of numerous books and articles, her scholarship has consistently focused on issues of racism, political economy, social justice, education and society. Among recent publications are: 'Decolonizing University Leadership: Transforming What it Means to Lead', in João M. Paraskeva (ed.), *Critical Transformative Educational Leadership and Policy Studies: A Reader* (2021); and co-wrote with Sharon Cronin, 'Reflections on the Decolonising Dance Praxis of Grupo Bayano', *Arts, Culture and Community Development* (2021). Through her writings, she has extended the contributions of Paulo Freire to our understanding of inequalities in schools and society. Professor Darder's critical theory of biculturalism links human development questions to issues of culture, power and pedagogy. Through her decolonizing scholarship on the body, ethics and methodology, she has contributed to rethinking questions of empowerment and liberation in the lives of subaltern populations.

Henry A. Giroux currently holds the McMaster University Chair for Scholarship in the Public Interest in the English and Cultural Studies Department and is the Paulo Freire Distinguished Scholar in Critical Pedagogy, McMaster University, Hamilton, Ontario, Canada. His most recent books include: *American Nightmare: Facing the Challenge of Fascism* (2018); *The Terror of the Unforeseen* (2019); *Neoliberalism's War on Higher Education* (2020); *On Critical Pedagogy* (Bloomsbury, 2020); and *Race, Politics, and Pandemic Pedagogy: Education in a Time of Crisis* (Bloomsbury, 2021).

Kemal İnal is Professor in the Department of Educational Sciences at Helmut Schmidt University, Hamburg, Germany. His research interests focus on Critical Pedagogy, criticism of the Turkish education system, the Kurdish Question in terms of language in education, secularism and religious education in Europe, and literacy. He has published on the critical analysis of the Turkish education system and sociology of pedagogy on teaching and teachers in Turkey. Professor İnal's most recent books are, *Literacy in the Digital Age* (2020); and *Village Institutes in Turkey* (2020).

Peter Mayo is Professor at the University of Malta, Msida, Malta. Professor Mayo is regarded as a leading international figure in critical pedagogy, adult education and on Paulo Freire and Antonio Gramsci. He has made distinctive contributions to Sociology of Education. He has produced twenty-two books, published by leading publishers such as Routledge, Rowman & Littlefield, Zed Books, Zer0 Books, Praeger, Brill-Sense, Bloomsbury Academic and Peter Lang. He is the author of *Higher Education in a Globalising World* (2019). Four of his books were translated into Turkish. His book on Gramsci and Freire was published in eight languages, with publishers including Argument in Germany and ArteMedicas in Brazil. Last year, he was inducted into the International Adult Continuing Education Hall of Fame.

Peter McLaren is Distinguished Professor in Critical Studies, College of Educational Studies, Chapman University, Orange, California, USA, where he is Co-Director of the Paulo Freire Democratic Project and International Ambassador for Global Ethics and Social Justice. He is also Emeritus Professor of Urban Educatfion, University of California, Los Angeles, and Emeritus Professor of Educational Leadership, Miami University of Ohio, USA. He is also Honorary Director of Center for Critical Studies in Education in Northeast Normal University, Jilin, Nanguan District, China. He is the author and editor of over forty-five books and hundreds of scholarly articles and chapters, including: 'Introduction', *Dialogues in Social Justice: An Adult Education Journal* (2021); 'Networked Religion: Metaphysical Redemption or Eternal Regret?', *Postdigital Science and Education* (2021); and co-authored with Petar Jandrić, 'From Learning Loss to Learning Opportunity', *Educational Philosophy and Theory* (2021). His writings have been translated into over twenty languages.

Fatma Mızıkacı is Professor and the Chair for the Curriculum and Instruction Division at the Faculty of Educational Sciences, Ankara University, Ankara, Turkey. Her recent books are: co-editor with Fatma Bıkmaz, *Curriculum, Teachers and Technology: A Turkish Context* (2021); *Higher Education in Turkey* (2019); translation editor of Michael Stephen Schiro, *Curriculum Theory: Conflicting Visions and Enduring Concerns* (2020); co-editor with Guy Senese, *A Language of Freedom and Teacher's Authority: Case Comparisons from Turkey and the United States* (2017). She has also published, 'The Challenges of Intercultural Understanding in the Central Asia Countries: Achieving Partnership through Higher Education,' in Peter J. Wells and Eric Gilder (eds), *Eurasian Inter-University Dialogue for Higher Education Development* (2011); and, 'The Role of Education and Ideology in Re-building Nation-States in Post-Soviet Societies, in Andrea Friedli, Aline Gohard-Radenkovic and François Ruegg (eds), *Nation-Building and Identities in Post-Soviet Societies* (2017).

Liv Mjelde is Professor Emeritus in Vocational Pedagogy in the Senior Centre, Oslo Metropolitan University, Oslo, Norway. She is a sociologist, specialised in Sociology of Education. Her research interests focus on the changing relations between vocational and general education from psychological, didactic and sociological perspectives. One of her main research fields is the gender divisions of labour. Her scientific work is published in several languages, and she is the author of *Secrets in a Pair of Scissors: Wartime Russian Women's labour and Life in Prison Camps in Northern Norway 1942–1945* (2018).

Arnd-Michael Nohl is Professor for the Foundations of Education in the Faculty of Humanities and Social Sciences at Helmut Schmidt University, and the University of the German Armed Forces, Hamburg, Germany. His research interests focus on systematic questions of education, qualitative social research, the materiality of learning and intercultural education. Professor Nohl has published on the methodology of qualitative research, transformative learning, directive education and foundations of education. He co-authored with Karin Schittenhelm, Oliver Schmidtke and Anja Weiß, *Work in Transition: Cultural Capital and Highly Skilled Migrants' Passages into the Labour Market* (2014) and co-authored with R. Nazlı Somel, *Education and Social Dynamics: A Multilevel Analysis of Curriculum Change in Turkey* (2019).

Nurcan Saltoğlu Özleyen is an instructor of English in the Department of Foreign Languages, at the TOBB University of Economics and Technology, Ankara, Turkey. Her interest areas are curriculum design, cultural studies, literature and media culture. As a Teaching English to Speakers of Other Languages (TESOL) certified instructor, she presented on various classroom practices at national conferences. Nurcan's publications include: 'A Tale of Professional Development', *TESOL Turkey Online Magazine*, 'Reflections on TESOL Experience' (2017); and 'Together Everyone Achieves More', *TESOL Turkey Online Magazine*, 'Reflections on a "Team Teaching" Experience' (2018).

Gamze Gonca Özyurt is a mathematics teacher and PhD candidate at Ankara University, Ankara, Turkey. Her research interests focus on adult education, numeracy and literacy and critical pedagogy. She has worked as an educator and a researcher in different public institutions and coordinated international projects in the field of adult education and youth. Gamze recently wrote a book chapter and it is published as a values education resource, 'Character and Values Education Approaches and Practices', in S. Tunay Kamer (ed.), *Character and Values Education in the Context of Society and Culture* (2021).

E. Wayne Ross is Professor in the Department of Curriculum and Pedagogy at the University of British Columbia, Vancouver, Canada. He is interested in the influence of social and institutional contexts on teachers' practice as well as the role of curriculum and teaching in building a democratic society in the face of antidemocratic impulses of greed, individualism and intolerance. Professor Ross's most recent book is, *Rethinking Social Studies: Critical Pedagogy and the Pursuit of Dangerous Citizenship* (2017).

Fevziye Sayılan worked as Associate Professor at the Department of Lifelong Learning and Adult Education at the Faculty of Educational Sciences, Ankara University, Ankara, Turkey, for many years and retired in 2020. She has also been involved in the Women Studies Centre at Ankara University. Professor Sayılan has published widely on issues relating to gender and education, popular education, transformative learning, neoconservative and neoliberal educational policies in several journals. She was on the editorial boards of the *International Journal of Critical Pedagogy* and *Journal of Adult Education* for many years.

Guy Senese is Adjunct Professor in Sociology of Education at Pima Community College in Tucson, Arizona, USA. He is Emeritus Professor in Educational Leadership and Social Foundations of Education at Northern Arizona University, Flagstaff, Arizona, USA. He was a Fulbright Visiting Scholar in Turkey at Ankara University, in 2014–15, and Guest Lecturer at Middle Eastern Technical University, in Ankara, in 2018. Professor Senese taught high school Social Studies at the first Native community-controlled public school, the Rough Rock Demonstration School, on the Navajo Nation reservation in Arizona. He has published in the fields of Native American education, critical theory and pedagogy, and autoethnographic critical studies in education. Professor Senese is the author of numerous publications, including: *Self-Determination and the Social Education of Native Americans* (1991); *Throwing Voices: Five Autoethnographies on Postradical Education and the Fine Art of Misdirection* (2007); with Ralph Page, *Simulation, Spectacle and the Ironies of Education Reform* (1995); and co-authored with Steven E. Tozar, *School and Society: Historical and Contemporary Perspectives*, 8th edn (2020). Guy Senese is the co-editor with Fatma Mızıkacı and associate editors Yasemin Tezgiden-Cakcak and Sharon Gorman, of *The Language of Freedom and Teachers Authority: Case Comparisons from Turkey and the US* (2017).

Ira Shor is Professor Emeritus at the Graduate Center, City University of New York, New York, USA. He wrote the first book-length text on adapting Paulo Freire's methods to North American classrooms, *Critical Teaching and Everyday Life* (1980). Ira was also the first educator to co-author a dialogic book with Freire, *A Pedagogy for Liberation* (1987), which was translated into Portuguese, Spanish, Greek, Hebrew and Chinese editions. Professor Shor had a long career teaching working-class students and travelling to give talks and workshops.

Yasemin Tezgiden-Cakcak holds a PhD and is a scholar at the Foreign Language Education Department of Middle East Technical University, Ankara, Turkey. Her research interests are critical pedagogy, language teacher education and critical applied linguistics. She authored a book on her own critical teacher education practices in Turkey, titled, *Moving Beyond Technicism in English Language Teacher Education* (2019).

ACKNOWLEDGEMENTS

The background to the idea of this book is the global phenomenon of the Covid-19 pandemic which is wreaking havoc on the world. In the turmoil of lockdowns, increasing global death tolls, closed schools, fights over human lives, commercializing vaccines and masks, I, Fatma Mızıkacı, could not be more than happy to talk to Peter McLaren, Guy Senese and Michael W. Apple, who helped me grow ideas to reunite. Deepest thanks to Eda Ata, the co-editor of this book and the moderator of Global Thursday Talks, whose energy and hardworking made this powerful project possible. It has been a great experience to work with her with joyfulness throughout the publication of this book. I am also grateful to Henry A. Giroux, Antonia Darder, Arnd-Michael Nohl, Liv Mjelde, Zeynep Ataman, Fevziye Sayılan, E. Wayne Ross and Ira Shor, who encouraged me to continue from the Global Thursday Talks to the book you are about to read. My special thanks go to Peter Mayo, who generated the idea of an edited volume covering the talks. This book could not be possible without the participants of the Global Thursday Talks, among them Eda Ata, Murat Ata, Ali Tansu Balcı, Nurcan Saltoğlu Özleyen, Gamze Gonca Özyurt, Zeynep Alica, Yasemin Tezgiden-Cakcak and Kemal İnal, who contributed to this volume with their reflections on the experience of constructing digital communities. I am thankful to the graduate students, research assistants and colleagues in the Department of Curriculum and Instruction at Ankara University. I have a special debt of thanks to my family, my niece Hazal Aksoydan, my sisters Müberra Mızıkacı, Emine Aksoydan, and my brother-in-law Levent Aksoydan, who wholeheartedly supported me unconditionally.

For my part, I, Eda Ata, am indebted to Fatma Mızıkacı for her guidance, support and belief over the years and her infinite patience, inspiration and wisdom throughout the Global Thursday Talks project. I am grateful beyond measure. I am also eternally grateful to my parents, Sultan Ata and Ömer Ata, for being amazing and always being there for me, especially during the pandemic, when we were away for over a year. Special thanks to my cat, Miço, for going through this 'critical' journey with me since 2012. I want to thank Nurcan Saltoğlu Özleyen, Sinem Günbay and Mehmet Cihan Oflu for their invaluable encouragement, kind-heartednes and support throughout and beyond the Global Thursday Talks and the publication of this book. And special thanks to my dearest brother, Murat Ata, who gave me Harry Potter books when I was a child to encourage me to improve my English and my imagination to discover the world. Eventually, we ended up as co-authors in this special book.

We, the editors of this book, are thankful to dearest colleagues Pelin Taşkın, Ayhan Ural and Fulya Soğuksu for their consistent participation and invaluable support of this project. We would like to thank Zeynep Akyol Ataman and João M.

Paraskeva for offering inspiring talks at Global Thursday Talks. In particular, we acknowledge the support of staff at Bloomsbury, Mark Richardson, Evangeline Stanford, Sarah Skinner and Anna Ellis, who laboured in cooperation with us in the publication and several stages of the final development of this book. We also would like to thank Merv Honeywood for his guidance and cooperation. We are also grateful to the anonymous reviewers for their invaluable contribution to the improvement of the book.

The editors and publisher gratefully acknowledge the permission granted to reproduce the copyright material in this book. Every effort has been made to trace copyright holders and to obtain their permission for the use of copyright material. However, if any have been inadvertently overlooked, the publishers will be pleased, if notified of any omissions, to make the necessary arrangements at the first opportunity. The third-party copyrighted material displayed in the pages of this book are done so on the basis of 'fair dealing for the purposes of criticism and review' or 'fair use for the purposes of teaching, criticism, scholarship or research' only in accordance with international copyright laws and is not intended to infringe upon the ownership rights of the original owners.

Fatma Mızıkacı and Eda Ata

INTRODUCTION: CONSTRUCTING COMMUNITIES OF CRITICAL PEDAGOGY IN TIMES OF CRISIS

GLOBAL THURSDAY TALKS

Fatma Mızıkacı

'There is enough bread for all except for the great humankind,' says Nazım Hikmet and continues, 'but the great humankind does have hope' (Hikmet 2008, 1,677), in his poem, the 'Great Humanity'. Nazım Hikmet, the great poet aged 119, and Paulo Freire, the great philosopher, pedagogue aged 100, the everlasting members of global community, are still lighting our way to struggle in solidarity.

Global crises like the Covid-19 pandemic have severe effects on all communities, particularly vulnerable, segregated, invisible and oppressed groups. With the recent global crisis, educators, teachers, students and learners of all ages have come under the pressure of loneliness, joblessness and non-connectedness as they are deprived of schools, campuses and community spaces. They were forced to act rapidly to adopt digital modes to keep connected. Academics and educators soon looked for platforms to meet for their food for thought. The Global Thursday Talks initiative is the fruit of such a pursuit. The book you intend to read now is the compiled documentation of the events organized in Global Thursday Talks, a community of critical pedagogues, public intellectuals and educators, who get together to construct critical consciousness and commitment to social justice in the time of the Covid-19 pandemic.

Before I continue, I would like to show reverence to the legacy of Paulo Freire on his hundredth birthday, which coincided with the publication of this book. It will not be an exaggeration to claim that almost all the chapters in this book are made up with/for Freire's legacy, in such a way that his intellectual, humanistic and education legacy is there planted and formed the ideas. Chapters were authorized by his colleagues, friends, students and those of us who are still being inspired by and learning from him. Freire is heralded in the chapters authored by Henry A. Giroux, Peter McLaren, Antonia Darder and Ira Shor explicitly and in all the other chapters in some other way.

The time when I started writing this chapter was a hard time to witness. The time of the trial of George Floyd's murderer, in March–April 2021, coincided with the tragedy of Daunte Wright, which was recorded as the 181st murder of black people by the police in the United States after Floyd's, and all happened within a year, between May 2020 and May 2021. It is impossible to imagine and accept for a normal human mind that 181 black people have been killed by the police.[1] Approximately a year ago from now, the world witnessed George Floyd's murder in sorrow and, soon after, tremendous uprisings in the USA and in the world. Later, protests, street demonstrations and anti-racist incidents spread all over the world in various ways. Godlee described it as a 'global outpouring of grief and anger at the killing of George Floyd in Minneapolis as either a distraction from or in conflict with efforts to contain the virus' (2020). Peter Mclaren (2020) was already writing articles criticizing these events. In our email exchange during these critical times, we discovered we had to reach out to larger groups, to our colleagues and students. McLaren agreed to attend an online meeting to talk about George Floyd's murder in a larger perspective of racism and the pandemic in relation to its implications for inequality, social justice and education. Then we organized a Zoom meeting on 11 June 2020. McLaren emphasized the quest: 'What kind of world is going to emerge after the Covid-19 pandemic and George Floyd murder protests?' The discussion was around the totalitarian regimes and their neoliberal policies, which have had and an influence on disadvantaged groups in society. McLaren identified these issues as follows:

- In 2019, Los Angeles school teachers went on strike for their rights and learning conditions for students.
- 15 per cent of the country's population live in conditions of poverty.
- 31.2 per cent of the population lacks critical media literacy. This made the discourse of President Donald Trump (2017–21) easily accepted by these groups.
- How people were called to go to church to pray about the coronavirus and went back contaminated by the virus.

McLaren's speech to a large group of graduate students, educators and scholars was not only a timely event but also a discovery of how such a gathering would work for our intellectual loneliness during pandemic. We decided to continue as the participants of the first event were eager to hear more from the public intellectuals. In the following gatherings, the simultaneous nature of the events gave us deeper insights. For instance, when Michael W. Apple appeared at the Global Thursday Talks, the Turkish community greatly appreciated him and he promised to attend another meeting. Similarly, Peter McLaren, Guy Senese, Peter Mayo, Henry A. Giroux, Antonia Darder, E. Wayne Ross and Arnd-Michael Nohl had an established relationship with the critical pedagogy groups in Turkey in different ways, they have been in the teachers' syndicate, conferences and universities and even in the street demonstrations during the Gezi Park uprisings in 2013. McLaren had been hit by the police in one of these demonstrations. Senese was teaching in Ankara when 301 coal miners were killed in a tragic mining

---

1. Katherine Fung, *Newsweek*, 21 April 2021, available at: www.newsweek.com.

accident in Soma,[2] then he became a part of the student protests at Ankara University. Apple worked with the Turkish Teachers Syndicate many times. After all, the ideas of the invited speakers have already long been in the graduate courses, in the discussion groups, in the reading circles, in the dissertations of graduate programmes and scholarly works.

As a matter of fact, the context of the global earth has expanded considerably by adding new uncertainties to the uncertainties from this process that started in June 2020. Diverse but focused topics were discussed within the framework of critical pedagogy at large. The prominent topics were social justice, problems related to the pandemic, racism in the axis of George Floyd's murder, migration, critical theory and class, public education, women's rights, body politics and education, schooling, home-schooling, participation and non-participation in distance education and the social gaps it creates, social movements, the isolation and changing roles of teachers in the pandemic, the effects of neoconservatism and neoliberalism on education, public advocacy, cultural studies, teacher organizations, resistance, political stance, vocational vs general education, curriculum and instruction in relation to the pandemic, empowering education and the agenda of critical pedagogy. These issues have been well emphasized in relation to the disparities, inequalities and injustice which are deeply felt but remain invisible in the times of Covid-19 (Steinberg 2020).

We have understood how important it is to come together even on digital platforms and what kind of power it can create in order not to turn into despair due to the increasing uncertainty due to the pandemic. The source of this strength was the feeling of resistance and solidarity arising from being together. This led us to an ethics of intellectual solidarity, an understanding that our contributions provide one another the tools of knowledge; that brings solidarity as a means to meet intellectual needs (Magill and Rodriguez 2021). At the same time, we felt the responsibility to continue these meetings and expand the space we opened up, and we feel that we have set a model for other platforms and entities, and this encourages us to continue and have different collaborations (Perng 2020). Then we heard that Global Thursday Talks videos are taught in graduate courses as an example of praxis and solidarity.

We are assured that Global Thursday Talks is a kind of praxis of its own with Bauman's definition of 'culture as praxis' (1999, ix) as it created and formed its own existence. The organizers, speakers and participants have formed a union so strong that they are also planning to share what they have witnessed with the future educators by organizing more events and turning what has been shared into a collective book project, thus achieving a safe and meaningful space for all to access, grow and walk together. Global Thursday Talks has reached an aim in an age that exaggeration, falsehood, lies and gossip are the characteristic of post-truth. In such an era, knowledge requires conditions of belief, truth and justification, while information requires none of these and misinformation and disinformation

2. Available at: https://en.wikipedia.org/wiki/Soma_mine_disaster (accessed 4 December 2021).

are fundamental categories of such information (Peters, McLaren and Jandrić 2020, 2; Mayo 2020).

At the time this volume is being projected, the community of Global Thursday Talks has enlarged its scope to the world, with thirteen talks with more than 3,000 participants and followers within nine months in 2020 (Figure 0.1). With this at

Figure 0.1 Collection of Global Thursday Talks posts in a year. *Source*: Fatma Mızıkacı, personal file.

hand, the idea of collecting what is done with and in this community in an edited volume came from the invited speakers and the participants, so that the movement would continue to communicate. The participants have reflected tremendously and mobilized the meetings. Due to the increasing interest in and expectations from the events, the idea of an edited book was created that would allow the speeches and discussions to be expressed in different ways, thus these valuable ideas can reach more people. We expect the readers to explore this extraordinary time – the pandemic – through the lens of critical educators worldwide, and to witness the praxis and reflection aspect of the events.

Organization of the book

This volume is organized into three parts, consisting of 19 chapters, which essentially represent intellectual perspectives and reflections from the field of larger critical pedagogy and cultural studies. The chapters are characterized by the contributors' critical approach to and experience in particular issues in relation to the controversies that emerged during the pandemic. Part I and Part II are constructed by the invited speakers' chapters, while Part III is a collection of participants' reflections on Global Thursday Talks. The chapters in Part I cover the general issues of cultural and social agendas of totalitarian regimes and their influence on education during the pandemic; the chapters in Part II discuss pandemic pedagogies, moving from the geographical perspectives to universal moments; while the chapters in Part III present the individual reflections on the ideas of the contributors of Part I and Part II. Thus, the logical organization of the chapters are mainly based on the interaction and solidarity in the space created through Global Thursday Talks. Authors focus on the Covid-19 crisis, the murder of George Floyd and racism, neoliberalism, neoconservatism, rightist ideology, capitalism, new cultural and social agendas of totalitarian regimes and their influence on education, schooling/home-schooling and its dangers, poverty and education, teachers and society, informal education, distance education, digital communities, interconnectedness, critical theory and practice in education, social justice, disembodiment, teaching the flesh, social gender inequality, women's rights, teachers' isolation, solidarity, social movements and critical race theory.

In Chapter 1, 'An Interview with Henry A. Giroux: Cultural Studies and Pandemic Pedagogy', Henry A. Giroux draws attention to the scope and meaning of critical pedagogy, especially as it is needed in the times of crisis like the pandemic. He first emphasizes what critical pedagogy is and states: it is a moral and political project, whose purpose is to equip students and others with the knowledge, the skills, the values and the sense of social responsibility that enables them to be engaged critical agents. Critical pedagogy keeps us aware of the questions that need to be asked about the relationship between knowledge and power, justice and critical agency, and values and the construction of specific forms of agency. The chapter presents an analysis of pandemic pedagogy from a larger perspective in cultural studies and critical theories with reference to Louis Althusser, Raymond Williams, Antonio Gramsci, C. Wright Mills, Pierre Bourdieu and Stuart Hall. Giroux suggests the realities of neoliberalism where educators, students, youth and social groups are degenerated, criminalized, dehumanized and commercialized. Creating spaces, getting together and hope in the meaning of reinventing sense of agency collectively in its struggle for justice, equality and freedom are the ideas pointed out throughout the chapter.

Peter McLaren's chapter, 'Radical and Hopeful Discussions about Times of Brutal Conservatism: Paths of Fight and Transformation in the Light of Paulo Freire', is an autobiographic journey of McLaren of an 'intellectual kinship' with Freire and a discussion of Freire's legacy in such difficult times for Brazil and the USA. Throughout the analysis, McLaren underlines the moment of extreme and violent neoconservatism that we are experiencing, and the paths of resistance that we need to take as educators and researchers to fight oppression, overcome inequalities and democratizing the university space. The chapter is adorned with the illustration from the book, *Breaking Free: The Life and Times of Peter McLaren* (2019), and photos from McLaren's personal collection.

Michael W. Apple, in Chapter 3, 'Critical Analysis and the Covid-19 Crisis: An Interview with Michael W. Apple', underlines the issues related to the unionization and solidarity of educators, especially in the times of crises, with specific focus on his own experience with various countries via teachers' syndicates and his connection with Turkey's Eğitim-sen (Education and Science Workers' Union). With reference to the threats on democratic schooling, especially in the times of the pandemic, Apple pointed out four groups who form the hegemonic bloc and become effective in the digitalized education: neoliberals, neoconservatives, authoritarian populists and social democrats. In all of this turmoil, Apple analyses the role of critical pedagogy and critical consciousness and unionization to resist against the hegemonic bloc that educators can refer to.

In Chapter 4, 'Higher Education in the Time of Corona', Peter Mayo discusses the challenges posed by Covid-19 to higher education. Mayo stresses the emergence and growth of university alternatives which offer tenured academics a relatively safe adjustment to the changed scenario in stark contrast to other people for whom the current situation presents a choice: exposure or starvation. Precarious academics working part-time and according to definite contracts and students coming from humble backgrounds also face problems in this age of corona. Furthermore, within the relatively safe 'middle-class' context of secluded and virtually mediated academic work and transaction, there are still issues to be considered, bearing in mind the future of higher education itself. The chapter is organized around these subtitle: 'Phantom City?'; 'University, Middle-Class Jobs and the Class/Ethnic Divide'; 'All into Proper Perspective'; 'Standard Corona Response'; 'Consumer Product or Public Good?'; and 'Covid-19 and Neoliberalism'.

Chapter 5, 'Freire and a Revolutionary Praxis of the Body: Countering the One-Dimensionality of Banking Education', authored by Antonia Darder, focuses on the ideas of the body within the pedagogical arena, and the importance of the materiality of body informed by a humanizing ethos that supports reflection, dialogue and solidarity in the flesh, as we labour for the common good. Darder's analysis continues Freire's humanizing praxis – a praxis fundamentally grounded in a larger revolutionary project for liberation, and makes the reader to think about how the human body is dehumanized during online classes. Darder organizes the ideas around these topics: 'One-Dimensionality of Banking Education'; 'The Politics of the Body'; 'The Estrangement of the Body'; 'Toward a Revolutionary Praxis of the Body'; and 'The Body as an Ethical Terrain of Struggle'.

E. Wayne Ross, in Chapter 6, 'A Dialogue with E. Wayne Ross on: A Crisis within a Crisis: Teaching, Learning and Democracy under Neoliberalism during the Pandemic', writes his own journey as an activist educator moving things around in solidarity, that is to say, he co-founded the Rouge Forum, and the journals *Cultural Logic, Works and Days, Workplace* and *Critical Education*. His early encounter with discrimination and racism essentially directed his focus to the idea of education for social justice in the educational and social context of the USA then. On his experience, Ross suggests that teachers and students critically explore their local and national communities, especially in the times of crisis. He points out that there are the risks of no school times for educators and for young learners as they become more fragile and bound to technology. As for the critical curriculum issues of today under the pandemic conditions, Ross discusses the concept of 'dangerous citizenship' and the idea that schooling is fundamentally about social control. Within the context of digitalization, he explains how these realities of schooling will shape the future of social studies curriculum studies.

Ira Shor, in Chapter 7, 'Paulo Freire at 100, Still Inspiring: An Interview with Ira Shor', presents a picture of Paulo Freire's struggle for critical consciousness over a bird's-eye view of a journey from Brazil to other Latin countries and Europe. Shor himself was lucky enough to spend more than 200 hours with Freire. The chapter then continues with the importance of critical consciousness, praxis, dialogue and problem-posing, especially in today's antidemocratic education settings. The chapter draws attention to new forms and understandings in education such as fake news reflecting in the classroom, reducing the teacher's authority and the ways to adopt critical consciousness against these neoliberal influences in education. The reader then contends what is needed more under the risk of a neoliberal blockade, empowering teachers and students through curriculum.

Guy Senese, in Chapter 8, 'Race, Plague and Resistance', starts a journey in a burger bar in Tucson, Arizona, USA, and questions the 'Black Lives Matter' milieu from the very heart of it, where almost all workers are of colour and have no citizenship and are close to deportation every moment they live. As a worldwide traveller, Senese takes the reader from Mexico to Turkey, the countries mourn for the loss of their young, 'The 43 of Ayotzinapa', from the symbolism of the distorted photos he is looking at to Guy Debord's image of a world made of copies. Eventually, he asserts, 'It is hard to tell which virus is spreading faster, Covid-19, or Hate, because they are now on stage together.' The critique Senese poses is centred around the politics of then US President Donald Trump and the media supporting his politics dangerously and its consequences on education and oppressed, segregated groups. This chapter consists of these subsections: 'Prologue: Dewey's

Dream'; 'Introduction'; 'Writing or Organizing?'; 'Refuge'; 'Murdoch's Fox'; 'For the Teacher'; *'Simit'*; 'Be Safe'; 'Reading *The Reading Girl*'; and 'Postscript: You Can't Live without Hope'.

Chapter 9, 'Liv Mjelde in Conversation with Fatma Mızıkacı and Eda Ata: A Pedagogy of Questioning: Vocational Learning: The Art of Reflective Curiosity', by Liv Mjelde, presents an analysis of the conception of vocational education from a critical perspective in a Scandinavian context. Mjelde explains how, between the end of the Second World War and to the present, vocational education has moved forward from being equally positioned with general education becoming an equality and social justice problem in the neoliberal age. Today, vocational schools are the places where gender, class and learning discriminations are persistently observed. Underlying the theoretical background to the social division of knowledge, Mjelde draws the attention to that of the unnatural idea of a contrast between mind and matter, man and nature, soul and body constructed today's injustice, gender discrimination and segregation in society and by the way of general and vocational education systems. The division of hand, mind and heart is a social construction of knowledge which has its different hegemonic ways of manifesting itself in different epochs of history.

In Chapter 10, 'Between *Bildung* and *Erziehung*: Mass Education during the Pandemic', Arnd-Michael Nohl makes an empirical analysis of the successive phases of directive mass education during the pandemic in relation to the concepts of German *Bildung* and *Erziehung*. Nohl elaborates theoretically on the suggested difference between 'Erziehung' and 'Bildung' and shows how, historically, *Bildung* became the dominant educational process in the democratic discourse of Germany. The question is whether directive (mass) education is at all a suitable means for democracy to bring about the willingness to act in the population or can it be tempting for politicians to become authoritarian. Nohl discusses this question concerning the social politics of the pandemic in the democratic German government in the following subsections: 'Introduction'; *'Erziehung* versus *Bildung'*; *'Erziehung'*; *'Bildung'*; 'Political *Bildung* in (West) Germany'; 'Mass Education, Phase I: A Means against the Pandemic'; 'Contact Ban and Mass Education'; 'Educational Sanctions'; 'Non-directive Education'; 'Educators' Disagreement'; 'The Fatal Success of Pandemic Containment'; 'Mass Education, Phase II: Authoritarian Relationship, Risk Areas and Collective Sanctions'; 'Superspreader'; 'Risk Areas and Collective Sanctions'; 'The Emergence of Co-educators'; Mass Education, Phase III: The End of *Erziehung*?'; and 'Some Critical Reflections on Mass Education in the Corona Pandemic'.

Fevziye Sayılan and Zeynep Alica, in Chapter 11, 'The Agenda of Critical Pedagogy during the Covid-19 Pandemic in Turkey', discuss how the crisis of capitalism, together with the crisis created by the pandemic, have opened up a period of most painful and radical changes. Sayılan and Alica go deep into the dramatic consequences of the pandemic in the following subsections: 'States, Schools and Rising Authoritarianism'; 'Education in the Distance'; 'Monopoly Capitalists in the Lead'; 'Public Education: Religionized'; and 'The Way Forward'. The authors emphasize that the crisis gives opportunity not only to the rulers but also to the critical educators, that is to say, for massive transformative experiences such as opening minds, seeing the unseen and seeing things from a different perspective. That is the work of critical educators.

Eda Ata, in Chapter 12, 'Transformative Power of Digital Communities: A Critical Educator's Perspective', presents an overall reflection of an organization member and participant of Global Thursday Talks. The chapter mainly focuses on the extraordinary nature of the pandemic and how solidarity via online communities turned out to be transformative and empowering, regardless of the problems faced globally. The chapter offers some background information, along with the effects of the online communities on the writer as a teacher (and an activist). A specific focus on the Global Thursday Talks series is given, with specific examples from the talk with reference to teacher empowerment via online communities. The chapter's subtitles are: 'Critical Student Becoming Critical Educator: Digital Spaces before and during the Pandemic'; and 'Hope as a Sustainable Asset: Where to from Here?'

Zeynep Alica and Yasemin Tezgiden-Cakcak, in Chapter 13, 'Grounding Critical Educators' Lives on Solidarity, Community and Friendship', tell us the story of how two critical educators ground their daily lives on solidarity networks they build with their colleagues and students. Authors describe their personal and professional experience and challenges during the pandemic and how they survive rough times with the support of their now new communities. Believing in the possibility of transformation even in difficult times, they think that (re)building relationships, community and solidarity through networks such as Global Thursday Talks is a cure for despair and alienation for it maintains nurturing dimensions of international cooperation and respectful relationship-building, all toward preserving our democratic public education spaces in these difficult times and circumstances.

Murat Ata, in Chapter 14, 'Coming to Terms with the Covid-19 Pandemic: Perceptions of a Language Teacher', discusses his own experience and reflections as a member of this community built in the times of pandemic. Ata underlines a questioning process he experienced in his teaching with these statements:

> experiencing the rapidly evolving nature of teaching practices, I, as a language teacher, have found myself questioning how the pedagogy I am supposed to follow is informed by the changing social structures and psychological development of learners and educators. The new normal initiated by the pandemic has introduced countless inequalities among students, highlighted the digital divide, caused psychological issues, limited social interactions, minimized mobilization and weakened the oppressed. I keep questioning around these issues.

Ali Tansu Balcı, Chapter 15, 'Rethinking Social Transformation from Informal Learning to Political Learning in the Covid-19 Pandemic', discusses the concept of learning in the context of the contradictions created by the crisis and the reasons for the crisis to occur. Balcı underlines the importance of informal learning, a self-learning process based on life experiences in the pandemic. Informal learnings, which come to mind first in this process, emerges in the field of education, health and work. During the pandemic, these discussions have become more crucial and generate new learnings. The author then discusses the potential of social transformation from informal learning to political learning in the context of critical education. The chapter has the following subtitles: 'Introduction'; 'Informal Learning in the Covid-19 Outbreak'; 'Political Learning in the Covid-19 Outbreak'; and 'Conclusion'.

In Chapter 16, 'Critical Pedagogy Confronts Technology: Responses to the Challenges of the New Education Reality during the Pandemic', Kemal İnal, addresses how critical pedagogy confronts technology and makes an analysis of the responses to the pandemic regarding uncertainty, the removal of time, distance, space and resource constraints. This chapter is constructed as an overall argumentation of the past, present and future critics of capitalism and its brainchild, technology, within the new education reality, with these subtitles: 'Introduction'; 'Critical Pedagogy on Technology'; 'The New Education Reality'; '"Education 4.0" and Expectations'; 'Critical Pedagogy: Responses to the Challenge'; 'Critical Pedagogy's Perspective on the Use of Technology in Education'; 'Increasing Kowledge by Technicalization'; 'Four Pandemic-Originated Challenges'; and 'Conclusion'.

Gamze Gonca Özyurt's Chapter 17, 'Cultural Resistance of Critical Pedagogy in the Age of Authoritarian Populism', is a reflection of the cultural power in critical pedagogy that encourages her to take action, which Giroux, Ross, Senese and Apple touched on in their Global Thursday Talks. Özyurt reminds us that critical pedagogues have crucial responsibilities as public intellectuals in authoritarian populism, where learning is generally not supported outside of the school, and schools are equipped with restrictive curricula by the state. The conservative/historical speeches and the manipulative information barrage (that feeds authoritarian populism) to children makes the culture-based struggle acute. This struggle must primarily serve the development of critical consciousness of the public, because the power of change and transformative critical pedagogy comes from the public movement. The chapter subtitles are: 'A Recipe I Got from Critical Pedagogy'; and 'Conclusion'

Nurcan Saltoğlu Özleyen, in Chapter 18, 'Rediscovering the Teacher's Voice in Higher Education in the Middle of the Covid-19 Pandemic', presents an overall reflection of a participant of Global Thursday Talks on teaching practices, material development, current social issues and the feeling of solidarity. While doing this, a summary of the time will be provided to familiarize the reader with the context in the introduction. In the rest of the chapter, following the sessions in the Global Thursday Talks, the shifts in perception of the writer about the aforementioned topics will be discussed in detail, referring to the talks in which they participated.

Chapter 19 by Fatma Mızıkacı and Eda Ata, 'Moving Forward', is an overall evaluation of the grounds that make the volume possible and a look forward to the post-pandemic era. Mızıkacı and Ata emphasize how the new era will be shaped by the need for more inclusion of larger communities and a wider scope of topics in various contexts. The authors close the chapter saying: 'We can call this as "the

Figure 0.2 This is how we started the idea of constructing digital communities, June 2020. *Source*: Fatma Mızıkacı, personal file.

era of hear and act" that has started as a post-pandemic case. Critical pedagogy communities will be empowered as we answer the questions: Hear what? Hear how? Act how?' The chapter subtitles are: 'Where are We Now?'; and 'Where are We Going?'. Figure 0.2 shows how we started the idea of constructing digital communities in June 2020.

Consequently, this volume offers a women's Initiative in Critical Pedagogy who gathered worldwide leading intellectuals, international pedagogues and scholars with graduate students and constructed a community for a common aim. As a product of timeless and placeless effort, this book involves experience and reflection on building a community of critical constructive pedagogy in the times of crisis. The community consists of global members from the USA, Canada, Turkey, Norway, Germany and Malta and participants from all over the world. Topics are inclusive and critical as they cover challenges to racism, neoliberalism, neoconservatism, rightist ideology, capitalism, new cultural and social agendas of totalitarian regimes and their influence on education, schooling/home-schooling and its dangers, poverty and education, disembodiment, social gender inequality and teachers' isolation.

References

Bauman, Zigmund (1999) *Culture as Praxis* (New York: Sage).

Godlee, Fiona (2020) 'Racism: The other pandemic', *BMJ* (2020): 369. Available at: https://www.bmj.com/content/bmj/369/bmj.m2303.full.pdf (accessed 30 June 2020).

Hikmet, N. (2008) *Bütün Şiirleri*, 4th edn (Istanbul: Yapı Kredi Yayınları).

Magill, Kevin Russel and Arturo Rodriguez (2021) 'Teaching as intellectual solidarity', *Critical Education*, 12 (1). DOI: https://doi.org/10.14288/ce.v12i1.186451 (accessed 10 March 2021).

Mayo, Peter (2020) 'The Corona challenge to higher education', *Culture e Studi del Sociale*, Special Issue, 5 (1): 371–6.

McLaren, Peter (2020) 'Pandemic abandonment, panoramic displays and fascist propaganda: The month the earth stood still', 1–10. DOI: 10.1080/00131857.2020.1781787 (accessed 30 September 2020).

Perng, Sung-Yueh (2020) 'Ignorance, exclusion, and solidarity in human-virus co-existence during and after COVID-19', *Dialogues in Human Geography*, 10 (2): 150–3.

McLaren Peter (2019) *Breaking Free: The Life and Times of Peter McLaren*, illustrated by Miles Wilson (New York: Myers Education Press).

Peters, Michael A., Peter McLaren and Petar Jandrić (2020) 'A viral theory of post-truth', *Educational Philosophy and Theory*. DOI: 10.1080/00131857.2020.1750090.

Steinberg, Shirley R. (2020) 'An interview with Henry A. Giroux and Joe L. Kincheloe', in Sheila L. Macrine (ed.), *Critical Pedagogy in Uncertain Times: Education, Politics and Public Life* (New York and Houndmills: Palgrave Macmillan, Cham), 203–7.

Part I

NEW CULTURAL AND SOCIAL AGENDAS OF
TOTALITARIAN REGIMES AND THEIR INFLUENCE ON
EDUCATION IN THE TIME OF THE COVID-19 PANDEMIC

Chapter 1

AN INTERVIEW WITH HENRY A. GIROUX: CULTURAL STUDIES AND PANDEMIC PEDAGOGY[1]

Henry A. Giroux

Global Thursday Talks (GTT)   We are honoured to have Henry A. Giroux today, one of the leading and most influential names in the world. A founding theorist of critical pedagogy, he is best known for his leading work in public pedagogy, cultural studies, youth studies, higher education, media studies and critical theory. Dr Giroux's work has also been translated into Turkish and we are looking forward to reading his latest book, *Race, Politics and Pandemic Pedagogy*, which will be out in February 2021. We prepared questions to ask Dr Giroux on critical issues in education.

The reason we are here now is mostly about the ongoing processes in the world. We are in an age of authoritarian populism, where capitalist cultures shape the society and the individuals' lives, hand in hand with neoliberal policies and now, with the age of [the] Covid-19 crisis. Within this context, how would you define critical pedagogy and its functions. Can it shape the new era of schooling?

Henry A. Giroux   I think one of the things you have to recognize is that one of the first casualties of authoritarianism, and in all of its forms, are the minds that would oppose it and it seems to me that what we have to recognize immediately is this is not just a political issue but also an educational issue. It means that questions of consciousness and learning, questions of knowledge and questions about power are quite central to how we understand the times in which we live. John Dewey used to say that you cannot have a democracy without basically having informed citizens. So, when we talk about critical pedagogy in its diverse forms, we are not talking about forms of education linked to both the older culture of positivism into the updated versions of commercialism, finance capital, and its more ruthless and updated versions of neoliberal fascism. Critical pedagogy is not a methodology;

1. This interview was conducted within the activities of the @globalthursdaytalks digital community on 13 August 2020, and is available at: https://bit.ly/3aDw1bo.

nor is it a preordained recipe. It is a moral and political project, whose purpose is to equip students and others with the knowledge, the skills, the values and sense of social responsibility that enables them to be engaged critical agents. Critical pedagogy keeps us aware of the questions that need to be asked about the relationship between knowledge and power, justice and critical agency, and values and the construction of specific forms of agency.

Critical pedagogy is directive and uses its authority in dialogue with students as part of the ongoing and crucial struggle over the acquisition of agency, values and the narratives that allow them to be reflective about themselves, others and the larger society. Talk about pedagogy is always related to how we define visions of the future. It is not only part of an ongoing dialogue about relations of power and knowledge, but also about the conditions necessary for creating informed and critical citizens who can act on the world. So, it seems to me that any talk about critical pedagogy always defines itself as a political and moral and political project. That is, it is taken up as a pedagogical practice that addresses both what it means to be in the world, while providing the meaningful contexts and critical preconditions for students and others to basically be able to intervene in the world. So, we are really talking about the relationship between power and agency as part of a broader pedagogical process. More specifically, critical pedagogy references what it means to understand the world and the conditions that shape our lives so at we have the knowledge, skills and tools to function as agents in the world.

We are talking about a political and civic project that highlights and addresses fundamental questions such as: 'What is the relationship between democracy and informed citizens?' 'How do you have one without the other?' 'How do you talk about schools as sites of struggle over power, agency, and assigned meanings?' 'What does it mean to basically talk about education as not just simply the production of ideas and knowledge, but a democratic public sphere that make critical education possible?' 'How do you talk about power with relation to teachers who clearly should have control over the conditions of their own labour?' 'How do you talk about education outside critical pedagogy outside of schooling?' 'How do you talk about it in the larger culture in the manner of Raymond Williams and his notion of *permanent education*?' In the manner of Althusser? In the manner of Gramsci? In the manner of Paulo Freire? In the manner of Stuart Hall? People who are vastly concerned, who are vastly concerned with the educative nature of critical pedagogy as the educative and fundamental nature and organizing principle of politics itself.

GTT Thank you. I want to emphasize a point you mentioned. It is critical pedagogy outside the classroom or outside schooling. Maybe, there are some areas that we can move or mobilize our students; maybe we can mobilize thinking outside the school. I remember in one of your writings that you took your students to movies and then how learning happened there. This experience, for example, can be a model for us and also there is art outside the school. Unfortunately, 'outside' or 'left out' at school and it is important, and it is not only school or only classroom, but also outside and critical pedagogy functions may well function outside school – maybe in these days, during pandemic and in isolation days. We may need this thinking more than any time.

Henry A. Giroux   I would like to thank you for the question. It is really a very important question and I am very pleased to have the opportunity to answer it. One of the things that I have been thinking about for a long time is how the role of culture functions as a pedagogical force and, clearly, I am not the first, but it seems to me that regardless of the origins of the question, again whether we're going back to Raymond Williams, Antonio Gramsci, Louis Althusser or Pierre Bourdieu, it is fundamental to recognize two things. The first one is that the pedagogical dimensions of learning are not limited to schools and that 'cultural apparatuses' that C. Wright Mills once talked about are really very powerful educational forces and I would argue in some ways more powerful today than probably schools – particularly when it comes to shaping the perceptions, values, modes of agency and forms of identification that take place in a society that is utterly committed to the regressive processes of commodification, privatization and the rise of a social media that has become an accelerant for the rise of right-wing extremism emerging across the globe, especially in the midst of a pandemic. I am not just talking about these cultural apparatuses as modes of entertainment; I am strongly identifying them as powerful and capacious modes of education.

The second issue is that these new cultural formations that extend from the digital media to the mainstream press are not just simply sites of domination; they are also sites of struggle. It seems to me for young people that's a particularly important issue because, unlike my generation, his generation is enormously savvy when it comes to these new social media technologies and I think that as educators we have a responsibility not only to educate them both as cultural producers and to be able to critically analyse the political dimensions of these apparatuses and the role they they play pedagogically in shaping the collective consciousness of the larger public on a global scal. Put differently, it is crucial to teach students to be more than critics but also cultural producers. They have got to learn how to produce plays, radio programmes, social media narratives, films and other modes of cultural intervention.

Of course, these new technologicsal formations and the pedagogical spheres they create have to be addressed within the massive degree of inequality that shapes different levels of access and accessibility for many groups operating within different and often grotesque levels of deprivation and privilege. Who has access? Who has the privilege of working from home and who does not? Inequality is central to a fascist politics because the latter thrives on resentment, the loss of dignity, community and the language of hope. Inequality is the main driver of a new fascist politics. Its division of groups into friends and enemies accentuates racial and class divides. Moreover, its call for racial purity and the logic of disposability reinforces its legitimation of what is nationalism. Neoliberal capitalism pushes more and more people into the abyss of poverty while concentrating wealth and power in the hands of relatively few people. What emerges amid this mix of inequality, poverty and a politics of disposability is the brutal face of racial capitalism, which is an updated version of fascist politics.

Pedagogy is one register for making visible power along with the micro-expressions and slow violence of racism. What is important here is to educate students in order to make them realize that pedagogy really counts as a tool of politics and resistance. In addition, it is crucial for students to understand that education exists outside of the parameters of schooling in a variety of cultural spheres. Education is now used to produce a cultural war, a war over the critical thought, rationality and equality. This is a war over civic possibility. This is a war over resistance, and this is also a space where young people can organize to challenge a screen and digital culture that in a dominant culture wants to isolate and privatize them. They can reach out, they can talk about sharing publications; they can talk about organizing direct forms of action; they can talk about what it means to make authority accountable but, most importantly, they can learn how to make power visible and to challenge it individually and collectively. So, it seems to me that pedagogical interventions with respect to the cultural sphere is enormously crucial.

GTT   As educators, we want to see something concrete here. As a consequence, I can summarize what you are saying. As educators we have the power – not to be confined, not to be limited with the distance education or what we are offered through distance education. This is a very, you know, common term these days and education is limited and restricted to distance education, but we should have our own agenda, our own curriculum out of this 'distance education' or the 'screen culture'.

And our next question is again about children and youth. You have so many influential ideas on how youth and children are being reshaped by some neoliberal ideologies and some different tools. Especially in this pandemic crisis, do you think this influence of neoliberal policies will be more influential or what direction can it go on children and youth?

Henry A. Giroux   Let us make something fundamentally clear about what it means to talk about youth in the neoliberal age. First of all, youth are a long-term investment in a democracy. The fundamental question that any democratic society has to ask is how you organize resources in a fundamental way to make sure that young people have a future that doesn't imitate the oppressive elements of the past or the present while providing the conditions for them for a life of dignity, fulfilment and justice. One in which the capacities necessary for them to be knowledgeable, to be literate, to be critical agents, are basically provided for them. Under neoliberalism, youth are viewed as a short-term investment, which means capitalist society does not make long-term investments in young people because they're viewed as a liability. I think that one of the ways in which we increasingly begin to understand a certain kind of dynamic between neoliberalism and what I call the 'social welfare state', is through its increasing criminalization and commodification of young people. As neoliberalism ascends and the welfare state is diminished, more and more social problems are criminalized. Hence, young people, particularly black and brown youth in schools, become a particularly vicious object of this kind of analysis – meaning that schools increasingly come to resemble prisons. You have police in schools, you have resources being taken away from the schools, you have schools that in many ways are punishing students with zero tolerance policies but, most importantly, you have the criminalization of social issues. A student will, for instance, doodle on a desk and, without warning, the police charge into the classroom and arrest that student for a trivial infraction. This marks the beginning of the student's entry into the criminal justice system. This horrifying practice is particularly true for black and brown students because this is not just simply about poor white students, this is mostly about the logic of racism in the United States and its impact on black and brown students.

Not too long ago, a film was released on the national news, in which an 8-year-old student in Florida was handcuffed because he had hit a teacher. The student is an 8t-year-old. They put his hands behind his back, but they couldn't put the cuffs on him because his wrists were too small. They then took him to court and charged him with a felony and it was only when that video became public that there was a massive uproar, and the charges were dismissed. This case is symbolic of something larger. There are four wars being waged against young people. The first one is the war of commodification. It's a war that says that young people should define themselves simply by the commodities that they buy and the commodities that they advertise. The second war is the criminal justice war. That is a war in which the forces of repression bear down on young people, particularly disproportionately, young people of color – poor young people of colour. That means that the punishing apparatuses bear down on students almost every day. Consequently, more and more students of colour are put in jail, more students are suspended from schools, more students are punished for trivial infractions, more students are basically suspended and more students are charged with criminal acts.

Add to this reign of terror directed against young people, is a war of surveillance. Moreover, with the addition of new sophisticated technologies, young people are being monitored in their schools, on the streets, through their cell phones, and in almost every other public space they inhabit. In the midst of the pandemic crisis, states are retooling the war of surveillance and expanding its reach. There is also the war of privatization which is part of an ongoing effort to individualize social problems for young people so that they cannot imagine what it means to translate their own problems into larger social considerations. They lose the possibility of translation and that is a direct attack on their self-esteem and is a direct attack on their sense of agency and, most of all, that adds up to a war of depoliticization. These students are being depoliticized. There is no question that the pandemic intensifies this. In 1977, I wrote a piece on the culture of positivism. Some of you are old enough to remember this phase, you know, in history, when everything was defined and relegated to the logic of empiricism.

This is a culture in which everything is instrumentalized. It is about rationalizing everything down to its lowest common denominator so that pedagogy is reduced to a force of enormous oppression that excludes questions of ethics, social responsibility, justice, power, values and the elements of a democratic vision. This is a very oppressive pedagogy, and we should not underestimate it. I think the great failure of the left, in my estimation, particularly in the United States, is its failure to take the question of education seriously as central to the notion of politics itself and to take the question of identification. What does it mean for us as educators to be able to talk to people in ways in which people can identify the nature of their own problems so that they can translate those problems in ways that give them a broader and more critical understanding of what the problems really are so that they don't end up with a form of right-wing populism or they don't end up sort of looking for the strong man or they don't end up believing that the only real problems facing society are the result of the behaviour and actions of black people or undocumented immigrants or women or people who have a different sexual orientation. These are crucial kinds of issues.

GTT   This reminds me, the 'Social Contract'. We should regain the social contract.

Henry A. Giroux   We not only need to regain the social contract, we need to do three things. First, we need to recognize that we are in a period of updated fascism that is almost unprecedented in its move from the margins to the centre of power. This is a fascism that embraces ultra-nationalism, militarism, the degradation of the other, racism, white supremacy, the language of dehumanization, and the concentration of power and wealth in relatively few hands. Secondly, I am concerned about the death of the social contract, but I am not concerned about the social contract within capitalism because capitalism believes anything that interferes with the market, including the welfare state, government regulation and the ethos of social responsibility are the enemy of freedom. I mean, if you can't develop an anti-capitalist understanding of what a new society would look like, a democratic socialist society, embracing the social contract is a dead end that modifies and updates capitalist reform rather than call for restructuring it entirely.

I have no trouble with liberal reforms in the immediate sense which might include raising the minimum wage or increasing food-stamps allocation for the poor. We cannot allow the poor and desperate to be thrown under the bus; people are dying, people who don't have food, people need food stamps. That's fine for me, but that should not be the end goal of a radical transformative movement. That is going to be able to address this new stage of neoliberal fascism in which we find ourselves. We need a restructuring. We don't need, basically, band-aid reforms. We don't need to look back to the fifties and say, 'Oh, that was great, we had a social contract and, of course, the 1 per cent only owned 30 per cent of the world's wealth instead of 50 to 60 per cent.' There is more at work here than a numbing nostalgia.

GTT   Thank you, Dr Giroux. Now, let's come back to critical pedagogy again, I don't want to downsize the critical pedagogy into geographic borders, of course, but how do you see critical pedagogy and its expanding, its borders or its limits in, for example, Mediterranean regions, [the] Middle East or in Asia. How do you see its situation and its positioning and its power all over the world?

Henry A. Giroux   Let me begin with a suggestion. I think it is a critical mistake to have ever suggested that critical pedagogy was simply the product of one particular region in the world. Critical pedagogy has been going on for a long time in many places: in Latin America, the United States and England, sociology of education in Africa, in Malta [addressing Peter Mayo among the audience]. In any way to limit it to a kind of nationalist logic, it seems to me imitates the worst dimensions of a kind of undemocratic ethos that seems to suggest something about the superiority of the North, and that is a colonizing logic. Let us move away from that and let's make it clear that it seems to me that those agencies that tend to define critical pedagogy in those ways share a very disrespectful, if not pathological, association with a form of colonization that works to silence the voices of others who, in fact, are making enormous contributions. By the way, let me clarify one thing, I am not the 'father' of critical pedagogy. I was just one of many people who at a particular time in history was dealing with the issue and we were able to seize that moment to put critical pedagogy on the agenda. I do know that Paulo Freire had an enormous influence on my work in the work of others and I know that Paulo would never have defined himself as the 'father' no less, never mind the masculine overtones here of critical pedagogy. Critical pedagogy is a political movement that operates in different contexts and, in its most fundamental stripped-down ideological perspective, it is about empowering people to learn how to govern rather be governed. It is about taking seriously questions of context, questions of power, questions of knowledge, questions of values, and questions of theory and organized resistance. Moreover, critical pedagogy is more than a classroom phenomenon and is central to how matters of agency, identity, values and visions are shaped in the larger society. Critical pedagogy has to be part of a movement of organized resistance, in which educators connect to social movements outside of the schools and connect with each other. Any transformative pedagogy cannot be reduced to closing a door in a classroom and being inventive about talking to students in ways that make something meaningful in order to make it critical, to make it transformative. Critical pedagogy is a project and a movement for both enlightenment, empowerment, and tied to the creation of a massively organized form of resistance that cuts across a wide variety of spheres and institutions; if it doesn't do that, it will fail and be reduced to simply a sterile method.

GTT   We have been talking in these events for a few weeks now, [about] organizational power, organization of, you know, educators, pedagogues in unions, for example, right now, all over the world, there are some unions and organizations and [they are] connecting each other. This is what we understand from partly from critical pedagogy and this is why we are here. Of course, there are no borders, there is no geography, it is all over the world where there's a need, there's a need for thinking, there is a need for mobilizing, for movements. Of course, the problems are having the same all over the world, so gathering into unions will be in the same form these days, especially these days we need to get together in such unions, in such gatherings and organizations. This is an international issue as a result.

Henry A. Giroux   Can [I] just say something about that? I may just build on your insight by referring to the work of Pierre Bourdieu. He argued that educators need an international movement for the protection of education and public goods. He argued for an international movement. We see some of that already with the Black Lives Matter, with the Palestinian movement for justice, and also where young people across the globe are coordinating and working with each other in ways to share their resources, share their insights and to share the pedagogical possibilities for organized resistance against various forms of authoritarianism. But I think that until unions and other social movements take the question of education more seriously and take it seriously not just simply as a national project but as an international global project, they will sabotage their efforts to build unions with an international reach capable of defending schools and public goods on an international level. Such actious would constitute a crucial move forward and it seems to me that it can be done in multiple ways. It can be done through the production and use of a range of alternative media, including the internet, print culture and various forms of audio culture such as podcasts; it can be done through the sharing of resources and acknowledging the particular kinds of forms of oppression under neoliberalism, in particular that universities have in common: the attack on governance, the attack on faculty, the privatization of students, the standardization of curriculum, and how we can work together to basically share research and work with other social movements to basically organize spaces of resistance both inside and outside of the schools.

I think that we agree that academics have an enormous responsibility here. Many of them, especially those who are tenured, work in very privileged positions, and I think that they have to be very careful about being seduced by power, especially when it comes to ignoring the rights of people who are not tenured for fear of losing their privileged positions. I think they have to be self-reflective about translating their work so as to make it rigorous and acceptable. This allows them to share their scholarship with public audiences while making clear the crucial link between higher education and the larger society. They have to, in some way, in a time of a pandemic crisis, speak very clearly to what it means to talk about how pedagogy is changing worldwide under the kind of standardizing logic emerging during the pandemic. The newfound emphasis on screen time, online teaching and endless technical refinements to the technologies involved have the potential to strip teaching of its most noble goals. Moreover, there are concerns about privacy rights, and the invasion of the corporate sector into these online projects. I mean these are all fundamental issues that academics as public intellectuals should be intervening in, their voices should be heard right now in conjunction with unions, social movements, youth groups, black groups, groups that are now being part [of this] who are moving and protesting against what I call 'the rise of the carceral state' and 'the punishing state'. These are very important issues.

GTT   Yes, the subject normally and naturally comes to public intellectuals here and academics and academic staff. As scholars, we are public intellectuals.

Henry A. Giroux   Something should be said here because I do not want to sound too Pollyannish. One of the first casualties of any authoritarian regime as we well know, is the attack on intellectuals. In Turkey, in Egypt, in the United States. In Turkey, over 500 intellectuals have now been either banished or put in prison. Opposition newspapers are being shut down and journalists who function in a critical capacity are either being killed or put in prison. Think about the way in which Russia and Saudi Arabia treat journalists and public intellectuals they consider a threat to their power. These attacks speak fundamentally to the fact that the first attack on the part of a fascist politics and the part of authoritarian societies is to eliminate those intellectuals and cultural workers who oppose it. We have to be very conscious of that and I think that means at some fundamental level, to be a public intellectual, we have to take risk[s]. You can't perform such work without being courageous, and you can't do it alone. Moreover, one has to fight for and provide safe spaces where we can support each other, and we have to find ways to mobilize the resources to be able to engage in such work. To be able to fight a machine, a capitalist machine that has so much power and so many resources can at times seem overwhelming and lead to cynicism. But we cannot withdraw or allow ourselves to fall into a defeatist mindset. This fight has to go on. It is much too important at this time in history.

GTT   I was really moved by the strong ideas that you have just mentioned. As Patti Smith would say, 'We have the power,' and we have the power, so we should come together.

Let's continue with other questions. I would like to move on with a focus on cultural studies and education. Dr Giroux, you have been introducing cultural studies into education and education into cultural studies. How should we revisit this merging of cultural studies and education? Especially under these circumstances.

Henry A. Giroux   I think what's particularly interesting about the merging of education and cultural studies, as many of you already know, emerges basically through the work of Raymond Williams and a number of other people who worked in adult education. They were working with workers trying to figure out how to redefine the question of education because education not only was meaningful in terms of what it might [mean]; what it might mean to address their problems and change their lives outside of a curriculum that basically had nothing to do with their problems or their lives and to make it relevant. They wanted to connect education to everyday life and popular culture. Eventually, the connection to education was lost and as cultural studies become more shaped by the rhetoric of high theory and ensconced in English Departments. All of a sudden, cultural studies, particularly in the United States and in the United Kingdom, became academicized in a way that removed entirely its connection with education in general. If you look at a number of texts that came out when the field of cultural studies, when it was at its most popular, many of these texts would provide definitions and associations of words and categories related to the field. I remember talking to Larry Grossberg once after I received a celebrated cultural studies book that included a number of alleged terms central to the field that he had edited with a number of other people in the UK. The words *pedagogy* and *education* were not included, and I asked him how this could have happened? I asked him how a text on cultural studies exclude[s] the categories *pedagogy* or *education* in it? He was apologetic, indicating that in spite of his support for including education and pedagogy, the editors rejected his position.

Of course, Stuart Hall clearly understood that the academicization of cultural studies and its incorporation into high theory was at odds with the initial spirit of cultural studies. Hall argued that the field had basically become so over-theorized that it began to resemble the language of scientific positivism. This was not an attack on theory as much as a criticism of the increasing use of jargon and deadening forms of theoretical discourse. Hall made clear that his comments were not an attack on theory per se, but on theory that loses its possibility for being vibrant, alive and able to speak to people because it resonated with their modes of identification, values and need for a critical and informed language. I think theory is crucial to inform what we do at the level of everyday life. Cultural Studies was crucial in that sense. It talked about everything, from the way working-class people interacted in stores and shopping malls and schools. It bore down on the problems in which diverse groups could recognize themselves while offering them a politics in which they could situate their lives in a more comprehensive understanding of politics. So, for me, the task was to reclaim cultural studies. At issue here was the need to argue that education is not simply about schooling, however important the latter, but to stress that pedagogy was central to politics; that is, to matters of consciousness, the struggle over agency and critical thought itself. How can you do cultural studies [and] not be concerned about the question of agency? How can educators address cultural studies and not be concerned with the politics of identification? How could we take up cultural studies and not take seriously what it means to be an organic intellectual? Gramsci once said that all politics is about education in some fundamental way.

What I am suggesting is that no field, including cultural studies, can run away from education. If you run away from education, then, basically, you end up believing that the only structures of domination that matter are economic. One consequence is that you lose or downplay any viable understanding of the terrain over struggle of values, ideas, pedagogical practices, etc. Bourdieu was right when he argued that those of us on the left should 'never underestimate the symbolic and pedagogical dimensions of struggle', which have always been forged as appropriate weapons of struggle. It seems to me that to take the question of politics seriously means recognizing that forms of domination are not only economic but also intellectual and pedagogical, as are weapons of resistance. I believe such an understanding should be a crucial organizing principle of cultural studies.

I once mentioned in *Theory and Resistance in Education* a basic precept of critical pedagogy that I still think has a lot of value. The point was: 'How do you make something meaningful to make it critical, to make it transformative?' Think about that. Think about what that means for theory. Think about what that means for teaching. Think about what that means for talking to people in a language that doesn't make it appear that you have no understanding of the experiences and level of competencies and narratives they bring to class. Think about the pedagogical value of being able accommodate multiple languages and narratives as part of a political project that enables people to narrate themselves. Think about what it means to respect the languages that people bring to the classroom or public sphere to both understand their need not to be voiceless and thus powerless, but also what it means to enter into dialogue with them and learn something. That's the essence of what Paulo Freire talked about in his various books dealing with politics, pedagogy and literacy. As educators, we have to learn how to learn how to be border-crossers. We have to move through multiple spaces and spheres, constantly developing a sense of what it means to be respectful and to recognize the limits of our own learning. I must tell you, for me, if I had to give you a definition of critical pedagogy that is somewhat abstract but seems to me to speak to something important, it is the recognition that critical pedagogy is not just about what you need to learn to be informed to be a knowledgeable and critically informed agent. It's also what you need to unlearn. What has this society made of us in a social order dominated by white privilege, a toxic masculinity, unchecked militarism and regressive notions of identity rooted in the dual logic of consumption and privatization. Dealing with such questions is a struggle in the challenge of being self-reflective, one we all have to engage in every day with ourselves and with others.

GTT Henry, just to add, we are experiencing this these days. How can we separate public health from economy? From politics? From education? From schooling? It's a matter of public health we are talking about these days.

Henry A. Giroux At the heart of an educational project that matters is creating the conditions for people to be able to exercise the capacities to not just simply learn how to survive but to live a good life with dignity in relationship to others. In order for that to happen, you absolutely have to have faith not just simply in the notion of the social contract, but in the notion of public goods. There are institutions that are so crucial to how we improve the quality of our lives that they cannot be turned over to market interests. This is obvious when we recognize that neoliberalism begins with the assumption that the market should be the basis for judging all relationships and defining all relationships and that it's the organizing governing principle is that everything is measured by the logic of profit. That's a predatory system. It's a cancer on the body politic. It undermines the public good. It undermines the basic institutions that people need as fundamental institutions that need to be safeguarded and put in the trust of the public good. Transportation, health, prisons, infrastructure, water, food, housing ... These are all institutions that in some way have to be taken on as part of a government responsibility that guarantees access. Nobody should be denied healthcare because they don't have the money. Where did that get us with the pandemic? It accelerated the pandemic, failed to deliver on essential goods, provide enough vaccines and protect the lives of the most vulnerable. Covid-19 made clear the failures of the market to deal with the plague while causing the deaths of over 33 million people globally. Capitalism has blood on its hands. Hundreds of thousands of people are suffering, dying, and suffering needlessly because of the logic of capitalism, because of its failure to address human needs over the accumulation of capital. This is a pathology. And as neoliberalism runs out of excuses to defend itself and suffers from a legitimation, it moves into the realm of white supremacy in order to provide scapegoats for its own failures. We have all seen how it then attacks how immigrants and other marginalized by class, race, and religion as are criminal and rapists. Allegedly, undocumented immigrants carry diseases; people who are refugees, fleeing from the worst kinds of economic and political conditions, become a scourge on humankind. Neoliberalism in recent years has found new and accelerated ways [to] find ways to dehumanize those considered 'other' so society does not have to invest in their wellbeing or future. This is a central element of a fascist politics, however updated. Consequently, as global capitalism becomes more vicious and crueler, it produces a fascist politics globally that far exceeds anything we have seen in a long time. At the same time, ignorance along with forms of social and historical amnesia are celebrated. And if we can't learn from history, the issue is not that we're going to repeat it. It is that we're going to become complicitous with it. And that's different.

GTT   Maybe I can go on with a note of hope as the last question. You wrote about higher education and neoliberalism in relation with the idea of the public intellectual. You also, like many of us, personally try to live your life as a public intellectual in an age [of] fake news, as you said, white supremacy, toxic masculinity, big lies and dumbing down. Should we be hopeful about a better climate for public intellectuals' work of teaching and research? How do you think about creating safe, creative and critical digital spaces that foster hope?

Henry A. Giroux   First of all, let me begin with the presupposition that there's no such thing as agency without hope. If we can't imagine a world beyond the one we live in, it seems to me that we either become cynical or we become complicitous. Secondly, it is important to do everything we can not to romanticize hope. Hope isn't, like, 'Oh, because I am hoping things will improve, I don't have to do anything else.' The latter is a not so innocent plaintive wish that things will turn out better simply by imaging it will happen. Hope is always engaged in a struggle with the dark forces of humanity. Hope is something that involves being educated. Hope means that you believe that people can basically come together to make the world a better place, but you have to find out how to do that and you have to make sure you know what the obstacles are to prevent that from happening. I don't believe you can act otherwise unless you can think otherwise.

That seems to me fundamental to the politics of hope; moreover, hope is a social and not merely an individual aspiration, but I also want to make it clear that when we talk about hope, we're talking partly about education, we're talking about consciousness or what I have called 'educated hope'. We're doing politics and we're talking about the spaces, ideas and institutions necessary to make it possible. How do we create those spaces? How do we bring people together? I mean, those spaces, to me, are both historical, literally meaning. How do we learn from the past? How have people struggled on the conditions not unlike the conditions that we are struggling under today? Moreover, what does it mean to realize rather than *think* about hope? How does hope become a project and a possibility that merges questions of critique with the questions of educated hope? How do we do that? Finally, it seems to me that I can't imagine living in a time of tyranny, given the era in which we live in, which those of us, who are educators, cannot reimagine the spaces in which we work as one of the few spaces left that really offer the opportunity to educate people; to unsettle common-sense assumptions; to push against the grain. In the Benjamin sense, it is crucial to think against the grain.[2] Intellectuals should cause trouble. We should cause trouble. We should unsettle.

You know, when I say 'safe spaces' should be safe, they should be safe in that they should allow people to be unsettled. They should be allowed people to cause trouble. They should be allowed, they should allow people to think critically. Sometimes, that's difficult and because it's difficult doesn't mean you can't or you shouldn't experience it. I don't believe that hope begins with trauma and ends with trauma. I think hope identifies trauma and then gets beyond it. I don't want to see hope collapse the public and the political into the personal. I want to see the personal translate into the political in ways in which hope goes beyond simply not only reinventing our own sense of agency but reinventing that sense of agency collectively in its struggle for justice, equality and freedom.

GTT   I know some people here who are very good in creating trouble.

Henry A. Giroux   Creating trouble should be the anthem for public intellectuals. James Baldwin once said, 'It is certain, in any case, that ignorance, allied with power, is the most ferocious enemy justice can have.' I think that making trouble, taking risk and making power accountable strike me as a central feature of politics. There's something about the joy of being with other people who cause trouble. There's something about the laughter. There's something about the drinking. There's something about putting our arms around each other. There's something about celebrating our dignity. There's something about not knowing that we're simply right but that knowing that love matters when it's political. That it matters. That desire is an element of justice. That justice without desire is empty. Politics without love is empty. That what we do is not just simply about wanting to change the world; what we do is about what Marcuse said is making the world a joyous place.[3] I'm not interested in intellectuals who are rigid, decry passion, live in circles of certainty and appear emotionally frozen. I don't believe in political purity, and any politics that matters should also not subscribe to such a ruinous notion of being in the world.

---

2. Walter Benjamin, *Illuminations* (New York: Schocken Books, 1969).

3. Herbert Marcuse, 'An essay on liberation', *An Anthology of Western Marxism: From Lukács and Gramsci to Socialist-Feminism* (New York: Oxford University Press, 1989), 234–47.

GTT   Yes, ... We had this, the combination of it, as a society, as a whole country seven years ago. We were in the streets for this joy and created a big trouble and we are still having it at an individual level, maybe in small groups. This is life, I think, and this is hope, this is joy.

Henry A. Giroux: Fatma, the greatest thing about the social is it brings us together and that's why right-wingers, market evangelicals and libertarian extremists want to destroy elements of the social; that's why they want to individualize every social problem; that's why they want to separate us and alienate us. Leo Löwenthal, writing with the Frankfurt School in the 1930s and the 1940s, said the worst element of fascism is social atomization. I believe that. Once we're separated, once we're individualized, once we're removed and disconnected from humanity, terrible things happen. And I think the good news is that these dictatorships never last too long, because they can't sustain themselves ideologically. They always end up simply operating on the side of repression, full-blown. Look at a guy like Trump, a buffoon and an authoritarian. He'll say anything and he's lost all credibility. We now operate in a time of a pandemic crisis, where capitalism has lost its legitimacy. It's suffering from not just a political crisis but suffering from a legitimating crisis, hence Turkey, Brazil, the United States. They're not attempting to legitimate themselves anymore. Now it's full stop of pressure and that actually opens up more spaces for resistance. It seems to me that's where the logic of possibility begins to bloom. They're not trying to control your minds anymore, just your bodies ...

GTT   Yes, there's this energy here. Thank you, Henry, that was so good to have you with us today. What would you like to say before we finish?

Henry A. Giroux   I think that it is crucial that we learn to work together, become border-crossers, invent a new language for politics and affirm the principles of democratic socialism. I think that these are dangerous times. (As my wife, Ourania, says), we have to fight the monsters and we have to fight them collectively and we have to do it through education and struggle and we can't despair because, in the long run, we have to win this struggle for justice and equality, we'll win. It'll just take time.

Chapter 2

RADICAL AND HOPEFUL DISCUSSIONS ABOUT TIMES OF BRUTAL CONSERVATISM: PATHS OF FIGHT AND TRANSFORMATION IN THE LIGHT OF PAULO FREIRE[1]

Peter McLaren

In a letter written in February 1994, Paulo Freire lovingly referred to the 'intellectual kinship' between people who are strangers from the blood point of view, but who reveal similarities in the way of appreciating the facts, understanding them, valuing them. This kinship is described by the wonderful feeling that invades us when we meet a person and we feel that we are connected to them by an old friendship. It is as if the meeting, in person, was a long-awaited reunion, in which the intercommunication takes place easily and the topics covered are apprehended through similar experiences of epistemological approach to them. Great friendships take root and thrive in this 'intellectual relationship', they cross time and resist possible changes. In that letter, Paulo Freire referred to Peter McLaren, an 'intellectual relative' who discovered and by whom he was discovered. After all, as Freire points put, 'no one becomes someone's relative if the other does not recognize the one as a relative' (2005, 247).

Freire had already read McLaren before meeting him in person and soon discovered that they belonged to the same intellectual 'family'. However, he made clear that this did not mean reducing each other, as the autonomy of both is what marks the true kinship.

1. Originally appeared as 'Interview with Peter McLaren: Radical and hopeful discussions about times of brutal conservatism – paths of fight and transformation in the light of Paulo Freire', *Praxis Educativa*, 16 (2021): 1–22, retrieved from: https://doi.org/10.5212/ PraxEduc.v.16.17204.010.

The interview was conducted by Lucimara Cristina de Paula and the translation of the questions from Portuguese into English and the introductory note was carried out by Bhianca Moro Portella.

Appears in this volume by the permission of Peter McLaren, Jefferson Mainardes, Chief Editor of *Praxis Educativa* and Lucimara Cristina de Paula.

When received the invitation to give this interview, Professor Peter McLaren quickly sent an affirmative answer, showing us great interest in discussing Paulo Freire's legacy in such difficult times for Brazil and the USA. Peter McLaren, one of the main representatives of Critical Pedagogy, was a professor at the University of California (1985–2013) and currently works at the College of Educational Studies, Chapman University. He works as director of the Democratic Project Paulo Freire and International Ambassador in Global Ethics and Social Justice and he is an expert in the following topics: Liberation Theology and Education in Catholic Social Justice, Revolutionary Critical Pedagogy, Philosophy of Education, Sociology of Education, Marxist Theory and Criticism Theory. He is the author and editor of nearly 50 books and his writings have been translated into more than 25 languages. Professor Peter McLaren is a scholar and activist whose educational work seeks to reflect objectives and practices developed by Paulo Freire.

In this interview, he tells us about his life and professional trajectory, how he met Paulo Freire and explains his 'intellectual kinship' with him, he brings deep discussions about the moment of extreme and violent neoconservatism that we are experiencing and about his Critical Pedagogy. He ends this interview by pointing out paths of resistance that we need to take as educators and researchers to fight oppression, overcome inequalities, democratizing the university space.

It is an honour for us to count on Professor McLaren (Figures 2.1 and Figure 2.2) in this dossier on Paulo Freire's centenary of birth. We appreciate his special contributions!

Lucimara Cristina de Paula (LCP)   Dear Professor Peter McLaren. It is with immense joy that we received your acceptance to grant this interview about Paulo Freire to our journal. We are grateful for your availability and generosity in sharing your experiences with Freire and his relationships with Critical Pedagogy in the United States.

Figure 2.1a Paulo Freire and Peter McLaren at the Rose Theater in Omaha, Nebraska, USA, 1996. *Source*: Peter McLaren, personal file.

Figure 2.1b Paulo Freire, Peter McLaren and Augusto Boal in dialogue at the Rose Theater in Omaha, Nebraska, USA, 1996, at the Pedagogy of the Oppressed Conference. *Source*: Peter McLaren, personal file.

Figure 2.2a Peter McLaren and students at Chapman University, Orange, California, USA (2017). (2017). *Source*: Peter McLaren, personal file.

Figure 2.2b A school building, in La Escuela Normal Superior de Neiva, named after Peter McLaren in Neiva, Colombia (2017). *Source*: Peter McLaren, personal file.

To start this interview, we would like you to tell us a little about your life and education, as well as how you met Paulo Freire.

Peter McLaren   I grew up in a working-class family in Toronto, Canada. My mother had some medical problems and had to have a hysterectomy when I was young, and so I was the only child. I did not enjoy school and in fact I barely remember much of my life in school until I went to college. I think I must have repressed much of this part of my life for reasons that I am unable to fully fathom. My mother was a wonderful woman, very kind and generous and my father was a gentle and kind giant at 6 feet 3. He didn't talk much about his six years in Europe fighting the Nazis but I am sure many of his experiences during World War II traumatized him. My uncle was a war hero with the Royal Navy, helping to sink the German battleship, *Bismarck*. The dominant adult males in my life were very conservative politically.

In the 1960s, everything changed, and I became a hippie. At 19, I hitchhiked to the US, to Los Angeles and San Francisco and participated in protests against the Vietnam War. I read my poetry in coffee shops and met some cultural icons at that time such as Allen Ginsberg and Timothy Leary. I met some Black Panthers in Oakland and took part in some political demonstrations. When I returned to Canada, I studied English Literature at the University of Toronto, majoring in Old English (Beowulf) and Middle English (Chaucer) and then went to Waterloo University to study Elizabethan Drama (Shakespeare). But during these years I kept up with what was happening politically, and some of my professors were American draft resisters who had left the United States for Canada to escape the Vietnam War. Many of my friends were taking drugs. My two best friends committed suicide.

Upon graduation, I took a job teaching grades 7 and 8 in a wealthy village. After one year I came to the conclusion that these young people from wealthy families were going to get into college and university despite whether or not they had good teachers, simply due to their class background. I went looking for another challenge. I took a job in an area of Toronto known as the Jane-Finch Corridor. It had a reputation as a dangerous neighbourhood. A cluster of government subsidized high rises flanked the school. Teachers did not last long in this school. But I loved the students and the principal was amazing. He took a sledgehammer to the wall of his office, and smashed it into pieces so his office could be easily accessible to all students. He replaced his steel desk with a small wooden table and replaced his chair with a rocking chair. All day long, students came to see him for a hug. He was known as the hugging principal. I followed his lead and threw out all of the desks and chairs in my classroom and filled the room with pillows and comfortable furniture. I found a pair of drums and for a month the students and I took turns drumming. Test scores went up. I wrote a book about my experiences, many of the pages documented violence and despair among the students. The book became a Canadian bestseller. However, I made the mistake of not analysing my experiences in the book. Later, after getting my Master's degree in Education at night, I was accepted to the Ontario Institute for Studies in Education, University of Toronto for a PhD. That is when I learned about Paulo Freire.

I had heard that Paulo had visited the university but I had missed his talk. And yet there was no mention of Freire's work in the official curricula for the courses that I was taking. Nor was their official mention of other critical scholars. I found out who they were by talking to students in other programs, and studied their works on my own. I finally was able to get a videotape of Paulo being interviewed. The year was 1980.

I met Paulo in person in 1985 at an annual meeting of the American Educational Research Association. He had filled an auditorium with 500 people. Clearly, North American educators were discovering who he was. I was close friends with Henry Giroux and Donaldo Macedo who were close to Paulo. I was surprised to learn from Paulo that he knew my work and spoke highly of it. I had no idea that he was familiar with my work. In fact, he wrote a Preface to two of my books. In one of the preface's he described me as his 'intellectual cousin'. That revealed to me the generosity of his spirit. He invited me to Cuba for a conference but when I arrived in Havana he had already left, but I was to meet many educators from Brasil, Mexico and other Latin American countries, who invited me to give talks in their home countries.

Paulo invited me to his home in Brasil and even helped to translate one of my talks in São Paulo. Other educators invited me numerous times to Brasil, to Porto Alegre, to Florianópolis, Santos, Rio de Janeiro, Santa Clara, Santa Maria (Rio Grande do Sul), Uberlandia, to Salvador in Bahia, and Cachoeira. I attended *Umbanda* and *Candomblé* ceremonies, thanks to Afro-Brazilian members of the Workers Party, and was able to visit many different favelas, and was even presented with a plaque for helping to defend Afro-Brazilian religion. I even watched a live football game between Brasil and Argentina. Brasil had captured my heart early on. Paulo had opened the door and made all of this possible.

LCP   In your narrative you seem to indicate that you got close to Freire since the time you worked at the Jane-Finch Corridor school. Your political and loving commitment to the transformation of students at this school already announced your 'intellectual kinship' with Freire, as he himself states in the preface to the book you wrote: Critical Pedagogy and Predatory Culture. How do you explain this 'kinship' and what has changed in your pedagogy, your intellectual production and your struggles since you got close to Paulo Freire?

Peter McLaren Yes, correct. I left teaching in the Jane Finch Corridor school in 1979. I first heard about Paulo in 1980. I eventually met Paulo five years later, in 1985. Yes, I did share some ideas about pedagogy and certain values about emancipation, freedom and the politics of liberation prior to reading Paulo's work. And yes, I would agree that I had a natural affinity towards Paulo's work. When I started to engage Paulo's work, I was determined to understand his ideas as best I could. Paulo brought a whole new range of meanings for me to consider, he opened doors to my understanding of politics and pedagogy in ways I had never managed.

LCP What I meant is that your affinity with him was natural and existed even before you two met. It was already expressed through emancipatory work and the ideal values you had. Your convictions brought you two closer, even before getting to know Freire. I have your book *Critical Pedagogy and Predatory Culture* translated into Portuguese and in its preface Paulo Freire mentions the 'intellectual kinship' he felt for you. Thank you for the explanation you sent anyways! It enriched your narrative for me!

Peter McLaren I felt a close affinity with Paulo, and was struck by his humility and his kindness. His was the most brilliant mind I had ever encountered and the tenderest of hearts. And the spirit of a warrior! When I first met him in one of the big hotels in Chicago during a conference, he was surrounded by dozens of admirers. When he entered a room, people stood up from their seats and there was loud applause. This happened everywhere he went. I think Paulo was surprised by the attention he received, and he always responded with patience, courtesy and humility. He would sometimes approach me in a fatherly fashion and offer me advice. Once I told him that I was discussing his work in talks I was giving in various countries in Latin America. In a friendly fashion, he cautioned me not to 'deposit' or 'import' his ideas across national borders but to invite teachers and activists from other countries to translate his ideas in the context of their own specific struggles (Figure 2.3).

President Chavez appreciated those of us who were working in Venezuela with Freire's ideas and once he emphasized to me that any critical pedagogy that would emerge from the struggle of Venezuelan communities would be Venezuelan. Chavez was an admirer of Freire and he knew enough about Paulo's ideas to understand the importance of what happens to theories when they 'travel' from one country to another. Paulo would always remind me that he saw the world through Brazilian eyes, and that the complex web of reality made it impossible to 'export' his work into other countries without considering the contextual specificity of the communities involved – he understood that people would take up his work in different ways and recreate and reinvent his ideas according to their own cultures and histories – including their

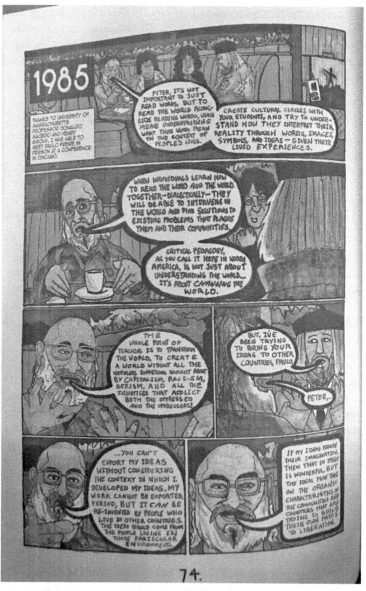

Figure 2.3 From the book, *Breaking Free: The Life and Times of Peter McLaren* (2019).[2]
Source: Peter McLaren, personal file.

2. Peter McLaren, *Breaking Free: The Life and Times of Peter McLaren*, illustrated by Miles Wilson (New York: Myers Education Press, 2019).

myths, and those forces that mediate their lifeworlds. He would always say, 'Peter, don't export me, but encourage my ideas to be reinvented' (Figure 2.4). He knew how important it was for struggling communities to navigate the contradictions inherent in asymmetrical political systems of power and privilege sustained by a patriarchal and colonial capitalist system. He exhorted those who took up his ideas to reread and rewrite him in their own ways, that is, in the ways in which they have come to read the word and the world. Freire did not want his work to be imposed on various groups through mechanistic, technocratic, or instrumentalized methodologies. When I gave talks about Paulo's work, I would restrict myself to discussing how Paulo's work influenced me in my North American contexts – how Paulo's ideas helped me to reread the word and the world in ways in which I had never considered. Likewise, other communities would judge the relevance of Paulo's work in relation to their own specific struggles.

Paulo's emphasis on praxis meant that such struggles could lead to outcomes that were achievable or potentially feasible. Paulo's work became a baseline for my work although I could never live up to the demands his work placed on me – such as Paulo's notion of unfinishedness and transcending our limit situations and transforming them into untested feasibilities as part of our ontological vocation to become more fully human and to create spaces where justice can be affirmed. Paulo's teachings sent me on a voyage of utopian dreaming for a socialist future,

Figure 2.4 From the book, *Breaking Free: The Life and Times of Peter McLaren* (2019). *Source*: Peter McLaren, personal file.

and I always tried to keep in mind Ernst Bloch's distinction between concrete and abstract utopias and the importance of an educated hope emerging through the praxis of revolutionary movements, among grassroots organizations. Paulo taught me to focus on concrete utopian thinking rather than abstract utopias which are often blueprints envisioned by bourgeois intellectuals to be put into effect at some distant point in the future. Abstract utopian thinking is often disconnected from the struggles of the immiserated, the impoverished, the disinherited.

Around 1995, I began to revisit Marx's writings and this helped to deepen my critique of political economy. We are all unfinished beings – and our purpose is not a Faustian bargain with the guardians of capital but rather humanization, which brings us closer to our goal of liberation. Revolutionary change means shifting the tectonic plates of unreason by dialectical thinking thus moving the geography of reason towards those precincts more hospitable to Marx. An historical materialist approach to understanding the role that capital plays in our social universe provides a crucial basis for overthrowing the present and inaugurating a new world, for issuing forth a novel present in which are planted the seeds of revolutionary socialism.

As Freire made abundantly clear, we need to transcend our limit situations, because beyond them is what Freire called untested feasibility, ways of being and becoming more human, where the words that we speak can hear themselves spoken. This helped me to focus on forms of human social reproduction that transcended value augmentation, the value form of labour, forms of existence that moved beyond forces and relations of capitalist commodification. Over time I became convinced that what we need is a robust transition to a new ecosocialist civilization. I began to consider the work of Marx and Freire in light of putting an end to the planetary destruction by the capitalist mode of production.

We live in the *Capitalocene* and under the influence of the negative consequences of the post-digital revolution, sometimes called the Fourth Industrial Revolution. How can we create an alternative to capitalism, combining the insights of eco-feminism and eco-socialism – this is still one of the major directions of my work. I became very interested in Raya Dunayevskaya's work, especially her notion of absolute negativity, the negation of the negation, and the positivity that can be extracted by the negation of the negation. But I don't want to get too theoretical here. I really do think we need to think of Marxism less as a mechanical approach that moves through prescribed stages, and more as a guiding myth, as the great Peruvian Marxist, Mariátegui, understood the meaning of the term. We need to feel we are part of a grand movement of change that is made more feasible in our daily efforts in challenging the system – such as in the recent protests we have seen in the United States and throughout the world after the murder of George Floyd by a Minnesota policeman.

Yet the pain and suffering that the immiserated, impoverished and disinherited strew throughout their personal narratives at this historical inflection point do contain instances of hope that a new day will be born. Consider the fact that these protests have been liberated from geographic rootedness: the demonstrations that broke out over the police murder of George Floyd sparked multiracial events in 2,000 US cities, where 26 million people participated. But the protests against police abuse, racism and social inequality also broke out at the same time in four dozen European and Latin American countries, including several African countries. This has been unprecedented. The protests became more differentiated and at the same time more collective, calling for prison reform, defunding the police, justice for transgender peoples, an end to sexual violence as well as to systematic racism, sexism and the school-to-prison pipeline.

It is gratifying to see such large multiracial groups rise up and protest the horrors of the growing slide into fascism that we are witnessing around the world at the moment, headlined by Trump, and Bolsonaro, who is sometimes called the Trump of the Tropics. I think we should take Trump and Bolsonaro in a *terreirode candomblé* and feed them each a bowl of Ayahuasca, and let Exú take them on a journey, similar to that of Dicken's *A Christmas Carol*, where they could both revisit their past, glimpse the future of the planet and be converted from fascist-loving tyrants into champions of democracy in the present. Having witnessed a devastated planet that has resulted from their shameful environmental policies and their inaction on climate change, they would witness generations of young people living disposable lives without futures, and they would undergo a personal commitment to an ecosocialist future. Yes, it is nice to live in a fantasy sometimes, to take away for a brief moment the sting of the present. But it is time that we wake up and realize that the only way to rid ourselves of these brutes is for the people to rise up and throw them out of office.

LCP   Professor Peter, your explanations made me think about various topics for us to talk about. But, as I need to choose one of them to go deeper, what really got me thinking was you said that Paulo Freire always told you: 'Peter, don't export me, but encourage my ideas to be reinvented.' And then you also said: 'When I gave talks about Paulo's work, I would restrict myself to discussing how Paulo's work influenced me in my North American contexts – how Paulo's ideas helped me to re-read the word and the world in ways in which I had never considered.' These specific parts of the answer brought me two big curiosities.

First, in what aspects did Paulo Freire influence your reading of the world and your reading of the word in the North American context? Second, what reading do you take of the world today, a world in which we see people like Trump and Bolsonaro come to power, and how to reinvent Freire's legacy as educators to seek the transformation of this world, helping to build less unjust and more respectful human relationships as he defended?

Peter McLaren   Paulo taught me to get in touch with my working-class roots, that go back to Ireland and Scotland. He turned my life as a teacher upside down. He helped me to understand my own racial privilege in a multiracial and multicultural society. He inspired me to visit Latin America, and to take lessons I learned there to the streets the United States – and this helped me to understand the systemic racism, sexism and class exploitation that was at the heart of the United States – the genocide of indigenous populations, the brutal and inhumane slavery that was embedded in the plantation economy, the ideological systems embedded in the mass media, the imperialist wars, the role of the CIA throughout the world, the hypocrisy braided into the concepts of American exceptionalism and the American Dream, the oppressive role played by the evangelical Christians who practice the 'prosperity gospel' that equates salvation which material riches. Paulo taught me how being a teacher means becoming involved in a path that requires a life devoted to an unrelenting pursuit of justice, despite the fact that the goal can never be fully foreknown or finally attained.

Paulo taught me to read history, the best I could, from the persepective of the victims, from the perspective of the people. I became an admirer of Howard Zinn's, *A People's History of the United States*. Paulo taught me to replace instrumental reason with critical, dialectical rationality, in order to enter a dialogical relationship with the oppressed and non-oppressed, and to foster popular dissent in the interests of building a society where oppression can be rooted out, and this required that I better understand the importance of workers and communal councils and community decision-making structures. Paulo risked his life to help those who suffered as a result of being disproportionately affected by the cruelty of capitalism's social relations of exploitation. Paulo taught me that education entails praxis, beginning with ethical action, not with correct doctrine.

This action is premised on a belief in the capacity for human goodness and begins with acting ethically. Human beings revise their thinking given various changes in their circumstances, and educators must themselves be willing to be educated. Revolutionary practice, or praxis, has to do with what Marx referred to as 'the coincidence of the changing of circumstances and of human activity or self-change'. That became clearer as I began to understand Paulo's work. Protagonistic or revolutionary agents are not born, they are produced by circumstances. To revolutionize thought it is necessary to revolutionize society. All human development (including thought and speech) is social activity and this has its roots in collective labour. Paulo sent me on a journey, and I am not finished yet.

I have not always been able to be a Freirean because Paulo set the standards so high. But Paulo's life and work helped me late in life to connect with the spirituality that informs all of our lives, whether we recognize it or not. Nita Freire also helped to inspire me. For me, it meant reconnecting with my Catholic faith and liberation theology. It has made me feel a deep sadness and anger at what Brasil's fascist president, Jair Bolsonaro, is doing to Brasil. He is a 'macho' man who is at war with the educational left of his country, whom he decries as 'cultural Marxists', and is playing the political fiddle as his country's Amazon rainforest goes up in flames. This is the same man who is trying to replace Paulo Freire as the Patron of Brazilian Education with a sixteenth-century Spanish Jesuit missionary, Saint Joseph of Anchieta, and who, armed with the logic of instrumental reason and the mental acuity of someone afflicted by an after-lunch stupor, has refused $20 million in aid money offered by G-7 nations to battle the fires that are wreaking havoc on one of the world's greatest sources of biodiversity, a refusal promoted by a slight on Bolsonaro by French President Emmanuel Macron.

Even the spirit of Chico Xavier, summoned from the dead by the followers of Allen Kardec, cannot halt the forces of deforestation any more than he can dampen the government's enthusiasm for the illegal 'sweetheart deals' it has struck with the Brazilian mining and logging industries. So, Bolsonaro doesn't seem to care about fighting 'anthropogenic extinction' or ecological collapse or climate change. How can we escape the probability of extinction, especially as it is aided and abetted by policies of the 'new barbarians' headed by Bolsonaro and Trump, policies designed to reduce environmental protections and to allow the destruction of four million hectares of forest in South America every year?

I am tired of Trump's juvenile theatrics and those of Bolsonaro. He can now boast he has survived Covid-19 because of his past as an athlete. So, he goes on trips to supermarkets and bakeries and shakes hands and takes selfies without gloves or a mask while Trump ridicules Joe Biden for wearing a mask. Trump has also survived Covid-19 and brags about how he was only sick for a few days because of his excellent genes. Bolsonaro has threatened to rid Brazil's education system of all 'Marxist rubbish' and to use a political 'flamethrower' to erase the historical memory of Paulo Freire throughout Brasil. Trump is now saying that education designed to help students understand white privilege and racism is un-American. He doesn't want white people to feel uncomfortable for their complicity in slavery, for systemic racism, for a capitalist system driven by racism. Create a safe space for the white people, for their complicity in racialized social relations! Here, Trump is pandering to his 'base' of supporters and enabling more racism to occur. He is 'normalizing' racism. He is 'weaponizing' white supremacy, and white militia movements armed with automatic rifles are growing under his leadership. They love Trump for making 'racism' permissible again. Let's keep the blacks and Latino/as from the suburbs! Make the suburbs great again for White people!

Both Trump and Bolsonaro need to take a seminar with Leonardo Boff. Maybe Boff can visit them and give them a tutorial on the life of Saint Francis when these leaders are both in prison.

What do you do when your *pai-de-santo*, your *babalorishá*, manifests *Exú* when you know *Exú* can be capricious as well as kind and loving? Once a lawyer from Brazil's *Partido dos Trabalhadores* told me that members of an *Umbanda* group where we once celebrated together a feast of *Pomba Gira* saved her daughter's life through a spiritual intervention when her daughter was undergoing a tonsillectomy.

These are questions I've tried to answer since my participation in *Umbanda* ceremonies decades ago. Does a scientific explanation really matter to those historically oppressed Brazilians who, during celebrations in their terreiros, are possessed by their orishas? I have never witnessed anything hateful at the heart of this religious practice. It is filled with outpourings of love and dedication to helping others. Umbandistas also worship Jesus. Yet they are constantly coming under attack, being falsely accused of practicing black magic. I would rather be in their company than with those prosperity-gospel, praise-the-Lord, fire-and-brimstone preaching protestant evangelicals who receive financial support from the US government to broadcast their missions throughout Latin America. Both the Brazilian and US governments are worried about liberation theology taking root again within the Catholic Church so they are happy to support fundamentalist evangelical protestants who preach patriotism, nationalism, and are pro-capitalist. The government of Bolsonaro, I am sure, does not want liberation theology to take further root in Brasil.

Because one of the foundational positions of liberation theology is that the exploitation and alienation of human beings from their own 'species being' results from the sin of greed, and the social relations and forces of capitalist production. Governments that pay total allegiance to the god of capitalism, whose leaders benefit from neoliberal capitalism, and that are led by fascists and authoritarian populists don't want the 'personal' Jesus of their citizens to meet Karl Marx. They must be kept wide apart for ideological reasons. Liberation theology emphasizes action over doctrine – what those of us in the critical pedagogy movement refer to as 'praxis' – and this term is very closely aligned with the revolutionary praxis of Marx and Freire.

I learned this from visiting the Landless Workers' Movement in Brazil, and from witnessing community initiatives throughout North and South America that have been influenced by the teachings of Paulo Freire. A Black Theology of Liberation has now a strong presence in African American communities, and there exists strong proponents of feminist theology, postcolonial theology, reconciliation theology. With Paulo Freire no longer in this earthly dimension of existence we must rely on those whose spirit and intellect have been touched by Freire – and I find this in the work of those teachers, community activists and priests who are living out Freire's pedagogical praxis in their barrios, favelas, communities and also in universities and theological seminaries.

They are helping us through their lived experiences and examples to better understand Freire's life and mission. In this way, Freire lives! The fascists can try to ignore Freire or attack Freire, but they will never kill Freire's spirit. Paulo Freire lives! Long after Bolsonaro and Trump are forgotten, Freire's spirit will be remembered and revered for his gift to humanity – a pedagogy of love!

According to Paulo, we become conscious of and transcend the limits in which we can make ourselves through externalizing, historicizing and concretizing our vision of liberation, as we challenge the psychopathology of everyday life incarnated in capitalism's social division of labour. Paulo advises us to refrain from separating the production of knowledge from praxis, from reading the word and the world dialectically. This taught me that praxis serves as the ultimate ground for advancing and verifying theories as well as for providing warrants for knowledge claims. These warrants are not connected to some fixed principles that exist outside of the knowledge claims themselves but are derived by identifying and laying bare the ideological and ethical potentialities of a given theory as a form of practice. This is Paulo's pedagogy of the concrete, his dialectics of the concrete.

We take our everyday social relationships and practices and try to examine their contradictions when seen in relation to the totality of social relations in which those particular relations and practices unfold. Thus, we have a backdrop against which we can read the word and the world historically. This enables us to live in the historical moment as a subject of history and, like Walter Benjamin's Angel of History, to see that human 'progress' has left a world devastated by violence and destruction. We link our own history to the struggles of oppressed groups. This process is not simply an effect of language but pays attention to extra-linguistic forms of knowing, forms of corporeal and praxiological meanings that are all bound up with the production of ideology.

Meaningful knowledge is not solely nor mainly the property of the formal properties of language but is enfleshed – it is sentient, it is lived in and through our bodies, the material aspects of our being. It is neither ultra-cognitivist nor traditionally intellectualist. Knowledge, in other words, is embodied in the way we read the world and the word simultaneously in our actions with, against and alongside other human beings. We can't transform history solely in our heads! But language is at the same time important. As Freire notes, 'Within the word we find two dimensions, reflection, and action, in such radical interaction that if one is sacrificed – even in part – the other immediately suffers. There is no true word that is not at the same time a praxis. Thus, to speak a true word is to transform the world.' True words require actions.

The world in which we speak our words must be changed in order for those words to be true. Words can only come to life when we use them to effect change. Do our words encourage dialogue and engagement with others? The words of Trump bring fear and hatred and division. His words are not true, they are shallow, they are hollow. The same with Bolsonaro. Freire teaches us to name our world and to humanize it. The words of Bolsonaro are spoken from above, from the precincts of power, they are dominative, not dialogical. They do not encourage reflection but only obedience. It is the same with Trump.

Paulo did not wish simply to organize political power in order to transform the world; he wished to reinvent power as power with the people, not power over the people. Political power, of course, is based on economic power. Freire believed that resources for a dignified survival should be socially available and not individually owned. The history of the rich is immortalized because their words are used to defend the interests and privilege of the ruling class. It is a fatalistic way of thinking about the poor that rationalizes poverty as a constituent condition of living in a class-divided society. Such a fatalism also leads to political immobilization as teachers focus on 'techniques, on psychological, behavioral explanations, instead of trying or acting, of doing something, of understanding the situation globally, of thinking dialectically, dynamically'.

Very often the rich are culturally progressive but economically reactionary. Freire taught me that dialectical inquiry should be at the heart of 'the act of knowing' which is fundamentally an act of transformation that goes well beyond the epistemological domain. It must reach into the real world of others. Dialogic education is, for Paulo, a path of providing opportunities for students to recognize the unspoken ideological dimension of their everyday understanding and to encourage themselves to become part of the political process of transformation of structures of oppression to pathways to emancipation – that is, to pathways to freedom. We cannot escape history. That is a powerful lesson that I learned from Paulo. Paulo wrote: 'You must discover that you cannot stop history. You have to know that your country (the US) is one of the greatest problems for the world. You have to discover that you have all these things because of the rest of the world. You must think of these things.'

I once wrote this description of Paulo for a book edited by Tom Wilson, Peter Park and Anaida Colón-Muñiz called, *Memories of Paulo*:

> He was a picaresque pedagogical wanderer, a timeless vagabond linked symbolically to Coal Yard Alley, to Rio's City of God, to the projects of Detroit and any and every neighborhood where working men and women have toiled throughout the centuries, a flaneur of the boulevards littered with fruiterers and fish vendors and tobacco and candy stalls, the hardscrabble causeways packed with migrant workers and the steampunk alleys of dystopian dreams.
>
> This man of the people was as much at home in the favelas as he was in the mango groves, a maestro who would cobble together the word and the world from the debris of everyday life, from its fury of dislocation, from the hoary senselessness of its cruelty, from its beautiful and frozen emptiness and the wrathfulness of its violence. And in the midst of all of this he was able to fashion revolutionary hope from the tatters of humanity's fallen grace. This was Paulo Freire.

Paulo Freire, he has found a place in our hearts, and as a fighter he has found a place in our protagostic struggle to build a better world.

LCP   Your answer makes explicit the profound influence of Paulo Freire in your Critical Pedagogy, the critical, revolutionary, radical pedagogy of Peter McLaren. So, I would like you to tell us about it (Figure 2.5).

We started this interview in order to learn about Peter McLaren's personal and professional trajectory, we talked about Paulo Freire and found out what Peter learned from Paulo. Now we return to Peter and his work in the second decade of the twenty-first century. So, tell us a little bit about how you put your critical pedagogy into practice at university and elsewhere in the USA. What results have you achieved with your work so far? Could you please send us photographs of you with Paulo Freire and also of your work to integrate and enrich the interview?

Peter McLaren   In 1995, my work became fundamentally Marxist humanist in orientation, and pedagogically I have always been a student of Freire. And I am a great admirer of Nita Freire, whose work has been helpful to many and to many of us in critical pedagogy. Donaldo Macedo's work with Freire has been very important in my understanding and appreciation of Paulo's work. I was very lucky to have joined the Paulo Freire Democratic Project at Chapman University (Figure 2.6) after being a professor at the University of California, Los Angeles. The professors who belong to the Paulo Freire Democratic Project are wonderful colleagues who have taught me how to engage with communities surrounding the university – Lilia Monzo, Suzanne SooHoo, Anaida Colon-Muniz, Jorge Rodriguez, Catherey Yeh, Kevin Stockbridge, Gregory Warren and Gerri McNenny. We believe critical pedagogy has the potential to rehumanize our future if we can challenge our dehumanized material (commodity) culture by a praxis-oriented

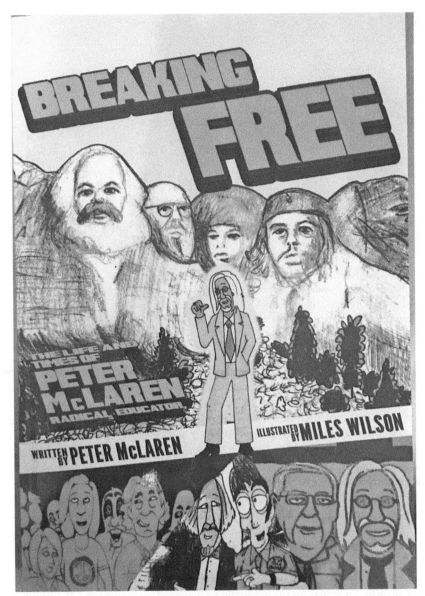

Figure 2.5 Graphic novel about Peter McLaren. *Source*: Peter McLaren, personal file.

pedagogy and are able to revolutionize the political and economic institutions in the public interest rather than for private gain. That means building for a socialist future. All education today needs to focus on building for a socialist future. Our planet is burning! We need to reclaim our humanity and the power of critique. Some are looking to communism as a new frontier, rethinking many of its major concepts, others are employing a socialist strategic offensive.

Figure 2.6a Peter McLaren beside the sculpture of Paulo Freire at Chapman University, Orange, California, USA. *Source*: Peter McLaren, personal file.

Figure 2.6b Peter McLaren at Instituto McLaren in Ensenada, Mexico. *Source*: Peter McLaren, personal file.

Now when you ask me what progress I have made, it's difficult to evaluate, because it is very difficult to make progress when you are a revolutionary Marxist and Catholic social justice worker who follows the path of liberation theology and is a major critic of the conservative wing of the Catholic Church – and live in the United States! My work appears to be more engaged outside of the United States. Here, in my adopted country, my ideas are seen by the majority of the population as radically extreme. That is because anti-communism and socialism have been weaponized by Republicans and many Democrats as the greatest threat to democracy. In fact, socialism in reality is the only hope for democracy to prevail. I am not the person to ask how successful I have been. That is a task for others to judge.

I have worked as part of a larger community of critical educators and together we have helped to build the field of critical pedagogy – there are courses in critical pedagogy in education, in the field of law, in psychology, in sociology, in English composition. Paulo's work has been engaged in all of these fields. He paved the way for all of us. Of course, in the academic field, critical pedagogy has been successful since the topic of 'social justice education' is now very common in teacher education and graduate classes in education. But there is still only a very few Marxists in the graduate schools of education and across other fields as well. Marxism and socialism continue to be attacked continually in the mainstream media.

I was accused of being 'the most dangerous professor in UCLA' back in 2005–2006 because of my support for Cuba and Hugo Chavez in Venezuela, and this attack on me and other professors at UCLA became an international story. And now it is worse in this country as we witness militarized forces attacking US civilians. Donald Trump is psychotic, clearly. Recently, he has criticized the important and illuminating revolutionary historian Howard Zinn and he has attacked critical race theorists and he has described Black Lives Matter protestors as 'terrorists'. In this respect Trump is as despicable as Bolsonaro, although Trump has the power to bring the world to ruins. Almost half the country supports a president who is racist, sexist, a misogynist, who is a white nationalist and white supremacist and who has turned the country into a pariah state. He is a malignant narcissist, is infected with misology, is a serial liar, and who lacks empathy for the poor. All of his decisions are predicated on what will get him reelected. He is basically a mafia leader, a criminal, a man-child who has divided the country to the point of almost tearing it apart. He has fired numerous inspectors general when they were beginning to investigate him. Then the federal attorney for the Southern District of New York, started looking into Trump's activities and Trump fired him. Trump's climate and nuclear policies could virtually doom the planet. He has abandoned arms control, and the arms industry is very pleased with Trump.

Trump has just mentioned that he will create a commission on educational patriotism, and insists that teachers must teach the greatness of the United States. I have been calling for a 'critical patriotism' which insists that the United States must recognize its many crimes as a country, through both its foreign and domestic policies. We do this through an historical materialist approach to understanding and interpreting historical events, through a dialectical engagement with what has transpired as a result of our activities in dealing with other countries. Of course, we can celebrate the good things about this country – I'm not against that – but not at the expense of recognizing its historical crimes which the country has too often carried on the back of a settler colonialism, a military nationalism, the notion of American exceptionalism and the belief that God has ordained the United States to exercise its power in whatever way it pleases in order to protect its material prosperity and its way of life.

Critical pedagogy has always been an outlier as far as education goes. It's been an oppositional 'way of life' that challenges the anti-Kingdom of those who worship money and who follow the God of profit. It does this from the perspective of the most vulnerable, the poor, the powerless, whom Frantz Fanon referred to as 'the wretched of the earth'. I have tried to work with many others as an internationalist educator in order to build alliances around the world, wherever it was possible. In my younger days I was able to visit numerous countries and I was able to see how capital dominates labour so powerfully. I think the recent protests in the US give us a powerful opportunity to make changes. Bernie Sanders, a socialist, was a highly popular politician before he was betrayed by the Democratic National Committee and I believe that we are closer to educating US citizens about socialism, although we have a long way to go. The social division of labour, or the realm of necessity, must be decommodified, and free of exploitation. We are a little closer to developing a counter-consciousness at one end, yet at the other end we face a growth in hate of the other.

I have been absolutely overwhelmed at and sickened by the pervasive and toxic racism that exists in the United States and how such large sectors of the population have fallen prey to neo-Nazi and white supremacist ideology. The Republican Party is the most dangerous political party in the world at this moment. The people have fallen victim to a dictator whom they actually believe cares for them. This to me is a stunning revelation. Herbert Marcuse asked whether the corporate state can be prevented from becoming a fascist state. With Trump, it is clear that no, it is not possible to prevent tyranny. In fact, it has happened in many aspects. We have capitalist overaccumulation and a failure of a reproduction of our labour force – so yes, capitalism is failing, it has failed! Our democracy has only a faint heartbeat, it is barely breathing. We need to resuscitate it through education – through revolutionary critical pedagogy. Through a critical pedagogy that benefits from the insights of Marx and Freire.

And, of course, Enrique Dussel argues that the modern violence of colonialism is legitimized by European, ego-centred philosophy. Which is why we must understand reality not from the center of the European socioeconomic-political-ethno-militaristic worldview but from the exteriority of the margins, of the oppressed, the periphery that is demanded of revolutionary praxis. Only through conscientization, denaturalization, de-ideologization, de-alienation can we appreciate the praxis of the oppressed, of peoples of the periphery, as they reveal themselves to us through a self-unfolding epiphanic experience that includes a relativization of self and other. Reflecting upon the peripheral otherness of the poor, of the 'wretched of the earth' relativizes the coloniality of power (Quijano) exercised by those who benefit most from the culture of domination, and reveals such a culture to be contingent and susceptible to change through the outlaw praxis of the marginalized, the oppressed.

Freire locates himself as allied with such decolonial logics and outlaw praxis which takes place, in theological terms, on the ground under the cross. Here, the question of 'proximity' (Dussel) becomes important. Here the ethical question takes precedence over the epistemological. When a voice cries out for help from the wilderness, the question, 'Where are you, where do you stand?', takes precedence over the epistemological question, 'Who am I?' Do you stand in solidarity with the oppressed? Do you have respect for their life-worlds? Or do you regard the 'other' as just as extension of yourself and your own Cartesion ego? Clearly the ethical question for Freire is the central one. European settler colonialism justifies its genocide, its ecocide, its epistemicide on the grounds of its superior role in God's providential plan for civilizing the world. And now its nuclear policy could take us on a path towards omnicide. While I can never fully know the experience of the other, I can stand in solidarity and commit myself to struggling to create the conditions of possibility for a social universe in which humanization for liberation is possible.

We are now confronting our Golgotha moment when we are about to re-crucify Jesus with teflon nails, transferring his salvific grace to Lady Luck's slot machines, all lined up like tin soldiers in some shiny Vegas casino. We have acquiesced to a neoliberal business model to manage our schools of education. Universities should be sites where we can actualize our potential as protagonistic agents of self and social change. Capitalism has become a deeply inculcated ideological belief around which we have organized our lives. Trump is demanding we sacrifice our lives by opening up schools and businesses without providing the necessary resources to protect students and teachers from the coronavirus. Some politicians have spouted social Darwinist remarks arguing that the virus is clearing out the dead wood from the forest, meaning that elderly people must be made expendable so Trump can recover the economy before the election. The increasing concentration of wealth in the hands of global elites is ingrained into the system and should not surprise anyone who has been studying the co-optation of government by business interests and austerity measures. What should concern us is the massive increase in the panoptic surveillance of private citizens under the guise of terrorist threats, and what Trump calls 'anarchy zones' in some cities such as Portland and Seattle. We cannot go backwards to neo-Keynesianism but must move forward to socialism. This means negating the barriers to socialism.

Self-movement is made possible through the act of negation by negating the barriers to self-development. But negation, is always dependent on the object of its critique. Whatever you negate still bears the stamp of what has been negated – that is, it still bears the imprint of the object of negation. We have seen, for instance, in the past, that oppressive forms which one has attempted to negate still impact the ideas we have of liberation. That is why Hegel argued that we need a self-referential negation – a negation of the negation. By means of a negation of the negation, negation establishes a relation with itself, freeing itself from the external object it is attempting to negate. Because it exists without a relationship to another outside of itself, it is considered to be absolute – it is freed from dependency on the other. It negates its dependency through a self-referential act of negation.

For example, the abolition of private property and its replacement with collective property does not ensure liberation; it is only an abstract negation which must be negated in order to reach liberation. It is still infected with its opposite, which focuses exclusively on property. It simply replaces private property with collective property and is still impacted by the idea of ownership or having something.

Of course, Marx thinks that it is necessary to negate private property. But this negation, he insists, must itself be negated. Only then can the *truly positive* – a totally new society – emerge. However, as Peter Hudis argues, in order to abolish capital, the negation of private property must itself be negated, which would be the achievement of a positivity – a positive humanism – beginning with itself. While it is necessary to negate private property, that negation must itself be negated. If you stop before this second negation then you are presupposing that having is more important than being.

Saying 'no' to capital, for instance, constitutes a first negation. When the subject becomes self-conscious regarding this negation – that is, when the subject understanding the meaning of this negation recognizes the positive content of this negation – then she has arrived at the negation of the negation. As Anne Fairchild Pomeroy notes, when a subject comes to recognize that she is the source of the negative, this becomes a second negation, a reaching of class consciousness. When a subject recognizes the positivity of the act of negation itself as negativity, then she knows herself as a source of the movement of the real. This occurs when human beings, as agents of self-determination, hear themselves speak, and are able both to denounce oppression and the evils of the world and to announce, in Freire's terms, a liberating alternative.

Freire was deeply religious. Freire was highly critical of the role of theologians and the church – its formalism, supposed neutrality, and captivity in a complex web of bureaucratic rites that pretends to serve the oppressed but actually supports the power elite – from the perspective of the philosophy of praxis that he developed throughout his life. For Freire, critical consciousness (conscientization) cannot be separated from Christian consciousness. To speak a true word, according to Freire, is to transform the world. The ruling class, from Freire's perspective, views consciousness as something that can be transformed by 'lessons, lectures and eloquent sermons'. But this form of consciousness must be rejected because it is essentially static, necrophilic (deathloving) as distinct from biophilic (life-loving), and turns people into sycophants of the ruling elite. It is empty of praxis. In other words, there is no dialectic, as conscientization is drained of its dialectical content. Freire calls for a type of class suicide in which the bourgeoisie takes on a new apprenticeship of dying to their own class interests and experiencing their own Easter moment through a form of mutual understanding and transcendence.

Freire argues that the theologians of Latin America must move forward and transform the dominant class interests in the interests of the suffering poor 'if they are to experience "death" as an oppressed class and be born again to liberation'. Freire borrowed the concept of class suicide from Amilcar Cabral, the Guinea-Bissauan and Cape Verdean revolutionary and political leader who was assassinated in 1973.

For Freire, insight into the conditions of social injustice of this world stipulates that the privileged must commit a type of class suicide where they self-consciously attempt to divest themselves of their power and privilege and willingly commit themselves to unlearning their attachment to their own self-interest. Essentially, this was a type of Easter experience in which a person willingly sacrifices his or her middle or ruling class interests in order to be reborn through a personal commitment to suffering alongside the poor.

This means examining poverty as a social sin. This means examining how the capitalist system has failed the poor and not how the poor have failed the capitalist system. If a person truly commits to helping the poor and the oppressed, then that is equivalent to taking down all victims from the cross.

LCP Your discussions bring up complex issues of our time, which lead us to countless reflections on how we reached this political, economic and social context that we live in Brazil and the USA, marked by the rise to power of inhuman, necrophilic, authoritarian, insensitive and violent people in several countries. One of the consequences of this context in Brazil is the dismantling and depreciation of public universities, both by the federal and by state governments, which aim the privatization of these universities.

So, now I ask you: what paths can be taken so that we can resist as educators and researchers, fighting oppression and acting to overcome inequalities by democratizing the university space?

Freire, among other announcements, indicated the path of unity in diversity - the union of the different in the fight against the antagonistic, which is not an easy task, but it is possible.

Peter McLaren This is an important question. We need to know where our leaders stand today, how they manufacture reality, and how they incentivize the public into seeing the world as they do. Even without Trump and Bolsonaro, the public universities were under assault by university administrators and boards of governors in the thrall of neoliberal business models. Almost the entire lifeworld of the planet has been colonized be neoliberal capitalism. Bolsonaro and Trump don't want public universities to succeed since they can better maintain control of the universities and the production of knowledge if the universities are private and for-profit institutions run by wealthy entrepreneurs who seek the stability of the market economy and private links to the ruling political party. But first we need to understand the political shifts in the larger political arena.

Trump's tabloid presidency may seem comical to some of its critics who often compare it to a circus clown act, but a closer reading should give any student of fascism serious pause. We need to turn the spotlight on Trump's fascination with being the übermensch, the strongman, a Nietzschean will-to-power demagogue, the Master of Chaos. Trump has purged his White House administration of non-loyalists, he has placed family members in positions of importance, drawing upon an us-against-them mentality; he has created an alternative reality in which the United States is under siege by Antifa and anarchists bent on death and destruction; he has lumped peaceful protesters with violent protestors, labeling them terrorists; he has used his political position to amass personal financial gain; he has withdrawn from international treaties and engaged in an isolationist politics; he brutally intimidates his political opponents; he has attacked the educational system for indoctrinating students with hateful leftist propaganda; he defines the nation around race, faith and white ethnonationalism as distinct from a humanitarian nation defined by rights and collective responsibilities; he has supported confederate statues and military bases named after confederate leaders.

Reaching a consensus with the left is deemed weak while the politics of brutality, force and the language of violence is championed. The theme of 'law and order' is frequently invoked as a means of quelling feelings of mass insecurity during times of economic or political crisis. Fascist leaders are adept at creating imagined communities of friends and enemies. Journalists are described as 'enemies of the people' and leftist intellectuals are declaimed as traitors, sabotaging the country. Fascists like to paint the country as targets of humiliation by other countries, enhancing the idea of the country being victimized by others, both by internal and external enemies. Fascists routinely discredit the election system and find ways to win the vote fraudulently.

In this climate, Freire's message of unity in diversity appears to the fascist leader as a politics of appeasement to the left. Fascists have no use for appeasement or diversity, they want racial unity, unity of white European blood. Hence, they often warn that the white race is being taken over in numbers by non-white races, which they argue will bring about the decline of civilization. Fascist leaders take a masculinist approach to politics, often borrowing from ancient archetypes of the hero, the father figure, the knight in shining armor, the protector of the people (meaning white people). Trump is all about atmospherics – his presidency is about hectoring, pugnacious energy, barbaric energy, demagogic energy, incendiary rhetoric, propagandistic energy, shambolic energy. This all suits Trump's logorrhea.

Trump has refused to denounce white supremacy in clear terms. Trump and Bolsonaro are social arsonists – they shatter and splinter the social cohesiveness necessary for any functioning democracy. Democracy is their enemy. This is why the Trump, the Racist-in-Chief, is attacking peaceful protestors and calling them terrorists. There have been more than 7,750 Black Lives Matter demonstrations held across the country in the last several months. Of those demonstrations 93 percent have been peaceful, according to numerous reports from Princeton University's Bridging Divides Initiative published in September. Trumpet-tongued Trump, the Imp of the Perverse, peers from the darkness of an Edgar Allan Poe nightmare, delighting in the deliciousness of the destruction. Trump is the Lord of Chaos, reveling in the death he has incurred, slurp-lipped at the thought of bodies writhing in pools of bloody devastation. He has fulminated against common sense, creating a world-wrenching apocalyptic narrative that he is protecting the United States from the evils of immigration and socialism.

Our universities have been colonized by the logic of neoliberal capitalism. To a large extent, the experience of the pandemic has derailed the academy's quest for certainty. Right now uncertainty and its twin – fear of the unknown – dominates the popular narrative. Our entire way of being-in-the-world has shifted dramatically. We have been made more vulnerable to the cajoling of rightwing demagogues to continue to define our very being through the prism of homo economicus, the predominance of linear succession, of technocratic rationality. Our ideas of teaching are shifting as we are faced with working solely through our computers. True, there are some advantages to digitally mediated schooling, once we are able to overcome the digital divide and provide high quality broadband to all students around the world. But digitalizing pedagogy is also like hanging the sword of Damocles over your head. Will it turn out to be the pedagogy of choice for many students after the pandemic, for those students who travel long distances to campus? Is the future of teaching hyper-flex models that are partially online and partially in person classes?

We need to be critical in how we understand the relationship between epistemology and ethics. We need to prepare for more chaotic disruptions, to anticipate them, and to study ways of preventing them. There will be more crises. There will be more economic disasters. There will be rising food prices and more famines in parts of the world, there will be geopolitical fights over water. There will be military invasions. There will be existential issues that demand answers. Universities need to begin to focus their curricula on trying to anticipate what these crises will be, address these issues using the best information and analyses possible, in order to prevent more crises. Fortunately, we have many strong Freireans working in our struggle to help defend democracy and socialism such as

Juha Suoranta, Peter Mayo, Antonia Darder, James Kirylo, Henry Giroux, Donaldo Macedo, Petar Jandric, Ana Cruz, Sheila Macrine, Sonia Nieto, members of the Paulo Freire Democratic Project – and many others too numerous to mention.

Thus, we need to rethink the epistemological and ethical underpinnings of education. We need to rethink how we utilize the resources of the planet and support public health, how we can seriously address climate change. The purpose of education must be refashioned towards addressing these issues. Can we envision a social universe outside of capital's value form which is value augmentation or profit-creation? Can we take advantage of the new abnormal? How can we undress the machinations of a capitalism that has absolutely failed humanity in this time of the pandemic? Can we move away from our laser-focus on postdigital technocracy, commercial interests and measurement and accountability schemes and place more value on dialectical reasoning, Freirean dialogue and revolutionary praxis? Can we shift away from the competitive branding and marketing of our universities to the pursuit of both truth and justice? Can we take seriously Freire's call for making education our ontological vocation for becoming more fully human? Can digitalization bring us closer together to becoming global citizens, and if so, at what cost? What does performing to standard mean with respect to online classes? Can it have a democratizing effect? Or can the rules and the interactive digital platforms that have been established favor the oppressor over the oppressed?

As a graduate student I took one class with Michel Foucault. It was the interactions I had with him when I took him to visit various Toronto bookstores that I valued more than the actual classes. For me, it was the cold breeze of walking the streets, watching Foucault's scarf billow in the wind, the comments he made about the city, and his sense of humor that would have been lost had the class been an online experience. It was the smell of peach brandy tobacco smoke that wafted through the office during my discussions with another professor that made the most impression on me. In fact, I became a collector of pipes after the class was over. Being in the physical presence of Paulo was an experience to which online communication could not have done justice. Teaching in real time and space is important. Meeting in cyberspace only allows for a small range of communication cues. But for those who do not have the opportunity of having an in-person mentor, online classes are often the only option. Debates will continue over whether embodied knowledge is ultimately more preferable than virtually mediated spaces and cultures of reasoning over long periods of time.

What needs to be done

Peter McLaren   Let's look at the curriculum. First, education must be focused on understanding the political economy of capitalism – from post-feudal times to present instantiations of financialization. Society, culture and social relations of production must be seen as interconnected. Systemic racism must be understood as inextricably linked to the legal system and the criminal justice system. Capital-perpetuated settler colonialism, sexism, racism, homophobia, and misogyny, misanthropy and misology must be examined for their interrelatedness, including the historically generated myths that have served to legitimize them. Classes must deal with the issue of climate change and scarcity, and technology-enabled extraction of natural resources.

I could continue but the point I want to make is that the main issue that drives the curriculum for liberation should focus on the various systems of mediation that have produced us as twenty-first-century compliant and self-censoring human beings who appear defenceless in the face of nationalist calls for war, for ethnic chauvinism, for narratives championing imperialism and the coloniality of power. There should be a study of revolutionary social movements that have challenged these systems of mediation, and why some groups succeeded and why many of them failed.

I have only scratched the surface here. Clearly, we need an education system that can move groups from a class-in-itself to a class-for-itself – that is, to a class that actively pursues its own interests. Certainly, we need a mass movement from below to counter the much more advanced digitalization of today's entire global economy and society which has utilized the application of fourth industrial revolution technologies led by artificial intelligence (AI) and the analysis of 'big data', machine learning, automation and robotics, nano- and biotechnology, quantum and cloud computing, 3D printing, virtual reality, new forms of energy storage, etc.). But that will not be an easy task. But it is a necessary one, since we will be struggling against the formation of a global police state.

The sociologist William Robinson has warned that in the time of the pandemic we are able to see the acceleration of digital restructuring 'which can be expected to result in a vast expansion of reduced-labour or labourless digital services, including all sorts of new telework arrangements, drone delivery, cash-free commerce, fintech (digitalized finance), tracking and other forms of surveillance, automated medical and legal services, and remote teaching involving pre-recorded instruction'. Hence, the giant tech companies and their political agents are able to convert great swaths of the economy into these new digital realms.

Robinson also notes that the 'post-pandemic global economy will involve now a more rapid and expansive application of digitalization to every aspect of global society, including war and repression'. We have an enormous task ahead of us. If we can make postdigital science work in the interests of the oppressed, rather the corporate elite, then we would be foolish not to try to strengthen our communal immune system. We have Paulo's legacy that will give us strength, both moral strength and intellectual strength. The strength needed to fight against repression in this time of fascist restoration.

References

Freire, Paulo (2005) 'Parentesco intelectual', in A. M. A. Freire (ed.), *Pedagogia da tolerância* (São Paulo: Editora UNESP), 245–7.

Chapter 3

CRITICAL ANALYSIS AND THE COVID-19 CRISIS: AN INTERVIEW WITH MICHAEL W. APPLE[1]

Michael W. Apple

Global Thursday Talks (GTT)   Dear Professor Apple, we are grateful that you honoured us for accepting this interview. We are excited to listen to your critical analysis and own experiences on the Covid-19 pandemic and its effects on communities, people, schools and education in general. This will be a great contribution to our community that you have been a member of for a long time.

To start this interview, we would like to ask you about your experience with critical educators in Turkey and other parts of the world, and their struggle for a just society and the right to education. How would you connect your profound observations and experiences in the US schools, where you thought earlier to your academic career, to the challenges here and there?

Michael Apple   I am the former president of a teacher syndicate and my first interactions in Turkey were with various teacher unions. Given the current situation with Covid, I do feel cut off from Turkey since Turkey has been profoundly important in my trying to understand what strong States look like. I don't want to see the world just through the eyes of the United States in order to understand what it means to have rightist mobilizations that are also deeply connected to conservative religious populations. As you know, that's been a key part of my analysis and part of my arguments over time. In some ways, it is both a pleasure to see some of you and to have this reunion. But it's sad because I don't want to talk about these kinds of things. and, of course, I am deeply distressed that this is happening all over the world. I am in contact with people in Hungary and Poland, Brazil, Korea, India and many other places. It is very clear that this is a very dangerous time. In my mind, we must not romanticize this. In responding to this crisis, I don't want to be too rhetorical. Unfortunately, all too much of critical pedagogical work throws words at it and is not

---

1. This interview was conducted within activities of @globalthursdaytalks digital community on 9 July 2020 and is available at: https://www.youtube.com/watch?V=Xv0Hh B_3gnq&t=2273s.

based on serious political economy or a serious understanding of the lives of teachers. As someone who has spent a lot of years teaching in rural and urban areas in the United States and elsewhere, I prefer that we ground our work in the daily lives of what is happening in those institutions called schools and in the lives of teachers, administrators and academics who are also in a school in some ways.

The plan for our conversation today is be something like this. I want to use the United States as a lever to pry loose and to open up a discussion about what the implications of our current dominant political-economic conjuncture are in terms of teachers' lives, kids' lives, and parents' lives. And then I shall rehearse some of the arguments I make in my book *Can Education Change Society?* (Apple 2013) about who is the 'we' and what can we do about these dominant relations. I want to be honest here. We only have a relatively short time for this discussion. and I will try to remember to talk slowly since unlike many of you I only speak English. But I am the product of the belly of the beast of the United States and even though we have always been a multilingual nation we refuse to understand that. I was taught two years of high school Spanish. I have forgotten all of it which is an immense tragedy. I know a few words in Turkish but I will not say them because they're not very clean words. I might normally say those Turkish words after some beer. (I hope that you will forgive my jokes but my last name is Apple. I spent three years in my early years of teaching as a substitute teacher under contract with the state. Every day I would go to a different classroom and every day I would have to introduce myself to children and say, 'Good morning children, my name is Mr Apple.' They would laugh for what seemed like four hours. In the process, I developed a teaching style that often has some humour. But let me remind you that there is nothing funny about what we're going to talk about today, about the complicity of the state and education in the murder of children, the murder of elderly people and putting teachers' lives at risk.)

GTT   Professor Apple, what is the struggle of those groups you mentioned here with neoliberal policies, neo-conservatism, or what you call 'conservative modernism'? In what ways our lives and kids' lives are risked by these policies?

Michael Apple   I want to talk about neoliberal policies and other policies and the formation of a new hegemonic bloc. Let me mention what I mean by that and then move on to say more about policies and practices in most nations of the world that have this odd combination, what I call 'conservative modernization'. There is a new alliance that is using education for its purposes. It's what again I call conservative modernization. This has four groups who have formed an alliance and we can find these groups in Turkey, certainly in the United States and many other nations but they certainly are present in Greece as well right now. The first is what we call *neoliberalism*. They believe that there's one simple thing about the world: the private is good and the public is bad and the task of schools is to efficiently produce workers. They valorize only the kinds of knowledge that they believe will support one of the world's (deeply unequal) economies. They are guided by a vision of a weak state.

The second group does not have a belief in the weak state, but is based on a commitment to a very strong state. For them, while they support capitalist economic relations and much of the neoliberal agenda, their position is based on the crucial importance of traditional 'cultural capital', on the crucial importance of winning the struggle over knowledge and values. This is what we call *neoconservatives*. In essence, they believe one simple thing. The problem is that too many minoritized people, too many women, too many progressives have now taken over the curriculum and the politics of knowledge. For neoconservatives, we must restore what they assume are the key elements of what it means to be Turkish or American or Brazilian as the core element of a curriculum. I will come back to the policies pushed forward by this group because these issues are important as Covid-19 provides an opportunity for these groups to mobilize. Because this is a group that wants a very strong state, it is behind many of the policies and assumptions that have led to the large increases in prison populations in the US and other nations. It is often both implicitly and overtly racist. It is anti-Kurdish and anti-immigrant in many nations.

In many nations, there is a third group that I want to call, following Stuart Hall, *authoritarian populists*. Populism can be good or bad. This is a group that says the people must decide, but there are good people and bad people. Good people are conservative religiously. They know what is right. God speaks to them but not to other people. We can see this in the formation of madrasas, of particular kinds of state funding for religious schools increasingly. In this notion, the separation between the secular state and religious forms is part of the problem. In Turkey, this is extraordinarily powerful and getting more powerful. Because of time constraints, as you know I will often not speak about Turkey today. (One of the reasons I have agreed to come back for a second session is so that you teach me about whether what I am saying fits. Again, I apologize for not being able to answer questions but that's why we're having the second session.) This group is behind the fastest-growing schooling in the United States right now which is not private schooling, it is home-schooling, which at times provides an opening for profit as conservative movements and publishers sell all of the things that parents supposedly need to school their children to be schooled at home. Home-schooling is not the same as madrasas. In the United States, currently, these are the parents of as many as 4 to 5 million children who have chosen to not educate their children in secular state schools or have even taken them out of religious schools, and are schooling them at home. Usually, these decisions are based on very conservative religious reasons and have their historical genesis in the resistance to anti-racist and anti-integration policies that outlawed racial segregation in the USA. It is grounded in a commitment to creating the gated community of the home. I want to come back to this because we are beginning to see increasingly in many nations a rapid growth of home-schooling for religious reasons as well. As we will see, this is becoming a site of for-profit schooling, giving the realities of Covid.

Finally, there is a fourth group that would usually not vote for conservatives, but still provide essential knowledge and skills for neoliberals and similar agendas. These are people who may be social democrats politically, but form a group that is devoted to the ideologies and practices of 'new managerialism'. It is part of the *professional middle class*. They believe one simple thing; if it moves in classrooms measure it and inside that classroom make certain that the teacher is teaching very efficiently. In order to accomplish this, we must have even more control of the curriculum so that we know what is going on. As we will see with Covid-19 there's increasing pressure on controlling the curriculum, and very importantly on controlling what actually goes on in the *home* as well as the school. As I noted earlier, this is odd because this group of people normally does not vote for religious conservatives but they provide the technical expertise for doing distance education, for the measurement that goes with it, for the national and regional examinations. They are, as Stephen Ball says, deeply committed to *performativity*. It is their cultural capital, one that they rely on for positions within the state and civil society.

Each of these groups in the alliance of conservative modernization can take advantage of the current Covid-19 crisis. As you know very well, this is not only a health crisis but it is a crisis even more in economic, ideological and political terms. Thus, we cannot understand what is happening in education and the often radical transformations that are occurring in so many aspects of education unless we sometimes shift the focus outside of education. These transformations in and to schools are part of a larger set of ideological, social and economic transformations. They involve powerful changes in what counts as the family, in what counts as a good school, a good curriculum and a good teacher. And, profoundly, all of these things are accompanied by a movement to create what I want to call an *epistemological fog* to make the inequalities that are created by the state's response to Covid-19 invisible. This means that, even if we cannot change many of the damaging things that are happening now, part of the task of critical educators is to challenge the epistemological fog and to make the invisible visible. It requires us to illuminate how both Covid-19 and the policies and practices of conservative modernization are creating some of the worst inequalities of your nation and my own.

Let me use the United States as an example. What is happening now is the mass destruction of the public sphere. It is grounded in a fundamental change in the very meaning of democracy. Democracy is 'de-socialized' so that it is private, a form of 'possessive individualism'. If we were to discuss a democratic public school, communities would have a voice, parents (but not only parents) would have a voice, teachers would have a voice, students would have a voice. This involves a collective understanding of what counts as democracy. Underpinning this is a vision of thick rather than thin democracy, one that is fully participatory, with the school becoming a central site for the practice of this thick form of democracy.

However, one of the effects of Covid-19 is the increasingly rapid embodiment of the neoliberal agenda of emphasizing choice, making it even more widely acceptable for the home to become the site of education. As schools become closed, there will be no physicality, no bodies in school, no collective sociality. The effects are actually quite a destructive form. School closures make the lived experience of schooling a site of social disconnection. There's an ideological transformation going on. It opens a space even more to making democracy now individual choice. Even though parents don't actually have a choice because the schools are closed, the evidence increasingly shows that the lived experience of being without the institutional forms of schooling in the usual ways has led large numbers of parents to reject state-supported schooling in general.

Other effects are becoming ever more evident. The closing of schools in most parts of the United States has created huge disparities and effects. Of course, as we know, this is going on in so many countries. Indeed, it would take hours just to list the ways that this crisis has created conditions where poor and working-class children often get little or no schooling whatsoever.

But let me paint a picture of some of these conditions. There's been a move to a hybrid form of home-schooling in many nations, with digital media replacing the schools. This has required resources that poor schools and poor families simply don't have. To take one example in the City of Milwaukee in the United States, the largest city in my own state of Wisconsin (but the same would be said for most cities or in rural areas), approximately 30 per cent of the students do not have a computer and do not have an internet connection. It becomes a fiction that we are distributing schooling in rural areas where there is no internet. As an example, my younger son was a secondary school principal in a rural school district in the northern part of my own state. In a town of 1,500 people, no one had an internet connection, there were no wires, none.

This situation is not unusual. It is exacerbated by the history of racial dynamics and colonial forms. Thus, if you're an indigenous person living on what we, unfortunately, call 'reservations' in the United States in the Native American rural communities in New Mexico and many other places, these reservations have been under attack technologically, economically and racially for centuries. The internet and the necessary technology to make it work is simply not there. The schools are underfunded, often understaffed, etc. To think that 'virtual schooling' doesn't create massive inequalities requires that one holds a utopian vision, that is based on historical amnesia. It assumes a reality that has never existed. Certainly, if we looked at Turkey in those areas that have a large minoritized population, a large population of immigrants from Syria, a large population of people who are poor and working-class who have lost their jobs, we will find similar conditions. These are the conditions in which Covid-19 enters. It is simply an impossibility to have schooling as we know it. It assumes resources such as internet connections, computers, even cell phones. Even more importantly, it has an ideological vision of what the home looks like and what family structures are. It assumes that there is a place in an apartment or a home where a student in a family of three or four or five or seven children that there is actually a place to do the school work.

I understand this personally. I grew up very poor as a child in a working-class and immigrant community, and my family's apartment was *very* small and there was no place to study, none whatsoever. The policies of virtual education in a time of Covid-19 crisis, is based on this ideologized space. Anyone who knows what it's like in the poorer neighbourhoods of your own nation as well will understand. This is simply not available in so many poor rural homes as well. The effects are worsened for other large groups of children, who are basically invisible. I refer here to homeless children. In in the city of New York, for instance, there are approximately 100,000 children who are homeless. Most nations have similar figures. In essence, what we are doing is saying you can have schooling. We'll call it 'distance education'. But you are living in a shelter or on the street or in some places in tents where there's not even electricity. In my own city, the city of Madison, Wisconsin, which is one of the wealthiest cities in the state of Wisconsin, there are approximately 2,000 children who are homeless. Many of them live on the streets or are in shelters, where they cannot distance themselves from other infected people. Hence, again, the virus then also has an effect in ways that are invisible where we have this vision of what it means to be human. Those students and families who are homeless or very poor are literally made invisible. It doesn't just desocialize schooling, it desocializes powerfully the ability of people to be part of being human. They are ignored; they're simply not seen. It is the politics of invisibility and that effect is absolutely central. It is the myth that makes the existence of the bodies themselves as well as the spaces that they inhabit or they don't have invisible as well.

It also means that without schooling, the children are sent back to the home, but there's a lack of food for children, since the school has provided not just 'food for the mind', but real material food in meals for the children. This has become a major crisis as well in many nations. In the US and other nations, there are what we call full-service schools, where children now get breakfast and lunch and are also fed after school before the children go home at say five o'clock in the evening. Thus, they are fed three meals a day. It is the only food they have since so many people now are out of work and many of them are losing their apartments or where they live. There is no food in the home. Food distribution centres of churches and mosques elsewhere are running out of food, so distance education is also a distancing of one's body in a different way. There is no food distribution for children. I don't know if I am being clear, but I want us to fully understand what all of this means. All of this and so much more has serious repercussions on what democratic and critical teachers can and cannot do, and on how we both understand the nature and depth of the crisis and its hidden effects – and on how we engage in actions to challenge what is happening. We cannot say what we should do unless we look at the very materiality of what is actually going on – and unless we are deeply honest. As one of my close friends who is no longer with us, Paulo Freire, reminded us, we need to critically confront the lived realities of oppressive circumstances. We, of course, need to openly 'bear witness' to the negativities of growing inequalities, exploitation and oppression. But, if the words are just rhetorical and theoretical, it's not sufficient (see Freire 1971; Apple 2010 and 2013; Apple, Gandin, Liu, Meshulam and Schirmer 2018). You will forgive me if I get a little emotional about this. As someone who grew up very poor, you will forgive me but I understand this in my body as well.

GTT   Then, in your analysis mingled with your own experience of childhood, this situation extends to other challenges on other groups in the society, that is there are other groups made invisible and segregated in the times of Covid-19. And it seems that hasn't changed so much since your time . . .

Michael Apple   This is where the pressures on parents then become important. It also means that this is where we cannot just talk about class, we have to talk about gender and race to uncover the pressures on parents. It is especially important to focus on mothers given the patriarchal structuring of domestic labour and how frighteningly intense their labour has become during a time of pandemic. Rates of child abuse and violence against women in the home are increasing in every nation that is going through this. These things are made even worse, given the necessity of adults and children to earn enough to survive in a time of famine. This is very evident in China and throughout Latin America for example. Many people there have become unregistered street vendors again. This includes migrant workers who have lost their jobs. It also includes their children. Even though in many places such labour in the informal economy is illegal, many people are selling almost anything so that they might possibly earn enough money to survive. Think about what it must be like to try to keep a home with a large family with children. Parents or extended family members have to make a choice between finding some way to earn enough money to survive. Yet, they also know that the only schooling available to their children is virtual and in the home (if they are lucky enough to have a physical home of their own). Think about whether their dire economic circumstances will 'make them lucky enough' to have a computer. And even if they somehow have managed to obtain a computer, virtual home-schooling carried with it a necessity for one or more of the parents to be in that home if it is to be even minimally effective to make certain that the children are actually engaged with schooling and are not in unsupervised dangerous realities. This is creating an exceptionally difficult moral choice where, no matter what, parents lose. Do we *all* work to keep a place to live and food for ourselves and our children, thereby sacrificing any serious schooling?

The effects of this critical existential choice on mothers are especially powerful in conservative nations and/or in those places with dominant conservative religious forms of gendered power. There, the idea is that all domestic labour and all labour that's done in the home is the role not of the man, but it is God's will that women must be those people who are taking care of children. Again, this is where the conservative religious movements not only mobilize support for these relations, but make them even more powerful in their effects both on children and on the daily life of women. We need to understand that women are often doing two kinds of labour. They labour outside the home, often in exploitative and uncertain positions, and then must engage in the unpaid and often unrecognized domestic labour. Not only is this dual labour exhausting, the realities of Covid-19 also have an increasing emotional cost. It also has resulted in increased physical danger to women and children.

I want to stress again, that much of what I have pointed to is not part of the official discourse associated with these hybrid forms of home-schooling. Yet, having argued for the crucial significance of making these causes and effects public, it is equally important to recognize that, like capitalism itself, these realities also create spaces for progressive alliance-building as well. Let me give an example. The turn to such hybrid forms of home-schooling has paradoxically made collective action even more imperative. It has made dealing with something I mentioned earlier – the loss of regular dependable meals for children in schools, especially for poor children. As I noted, food is not being made available within schools, because the schools are closed. But, right now, in many parts of the United States, in Brazil and elsewhere, teachers, parents and community activists have organized an alliance for food distribution to community centres and to families. This alliance may last as more collective identities are being formed, ones that cut across class and race divides. That's actually quite crucial since this provides a space for building alliances that are counter-hegemonic in other areas of social life. I don't mean this to be rhetorical. Right now, we are witnessing similar movements in many places in the United States in slums and favelas in Brazil and in many places in South Africa, throughout Latin America and elsewhere. This gives me reasons for hope.

GTT   This is striking, Mike. We also witness that people are organizing against pressure and discrimination inflamed by tragic murders such as the Black Lives Matter movement that turned into an overall reaction, deep into the historical background of racism. And then, other small groups started mobilizing against discrimination and racism, etc. What about this side, the resistance side? Can it be turned into an effective post-pandemic movement?

Michael Apple   These, too, give me reasons for hope. There is now a mobilization that cuts across ideological boundaries, where parents and communities are mobilizing with teachers who have an ethical commitment to their children to support the Black Lives Matter movement, for instance. The teachers, students and communities are extending this to also mobilize to stop the violence against women. I want to take that seriously: when this is over (if it is ever over). It is important to ask: Does this provide a space for alliances to support teachers at a time when many governments and many authoritarian leaders are saying, 'anybody can teach,' 'We don't need teachers, we don't need teachers' syndicates'? So, does this open a possibility that we don't think enough about? I will come back to that later, okay?

GTT   Yes, is this related to the effort to normalize isolation thus the idea that we can live without school? What do you think will be the cost of isolation for parents, teachers and students?

Michael Apple   There's another major effect that comes out of this. The isolation of people in the home and the isolation of teachers is going on. This does mean in most places right now that there's a loss of momentum, loss of mobilization, and this threatens the building and defending of social movements to challenge state and local conservative and neoliberal policies. This is very important. We know one thing, teachers and administrators do not change schools by themselves. Let me repeat that, because it is tough as an educator for me to say it in public. Teachers and administrators by themselves cannot make large-scale transformations of educational policies that extend beyond their schools. Now, don't misunderstand me. In the life of schools and teachers, it is crucial to interrupt, every day, one's undemocratic experiences. But we do know that teachers as parts of social movements, larger movements of parents and activists together, put pressure on governments, are saying, 'No you cannot do this anymore.' And we will fight for alternatives. That's the history of Turkey's teachers' unions. However, when you are no longer physically together, when you cannot even have lunch together, when Zoom gets tiring and when your everyday conditions are isolating in so many ways, will there be this momentum for building the alliances between teachers and communities? What will happen to teachers' syndicates and teachers who are no longer together every day? To me, this is crucial because teachers in syndicates are absolutely central to changing the curriculum and to defending the rights of teachers for better pay, for healthcare, for respect. So, isolating people in their homes makes it much harder for social movements to build. In addition, all of this creates even more difficulty for parent mobilizations and community mobilizations.

As you know, I am a deeply committed political activist and this is a time of Black Lives Matter and similar mobilizations in the United States and other countries. I am usually speaking at these things, mobilizing with them, learning from them, marching, giving money. As an example, I get no money from my books, even books like, *Democratic Schools* and *Ideology and Curriculum*, which have sold over a million copies. The money goes to community mobilizations. I have a salary and I can live on it. But I am now prevented from joining the mobilizations because I am sheltering at home. Even if we say someone like me, who spends a good deal of my life on writing and speaking. Am I also engaged in other political work or is it only my writing? Writing is crucial, of course, and I never want to diminish its importance. But we again have to ask what is the effect on daily life of these kinds of isolating conditions, not only for people like myself but for an entire range of other groups. A good example is youth. We are also isolating youth. Youth mobilizations are absolutely crucial in so many nations. If even youth are sheltering at home, what does it mean for youth mobilizations? What kinds of education are these students experiencing – and *not* experiencing? What does this mean for their identities as *social* beings?

Let us think about this more. We are seeing that curriculum and teaching now increasingly are delivered electronically. This means that the content and processes of education are becoming standardized even more. This was increasingly seen as a very real opportunity by media and large publishing houses. It was recognized as an even greater arena for the generation of profit as even more things become commodified than before. The schools were seen as sites of profit under neoliberal regimes as more and more teachers didn't have time to build curriculum. Added to this, was the power of state testing – where the state test, in essence, embodied a position that said, 'I am sorry, but we don't want teachers doing this; you have to prepare students for the all-important high school entrance examination.' Now, even more, those tests are published by Pearson Company or other large multinational corporations. And, with distance education, we are already seeing that these large corporations are hiring people who create curricula and tests for all kinds of things to make certain that they make a profit off of the distance education programmes. In the process, increasingly the curriculum becomes commodified. The home then becomes like the school. It increasingly becomes a site of profit generation. It creates a situation in which something is good if it makes a profit, whether or not it connects to the real lives of parents and children. This subsidizes in many ways neoliberal ideological forms, and makes more legitimate the idea of democracy as the gated home. It is the individuated family as consumer, not the community, since the community is diminished.

There are other increasingly powerful effects. That would mean that teachers lose their autonomy. That autonomy was of course already limited. But it makes it even more difficult to teach counter-hegemonic and critically democratic material and, just as importantly, to have the ability to connect what they teach and how they teach it to the lives and cultures of students and their communities. This is significant for nations such as Turkey. Let's think about the population right now of Turkey. The nation is increasingly diverse. Its population and its cultural assemblages are in motion. This is not actually new. Turkish culture has always been multiple. It is a fiction that there is one Turkish culture. In the same way, there's a fiction that there's one Greek culture or one US culture. Culture is not a noun it is a *verb*. It is constantly in motion. Millions of people from Syria have moved to Turkey to protect their lives. These are among the children that if I am a teacher I must deal with. We know what has happened with Kurdish and other minorities in the history of Turkey. (I will let you deal with the politics of that statement. I think people know where my sympathies are.) But what does this mean, then, if all curricula are digitized and, if I am lucky enough to have a real school and a classroom, I am faced with a curriculum and a set of tests that have no relationship to their lived experience, their hopes or fears, their language, their dreams, etc.? For teachers, what does it mean for the lives of children in the future? Good teaching, and especially critically democratic teaching, begins with that. It doesn't only end with it. It starts with whom am I working now. That means that critical pedagogy becomes an almost impossible practice., Of course, no teacher is a puppet, no administrator is really a puppet. But the material and ideological realities they will face because of these transformations creates a truly difficult situation.

GTT   You say critical education is a struggle itself. From here, can we continue with the role of critical education and critical educator under these new conditions. What is endangered for teachers by Covid-19? Though you mentioned the new risks added by the pandemic conditions, can you open it up please?

Michael Apple   Yes, as I just noted, we must ask then what are the material conditions for doing critical education and what makes it possible and impossible. I will come back to that. This also leads to what I want to call an intense epistemological war. The areas of knowledge and ways of presenting them that can be more easily commodified and packaged for profits will be stressed even more. Today, when faced with this, many teachers are saying this is not teaching. But, this is not all that is happening. What it has done increasingly is to make it even more difficult for teachers to keep the skills that they have already developed. Critical pedagogy is not simply rhetorical, it requires skills, requires that we teach each other what works and what doesn't. Let me use a slightly masculine example. Even though I play basketball on a shared men's and women's team, if you will forgive that binary term, I hurt my leg a few years ago and could not play basketball for six months. I am supposed to be relatively skilled at playing basketball. Yet, when I got back on a basketball court, it was as if I had never played ever before in my life. It was embarrassing. This is similar to the fact that a number of my friends who are engaged in knitting – that is making sweaters and other kinds of things and clothes for their children – who have injured themselves with things like a broken arm and can no longer do that for three or four months tell exactly the same story. When they were called upon to sew or to do things like that or to make aesthetic forms out of their knitting and weaving, they had to relearn the skills and it took a very long time for them. Today, what happens to teaching when the skills that are counter-hegemonic, skills of connecting to children's daily lives, connecting to communities, connecting to the social transformations that you want to come from a critical education, but you don't have the capacity to do them anymore? You slowly lose them. As I have said multiple times, long-term effectiveness to make critical pedagogical work a reality can't be simply rhetorical. It requires practice and constant use to keep them and to extend these skills and values. However, the increasingly commodifying 'solutions' and material conditions now being normalized make it harder. The art form and skills of actually doing it, of remembering how it has done so that it is 'natural', may slowly atrophy and risk being lost.

We need to see this as a collective, not only an individual, problem. We must be able to support each other so that we continue to keep our skill levels and artistry levels in counter-hegemonic forms alive and worth doing. And here there are possibilities that arise from the conditions I have been criticizing. Paradoxically, we are being presented with a technology that, oddly enough, may make it somewhat easier for us to connect with each other, to share our stories of success and of the accounts of going beyond the knowledge, values and commodified logics that are becoming more prevalent. We need to become skilled at creatively using these technological tools and media ourselves and employing them to rebuild critical communities and to defend the traditions of critically democratic education.

Let me now turn my attention to teachers as parents. The lives of many teachers are not only devoted to teaching. Teachers are often parents as well. Thus, with schools being closed and education being shifted to the home, just as most parents are now having to do dual duty, large number of teachers must also engage in domestic labour and at the same time do their time-consuming teaching electronically. When I speak to my friends who are deeply involved in this, they say, 'we are going crazy'. One of my favourite quotes from a teacher is, 'we didn't even have time to go to the bathroom. My life has become so intense, I am trying to work with my classroom electronically, and my kids want my attention.' This embodies the material conditions involved in both wanting to be an ethical and caring parent and an ethical and caring educator. Often, in this country and a number of others, teachers have lost their jobs because of the decisions they were forced to make during the pandemic. In many school districts, teachers were forced to return to school even though the rate of infection in collective settings was very high or they were forced to continue teaching their very time consuming virtual lessons at a distance for other people's children even though their own children were ill. This is certainly true in the United States. Those teachers basically said, 'I am sorry I cannot teach my lessons today with the students who are in my classroom or who are now at home. My kids are sick.' In response to this, the school authorities, in essence, said, 'Well you have a choice, you can be a teacher and we will send you a paycheck or you will be fired. It's your choice. If your kids are sick, you still must find a way of dealing with this. Why should we pay you when you're not working?' This, oddly enough, has now created mobilizations among teachers, creating movements, in which teachers defend their autonomy.

This has important implications for how we think about the contradictory effects of the political situation I have been discussing. One thing we should always remember is that this is not just a one-way set of effects, where neoliberal Covid-driven interests and policies win. As Marx and others reminded us, capitalism is contradictory. One of the effects is that these policies and managerial demands also open spaces for counter-hegemonic work. As a result of some teachers being told, 'make a choice: your children or your job', they collectively mobilized and said that this is a choice: 'that we will not accept. You cannot tell me that I must go into the school to teach every day during a time when infection rates are high and could then infect my family and then also say, "if I care for my kids that I no longer have a job"'. Again, this counter-hegemonic possibility is growing.

GTT   Okay. What should we understand from the mobilization of teachers? It has to be a collective action, right? Can we go back to our discussion about the importance of syndicates, here and there and worldwide? Teachers' unions have been in charge in in teacher strikes in the States . . .

Michael Apple   In the midst of all of this, other things are going on that need to be included in our understanding. First, there is the economic crisis that is creating intense pressures on many states to look for ways to save money. This is made even more powerful by the growth in influence of conservative legislatures throughout the nation. Given this, it is going to be much harder for teachers and other educators to defend their jobs and to secure benefits. The hidden effects of this would be not just be on teachers and teaching, but on the things that make unions so necessary. As people lose their jobs and the rates of unemployment rise to crisis levels, the money that people will pay in taxes no longer goes to the state. That is a crisis of immense proportions both economically and ideologically given neoliberal and conservative control of the media and government at so many levels. There are very damaging cuts in healthcare. Social workers, community-based programmes, literacy and library programmes, cultural institutions, assistance for immigrants and homeless people and so much more, as well as teachers and other educators, will not be seen as important enough for the dominant neoliberal agenda to be given support. What will not be cut will be the support of businesses and financial capital. The building of new state-supported madrasas will not be cut. In general, what will be cut is the public sector. That means that we have to face the fact that teachers (and nearly all public service workers) may lose crucial benefits like healthcare. Class sizes may rise. Things that are truly essential for quality education like having time to plan will be lost. And, most certainly, these neoliberal and conservative transformations may lead to further attacks on future unions. We are already seeing such things. And more effects are on the way. But it is essential that we not wait for those things to intensify. We need to mobilize around efforts to defend the democratic gains that have been made in education and in so much else. Critical teaching is not just one teacher, in a setting with children or adults. It requires collective mobilization. We need to better understand the importance of confronting what is happening collectively – at the same time as we as individual educators strive to build critically democratic realities in the classrooms and other institutions and spaces where we work.

GTT   Among many effects of Covid-19 on education, there is home-schooling, right? As it has already been a common legitimate practice in the States, can we say it is inflamed worldwide in the times of distance education? And what would be the consequences of home-schooling for the individual, for the society?

Michael Apple   This growth is one of the other long-term effects that is growing in the United States, England and Germany, and you will have to tell me whether this is growing in Turkey, but it is growing, oddly enough, in China right now. This surprises me, because in China, educational policies are top-down and state-controlled. I mentioned before that approximately 4 to 5 million children in the United States are currently experiencing some form of home-schooling. The official data say two to three million. But that's wrong since many children are counted as being enrolled in public schools if they are part of a sports team organized by the school, for example, even if none of their actual schooling is done in the school. The curriculum of home-schooling is often very religious. Approximately 80 per cent of home-schoolers are doing this for conservative religious reasons or conservative political and cultural reasons. Even though the public school's commitment officially in the many parts of the United States and many other nations is to promote anti-racism and diversity, to be anti-homophobic and to aim toward the creation of critical citizens, in all too many schools these goals are often largely rhetorical. However, even when they may be rhetorical, these goals and the educational practices associated with them are much less likely to be found in home-schooling.

One of the effects of Covid-19 is the normalization of home-schooling, even if the parents are not yet totally connected to conservative movements. Many parents are saying, 'It was bad economically before, but now I cannot afford to pay my rising taxes My job is insecure or lost so I am going to school my child at home.' There are large numbers of people now facing that. Interestingly, this at times also cuts across ideological lines. The fastest-growing statistical populations in the United States doing home-schooling. are in two groups. The largest is made up of conservative evangelical parents who see the school as a site of secular danger. I quote from one of the most radical of them: 'Teachers are tools of the devil.' To say the least, that makes me a little nervous. The second group is black and brown minoritized people. They don't like Donald Trump at all. They know that they're being hurt. They are increasingly mobilizing and may actively participate in such movements as Black Lives Matter demonstrations. They are also rightly worried about the schooling of their children and are increasingly conscious of what they want and do not want to go in schools. They now are even more conscious of how racist the school system can be. Thus, a significant number of them have decided to school their children at home, even when schools reopen.

The larger anti-racist struggles in which minoritized parents and activists are engaged are movements that I strongly support. I march with them. I donate the royalties for my books and lectures to their organizations. But the issue of home-schooling makes this complicated. Many of these same parents and activists have been drawn to home-schooling. Given what I have said before, I am concerned about the long-term effects of this. One of the hidden results could be that a neoliberal identity will be formed, one that is based on what is called possessive individualism. The home, and the family, is the limit of one's social consciousness. Now that's also true already for many white people increasingly. If we normalize home-schooling, it means that possessive individualism – with all its damaging effects – can be seen as even more legitimate. I write about this in *Educating the Right* Way (Apple 2006; see also Apple et al. 2018). Let us remember that 80 per cent of home-schoolers engaged in this for very conservative reasons. They do not want even progressive rhetoric, let alone progressive and critically democratic practices. A vision that immigrants are good, anti-racism, anti-homophobia, anti-patriarchal forms, a much more open and honest curriculum – they are opposed to all of that. What critically democratic educators are doing in schools then represents to them the secular world that is a sight of danger. That's clearly already strong in Turkey and many other nations.

What happens when we now make home-schooling an increasingly legitimate and widespread form? What happens to people's identities? What and whose knowledge will be taught (see, for example, Apple 2014 and 2019)? One of the results that may increasingly be seen is that it will be even harder to mobilize around *critical* social and educational issues. Thus, I fear that minoritized parents may then lose in the long run as 'whiteness' and a safe curriculum for dominant groups becomes even harder to challenge. The ideological forms that will be accepted as the only legitimate ideological forms will be possessive individualism – or the deeply conservative religious forms that exclude any recognition of the importance of diversity. As long as my child does well and accepts the normative common sense that remains unquestioned, all is fine (see Verma and Apple 2021). Social justice will 'take care of itself'. This is, indeed, very worrisome.

GTT   Professor Apple, as we are approaching the end of this interview, can we talk about your experience of praxis as a critical educator? This would be a model for us and this will get us out of the state of feeling helpless, especially these times that we need to feel we are not alone.

Michael Apple   Let me end with some possibilities. Of the many of the things I have mentioned so far, some have undoubtedly depressed everyone. Let me remind you again of what I said before. In the midst of all these rightist mobilizations and hidden and overt ideological transformations that are going on, no one is a puppet. Teachers are using the technology that they are now getting to develop skills that they didn't have before, often sharing powerful lessons and building allies. Parents are using Zoom in similar ways that were unheard of earlier. Black parents are, in fact, doing anti-racist mobilization. Teachers are doing counter-hegemonic work. Yes, the intellectual labour and emotional labour that parents are now having to do is growing and is making their lives more difficult and intense. But one of the positive effects is that an understanding of the importance of teachers' work that is also growing. This is very important. Thus, people like Trump and similar authoritarian (faux) populists were and are mobilizing in anti-school and especially anti-teacher and anti-teacher union ways. In Brazil, there were and continue to be attacks on teachers and attacks on any elements of the curriculum that are critically democratic. The conservatives there want to actually take away anything that recognized the significance of Paulo Freire. Elements in the Congress of Brazil have proposed legislation to take away the awards, the honorary doctorates, everything of Paulo Freire. Teachers and others who supports him and who keep his legacy alive in schools and communities risk losing their jobs. All of that is going on.

But, at the same time, we are seeing increasingly that these authoritarian rulers are losing support as parents and communities are understanding now how much hard emotional and intellectual labour it is to be a teacher, to be an administrator. They recognize the economic effects of neoliberal policies and what they are and their children are losing. Thus, paradoxically, the same forces that are making it so hard to be a critical and democratic teacher are creating a situation where teachers are gaining more respect, and parents are mobilizing with teachers to support teachers and schools. Now, that's absolutely central because it means we are not starting from zero in the midst of these powerful mobilizations. This has also led to an increased understanding among teachers and critically minded academics and activists that part of our task is to take leadership from and mobilize with these groups. This carries with it certain responsibilities. It means we have to learn how to talk and write in ways that do not require the listener and reader to do all of the hard work. It requires that we see ourselves not as 'isolated individuals', somehow cut off from the rest of society, but as 'public intellectuals'. Thus, we have to keep going on our efforts to be understandable, to continue the process of learning how to speak in different ways.

As an example, when I am working with my PhD students in what is called my Friday Seminar, which has people from all over the world speaking multiple languages, I quote from Marx, Gramsci or Foucault, and, of course, from Paulo Freire as well. The students respond positively, saying give me more critical theory. However, if I am working with or giving a talk at a protest rally or with a group of parents or a group of deeply committed teachers, this requires a different way of speaking. The teachers may say to me, 'Look, here's my curriculum. It's based on a view of kids as active and critical knowers. Given the pressures on me now to do everything virtually, how do I get some of this to be electronically legitimate?' My response will not be to quote from Foucault or from Gramsci's, *The Prison Notebooks*, one of my favourite books. Their eyes may get a little glassy if I do. I need to take their critical but practical concerns seriously. Having spent years as a teacher in schools in very poor urban and rural areas, I understand what they are going through – and I need to work with them to try to answer their very real questions and still point them in further critical directions. I don't want to be misunderstood here. My point is not to be anti-intellectual at all. That should never be our approach. Rather, the keyword is *praxis*. How do I combine theory and practice together? But that means I must put myself in a position where I am in honest and dialogical interaction with the teachers and educational and community activists who will be called upon to do this. That means I cannot simply be isolated on the balcony of the university. It means that I must be deeply connected to journals in the United States, like *Rethinking Schools*, a journal not only for academics but definitely as well for teachers, administrators and community organizers writing for and teaching each other. There's much more I could say about this. But this is one of the tasks of the 'critical scholar/activist' that I describe in much more detail in *Can Education Change Society?*

Unfortunately, I need to close now. I feel as if I have spent our entire time together trying to discuss much of what I include in an entire course! I teach a course in critical pedagogy. And you've now had the whole course in 57 minutes. I apologize for trying to do all of this together. Again, what we will have to do is meet again soon. When we meet the next time, which I hope will be soon, I would welcome comments, criticism and substantive dialogue. Freire was clear when he said, 'Any teacher who is not a learner is not a good teacher.' I welcome being taught by you the next time we get together and with that, you will forgive me. I must leave very soon. I hope I have been helpful and, again, I hope that your own struggles are successful as time goes on. I must say goodbye to you and to Fatma and my other friends. Keep strong.

GTT   Professor Apple, thank you so much this was very good really, as you said it was the whole class that we learned from you. We are honoured to have your class, but there will be next time with you and to say a lot, you know the keyword, you said, it is 'praxis'. Can we count this community, this digital community, as a praxis or a part of praxis?

Michael Apple   This is an example of using the media that we have been given to try and deal with a crisis in ways that build communities and also create a learning community that is deeply committed socially, that's where we begin. Thank you. See you next time. Bye-bye.

GTT   Thank you so much for this special interview and your support to empowering our community [in] which you have been an active member. This has been a remarkable moment for us listening to your analysis of social and educational issues with a particular focus on the pandemic challenges. Before we say goodbye, I am going to ask the participants to stay more to ask questions to Professor Apple. Because we're going to collect the questions, comments and critics, as he stated, for the next meeting.

References

Apple, M. W. (2013) *Can Education Change Society?* (New York and London: Routledge).

Apple, M. W. (2014) *Official Knowledge: Democratic Education in a Conservative Age*, 3rd edn (New York and London: Routledge).

Apple, M. W. (2019) *Ideology and Curriculum*, 4th edn (New York and London: Routledge).

Apple, M. W. (ed.) (2010) *Global Crises, Social Justice, and Education* (New York and London: Routledge).

Apple, M. W., L. A. Gandin, S. Liu, A. Meshulam and E. Schirmer (2018) *The Struggle for Democracy in Education: Lessons from Social Realities* (New York and London: Routledge).

Freire, P. (1971) *Pedagogy of the Oppressed*, 4th edn (London: Bloomsbury).

Verma, R. and M. W. Apple (eds) (2021) *Disrupting Hate in Education: Teacher Activists, Democracy, and Global Pedagogies of Interruption* (New York and London: Routledge).

Chapter 4

HIGHER EDUCATION IN THE TIME OF CORONA[1]

Peter Mayo

Introduction

Higher education is constantly being exposed to several challenges in this day and age. The Covid-19 pandemic has offered a series of challenges which has plunged many in the academic community, tenured/non-tenured faculty, and students alike, into modes of delivery and interaction, that differ considerably from the hitherto established norm. As I will argue in this paper, university alternatives offer academics a relatively safe adjustment to the changed scenario (some have been attuned to this for quite some time before the outbreak) in contrast to other people for whom the current situation presents a choice: exposure or starvation. Even within the relatively safe 'middle-class' context of secluded and virtually mediated academic work and transaction, there are issues to be considered with regard to the future of Higher Education itself.

Phantom city?

Desperate attempts to curtail the spread of the Corona Virus are said to have been turning many localities in different parts of the world into seemingly phantom cities. For some this is a spectre of an 'unreal city'. For others it lays bare the clear and unadulterated design of the city itself, city centre or square. There are those who hailed city vistas, including open spaces, as things of beauty untrammelled by such paraphernalia as ticket booths, market stalls, coffee tables, chairs and umbrellas. Others underline the eeriness of the sight – a setting in which strange matters can unfold and which fuels the imagination.

1. Originally appeared as P. Mayo, 'The Corona challenge to higher education', *Culture e Studi del Sociale*, Special Issue, 5 (1) (2020): 371–6, retrieved: http://www.cussoc.it/index. php/journal/issue/archive.

University, middle-class jobs and the class/ethnic divide

University and other higher education campuses have not been immune to this process. They are 'closed' institutions with administration reduced to skeleton staff and academics urged to seek alternative ways of interacting with students. As Donatella della Porta underlined in a Facebook remark, middle-class work allows for such contingencies as being able to work from home, a possibility not allowed to many working-class and certain service-oriented middle-class professionals, the latter, I would add, including medical doctors, nurses and pharmacists. 'The pandemic has complicated the class divide, by singling out a privileged class of those who can work from home in a secure labour condition'[2] (della Porta 2020). She raises an important sociological question for those engaged in exploring the nature of class stratification in this day and age: 'Who is producing and distributing all those products that keep those who can [be] comfortable at home . . .?' (ibid.). So, in effect, we might argue that these centres in the city and adjacent streets are not as barren as certain pictures shown on the social media and newspapers would have us believe. There are moments when they are full of people scampering around as their livelihood depends on this. This is a time when abuse and exploitation of those engaged in the informal economy, necessary in certain countries or regions to keep the formal economy going, reach an unprecedented level (Borg 2020). The 'realm of necessity' has not receded into the background for certain people. Others do so because of mental health issues arising from living in a restricted room or two, or outside sleeping in tents or under cardboard covers, in shacks or beneath bridges (Rosa Luxembourg's most tangible form of 'barbarism' today) – all this as opposed to the palatial settings of certain dwelling places.

This, in effect, represents a demarcation with regard to those who can work safely and continue to live and survive the virus and those who have had their odds on doing so lengthened. Social class and, I would add, ethnicity become important variables in the chances of overcoming or succumbing to the virus, especially in the area of menial and intermittent, often clandestine, work carried out by immigrants especially undocumented immigrants. One would have to add here the intersections of social class, ethnicity, gender, citizenship/non-citizenship (including *sans papiers*) and age. Elderly people without help or assistance and living on their own are particularly vulnerable in this regard, and one has to see how older adulthood intersects with many of the other variables.

The choice for these is between exposure and starvation; and people who have risked the vagaries of the desert, the anarchic state of Libya and the ocean, are most likely to be ready to risk exposure to the virus. Some were less fortunate as the pretext of Corona prevented their hitherto resilient bodies to enter Southern European ports, a number succumbing to the fatality of dehydration or drowning – a sad and tragic end to a brave but doomed saga. This is compounded by the

2. See at: https://www.facebook.com/donatella.dellaporta.73.

stubbornness of uncompromising governments intent on forcing a bigoted, self-interest driven European Union to share in the responsibility of taking migrants. At a time when a pandemic increases the call for cooperation and compassion, giving the lie to Maggie Thatcher's mantra, 'There is no such thing as society,' there are those who persist in a 'dog eat dog' mentality. Self-interest lies at the heart of not only individuals, under neoliberalism, but nation-states as a whole.[3]

All into proper perspective

All this is to place the travails of higher education in the time of Corona into proper perspective. In many respects, universities are privileged places. Of course, there are some noticeable exceptions: students surviving the fees regime and other higher education conditions by the skin of their teeth, living in crowded spaces where the tranquillity of online learning and home study in general is a luxury 'devoutly to be wished' but difficult to realize – all this assuming that they can afford a computer and its accessories. There is then the case of adjunct faculty often paid at piece rate. They cannot benefit from the time and space afforded their full-time colleagues for research as they are overburdened by excessive teaching and marking loads. Some need to juggle university teaching with other jobs. Adjunct faculty, working in precarious conditions, are an increasing feature of contemporary higher education [HE] in many parts of the world. This is how the post-1968 mass university or HE institution copes with increasing numbers of students.

These are important considerations that have to be taken on board when exploring higher education alternatives in a time of Corona and after. My guess and fear is that all this will continue to be given short shrift. Higher education, and especially university education, by and large still accommodates a middle-class viewpoint. Despite laudable and interesting experiments among peasants in Latin America[4] (Santos 2017; Connell 2019; Mayo 2019; Mayo and Vittoria 2017) and also in Western Europe (Neary 2014; Earl 2016), the institution as we conventionally know it, and in which most of us academics work, remains a bourgeois institution with an unmistakably bourgeois ethos. Many institutions have come a long way since the exclusive and exclusionary days of old, though the few elite bastions that survive and thrive on endowments, elite residues from that period, persist in their social selection – your *Grandes écoles* and Oxbridge colleges. The general ethos, however, as with the whole competitive educational ethos, remains what it was when we frequented the institution as undergrads. What follows therefore can

3. So much for the so-called receding of the nation-state through the intensification of globalization (Mayo 2019).

4. These include higher education institutions connected with social movements as is the Escola Nacional Florestan Fernandez connected with the Landless Workers Movement (MST) in Brazil and the UNITIERRA in Chiapas, Mexico.

come across as the mumblings of a relatively privileged commentator. And yet there are issues to be raised with regard to the future of these institutions, the epistemological foundations of the knowledge they promote (Santos 2017) and their chances of engaging wider communities (Walcott 2020), in short, their greater, genuine democratization.

Standard corona response

During this period of Covid-19, academics have been urged, if not compelled, irrespective of their training for this purpose, to place their courses and carry out their teaching online. This has led many to herald the 'brave new world' of online learning as the panacea for the crisis. There are those who would consider the present period as the potential watershed in establishing this already widely practiced mode of delivery as the dominant form of teaching in higher education. This reaction, couched in phrases such as 'every cloud has a silver lining', is to be expected and falls in line with the neoliberal tenets that have been underlying most common sense thinking about mass-oriented higher education. I argue for caution in this regard.

The history of education is full of episodes whereby necessity, through crises in the form of occupation, led to ingenuity. Under Nazi occupation, Polish universities went underground; material moved from one place to another. This echoed the earlier 'flying university' of the Partition period, when Marie Curie (Puiu 2020) and Janusz Korczak were among the students. It was innovative and attested to the resilience of the Polish academic community (students and professors) involved. It resurfaced when Poland was under Soviet control.

The good thing about the present crises is that it makes those who are resistant to modern digitally mediated technology take the plunge, whether adequately trained for this purpose or not. Many academics from Greece, Italy, Cyprus and the UK revealed that online learning is a new experience foisted on unprepared academics. It might enable them to transcend archaic ways. It is common knowledge that most universities throughout the world have placed their courses and are delivering their teaching online. Some universities already have had adequate preparation for this as a good percentage of their students are distance-learning students. It is likely that the teachers involved have had adequate training. A former tutor at the UK's Open University, which backs distance learning with a variety of other approaches, including tutorials carried out by academics ensconced in different parts of the country, spent a year's preparation period before joining the university staff. The present crisis however recalls, in certain cases, the situation during the immediate post-revolution literacy campaigns in Latin America and elsewhere when young literacy workers were rushed to the field without adequate preparation (Arnove 1986).

This mass-scale online learning approach can have the same effect. It can extend beyond a crisis response as the institution begins to see the lucrative side of it, a means of spreading one's net far and wide. Now it would be foolish to overlook online learning's positive aspects reaching communities at the furthest remove from universities and centres. It reaches communities with problems of physical access and time.

However, once the dust settles, will there be space for critical reflection as to how technologically mediated delivery complements what is good about 'face-to-face' delivery and adequate teacher student human interaction? Online learning can address mass students anywhere and at any time throughout the world. Academic staff, therefore, really need to think about the appropriate pedagogical approach to take and how to use most modern technology in appropriate ways. Development of good learning environments requires specialist skills and is a team effort that requires collaboration between academics, communities and learning designers. There is also the danger of surveillance with these sessions especially when recorded for the benefit of those who could not gain access in real time. The fear of recordings and of outside parties gaining access to the conversations might make participants hesitant to talk freely in the virtual classroom conversations, especially students hailing from countries abroad with a poor track record when it comes to human rights and civil liberties.

To what extent is online leaning part of the blended approach to learning which reserves space for different forms of interaction including human to human and human to earth interaction? The push for a lucrative share of the global education market can easily make institutions forget the second aspect of the blended learning approach. Meanwhile, elite schools continue to enjoy a monopoly in the latter type of university learning.

Consumer product or public good?

How do we strike a happy medium between online and face to face teaching? Will online learning continue to drag higher education along the business route (Giroux 2014)[5] or will it play its part in an overall conception of education as a public good? And if it is to be part of education as a public good, what provision is to be made in conditions of 'normality', that is when higher education institutions reopen their doors, to ensure that all students have access to the resources necessary for a

---

5. Quite interesting here is the development of MOOCS (Massive Open Online Courses). Do they represent a case of 'testing the waters' for a business approach to higher education? Sarah Speight (2017) indicates the gradual mainstreaming of MOOCS. They are becoming part of degree courses offered at a considerable financial cost. Speight argues that MOOCs target people with a good education and familiar with basic learning modalities and who can afford the 'state-of-the-art' facilities that enable them to cope with the online provision – a case of giving more to who already has? Is this a CPD (continuing professional development) outlet? The fee structure for courses is steep, according to Speight (2017). MOOCs are considered a key feature of the Fourth Industrial Revolution (4th IR) (Xing and Marwala 2017).

genuinely good quality higher education to which they are entitled (face to face or blended)? To strike an optimistic note, as hope springs eternal, I reproduce the words of one of the USA's most prominent critical educators, Ira Shor who wrote to me on this matter, stating: 'Critical teachers who question the unequal, toxic status quo will deliver critical education no matter the delivery system' (Shor in Mayo 2020).

Covid-19 and neoliberalism

It is the uncritical educators, those who go with the flow, taking on new fads uncritically, that are of great concern to me. There is a terrible and unequal world out there that needs to be confronted. Covid-19 has shown the true face of neoliberalism as years of reneging on and shredding of the social contract have finally taken their toll with few public resources available to counter such a calamity. Hopefully, the newly rediscovered sense of solidarity among certain academics will enable them to rethink their mission as people who not only *interpret* the world but contribute towards *changing* it. To do this, the genuine human factor in research and thinking remains paramount. The virtual classroom might have served its purpose as a contingency during the crisis. Once this is over, it should be only part of a more holistic approach which foregrounds face-to-face encounters, one in which even an approving eye contact can be enough to encourage a shy or hesitant student to express what the body language suggests but which would otherwise remain suppressed. The holistic approach would also include engagement with communities (Walcott 2020) and ever-changing communities at that – migrants are important agents here (Mayo 2019). This applies to all disciplines for as a science student is on record as having said, during the pandemic, 'now, when the world's attention is on a virus – a topic I've spent my whole adult life studying – what I think about most are social structures, inequality, and sacrifice. I think about people' (Quizon 2020). This might place the onus for societal relevance on the Humanities and Social Sciences but I would argue that it should apply to most university and higher education areas as they all impact on society and the rest of the environment.

References

Arnove, Robert (1986) *Education and Revolution in Nicaragua* (Westport, CT: Praeger).

Borg, Carmel (2020) 'Analiżi: Il-pandemija żiedet l-abbuż u l-isfruttament fuq il-ħaddiema fl-ekonomija "informali" daqs qatt qabel' (Analysis: The pandemic has increased abuse and exploitation of workers in the informal economy as never before), *illum*, 29 April (in Maltese).

Connell, Raewyn (2019) *The Good University: What Universities Actually Do and Why It's Time for Radical Change* (London: Zed Books).

della Porta, Donatella (2020) 'The pandemic has complicated the class divide . . .' posting, Facebook, 3 May.

Earl, Cassie (2016) 'Doing pedagogy publicly: Asserting the right to the city to rethink the university', *Open Library of the Humanities*, 2 (2): e3.

Giroux, Henry (2014) *Neoliberalism's War on Higher Education* (Chicago, IL: Haymarket Books).

Giroux, Henry and Susan Searls Giroux (2004) *Take Back Higher Education: Race, Youth and the Crisis of Democracy in the Post-Civil Rights Era* (New York and Basingstoke: Palgrave Macmillan).

Mayo, Peter (2019) *Higher Education in a Globalising World: Community Engagement and Lifelong Learning* (Manchester: Manchester University Press).

Mayo, Peter (2020) 'Higher education in the time of Corona', *RSA*, 23 March. Available at: https://www.thersa.org/discover/publications-and-articles/rsa-comment/2020/03/higher-education-in-the-time-of-corona?fbclid=IwAR3O4r8JhzaKRQu4HlKiZrIuGtPEaSrxFxnLYTjOf6Haq07b_hRQAUksvYk.

Mayo, Peter and Paulo Vittoria (2017) *Saggi di Pedagogia Critica. Oltre il neoliberismo. Analizzando educatori, lotte e movimenti social* (Essays in Critical Pedagogy: Beyond Neoliberalism: Analysing Educators, Struggles and Social Movements (Florence: Società Editrice Fiorentina).

Neary, Mike (2014) 'The university and the city: Social Science Centre, Lincoln – Forming the urban revolution', in P. Temple (ed.), *The Physical University: Contours of Space and Place in Higher Education* (Abingdon: Routledge), 203–16.

Puiu, Tibi (2020) 'The story of Poland's secret "Flying Universities" that gave men and women equal chance, Marie Curie among them', *ZME Science*, 5 May. Available at: https://www.zmescience.com/science/flying-universities-poland/.

Quizon, Kaye's tweet: 'I didn't get why we were required humanities in undergrad . . .' Available at: https://www.facebook.com/photo.php?fbid=3020940784640059&set=a.248930831841082&type=3&theater.

Santos, Boaventura de Sousa (2017) *Decolonising the University: The Challenge of Deep Cognitive Justice* (Newcastle upon Tyne: Cambridge Scholars Publishing).

Speight, Sarah (2017) 'The mainstreaming of Massive Open Online Courses (MOOCs)', in M. Milana, S. Webb, J. Holford, R. Waller and P. Jarvis (eds), *Palgrave International Handbook on Adult and Lifelong Education and Learning* (Basingstoke and London: Palgrave Macmillan).

Walcott, Rinaldo (2020) 'During the Coronavirus, academics have found themselves in a crisis of their work', *Macleans*, 15 April. Available at: https://www.macleans.ca/opinion/during-the-coronavirus-academics-have-found-themselves-in-a-crisis-of-their-work/?fbclid=IwAR3tTWzo41aA1cD87W0Ge-fP_ZnV4JVfbdSzQabT3L-P1xZNJr1sBLhFgDk.

Xing, Bo and Tshilidzi Marwala (2017) 'Implications for the Fourth Industrial Age on higher education', Paper, Cornell University Library. Available at: https://arxiv.org/abs/1703.09643; and https://arxiv.org/ftp/arxiv/papers/1703/1703.09643.pdf.

Chapter 5

FREIRE AND A REVOLUTIONARY PRAXIS OF THE BODY: COUNTERING THE ONE-DIMENSIONALITY OF BANKING EDUCATION

Antonia Darder

It is the human body, young or old, fat or thin, of whatever colour, the conscious body that looks at the stars. It is the body that writes. It is the body that speaks. It is the body that fights. It is the body that loves and hates. It is the body that suffers. It is the body that dies. It is the body that lives!
—Paulo Freire (in Freire and Faundez 1989, 18)

Over the years, Paulo Freire began to speak more openly and passionately about the relationship of the body to humanizing praxis. His critical understanding of the body encompasses a pedagogical perspective that focuses on the political primacy and social power of our bodies in the construction of critical consciousness. Freire and other critical education scholars (Shapiro and Shapiro 2002; Shapiro 1999; McLaren 1999) who have chosen to engage ideas of the body within the pedagogical arena also point to the importance of the materiality of body, informed by a humanizing ethos that supports reflection, dialogue and solidarity in the flesh, as we labour for the common good. As teachers and students participate in the dialogical process of communal learning, the body and the mind must be understood as rightful allies in the formation, expression and evolution of collective consciousness.

For Freire, critical consciousness, as a social and material phenomenon, constitutes far more than simply a cognitive abstraction. Of this, Freire argued that the development of critical consciousness and 'true education incarnates the permanent search of people together with others for their becoming fully human in the world in which they exist' (1983, 96). Education is conceived then as a vital communal arena, in which expressions of the body are inextricable to the construction of knowledge, the evolution of consciousness and the formation of our humanity. With this in mind, the following considers some of the salient ways in which the body was central to Freire's humanizing praxis – a praxis fundamentally grounded in a larger revolutionary project for liberation.

One-dimensionality of banking education

Dehumanizing conditions of hegemonic schooling reduce students' bodies to passive objects, given the one-dimensional nature of banking education, where teachers are expected to fill students minds with official knowledge. Yet, we cannot ignore that the materiality of the body is widely implicated in students' repetitive interactions with dominant curricular and relational values and norms routinized and normalized as commonsense (Butler 1993; Mauss 1992 [1934]). Within the mainstream classroom experience – beyond the process of socialization and adaptation – there is a hidden curriculum or pedagogy of domestication that disciplines the body to adopt dominant forms of knowing and being. The one-dimensionality of banking education is systematically predicated on the logic of a colonizing educational practice marshalled through control of the body. In Freire's work, for example, the culture of silence signals one of the primary ways that the bodies of the oppressed are disciplined, controlled and repressed, limiting their pedagogical opportunities to voice and enact their lived histories, cultural sensibilities and collective ways of being.

This culture of silence is inherent in the Eurocentric epistemology that informs Western pedagogical views (Santos 2014), where students are perceived as decontextualized individuals, who are expected to abandon their pre-existing cultural values and norms (most often reflected in one's use of the body), which lie outside the purview of hegemonic educational expectations. In contrast, Freire's (1989a, 1993, 2002) problem-posing pedagogy counters the limits of the one-dimensionality of the banking pedagogical tradition, which abstracts knowledge and negates the role of the body in the process of teaching and learning. Furthermore, Freire understood this tradition to be tied to the intellectual history of the West, where the Cartesian mind/body split deems the heart and mind as antagonists to intellectual formation.

While emancipatory schooling embraces the multidimensionality of our humanity and the materiality of the body as significant to the development of consciousness, this integral view is summarily curtailed by banking education. Accordingly, a more complex understanding of the body and its significance to teaching and learning is generally absent, unless it is directed toward the corporal management and control of students. Here, this one-dimensional epistemological focus privileges cognitive approaches to education, disregarding other forms of knowing. In the process, cultural voices and physical movements of the body that fall outside the mainstream cultural register are systematically marginalized. It is also worth noting that this phenomenon is predicated upon prevailing Western notions of the individual as primarily a psychological self, whose intelligence and 'ego strength' is supposedly gauged by the ability to function effectively, irrespective of external conditions. Nowhere do we see this phenomenon more at work today than in the disembodied and virtualized pedagogy of on-line teaching that has become commonplace in the era of Covid-19.

This pedagogical culture of disembodiment has historically promoted anti-dialogical relationships, curricular practices, and forms of socialization that alienate students. Too often, for example, typical seating classroom arrangements require students to remain immobile for the majority of the day, despite the fact that this ignores the needs of kinesthetic learners, who learn best through their bodies and sense of touch. Within the context of online education, the issues seem self-evident, including the difficulties faced by children who cannot sit still, hour after hour, with eyes glued to a screen. Beyond the apparent inequality in access to technology associated with virtual learning, students from more affluent communities – where greater emphasis is given to abstract ways of knowing the world – will be far more apt to succeed academically. Yet, despite such underlying exclusions, seldom are educators prepared to contend with the cognitive injustices perpetuated by instrumentalized and marketized approaches to learning – approaches that undermine student opportunities for meaningful participation in their own learning.

Concerned with the impact of such oppressive classroom practices, Freire (1998a) argued that the one-dimensionality of banking education functions to disable the critical formation of voice, social agency and democratic solidarity, which generally is even more disabling for students from racialized and working-class communities, who seldom receive the resources or opportunities enjoyed by their more affluent counterparts. In contrast, a critical pedagogy of the body integrates an underlying commitment to (re)inventing social and material classroom conditions in ways that offer teachers and students the opportunity to learn, as Marx proposed, *according to their abilities* (Wallimann 1981). This political commitment cultivates a pedagogical environment where the body is understood as *our medium for having a world* (Merleau-Ponty 2002) and teachers are free to develop forms of revolutionary classroom praxis where students are neither asked to deny the wisdom of their cultural bodies nor to estrange themselves from one another, in the name of meritocratic competition, individual academic success or social mobility.

The politics of the body

Human bodies are continuously being molded by a matrix of power relations and the cultural practices of communities, social groups and organizations in which they participate. Therefore, the body can be comprehended as a political material force with which we can either wage liberation or domination. In his writings on the control of body movement, for example, Marcel Mauss (1992 [1934]) contends that there exists a process of normalization, 'a mechanism inhibiting disorderly movements (ibid., 474) within the classroom and society. Cruz and McLaren (2002) argue that this assertion helps to illuminate significant organizing elements of a pedagogy of the body, particularly within the context of late capitalism. They argue: 'it is imperative that we view the physical body as a site of meaning-making; and that we read the body's contradictory and often agonistic discourses as a social relation linked to the forces of revolution' (ibid., 188). The process of teaching and learning must then be acknowledged as human labour overwhelmingly influenced by the political intricacies of our materiality – a materiality that exists prior to the emergence of our social agency and expressed through the different cultural processes that influence our direct engagement with the world. Hence, diverse student populations and their communities are profoundly shaped in differing ways, given the political nature of their life experiences, economic conditions and cultural histories of survival.

In concert with the ideas of Jose Ortega y Gasset on sensualism and Merleau-Ponty's opposition to the dualism of consciousness and the body, Freire (1993) refused to dichotomize or marginalize the body's sensuality from the development of critical consciousness. He argued persistently for the indisputability of the body in the process of teaching and learning, pointing to the political significance of 'a certain sensualism . . . contained in the body'; a sensualism inseparable to 'rigorous acts of knowing the world' and our passionate ability to love and know the world around us. Not surprisingly, it is precisely this passionate sensual freedom, from which we produce revolutionary thought and action, that is held hostage by the deeply fragmented, objectified, and instrumentalized neoliberal curricula administered to oppressed student populations. Freire's perspective on the politics of the body also echoes aspects of Herbert Marcuse's (1955) thesis in *Eros and Civilization*, where Marcuse boldly argues for a widening of our experience of the body through embracing a *polymorphous sensuality* – a sensuality more in line with our human capacity to emerge as freely empowered and conscious subjects of history. Unfortunately, conscious and enlivened sensual bodies that could potentially resist and defy the perversities of capital, are often thwarted in the classroom, abstracted, disempowered and conditioned to normalize the depravities of a neoliberal logic in exchange for academic success.

Yet, despite the common phenomenon of fettered bodies – anchored in the Western classical tradition of Cartesian dualism or the mind/body split – the colonizing dynamic of banking education seldom is carried out without protestations. Notwithstanding major institutional efforts to control the body's desires, pleasures, sensuality and mobility within the classroom, students seldom fully surrender their bodies completely or readily acquiesce to authoritarian practices – practices which, in themselves, can provide the impetus for resistance and self-determination, especially for those students whose dynamic histories are excluded within the hegemonic curriculum of schooling under capitalism (Darder 2012 and 2014; Paraskeva 2011; Shapiro 1999). Instead, many students engage in the construction of their own cultural forms of resistance – forms of resistance which may or may not always function in their best interest. Typical expressions of student resistance globally are often expressed through counterculture alterations of the body – be this through clothing, hairstyles, postures, ways of walking, manner of speaking, or the piercing or tattooing of the body. These physical alterations, moreover, which represent not only acts of resistance but alternative ways of experiencing and knowing the world, are generally perceived by officials as both transgressive and disruptive to the social order.

Teachers, whose bodies and sensuality are similarly restricted, alienated and domesticated by their workplace, are also under enormous pressure to constantly police policies related to the movement of student bodies in the classroom, while simultaneously dispensing pre-packaged curricula and testing protocols that further dehumanize student learning. In the process, critical approaches grounded in the actual needs of students are seldom initiated, unless students are of more affluent communities. Yet, given the impact of disembodied practices, particularly in the current online pedagogy of the pandemic, teachers generally experience an uphill battle in meeting standardized mandates that physically alienate students from their learning. Nowhere is this more apparent than in low-income schools, where teaching-to-the-test tends to be the curricula of choice, even within colleges and universities.

Consequently, teachers who, consciously or unconsciously, reproduce a variety of one-dimensional authoritarian classroom practices in the name of classroom management, seldom find it easy to maintain physical control of their students or to persuade them to complete meaningless educational tasks. Moreover, teachers in the repressive climate of banking education struggle to implement more liberating strategies, in that they are often forced to become masters of deception – saying what the principal, director or district office wishes to hear, while they try to do behind closed doors what they believe students actually need. The experience of duplicity that this engenders can becomes intolerable, driving some of the most effective teachers away from their chosen vocation, irrespective of their political commitment. Meanwhile, others who begin to sense defeat, in frustration, adopt more authoritarian approaches to manipulate and coerce cooperation, while justifying their means, in the name of helping students succeed academically. What cannot be overlook here is the manner in which authoritarian practices are designed not only to 'blindfold students and lead them to a domesticated future' (Freire 1970: 79), but also to estrange teachers from their labour as well.

Concerned with the need to restore greater freedom, joy and creativity in the classrooms, Freire urged teachers to reject this domesticating role within their classrooms 'by demythologizing the authoritarianism of teaching packages and their administration in the intimacy of their world, which is also the world of their students' (1998c, 9). Freire's (1993) pedagogy of love challenged the necrophilic grip of hegemonic schooling, highlighting the ways in which students from oppressed communities, in particular, are expected to engage their studies as objective and impartial observers, even when the object of their study may intimately link to conditions of human suffering that may be part of their everyday lives. Here, traditional academic expectations affirm that feelings and intuition corrupt the process of teaching and learning and are suspect in formulating truth. Of this, Freire argued, 'the categorical negation of emotion and passion, the belief in technicism, ends in convincing many that, the more neutral [or estranged] we are in our actions, the more objective and efficient we will be' (ibid., 106). Hence, it is not surprising that the university formation of students is, more often than not, tied to an epistemological logic of physical estrangement, which expects they learn to labour as uncritical, descriptive, 'neutral' researchers, disembodied, objective and dispassionate.

The estrangement of the body

In *Pedagogy of Hope*, Freire (2002) made a variety of references that reflect his recognition that the material conditions of estrangement that shape the lived histories of oppressed students, workers, and their communities are profoundly visible through the body. This can be witnessed, as noted earlier, in their skin, teeth, hair, gestures, speech and cultural movements of the body. As such, bodies provide meaningful maps of cultural, class and gendered identities and offer powerful insights into the tensions, struggles and needs that shape the lives of students from oppressed communities. In concert with Marx, Freire (1998a) argued that hegemonic schooling is founded on a politics of estrangement, which, like that of estranged labour, functions to alienate students from their bodies and the natural world. Further, he suggested that this pedagogical estrangement of the body is akin to 'that invisible power of alienating domestication ... a state of refined estrangement ... [and] of a loss of consciousness' (ibid., 102).

Unfortunately, educators prepared in the one-dimensionality of banking pedagogy seldom possess the necessary political knowledge about the body to counter deficit notions that become embedded commonsensically within the classroom. This further incapacitates the human sensibilities necessary for critical engagement of the larger conditions of inequalities that impact the lives of students from historically oppressed populations. Common authoritarian responses to student physicality also ignore or often misinterpret the meaning and intent of student behaviours outside the mainstream, converting the body into an object that must acquiesce to the teacher's will or be expelled (Darder 2015). In the process, little attention is given to the dialectical relationship that students have with their social and material world – a relationship that for working class youth of colour, for example, requires constant navigation of the minefields of structural oppression perpetuated by racism, poverty and other forms of social exclusion. The unfortunate consequence is that the disembodied knowledge of the curriculum seldom assists teachers and students to grapple critically with deeper moral questions of education, which would undoubtedly challenge colonizing views and practices that sustain inequities.

Correspondingly, banking education exists as an arena of domestication, where abstract knowledge and its constructions are decontextualized, disembodied and objectified. In response, students are forced to acquiesce to its alienating function, limiting rationality and technocratic instrumentalism. In response, Freire asserted in *Pedagogy of Freedom* that it is insufficient to rely on abstract approaches to learning, where disembodied words and texts are privileged in the construction of knowledge: 'words not given body [or made flesh] have little or no value' (1998a, 39). Moreover, Freire underlined the manner in which educational processes of estrangement cause false dichotomies that alienate students from their material world – the only true realm in which cultural, political, and economic liberation can be forged.

Given the significant role of the body to the pedagogical process, Freire was troubled by the manner in which the ontological and epistemological estrangement of the body in banking approaches interferes historically with the capacities of students to know themselves, one another, and their world. Often ignored is the obvious fact that our lives unfold within the vital historical experiences of the flesh and its sentient capacities. Instead, the body is seen as an object to be controlled, contained or transcended, given its potential to disrupt the hegemonic order. This negation sidelines the affective and relational needs of student bodies that must endure, resist and struggle to become free from the social and material entanglements of a society that imprisons them, both ideologically and corporally. Furthermore, repressive views of the body and sensuality within education undermine, overtly or covertly, the cultural knowledge and wisdom of oppressed populations, whose distinct epistemologies and cultural expressions of the body may differ substantially from hegemonic notions about the body, learning or consciousness. Epistemologically, this alienates and undercuts the pedagogical experience of students who arrive at school with ways of knowing that are perceived outside the limited scope of the hegemonic lens, whether these differences are predicated on class, gender, ethnicity, sexuality, skin colour, physical constitution or spiritual beliefs (Paraskeva 2011).

Even more disheartening are disembodied views of teaching and learning that reinforce attitudes and practices of pedagogical estrangement that subject the oppressed to psychological or physical violence. Accordingly, inequalities are reproduced through class, racialized, gendered, ableist and heterosexist perceptions and distortions embedded, wittingly or unwittingly, in the hegemonic culture of schooling and society. This brings to mind deficit assumptions and preconceptions about student intelligence or what is accepted as legitimate knowledge. These assumptions are generally projected implicitly upon both teachers or students from oppressed communities whose appearance or physical movements are exoticized or perceived antagonistic to the classed, racialized, patriarchal, heteronormative, abled or spiritual ideologies that conserve the interests of the capitalist state. Consequently, students from working-class and racialized communities – where the body's spontaneity is often given greater primacy and freedom of movement – are expected to sacrifice their body's creative, imaginative, and sensual knowledge to an atomized and objectified logic of being. In response, Freire challenges conservative ideologies of historical erasure and social control associated with hegemonic pedagogical traditions that discount the body's pedagogical relevance. This again signals the importance of a multidimensional reading of students' bodies in our revolutionary efforts to dismantle the dichotomies, contradictions and exclusions that obstruct students' capacities for self-determination and for participation in a more just and loving world.

Toward a revolutionary praxis of the body

Freire's ideas on the body confirm the need for teachers and students to labour in the flesh. This is to say that emancipatory forms of teaching and learning must be rooted in the materiality of our human existence, as a starting place for a revolutionary praxis. Freire argued, 'It is this process of change, of transforming the material world from which we emerged, that creation of the cultural and historical world takes place' (1993, 108). However, there is nothing automatic or 'natural' about a revolutionary process of social change nor is it a process that can solely rely on calculating logic or cold rationality. In fact, it is the sentient and organic qualities of the body that overwhelmingly shape individual and collective consciousness when we resist or desist, adjust or rebel, rejoice or despair in the passionate search for the freedom to be.

As noted throughout this discussion, historical and cultural experiences are deeply imbedded in the materiality of the body. Thus, our memory of lived conditions of repression or trauma are dialectically held within both our body's cellular memory (physical body) and our relational memory (social body). Hence, the material, emotional, psychological, and political experience of the pandemic lockdown, for example, will remain indelibly marked in the bodies of all who have experienced this moment, whether we are conscious of this phenomenon or not. With this in mind, a revolutionary praxis of the body supports teachers in building democratic educational conditions where students can engage the actual historical events transpiring in their everyday lives, as they learn together within an embodied spirit of human kinship and community. By so doing, teachers create pedagogical spaces that support students in becoming critically conscious of the social and material conditions that can potentially retraumatize, isolate, marginalize and alienate them in their lives. This pedagogical link between the body and communal life was key to Freire's understanding of *conscientização*, which can only unfold and evolve within the context of political participation and solidarity – a revolutionary form of cultural action that must be enacted in the flesh (Darder 2015).

In *Pedagogy of the City*, Freire again referred to the undeniable centrality of the body and its 'passionate ability to know' (1993, 87). Freire's own passionate way of being in the world and his many references to the 'beauty of the body' and 'the restlessness of bodies', bore witness to the ways in which the body's sensuality and sexuality have a determining impact on consciousness and reason. In *Pedagogy of the Heart*, for example, Freire commented on the 'gradual improvement in performance on the part of the student, as the pedagogy of questioning started to gain ground against the pedagogy of answers, and as issues around the body were addressed' (1998b, 62). Toward this end, a revolutionary praxis conceptualizes students as fully embodied subjects of history (Darder 2014), who enter the classroom with preexisting cultural capacities to express community forms of embodied knowing. This emancipatory pedagogical sensibility again acknowledges as essential, right from the start, the dialectical relationship between the physical body and the social body, a relationship that shapes our understanding of who we are as human beings.

Freire steadfastly argued, 'What is important in teaching is not the mechanical repetition of this or that gesture but a comprehension of the value of sentiments, emotions, and desires ... and sensibility, affectivity, and intuition' (ibid., 48). This pedagogical assertion of the power of human sensibilities, beyond reason, in the struggle for our liberation is, indeed, a hallmark of Freire's revolutionary praxis. As such, teachers committed to a revolutionary praxis of education must enter the classroom prepared to contend, in the flesh, with the embodied sensibilities of the oppressed, along with the social and material forces of oppression that shape their classroom labour. The difficulty here, of course, is that these two pedagogical questions of embodiment are generally silenced within the one-dimensionality of banking education. Hence, the pedagogical absence of the body functions effectively to undermine teachers and students' social agency, inhibit their development of critical consciousness, and reinforce their hegemonic induction into the repressive and consuming culture of capitalism.

It is also significant to note here that the genesis of revolutionary thought often emerges from the critical pedagogical nexus where student bodies confront the repressive culture of capitalist schooling. For students from racialized and working-class communities, for example, critical consciousness most often emerges and is expressed through their critical efforts to make sense of the oppressive material conditions and social relations of power that shape the limitations they face daily. This vital genesis of resistance signals an essential break from the one-dimensionality of hegemonic schooling, in that it propels teachers and students toward greater critical engagement with the diverse social and material forces that mold, inhibit and control their sensuality, physical movements and political participation.

Therefore, despite classroom practices that serve to repress and control the movements of racialized and working-class bodies, Freire noted that, in the struggle for freedom, students who are oppressed will 'try out forms of rebellious action' (1970, 64), engaging in the construction of their own cultural forms of resistance, as noted earlier. In a footnote in *Pedagogy of the Oppressed*, Freire points to the pedagogical significance of this phenomenon by noting that teachers cannot 'see youth rebellion as a mere example of the traditional differences between generations. Something deeper is involved here. Young people in their rebellion are denouncing and condemning the unjust model of a society of domination. This rebellion with its special dimension, however, is very recent; [in that] society continues to be authoritarian in character' (ibid., 154).

Despite progressive educational efforts of the past, authoritarianism remains a central feature of banking education as an effective means for mitigating longstanding institutional fears associated with the real potential of oppressed bodies to disrupt and subvert the status quo. With this in mind, Freire turned to a humanizing ethical commitment to counter authoritarianism and its disembodiment of our humanity – a commitment that also lies at the heart of his revolutionary praxis. To endure daily confrontations with oppressive forces, Freire (1998a) urged us to struggle ethically against the social and material conditions in our lives that shape, disable and distort our experiences of the world, causing our bodies, both individually and collectively, to suffer under regimes of power that perpetuate political and economic marginalization, exploitation, disempowerment and violence.

The body as an ethical terrain of struggle

As an ethical stance, Freire embraced the totality of the body in the act of knowing, insisting, 'It is my entire body that socially knows. I cannot, in the name of exactness and rigour, negate my body, my emotions and my feelings' (1993, 105). The human body then constitutes an important ethical terrain of struggle from which all emancipatory knowledge unfolds and critical consciousness develops. Without the materiality of the body, our teaching and learning is reduced to fractured processes of abstraction that falsely render knowledge a neutral and objective phenomenon, absent of history, ideology and contestation. Without critique and resistance, we are too easily moulded and shaped by the structures, policies and practices of economic domination and social exclusion that violently insert our bodies into the alienating morass of an intensified global division of labour. In contrast, Freire (1993, 1998a, 2002) asserted the ethical body as a revolutionary means for our existence as subjects of history and as politically empowered agents of change. Most importantly, it is through our embodied collective labour and struggles that political consciousness is born and societies transformed. Hence, the integration of the body serves as an overwhelming ethical feature of revolutionary praxis, in that, ultimately, it is the body that lives, struggles and holds the potential for our individual and collective liberation.

Forging a revolutionary praxis of education and society beckons us all back to our bodies, in a world where all aspects of our daily life – birth, death, marriage, family, school, work, leisure, parenthood, spirituality and even entertainment – are monitored and controlled. This historical colonization of our bodies has left many of us numb, alienated and fragmented and defenseless and at the mercy of capitalism – a totalizing force that generates a variety of oppressions (racism, sexism, poverty, etc.) inextricable to the economic accumulation of a few, at the expense of the many. The consequence is a deep sense of personal and collective dissatisfaction, generated by a marketplace that cannot satisfy the human needs of the body – needs that can only be met through relationships that break the alienation and isolation so prevalent in our lives today.

Moreover, it is the absence of a truly ethically democratic language and practice of the body that can stifle our capacity for social struggle. For example, many educators across the country bemoan, justifiably so, conditions created by the privatization of education, and accountability regimes of high-stakes testing and standardized knowledge, which negatively impact not only the education of racialized and working-class students but also the labour of teachers themselves. Rather than a language of economic efficiency and neoliberal accountability, what is most needed is the development of an ethical political language of educational struggle that can safeguard the dignity and integrity of all human beings, but in particular those populations who have historically suffered the brunt of economic exploitation, through the racialization of communities, the dispossession of lands, the genocide of minority languages and cultures, and the over-surveillance and imprisonment of racialized working-class populations. In the present climate, of course, there is growing concern that the extensive measures of social control introduced during the coronavirus outbreak will widen and become firmly entrenched after the crisis is over, limiting the future opportunities and movement of oppressed populations worldwide.

By connecting the body to revolutionary praxis, we can better comprehend why Freire believed that education can serve as a fundamental vehicle for the political formation of citizens and the making of a more just society. His work points to a revolutionary praxis that prepares students from oppressed communities for voice and participation in civil society, as well as for ethical decision-making in all aspects of their lives. For Freire, the purpose of a revolutionary praxis of education is to support the evolution of critical consciousness with an explicit aim toward the establishment of a more loving and just world. This begins with a fundamental realization that we live in an unequal world and our commitment to liberation, which entails a collective 'struggle for our humanization, for the emancipation of labour and for the overcoming of our alienation' (Freire 1970, 28). As we courageously move to break our alienation and estrangement of the body, we come to affirm ourselves as full political subjects of our destinies. Indeed, such a revolutionary praxis of education demands an on-going political process, which can only be sustained through our embodied and collective labour – labour born of faith, love, and our unceasing political commitment to know, through both theory and practice, the nature of the beast that preys on our humanity.

References

Butler, Judith (1993) *Bodies that Matter* (London: Routledge).

Cruz, Cindy and Peter McLaren (2002) 'Queer bodies and configurations: Toward a pedagogy of the body', in Sherry Shapiro and Svi Shapiro (eds), *Body Movements: Pedagogy, Politics, and Social Change* (Creskill, NJ: Hampton Press), 187–207.

Darder, Antonia (2012) *Culture and Power in the Classroom*, 2nd edn (New York: Routledge).

Darder, Antonia (2014) *Reinventing Paulo Freire: A Pedagogy of Love* (New York: Routledge).

Darder, Antonia (2015). *Freire and Education* (New York: Routledge).

Freire, Paulo (1970) *Pedagogy of the Oppressed* (New York: Continuum).

Freire, Paulo (1983) *Education for Critical Consciousness* (New York: Seabury Press).

Freire, Paulo (1985) *The Politics of Education: Culture, Power and Liberation* (South Hadley, MA: Bergin & Garvey).

Freire, Paulo (1993) *Pedagogy of the City* (New York: Continuum).

Freire, Paulo (1998a) *Pedagogy of Freedom: Ethics, Democracy and Civic Courage* (Lanham, MD: Rowman & Littlefield Publishers).

Freire, Paulo (1998b) *Pedagogy of the Heart* (New York: Continuum).

Freire, Paulo (1998c) *Teachers and Cultural Workers: Letters to Those Who Dare to Teach* (Boulder, CO: Westview Press).

Freire, Paulo (2002) *Pedagogy of Hope: Reliving Pedagogy of the Oppressed* (New York: Continuum).

Freire, Paulo (2005) *Pedagogy of the Oppressed*, 30th anniversary edn. (New York: Continuum).

Freire, Paulo and Antonio Faundez (1989) *Learning to Question: A Pedagogy of Liberation*, trans. T. Coates (New York: Continuum).

Giroux, Henry (1998) 'Teenage sexuality, body politics and the pedagogy of display', in J. Epstein (ed.), *Youth Culture: Identity in a Postmodern World* (Malden, MA: Wiley-Blackwell), 24–55. Available at: http://www.henryagiroux.com/online_articles/teenage_sexuality.htm.

Marcuse, Herbert (1955) *Eros and Civilization* (Boston, MA: Beacon Press).

Mauss, Marcel (1992) 'Techniques of the body', (originally published in 1934) in J. Crary and S. Kwinter (eds), *Zone 6 Incorporations: Incorporations* v. 6. (Massachusetts, MA: MIT Press), 455–77.

McLaren, Peter (1999) 'Foreword', in S. Shapiro (ed.), *Pedagogy and the Politics of the Body* (New York: Garland), ix–xvii.

Merleau-Ponty, Maurice (2002) *The Phenomenology of Perception* (New York: Routledge).

Paraskeva, Joao (2011) *Conflicts in Curriculum Theory* (New York: Palgrave).

Santos, Boaventura de Sousa (2014) *Epistemologies of the South: Justice against Epistemicide* (Boulder, CO: Paradigm).

Shapiro, Sherry (1999) *Pedagogy and the Politics of the Body: A Critical Praxis* (New York: Garland).

Shapiro, Sherry and Svi Shapiro (2002) *Body Movements: Pedagogy, Politics and Social Change* (Cresskill, NJ: Hampton Press).

Wallimann, Isidor (1981) *Estrangement: Marx's Conception of Human Nature and the Division of Labor* (Westport, CT: Greenwood Press).

Chapter 6

A DIALOGUE WITH E. WAYNE ROSS ON:
A CRISIS WITHIN A CRISIS

TEACHING, LEARNING AND DEMOCRACY UNDER
NEOLIBERALISM DURING THE PANDEMIC[1]

E. Wayne Ross

Global Thursday Talks   Dear Professor Ross, first of all, we would like to welcome you with our gratitude, thank you for accepting our invitation. We are passing through strange days, where we need more solidarity in our communities, and we need to get together in digital communities like this one. Our first question is about your journey into being an education activist. We know you as an activist scholar. To start this interview, we would like you to tell us a little about your journey as an activist educator, your active involvement and your moving things around such as co-founding the Rouge Forum, [and the journals] *Cultural Logic, Workplace, Critical Education*. How did you start? What was your drive? What life experiences shaped your thinking? Whom have you supported? Have your institutions (like UBC [University of British Columbia]) backed your activist standing?

E. Wayne Ross   Thank you for that question. I think it's a good one and it causes me to do some soul-searching, which I've done over the years. First of all, I'll say that I think of education as a process of becoming, it is a process of personal transformation and when I look back across my own experiences, that is what I see. I was born and raised in the Southern United States, in South Carolina and North Carolina. Having been born in the mid-1950s, I grew up in the 'Jim Crow' era, which was a society based on racial discrimination and white supremacy and I can't separate who I am from those origins. The context of a white supremacist society as well as the context of being raised in a family that was ultra-conservative evangelical Christian fundamentalist – my father was a Pentecostal minister – those two embedded contexts really shaped my

1. This interview was conducted within the activities of @globalthursdaytalks digital community on 10 December 2020 and is available at: https://youtu.be/VGsNemNRkiM (accessed 11 December 2020).

world view in an unusual way. Because growing up in church culture was like a 'total institution' – if you've ever read Erving Goffman, the sociologist, particularly his book, *Asylums* (2017 [1961]), he talks about these worlds that are captured within worlds and I was from very early in my life quite aware of the racial discrimination and segregation that I was living in as a white person, but then simultaneously in a ultra-conservative Christian community that itself was separated from what I saw, as a child, as the 'normal' community. Growing up, my family had very strict behavioural guidelines, so I think, for me, my sense of justice and equality was really shaped by being, by growing up in an apartheid society. It wasn't until I was in secondary school that I went to a racially desegregated school, in Charlotte, North Carolina. Experiencing the violence and the tensions of racial desegregation in the South had a huge effect on me, so the sense of place was very important to me and one of the things that I have done in recent years is write about through those experiences in intellectual memoirs (Ross 2014 and 2015).

What has been really important to me are the academic colleagues I have had an opportunity to work with. In particular, Rich Gibson who worked at Wayne State University in Detroit and then at San Diego State University; Kevin Vinson, who taught at the University of Arizona and then the University of the West Indies; Valerie Ooka Pang at San Diego State University; David Hursh at the University of Rochester; Perry Marker at Sonoma State University in California. I've been lucky to have a partner – Sandra Mathison – who is also an academic and that's been an important source of support for me and my close colleague Stephen Petrina at the University of British Columbia (BC). So, all of those people and others have been important sources of support and collaboration in my work.

Rich Gibson and I, along with a few other people, started the Rouge Forum in the 1990s. The origin story of the Rouge Forum comes out of a professional meeting in Phoenix, Arizona, in 1994 at the National Council for the Social Studies (NCSS), which is the US professional association for social studies educators (Gibson, Queen, Ross and Vinson, 2007). There are two events that happen in Phoenix that really brought a group of progressive social studies people together. First, was the arrest of Sam Diener, a teacher, who was peacefully leafleting at an outdoor concert by the US Marine Corps Band that was sponsored by NCSS. Diener's leaflets were about keeping the military out of schools. The president of NCSS – Robert Stahl, who was at the time a professor of Social Studies Education at Arizona State University – asked the Phoenix police to arrest Diener for trespassing. Diener ultimately went through years of hearings and a trial and was found guilty of trespassing. His arrest really galvanized a small group of social studies educators attending the NCSS conference to support Diener and also join him in his leafleting activities. The second important event at NCSS in 1994 was related to California Proposition 187, which was an anti-immigrant law that required all government employees, including social workers and teachers, to report undocumented people to the US Immigration and Naturalization Service. We had proposed a resolution to the NCSS that the organization condemn Proposition 187 and refused to meet in California until the law was repealed. NCSS rejected our resolution. These two events galvanized a small group of social studies education to create a collaborative force that was both activist-oriented and scholarly at the same time. We met in Detroit at Wayne State University and the Rouge Forum grew out of that meeting and developed in collaboration with two other progressive groups of scholars – one group from the National Council of Teachers of English called the Whole Language Umbrella and a group of special educators that had formed what's called the Whole Schooling Consortium. What all of these groups had in common was a focus on education for social justice, so the Rouge Forum was really a collaborative effort that grew out of instances of injustice within a professional society or indifference to it.

I will briefly discuss the journals I work on. *Workplace: A Journal for Academic Labor* (https://ices.library.ubc.ca/index.php/workplace) is a journal I got involved with because of my interests and activities in labour organizing, in particular at the higher ed level when I was at the University of Louisville. *Workplace* was one of the very early online open-access journals and it was founded by members of the Modern Language Association's Graduate Student Caucus. I co-edited an issue called, 'Building a K-16 Movement', for *Workplace* that was about labour organizing and labour issues in K-12 schools – primary and secondary schools – as well as the university. Addressing the question regarding support from institutions for activism, I have not had any such support, in fact *Workplace* as well as the journal *Cultural Logic* were shut down by university administrations. *Workplace* was housed at the University of Louisville and the order to shut it down came from the dean of the College of Education and Human Development, Robert Felner. *Workplace* was shut done while I was moving from Louisville to the University of British Columbia. Steven Petrina and I reconstructed the journal from scratch and it's now hosted at UBC. I will add this about Robert Felner, he was convicted of embezzling money from the US Department of Education (over $2 million dollars) and spent five years in prison for that. So, these are the kind of people that you can end up dealing with in higher ed! I know it seems like an odd thing, but this is a good activist story. Here's alinktosomestuffaboutthatepisode(http://blogs.ubc.ca/workplace/?s=robert+felner).

Cultural Logic (https://ojs.library.ubc.ca/index.php/clogic) was started by members of the Radical Caucus of the Modern Language Association and I got involved with the journal when Rich Gibson and I guest edited a special issue on, 'Marxism and Education', in 2000. *Cultural Logic* is an online open access journal that started in 1997. I came on as a co-editor after editing the 'Marxism and Education' issue. Rich and I then guest edited another issue together called, 'Education for Revolution', in 2013 that was co-published with *Works & Days*. *Cultural Logic* was for years hosted on a server – eserver.org – at the University of Iowa, along with many other humanities-oriented journals, with over 10,000 articles and the administration at the University of Iowa shut down *Cultural Logic* and the entire e-server in about 2016. I worked with David Siar, who teaches at Winston-Salem State University in North Carolina, to reconstruct the journal and I brought it to the University of British Columbia, too.

Work on these journals were all collaborative efforts. Scholarship published in *Cultural Logic* and in *Workplace* is typically antithetical to mainstream thinking. *Cultural Logic* focuses on Marxist theory and practice, which in the United States is very marginalized, even within university settings. *Workplace* focuses on academic labour and organizing. I don't think that the journals were targeted specifically, well *Workplace* was by a particular individual, but I do think it illustrates the barriers that must be dealt with by academics working in critical frameworks, particularly if you're working independently, that is not with a corporate publisher or a university press. These are journals that are completely independent and that are run on donated labour. Stephen Petrina, Sandra Mathison and I established *Critical Education* (https://ices.library.ubc.ca/index.php/criticaled/), which is a flagship journal of the Institute for Critical Education Studies (http://blogs.ubc.ca/criticaleducation/) at the University of British Columbia. We established *Critical Education* eleven years ago because we saw that JCEPS, the *Journal of Critical Educational Policy Studies*, in the UK was so successful and felt we needed a North American journal that didn't try to replicate what JCEPS was doing but provided a space that might attract more North American authors working in the critical tradition. *Critical Education* is not as explicitly Marxist as JCEPS, rather the journal is open to centre and left-oriented of scholarship and we've been trying to provide that kind of space to have a community where voices that are oftentimes marginalized in the education and political discourses in North America can have a place to publish. All of the work that I've done in organizing and journal editing has really been about trying to tap into shared interests with people who were willing to volunteer their labour to create these spaces for political and scholarly perspectives that might not have a home elsewhere.

GTT This is really very interesting, you know, to hear about the story behind all these movements, especially the Rouge Forum is unique in itself and it takes a real struggle. I think *Cultural Logic, Works and Days*, especially *Workplace* took a struggle, a real struggle, and Wayne, what about inviting our participants to visit these sites? They're all active now and some of them are publication-based, some of the sites are more activity based and please visit all these sites and let me repeat them: the Rouge Forum, *Cultural Logic, Works and Days, Workplace* and *Critical Education*. I'm sure you know *Critical Education* better than the others and Wayne is the founder of this initiative and he told the story about it.

You have always been in collaboration with other scholars and educators. What is the importance of collaboration of educators, scholars and students, especially in the times of [the] Covid-19 pandemic? Can an online collaboration be functional? Can direct action be possible? Can we talk about an online activism? You suggest that 'teachers and students critically explore their local and national communities'. Can this idea be adoptable in digital communities?

E. Wayne Ross Oh, yes, absolutely. I think what we're doing right now – Global Thursday Talks – is a great example. Global Thursday Talks, the ways in which we can use the internet and other kinds of digital media to engage in activism and discuss scholarship and stay connected. I don't think that the digital environment is significantly different from other kinds of face-to-face in-person activism. I mean, it can be reduced to, like, 'clicktivism', where we're just kind of performing activism that is not very deep. That happens in face-to-face activism, too. I'm talking about people who engage in bumper-sticker activism or performing activism without actually integrating the principles into their work and carrying it forward in serious ways. Global Thursday Talks is a great example and the journal work, those are internet-based and people contributing to them, the editors and editorial board, have always worked in a digital format, those are solid examples that we have great experience with.

I'm not saying that the digital connections can completely substitute for in-person connections, but I think one of the things that we need to be looking at in these new and strange times are how we can pivot and rethink and reshape our activism so that we can have an increased impact. There are people in the streets, of course. There have been people in the streets in Portland, Oregon, around Black Lives Matter and protesting police violence issues for months. They're still there. You can find on Instagram, called @blackpowderpress, with videos of barricades that were built just yesterday and the day before, closing off streets in Portland; anarchist attacking police with paint. I mean there is still in-person activity happening Paris, France, we can see that there's still a space for being in the streets. We can learn from these protests and we can learn from, and I think we do learn from, those activities as well as from the protests around the deaths of George Floyd and Breonna Taylor (Ford 2015; Ross 2020a).

There are pedagogical opportunities to be found in the Columbia University students, who are currently organizing to withhold their tuition fees as a response to the way that they've been treated during the pandemic (Helmore 2020). That's happening right now. There are rent strikes going on in the UK with students at Manchester Metropolitan University who got a 30 [per cent] reduction in their housing fees. Now, that was a combination of digital and also going out and tearing the fences down and occupying the residence halls (Hall 2020). The strike has spread, so now there's a number of universities in the UK where students are organizing rent strikes (Wall 2020). Plus, you have various other kinds of labour strikes that have happened during the pandemic, so I don't want to create an either-or dichotomy, but I think there are ways for us to imagine the advancement of our activism and building our communities online that could actually strengthen our in-person activist stances. Of course, there are real risks involved now with being out in the streets. As we were talking about this right before the audience joined us online that I've been very conservative about my associations during Covid-19 and keeping a very small bubble of people. But, hopefully the situation that we're in now is going to improve and our isolation is going to ease. We should look to the strategies and tactics that we've used digitally, using Zoom, Skype, social media and try to take a greater advantage of those opportunities, both in terms of activism and also pedagogically. I know many of us have been in a learning mode about remote teaching. I've learned quite a bit and think that what I will carry forward from my experiences around remote teaching is going to have a profound effect on my pedagogy once we're back in the classroom again. Hopefully, we will find other ways, new ways, to be engaged in online activism, because every day we experience something new and every day we can learn lessons from this experience. It's really different for all of us but we are getting used to it and we are creating something new every day.

GTT Thank you. So, you know speaking of online experience in terms of activism and our pedagogies I would like to, as a teacher myself as well, it has been almost two semesters now that education has been online globally, so my question is: what are the risks of no school times for educators and for young learners, children and do you think they become more fragile and bound to technology? We know that technology is controlled by the big corporations, so how do you think educators and students have been affected by online teaching?

E. Wayne Ross Our increased reliance on technology for instruction during the pandemic is really a double-edged sword. I'll start with some of the things that I think are problematic. Certainly, when we think about technology, it has been and it continues to be, a backdoor threat to education. In British Columbia, we've seen this prior to the pandemic, with the use of software for student assessment that's been adopted by the government, as well as the government funding for private schools that offer distance learning. This was before the pandemic, so we can see the threats that technology offers in terms of privatization (Kuehn, Mathison and Ross 2018).

The pandemic's really been a significant disruption and it highlights the central role that public education plays, especially regarding the economic, social as well as political lives people lead. The key role of schools in society has become much more obvious. We are experiencing this trauma, this public health trauma, this social trauma that has created opportunities for us to learn and to consider some of the ways in which we might capitalize on the role public education can play in envisioning change in an unprecedented time. The disruption the pandemic has caused has to be seen, not as something that we need to get over and through so that we can go back to the way things were. We need to think about our current circumstances as an opportunity to pivot in our thinking, to see what it is about how we've had to move to remote teaching that we can carry with us in a positive way. So, what are some of these things that are potential positives? I would say the diversification of the way learning occurs outdoors and at home. How can we hold onto that? How can we hold onto the importance of place in teaching and learning? In Canada, there's been a huge emphasis on meeting the needs of the most vulnerable students because this has exposed the necessity of vulnerable students having access to schools that provide a whole range of services to them. How can we hold onto prioritizing responding to the most vulnerable students? Thinking about the diverse modes of delivery either hybrid or completely online. How does that affect our roles as teachers?

There are already discussions at UBC among faculty who hated the idea of teaching online prior to the pandemic, but now they love it and they want to have an option to continue doing it. That's one discourse that's happening now. Thinking about who educates, it's not just the teacher in a transmission mode rethinking what student progress means, which maybe gets more directly back to your question about the impact of students. Rethinking school timetables and the way schools are organized. I know that's been done in British Columbia schools, where some students are meeting face to face, but the students are going to school in cohorts and the timetables have changed, so they take fewer courses at a time. How can we foster informal learning? Parents have become even more actively involved. How can we tap into that thinking about schools as community hubs or the caretaking and public-safety role of schools? What about the critical issue of providing food to students? These are all things that the pandemic has given us an opportunity to consider as we move forward. It's a totally incomplete list of things that we could think about, areas where we've had to pivot and respond. Hopefully, our responses give us an opportunity and a platform to bring different approaches into schools when they return to normal. But I'm not so sure I want schools to be normalized again.

This leads me to another area. I don't say this often, but I don't like schools. In fact, I kind of hate schools, but I love the idea of education. We don't often interrogate the differences of what we mean when we compare schooling with education. The pandemic can provide us an opportunity to make some clarifications about that now. Of course, the pandemic has emphasized the digital divide, not just for students, but even for teachers. In the US, 30 per cent of public K-12 students live in households either without an internet connection or a device adequate for distance learning at home. There are nearly 400,000 K-12 teachers without adequate internet connectivity, roughly 10 per cent of all public school teachers in the USA. And 100,000 teachers lack adequate home computing devices (Rosen 2020).

Why is this the case? Well, it is because of capitalist thinking about bandwidth, the airwaves and the other commonly held resources that have been sold off to private interests. We have a digital divide, where 150,000 students in New York City alone that don't have internet access at home. This is an amazing thing in a nation of such great wealth. There are 500,000 households in New York City that don't have any kind of Wi-Fi access and, with lockdowns, there are fewer place[s with] access to Wi-Fi off from restaurants or coffee shops or libraries. Much of that disappeared.

We have teacher burnout because – I don't know about you guys, but when we pivoted to remote instruction, we didn't get any release from other responsibilities. I spent the summer planning my teaching for the fall, which is typically the time I have, and it is expected that I write and research and publish. I was trying to do that while planning for my online courses in the fall. I'm now teaching my courses online, for the first time, while I'm trying to plan for new courses to go online in the spring. But the university's criteria for judgement of merit and success haven't changed. There's no extra pay. And teachers in schools have faced the same thing as they're teaching in hybrid models where, in the morning, they're face to face with kids and worried about, not just pedagogical and curricular issues, but the safety issues around Covid-19. And then, in the afternoon, they are teaching online to students that aren't in schools. The result is 13-, 14-hour days for teachers. And what does all of this do in terms of teacher burnout? National Education Association, which is the largest labour union in the United States, it's a teacher union with 3 million plus members, they're reporting that almost a third of their members are considering leaving the teaching profession now or taking early retirement. In Minnesota, there has been a jump in the last few months of teachers applying for retirement, an increase of 20 per cent over last year. In Pennsylvania, there's been an increase in applications for early retirement that's 60 per cent higher this year over last year (Singer 2020). All of this effects, not only the quality of teaching, but the supply of teachers.

Now, I'll get back to the question about vulnerability of students. Of course, they're the most vulnerable of all. And if teachers are compromised, then the instruction that students receive is affected. I'm not saying that it's necessarily poor instruction, but when teachers are stressed, then their practice is also stressed. So, yes, absolutely, students are in a very vulnerable position. I do reject, though, the often stated assumption that because of the pandemic and the shifts to online teaching or to new kinds of school schedules that children are 'falling behind'. That is a neoliberal narrative that quantifies education or makes it commodity. Just as we can take advantage of digital activism as an alternative, we take the pandemic as an opportunity to extract ourselves from the accountancy of bureaucratic outcomes-based education – where the focus is on test scores and ticking off learning outcomes. And if we focus on the experiences students bring to the classroom, if we focus on the knowledge that students bring to the classroom, if we focus on the capacity that students have – and I'm talking about even with the youngest students – and we make those starting points for what we're trying to do as educators in either online or face to face in a classroom, we now have an opportunity to break out of the neoliberalized formulaic, numbers-driven, narrowly achievement-driven idea of what teaching and learning is about. We need to start with students' needs and what they bring to the classroom.

Adultism is central to the neoliberal narrative of education – the notion that students come to schools as blank slates and that teachers are supposed engage in a banking model education, as Freire called it, filling students' heads with stuff and then certifying them as having achieved certain rungs up the ladder. The disruption of the pandemic gives us a reason to prioritize the social, emotional, economic context that our students live in and for them to share and explore their own questions, their experiences and their needs. And teaching and learning that begins at that point is a much more meaningful experience for students. So, yes, students are vulnerable and the disruption of schooling during the pandemic is a critical issue because of that vulnerability – hunger and food insecurity, relief from abusive households for example. We've seen the heightened importance of schools and other social institutions in the pandemic, especially with lockdowns and the meteoric rise in domestic abuse that's happened because people are trapped at home. These things are happening to teachers and to students. We all are more fragile, but at the same time, that fragility should give us an opportunity to call into question some of the frames that govern the way we interact with students in schools and to create new ways of interacting with them.

GTT Yes, thank you for this answer because you know you inspired our participants' comments and questions are flowing on the chat part and our participants share your ideas. You touched upon a very common challenge, you know, all over the world, in different countries, from Africa to, for example, New York. Anna says on Monday in New York all schools will be reopened, and it's a common thing, not only in New York, in maybe Canada, in Africa. Our participants are sharing their ideas because you inspire them to share common problems all over the world. Thank you for your contribution. In Turkey, we had opened the schools first and then, after a month, we closed down. Of course, vulnerable groups are being influenced; it is different implementations but there are common things.

Thank you. Now, let's continue with curriculum issues, which is your expertise. Curriculum is a big issue, especially these days we have to touch with the curriculum, I will ask you some deeper questions about your curriculum perspective, your curriculum studies, but first, please, explain [to] us what is 'dangerous citizenship'?

E. Wayne Ross I'll start by saying that dangerous citizenship goes back to the issue of schooling. And as I said earlier, I hate schools, but I love education. I think there's only one other person I've ever read who basically says the same about schools, sociologist Willard Waller, in 1932, in his book, *Sociology of Teaching*. I know we don't usually read stuff that's almost 100 years old but I highly recommend it. Schooling, fundamentally, is about social control. And curriculum is about social control. It's usually about the transmission of facts; it's about the transmission of national narratives and myths; it's about the inculcation of dominant values. Schools are about social control and contemporary capitalist democracies are about social control. We typically think about social control being exercised by governments as being forthrightly authoritarian governments, such as the Democratic People's Republic of Korea. But it has been demonstrated quite well by Edward Herrmann and Noam Chomsky that we do have thought control in democratic societies. Manufacturing consent or thought control in democratic societies is Hermann and Chomsky's idea, which focuses on the media, but the propaganda model offered in *Manufacturing Consent* (1988) – a brilliant book and an excellent documentary film by the same name by Canadian filmmakers, Mark Achbar and Peter Wintonick (1992), – the manufacturing of consent happens in schools, too. It certainly happens within the curriculum area that I'm most closely associated with and that is social studies education.

Dangerous citizenship is really a container for ideas that could fall under different names such as critical pedagogy – or at least certain strains of critical pedagogy – or from anarchist education, aim at a levelling of society, creation of a non-hierarchical society based on mutual aid. It's a concept that I developed with my colleague Kevin D. Vinson. In a nutshell, dangerous citizenship is a radical critique of schools as social control. It is also a collection of strategies used to disrupt and resist the conforming, anti-democratic, anti-collective and oppressive potentialities of society and schooling (Ross 2017). It is also a critique of what counts as political participation within social studies, civics or global citizenship education. Of course, the context of teaching about democracy in schools is one where teachers lack academic freedom and there are policy regimes and official curriculum that strongly discourage critical social analysis.

And beyond education, dangerous citizenship is a critique of the supposed representative governments that are presented as democracy. What we call democracy in contemporary times has nothing to do with the rule of the people and everything to do with legitimizing the interests of capital. That is putting corporations at the forefront and creating an illusion of real participation on the part of the people. Fundamentally, the idea here is that capital dominates and perverts the idea of democracy as the rule of the people.

Dangerous citizenship posits that it's important for us to have critical consciousness about our surroundings. Critical consciousness might be approached from a Freirean (1970) notion of critical consciousness – conscientization – and/or from Lukács' (1971) notion of class consciousness as class struggle. So-called democratic societies frame political participation in very narrow ways and with very narrowly conceptualized ideas of dissent. Dissent has to happen within a regulated framework, within a legitimized framework, if it happens at all. As a result, students are taught to be obedient. Civil obedience is the key framework for participation in democracy. This a very shallow notion of democracy and dissent. Democratic participation is reduced to a choice from a menu. Sometimes, there are two choices: Column A, Column B. Sometimes, there are three, sometimes, or five, sometimes there may be ten. When there is a multiplicity of choices or even when there are only two choices, we are told that we need to be strategic about what is possible. 'You'll waste your vote, if you vote for a party that doesn't have the potential to win.' These are ways in which civil obedience becomes the core of what it means to be a democratic citizen.

The final premise is that the problem with democracy in societies as well as in the way we teach about democracies in school, is we have too much civil obedience and we don't have enough civil disobedience. What's dangerous about dangerous citizenship is that being a dangerous citizen is being dangerous to the status quo, being dangerous to the hegemonic ideas that exist in society and that goes from the smallest kinds of disruptions that might be mundane to large-scale disruptions such as we see currently in Portland, Oregon. Attacking police because of police brutality and police executions that are all too common in the United States – that's civil disobedience. It's also civilly disobedient to steal time from work to do things, not that are for your own personal gain, for example teachers who are teaching in highly regulated classrooms and expected to prepare students for examinations who suspend that kind of direct teaching activity to address the needs and interests of the students on topics that are not part of the official curriculum. That's civil disobedience, too. It might be more mundane than taking to the streets, but it's really important. As with critical pedagogy, there's not a recipe or a formula with the idea of dangerous citizenship.

Dangerous citizenship is a container for ideas that can be useful in a lot of different ways, depending on where you are. Because, what it means to be dangerous if you're teaching from a critical perspective in Egypt is quite different from what counts as being dangerous if you're teaching from a critical perspective in Vancouver, BC. When I teach with my pre-service social studies teachers, I talk with them about this idea and say that what we really need to do is look for other kinds of imaginaries to draw on as pedagogical imaginaries. I've been very interested for a long time in left-anarchist, arts-based, political activism groups such as sub rosa, Yes Men, Clandestine Insurgent Rebel Clown Posse, Surveillance Camera Players – see the book, *Beautiful Trouble* (Boyd and Mitchell 2013) and a website (beautifultrouble.org). *Beautiful Trouble* presents tactics, principles and theories that can be sources for rethinking, disrupting our pedagogical approaches.

I want to give you a concrete example of what I'm talking about. For example, Temporary Autonomous Zone (TAZ) is an idea that developed by Hakeem Bey (1985). You may not have heard of TAZ, but you may have heard of an event that happens out in the desert in California that's called 'Burning Man' (burningman.org) and it's basically a community that rises up out of nothing and exists for a few days, there are really no rules, there's lots of drug-taking, there's lots of music, there's lots of kinds of behaviour that wouldn't be tolerated in everyday life in a typical community, but it pops up for a few days and then it disappears. The point of Burning Man is not to try to create policy changes; it's not to confront the government; it's not to foment a revolution; but it's to create a space for free activity to happen, freedom of thought, freedom of behaviour, even that which some might think is bizarre or dangerous.

There's something pedagogical that can be taken from the idea of TAZ. For example, in a mundane way for a classroom teacher. What if I start to think about my classroom as potentially being a TAZ, in which I can subvert what's required of me whether its teaching to a test or preparing students for an examination or just transmitting facts, if I can create an open space, an ephemeral space – not a space where I'm trying to say I'm a revolutionary radical teacher that wants to change the way things happen in my school or in my school district you're not doing that – rather, you're just asking, 'What would serve the interests of my students?' An important part of dangerous citizenship is teaching and relating to others with the intention of instigating human connection. It's about collaboration and fostering equality. And it's about thinking of the needs of others.

Here's another example of teaching from a dangerous citizenship framework that's different, but related to Bey's TAZ, Michele de Certeau, who is known as a philosopher of everyday life. In his book, *The Practice of Everyday Life* (1984), he describes a concept that he calls *la perruque*, pardon my French, it means 'the wig'. De Certeau gives examples of *la perruque* such as a secretary in the office typing a love letter, on company paper, on the company typewriter while she's being paid to do other work. Another example he gives is of a carpenter who uses a lathe and a piece of wood to make something for his own personal use using his employer's tools and supplies. De Certeau says that *la perruque* is not about pilfering, it's not about making profit, but it's about diverting resources of your employer to a different end. I think really a potentially useful pedagogical imaginary for teachers. How can I engage *in la perruque*? How can I divert the resources of the school to creative aims, aims that interest my students? How can I divert school time from teaching to the objectives that the school wants me to teach to in a way that responds to the experiences of my students, to interests and capacities of my students, to the knowledge that my students bring with them from outside school?

How can I instigate a connection with them? So that I'm no longer teaching a subject, but am engaged in a learning exercise with the people who are in front of me. Those are two examples of how we can find pedagogical imaginaries outside of the context of education and bring creative and activist ideas to bear on rethinking teaching. Dangerous citizenship doesn't have to be 'revolutionary', you can think of this approach to teaching as insurgent.

Can you think of subversive and creative acts – that may be very mundane acts – that aren't necessarily intended to transform relationships, but they do. Acts that creatively disrupt everyday life in the classroom. Sandra Mathison (2019) describes how small, everyday resistance can change lived experience in schools and through accumulation and storytelling can even lead to broader levels of social change and class struggle.

GTT　This is about what our students really do need to see. Maybe every teacher here, every educator here, should create their own curriculum in their classroom, right under these conditions?

Do you think curriculum (studies), teachers and teacher educators have lagged behind the digitalization era, technological revolutions in artificial intelligence (AI) and other innovations like the analysis of 'big data', machine learning, automation and robotics, nano- and biotechnology, virtual reality and new forms of energy storage? Are these related to the content of curriculum or methodology of curriculum? Within this context, how do you see the future of (social studies) curriculum and curriculum studies? Should we involve or resist these developments?

E. Wayne Ross　Yes, absolutely, teachers and teacher education have lagged behind in these areas. Do I think that's a bad thing? No. Should we ignore these developments? No. But, I believe that technology itself is neutral. It's a tool, so I don't think we should feel threatened by AI or we shouldn't be threatened by 'big data', in and of itself. But what we do need to do is question the objectives and aims of the way technology is used.

The first question to ask is always, who benefits from this? If we look at the way EdTech is used now, there are beneficial aspects to sustaining education in the pandemic. What we're doing right now – Global Thursday Talks on Zoom – we can't separate from the tech movement. But when EdTech is used to commodify education, curriculum, and learning; to create a product to be sold, then we need to ask questions about who's benefitting from that. If technology is used to control behaviour, if it's used to surveil teachers and students, we need to ask questions about that. At my university, there is controversy over use of technology to proctor online examinations. What happens when students are taking exams and their webcam is used to track their eye movements and behaviours and if there is a certain algorithm indicating that that student is engaged in behaviours that looks like they're cheating? Well, that person is flagged. Is that ethical? Even accurate? Should technology be used in this fashion? An EdTech specialist in the Faculty of Education at UBC spoke out about the remote-testing software used at the university to surveil students and now he's being sued by the tech company, Protorio (Alden and Ha 2020). We definitely need to be asking questions about this because this is a level of surveillance, this is problematic.

Anything that we do to advance, to instigate and to develop human connections, even as if it's via technology, is a positive thing. But then, I mean this can connect to the distinctions between schooling and education I made earlier, if I think of education as a process of becoming, that is transformative of self – and it can be fundamentally transformative of the way we understand ourselves, others, the world, our relationship to our environment – and technology can play a part in that, but I think the controlling aspects of technology are the areas of serious concern as is how technology can serve commodify aspects of education.

GTT   Can we continue to discuss universities? What's your perspective regarding the universities moving in the direction of corporations, operating in the interest of corporations? Why do you think corporations are interested in universities?

E. Wayne Ross   That is the easiest question I've ever been asked, and I'm not criticizing because it's a great question. The answer is, just follow the money. The education market, the global education marketplace, is estimated to be in by 2030 worth $10 trillion (Holon IQ 2018). $10 trillion! It's a massive amount of money.

The efforts to privatize public education, all over the world – as Pasi Sahlberg (2012) calls it GERM or Global Education Reform Movement – is driven by the interests of capitalism, neoliberalism and the opening of markets. GERM is connected to attacks on public education. Historically, public education was a public service, it remained in the realm of the commons. Education was a resource that was shared by all. People paid taxes. That tax money went to ministries of education and was redistributed to the schools. It paid for teacher salaries and it paid for resources to educate students who went through school and attended university.

This cycle or circulation of public funds to support public services like education stayed pretty closed, but what neoliberalism does – it hates the enclosure of an economy that serves the commons – its interest is profits, it wants to destroy the commonwealth. Neoliberalism aims to transform the commonly held wealth of the people into privately held wealth, so it has to disrupt this cycle of public schools serving the public interest. What happens is at the 'discourse level' is that attending to university is no longer about obtaining an education and expanding your mind, now it's about 'investing in yourself', and 'developing skills' so that students can enter the marketplace and sell their labour. Neoliberalism is about the extraction of commonwealth. It's about moving the commonly held wealth into private interests, whether it's corporate shareholders or individuals. That is why corporations are interested in education and educational institutions. They are not interested in education at all. They are interested in the credentialling process. They are interested in patents that are produced at universities. They are interested in selling textbooks. They are interested in building school buses. They are interested in shaping the curriculum so that education becomes, not about a process of understanding yourself and society, but it becomes a process of preparing a workforce to serve the interests of corporations. It's about the creation of education as a commodity.

I'll give you a couple of examples that are specific to my locality, the province of British Columbia on the west coast of Canada. After years of cuts to the education budget, the Ministry of Education altered the School Act in British Columbia to allow school districts to sell seats in public schools in the international marketplace. Public school districts sell seats for, well, the basic costs, anywhere from $12,000 to $18,000, depending on whether it's [an] elementary student or a secondary student. The main target market is the Pacific Rim and, of course, People's Republic of China. As a result, there is an influx of students in popular districts, mostly wealthy districts, so much so, that sometimes, if a Canadian student moves into the school district, there's no room for them. Selling seats in schools is clearly an entryway of privatization into public education. The government cuts the budget for public schools, then forces them into the international marketplace, in an effort to bridge their budget gaps.

This phenomenon occurs in universities. The University of British Columbia has one of the largest percentages of international students in the world – and it's a great thing. Despite what our president says about our international campus, the bottom line is international students at the UBC pay seven times more tuition than a Canadian student. The university has also been subjected to public-funding cuts and is doing the same thing that the public schools are doing, only on a more massive level. Percentages of international students are rising every year because the university is addicted to the revenue, so much so that the board of governors decided a few years ago to create a new college within the university – called Vantage College – for the international students who have the money to pay the massive tuition fees to attend UBC but cannot meet the entrance requirements. These students attend Vantage College for a year or maybe two, pay the same tuition as regular international studies, plus an additional $6,000 to be in the Vantage College, where they work on their English skills, work on math skills, whatever it was, that kept them from being regular first year students. Instead of four years to their degree, they now pay tuition for five or six years, which, of course, increases the revenue taken in per student for the university. Vantage College allows the university to bring in more profits from selling a product on an international market. While there are many advantages to having international students on campus, revenue has become the driving force. So, there are two examples from British Columbia on the commodification of education and how [the] $10 trillion market gets tapped into – the market is not for investors or corporations, but it's from public institutions that are pressed into competing in the marketplace because of funding cuts driven by neoliberal social policies that eschew public interest for private gain.

In British Columbia, we have had a long history of neoliberal government. From 2001 until 2017, [the] BC government was strongly driven by neoliberal ideology. Our extensive ferry system which used to be run by the government was privatized and guess what happened? Ferry fees dramatically increased and the number of voyages was significantly reduced. What used to be considered part of the public highway system, which had a subsidized user fees for travel from the mainland to the islands or between the islands, became a profit-making adventure, an American CEO with a $600,000 salary. BC government did the same thing with the publicly held railway system that was sold to a privately held company. A transaction that produced scandal involving the kickbacks to legislators, which still has not resolved.

These are all examples of public-policy actions driven by the ideology of neoliberal capitalism – the idea that the market is the framework for everything. Intellectually, neoliberalism is an ideology that developed from [the] work of Hayek and von Mises in the middle of the twentieth century and the creation of the Mount Perlerin Society, an intellectual movement that was against Keynesian economic policies of the post-World War, when governments were trying to put money into public projects and creating a social safety net. Then, politically, neoliberalism is adopted in the 1980s by Thatcher in the UK and Ronald Reagan in the US. Now, neoliberalism [is] ingrained in our imaginations, it's part of the water that we live in. We've lost our reference points for anything other than a neoliberal market-based concept of the world.

At a personal level, neoliberalism produces a quantification of our lives. Think of Fitbits, for example. Or, when I run, I have my Garmin watch and that tracks where I run, my heart rate, speed, distance, etc. I can't decide whether or not that was a good run until I look at my statistics. Do you know what I mean? We do the same thing with schools and university ranking in league tables. These metrics have huge impact on how we understand student achievement, impact of scholarly research, judgements of productivity, etc. In this way, neoliberalism is like the water we swim in. The old proverb of the fish that jumps out of the water and asks, 'Well, what's this?' we often lack awareness of the impact of neoliberalism, we're in it every day and we embody it. It comes through in terms of the way we think about school achievement, university prestige, credentialing, ideas like '21st-century skills', league tables that [are] ranking the 'best' universities or schools. All of that is a function of a neoliberal way of thinking. In a recent article [in] *Canadian Journal of Action Research*, I explore how neoliberalism, with its key principle that competition is the defining characteristic of human relations, reshapes our work as educators and researchers, and discuss how action research can help us, not only better understand our world, but also resist the deleterious effects of neoliberalism on our work and workplaces (Ross 2020b).

Universities and schools are now governed by an accountancy, what I call 'bureaucratic outcomes-based management' or 'new public management' in governmental agencies. Student achievement or scholarly impact is reduced to metrics. University promotion committees focus on the metrics rather than the substance of their colleagues' work. The unit of scholarly output that matters is journal articles rather than books or other kinds of work because of the importance of metrics produced by World of Science, for example.

Neoliberal values have reshaped education, teaching, learning and research. It is crucial to create awareness about why things are the way they are in universities and schools and how neoliberalism governs our lives as the teachers and scholars and find ways in which we resist.

GTT   Let's underline this, Web of Science is one of the biggest corporations in the world, right, and we are suffering from the same problems. Thank you so much, but I want to ask to summarize your last comments about university and corporations and these complex relations, actually very complex and not easy to understand and the amount of money you mentioned is beyond understanding. You know, beyond the imagination of a most people. All these complex issues and none of them has nothing to do with public good, nothing to do with welfare of individuals.

E. Wayne Ross   What neoliberalism does is it takes the discourses that we use in education and it narrows them down, so education becomes more about skills education You've no doubt heard the discourse of '21st century skills', which is really a corporatized idea of what education should be, that is workforce preparation. Education is not preparation, it's a process of becoming. I think about education as a process of self-understanding; understanding yourself in relation to society as well as your capacity or agency to act on society. When the neoliberal discourse on education is about credentials, numbers of graduates. If you look at some of the global education market analysis companies, what you'll see is they talk about the number of post-secondary graduates that are going to be produced in the next decade. How many teachers are needed to teach the number of students that are coming into schools. Credentials are a commodified version of the education. What matters in the marketplace is not the intellect, not the thought process, but the accumulation of the credentials. The focus is on the commodity.

If education is a process or becoming, it's a process of transformation. Neoliberal education is not about becoming or being, but rather appearing to be. Within neoliberalism, education is reduced to a commodity to be traded, grades for credentials, credentials for jobs. Education as enlightenment, evolution of self, is degraded to mere appearances.

Neoliberal does the same thing to democracy. In *Brave New World Revisited*, Aldous Huxley describes a dystopian world in which democratic institutions still exist (e.g. elections, parliaments, courts), but of the ideals of democracy – egalitarianism, justice, democratic social relationship – had all been disappeared. That's what has happened to democracy. We don't have a rule of the people, we have plutocracy, a rule of the rich. Or, perhaps, a corporatocracy, rule of corporations, not a rule of the people. The discourse of democracy has been stripped of its substance, democratic participation has been reduced to voting rather than thinking about democracy as being an associated way of living, conjoint communicated, experience where people are aware of what they think, say and do and its impact on other people. In a nutshell that's how philosopher John Dewey (1916) saw democracy. Not democracy as elections that are a corporate spectacle, driven by millions of dollars to promote a personality; creating a menu for voters to select from. Democracy today is like the parable of the chef who calls all the animals into the kitchen – he's got the chicken, the pig and the cow there – and he asks them, 'What kind of sauce do you want to be cooked in?' The animals protest, 'We don't want to be cooked.' Chef says, 'That's not the question. You just get to choose the sauce!' Democracy has been degraded to voters choosing the sauce they will be cooked in.

How often do any of us have democratic experiences in everyday life? We don't have democratic universities – we used to have something approaching it with 'shared governance' or at least that was an idea that existed in North America when the faculty made decisions about the curriculum and were consulted on other decisions, but faculty don't even have that level of involvement anymore. In the corporate university, all important decisions come down from the top managers. Benjamin Ginsberg (2011) described this as the fall of the faculty and rise of the all-administrative university. Schools are certainly not democratic and never have been – even though, paradoxically, schools are where democracy is probably going to be most discussed, but typically only in its idealized form, which is a reason students become alienated from political participation, they have never had any serious democratic social experiences in their life. They are just told about an ideal democracy (which doesn't exist) and the only 'democratic experiences' they have [are] very shallow. Can we envision a Deweyan democracy – a strong democracy that goes beyond elections and voting to cultivate shared interests among people?

GTT This has been a very interesting and very stimulating talk. We are having so many comments, so many people sharing in the chat, many questions, but, unfortunately, we are approaching to the end and we have to stop here. It's been a very good dialogue between you and our participants, welcome to our club, welcome to our network, by the way, and would you like to add something for New Year, something hopeful?

E. Wayne Ross I hope I have been hopeful at points! I've tried not to be all negative, all the time. This is a wonderful experience for me. I think this illustrates that we can instigate human connection even when we're physically apart and we are restricted in our travels. I implore everyone to think about how we can hold onto our human selves. How do we increase the humanness of our pedagogical experiences? That's something that we need to keep at the forefront of our minds as we're dealing with these strange times. I wish everyone good health and I hope that we can get through the pandemic in a way in which we have strengthened our human bonds. Not just our human bonds, but our bonds with non-human animals, too. That we come out on the other side of this experience with an increased level of consciousness, that's my hope.

GTT Thank you for these wishes that we need to hear more these days. Nice to have you here, nice to host you. Thank you so much, Wayne. Thanks everybody, all participants, a New Year comes with hopes and greetings.

E. Wayne Ross Happy New Year!

References

Alden, C. and A. Ha (2020) 'Proctorio sues UBC staff member for tweets sharing "confidential" information about the software', *The Ubyssey*, 3 September. Available at: https://www.ubyssey.ca/news/proctorio-sues-linkletter/ (accessed 5 December 2020).

Bey, Hakeem (1985) 'The temporary autonomous zone, onological anarchy, poetic terrorism'. Available at: https://hermetic.com/bey/taz_cont (accessed 8 December 2020).

Boyd, Andrew and David Oswald Mitchell (2013) *Beautiful Trouble: A Toolbox for Revolution* (New York: OR Books).

de Certeau, Michel (1984) *The Practice of Everyday Life*, trans. S. Rendall (Berkeley, CA: University of California Press).

Dewey, John (1916) *Democracy and Education* (New York: Free Press).

Ford, Derek R. (2015) 'Studying in the streets: The pedagogy of throwing bottles at the cops', Black Agenda Report. Available at: https://www.blackagendareport.com/studying-in-the-streets (accessed 10 December 2020).

Freire, Paolo (1970) *Pedagogy of the Oppressed* (New York: Continuum).

Ginsberg, Benjamin (2011) *The Fall of the Faculty* (Oxford: Oxford University Press).

Goffman, Erving (2017 [1961]) *Asylums: Essays on the Social Situation of Mental Patients and Other Inmates* (London and New York: Routledge).

Hall, R. (2020) 'Manchester University students win 30% rent cut after Covid protests', *The Guardian*, 26 November. Available at: https://www.theguardian.com/education/2020/nov/26/manchester-university-students-win-30-rent-cut-after-covid-protests (accessed 12 December 2020).

Helmore, E. (2020) 'Columbia students threaten to withhold tuition fees amid Covid protest', *The Guardian*, 5 December. Available at: https://www.theguardian.com/us-news/2020/dec/05/columbia-students-tuition-fees-covid-protest (accessed 5 December 2020).

Herman, Edward S. and Noam Chomsky (1988) *Manufacturing Consent: The Political Economy of the Mass Media* (New York: Pantheon Books).

Holon IQ (2018) '$10 trillion global education market in 2030', 3 June. Available at: https://www.holoniq.com/2030/10-trillion-global-education-market/ (accessed 15 December 2020).

Kuehn, L., S. Mathison and E. W. Ross (2018) 'The many faces of privatization', Institute for Public Education/British Columbia, Occasional Paper No. 1, 5 June (Vancouver, BC: IPE/BC). Available at: http://instituteforpubliceducation.org/wp-content/uploads/2018/06/Many-Faces-of-Privatization-IPEBC-Occasional-Paper-1.pdf (accessed 21 December 2020).

Lukács, Georg (1971) *History and Class Consciousness: Studies in Marxist Dialectics* (London: Merlin Press).

Mathison, Sandra (2019) 'Resistance in the quotidian life: With special attention to daily life in schools', *Cultural Logic*, 23. Available at: https://ojs.library.ubc.ca/index.php/clogic/article/view/192128 (accessed 26 December 2020).

Rosen, D. (2020) 'Covid-19, schools and the digital divide', *CounterPunch*, 2 December. Available at: https://www.counterpunch.org/2020/12/02/covid-19-schools-and-the-digital-divide/?fbclid=IwAR3Z69GubE2Nf_l8V7fNp1dXtypdmz2GApdMXjQRKCgwpdU2rq_v_HR0yPY (accessed 5 December 2020).

Ross, E. Wayne (2014) 'A sense of where you are', in C. A. Woyshner (ed.), *Leaders in Social Education: Intellectual Self-Portraits* (Rotterdam: Sense Publishers), 163–78.

Ross, E. Wayne (2015) 'Dr. Dewey or: How I learned to stop worrying about where ideas come from and love critical pedagogy', in B. J. Porfilio and D. R. Ford (eds), *Leaders in Critical Pedagogy: Narratives for Understanding and Solidarity* (Rotterdam: Sense Publishers), 141–55.

Ross, E. Wayne (2017) *Rethinking Social Studies: Critical Pedagogy in Pursuit of Dangerous Citizenship* (Charlotte, NC: Information Age Publishing).

Ross, E. Wayne (2020a) 'Μπορούμε να πάρουμε μαθήματα από τους δρόμους [We can learn lessons from the streets]', *Documento*, 6–7 June, p. 37. Available at: http://blogs. ubc.ca/ross/2020/06/can-we-take-lessons-from-the-streets-interview-with-documento-athens-greece-on-uprisings-in-the-usa/ (accessed 10 July 2020).

Ross, E. Wayne (2020b) 'Why are things as they are? Action research and the transformation of work and education in the neoliberal age', *Canadian Journal of Action Research*, 21 (1): 10–26. Available at: https://journals.nipissingu.ca/index.php/ cjar/article/view/515 (accessed 25 December 2020).

Ross, E. Wayne, Rich Gibson, Greg Queen and Kevin D. Vinson (2013) 'How do I keep my ideals and still teach', in Emily A. Daniels and Brad J. Porfilio (eds), *Dangerous Counterstories in the Corporate Academy* (Charlotte, NC: Information Age Publishing), 203–23.

Sahlberg, Pasi (2012) 'How GERM is infecting schools around the world'. Available at: https://pasisahlberg.com/text-test/ (accessed 11 December 2020).

Singer, N. (2020) 'Teaching in the pandemic: "This is not sustainable": Teacher burnout could erode instructional quality, stymie working parents and hinder the reopening of the economy', *The New York Times*, 30 November. Available at: https://www.nytimes. com/2020/11/30/us/teachers-remote-learning-burnout.html (accessed 15 December 2020).

Wall, T. (2020) '"We won't be cash cows": UK students plan the largest rent strike in 40 years', *The Guardian*, 5 December. Available at: https://www.theguardian.com/ education/2020/dec/06/we-wont-be-cash-cows-uk-students-plan-the-largest-rent-strike-in-40-years (accessed 20 December 2020).

Waller, Willard (1932) *Sociology of Teaching* (New York: J. Wiley & Sons).

Wintonick, P. (director) and M. Achbar (director) (1992) *Manufacturing Consent: Noam Chomsky and the Media*, film, Zeitgeist Films.

Chapter 7

PAULO FREIRE AT 100, STILL INSPIRING: AN INTERVIEW WITH IRA SHOR[1]

Ira Shor

Global Thursday Talks (GTT)   Dear Professor Shor, we are honored to have you at our community and excited to hear about your experience with Paulo Freire, who will be at the age of 100 next year. You had the opportunity to meet and learn from Freire, in some hundreds of hours spent in dialogue with him, and then it turned into a 'talking book' (Shor and Freire 1986). You describe your experience with him as 'the most intense education I ever had'. It would be historically momentous for us to listen to you about him and your experience with him.

Ira Shor   Paulo Freire died suddenly in May, 1997, and I still miss him. I was very fortunate to spend many hours and days with him in the last two decades of his life, especially when we worked on our book, *A Pedagogy for Liberation*. I also took part in seminars and public meetings with Paulo across ten years. Mealtimes were special for the conversation over food. Paulo loved Brazilian cooking most of all, especially regional dishes from his native Northeast; he liked having beans with every meal (especially the Brazilian bean stew called *fejoado*); his favourite green was *arugula*, which he liked to eat at dinner. Among wines, Portuguese *dao* and French *Beaujolais* appealed most to him. Good food and good companions moved Paulo to tell stories from exile, childhood and teaching among Brazilian workers and peasants. He told these stories with such drama that [would] Paulo say, 'Look, I am sweating from the memory.'

English was sometimes a challenge to him, especially at the end of a long public session. Occasionally, he would say impatiently, 'This English!' When abroad, Paulo would have looked forward to speaking Portuguese for an hour or two at the end of a workday, to recharge his voice and brain. I listened carefully to how he

---

1. This interview was conducted within the activities of @globalthursdaytalks digital community on 12 November 2020 and is available at: https://www.youtube.com/watch?v=AsElLmwg8Rc (accessed 1 May 2021).

chose words, composed sentences and edited his remarks aloud in progress to restate a thought two or three times, trying to get closer to the meaning he wanted.

Of course, co-authoring our book involved an intense focus on his words and mine. Our composing sessions lasted hours. Whenever he came to North America, I would travel to work with him, then take home our revisions to prepare a new draft for our next meeting. I understood then that this was an educational chance of a lifetime for me, so for years I put this work ahead of everything else. I also intuited the long-term commitment to critical pedagogy and social justice I would need to make in the years to come to justify the good fortune of co-authoring the first book Paulo Freire published with a collaborator.

Paulo put texts, theories, themes and practices into their historical and political contexts. He situated theory in power relations as well as into concrete practice. Knowing the influence of liberation theology on Paulo, I saw in his speech and writing 'the word made flesh', because he gave abstract and symbolic references a materialist connection. That is, Paulo philosophized experience and experientialized philosophy. To him, the academic discourse was too much 'a dance of the concepts', too abstractly distant from immediate reality. Dialogue and critical pedagogy were tools to 'passionately know the world' (as his daughter, Maddalena, put in when writing about her own teaching). Questions, problems, contradictions, conflicts and social conditions were materials for deep feeling and action. When Paulo was moved by the illuminating force of an utterance or text, Paulo's body, face and voice registered an intensity, animated by the word made flesh, the symbolic made actual, the theoretical become concrete.

His passion of knowing the world was apparent one night in Amherst, Massachusetts, in 1984. After a long day of sessions, we watched on TV the film, *Judgment at Nuremberg*, the famous movie about the trial of Nazi leaders after World War II. The story of murderous leaders brought to justice moved Paulo to speak about the generals in Brazil who were never held accountable for their brutal coup in 1964. He relived this sorrow and anger again when I brought news that the dictator of Argentin,a General Galtieri, had been arrested after the defeat in the Falkland Islands. Such moments revealed to me how deep a wound Paulo carried from the worst moment of his political life, the coup of 1964, which destroyed his emerging national literacy programme. Fired from his job as director, jailed, interrogated, then forced out of his beloved Brazil, Paulo became a global exile without a country, a figure he sardonically called 'a peregrine of revolution'. I saw in Paulo, then, a political man fighting on with a deep wound. The terrible coup ripped from him and Brazil a future within reach when he was in the prime of life. Older when he finally came home, he dove again into the political contentions.

Paulo was a passionate advocate for social justice and a modest person at the same time. Humility was a cardinal virtue to him. 'I am still trying to be a good Christian,' he would say. Unassuming, he was often uncomfortable with the celebrity status that greeted him wherever he went. After speaking at a conference in Vermont, for example, he said that he was grateful because the attendees there treated him like a human being, not as a star. I never heard him take credit for anything or boast about any accomplishments. He insisted that it was important to listen to others before we spoke to them, and to be 'humbly militant and patiently impatient'. Yes, humility and respect were ways of being he taught by example. My own arrogance as a white North American man became embarrassing to me as I interacted with Paulo over a span of years. I felt obliged to recognize my own arrogance, self-centredness and aggressiveness; finally, I called Paulo in early 1994 to tell him that I was living alone in a mountain cottage to study humility. Paulo said to me, 'I am sure it will make you a better person.'

At the same time, Paulo also advised me to travel as much as possible, again for learning humility, to deal with the arrogance he thought was culturally embedded in the greatest global power. Paulo urged me to listen to and learn from as many others as possible, in other nations as well as from social classes without PhDs.

Paulo slept with a crucifix above his bed and crossed himself each time we passed a church. When I stayed in his home in Sao Paulo, the phone rang constantly, the postman daily delivered a stack of letters, books, proposals and invitations. He had become so important to so many people, so his sad passing in 1997 left a hole in the world no one else has been able to fill.

When he was young, Paulo came of age when Brazil was in a prerevolutionary moment; popular forces were gathering from the bottom-up to gain democratic power. This is what's so special about Paulo's literacy method, that his way of teaching reading and writing fed into and fed from the democratic upsurge from below. His pedagogical work was political in itself and in its integration with the mass movements then consolidating in Brazil. When Paulo developed his literacy method, Brazil was ruled under the Constitution of 1932, which had finally extended voting rights to women but only if they could read and write, the same restrictions which the earlier Constitution of 1889 had applied to men. Only literate adults could vote in elections, thus disenfranchising newly freed slaves, peasants and labourers who had no access to instruction. In the early 1960s, in Brazil, there were some 70 million adults, of which about 20 million were illiterate, according to historian Andrew Kirkendall. An enormous piece of the electorate was disqualified from voting, mostly poor and working class, legally excluded from exercising formal political power. So, when Paulo used his famous phrase, 'the culture of silence', he was referring to the enforced political muteness imposed by the dominant elite on the bottom of society.

Paulo's generative theme/problem-posing method, which he spent over a decade developing, was by the early 1960s ready for national implementation. This method was inexpensive, effective and fast, insofar as only 40 hours of group instruction were needed to achieve basic literacy in adults. Illiterate adults could gain literacy and thus qualify to vote in 40 hours of instruction, using low-cost slides displaying hand-drawn pictorial prompts on whitewashed walls with cheap imported projectors. With volunteer teachers trained by Freire himself from high school and college students, the costs were attractively low.

The historic debut of Freire's method took place in the poor Northeastern village of Angicos in April 1963; it was a graduation ceremony of the first 299 adults in the programme, who made presentations in front of the attending President of the Republic Joao Goulart. The president brought his entire cabinet with him.

Impressed by the students and by Freire's remarks, Goulart appointed Paulo to head a national literacy project to set up 20,000 literacy circles. The goal was to produce 5 million newly literate voters in time for the national elections in 1965. These millions of new voters, drawn from the poor and working class, would very likely vote for the democratic and left-wing parties that had been fighting for their needs. Thus, a literacy programme closely allied to class-based movements for social justice would serve as a powerful political instrument for democratizing the state and society. When the oligarchy and the military saw this looming threat to their unaccountable power, along with street agitations and strikes breaking out then, they decided to suppress them even though Paulo and his literacy programme did not advocate violence.

Paulo did not speak often about the coup and its aftermath but when he did it was an obvious painful and unhealed wound. He repeated one lesson from the violence of the coup, that questioning the status quo is not a weekend on a tropical beach; that opposing what he called 'the power now in power' involves unavoidable risk. He described such opposition as a choice we make because we cannot stand injustice and cruelty, inequality and poverty. Opposition was for him a moral choice, fundamentally based in his Christian commitments, which he said walked hand in hand with his Marxist understandings of injustice. Militantly opposing an immoral status quo, we have to expect authorities to punish us, Paulo indicated. Those in power won't quietly give up wealth and privilege, the lesson of the coup.

Paulo's remarks about the violent coup connected to his comments on fear, a subject often raised by teachers practicing critical pedagogy in hostile locations, to which we devoted a chapter in our book, and which Paulo used for the title of our book's Portuguese edition (*Medo e Ousadia: O cotidiano do professor – Fear and Courage: The Daily Life of the Teacher*). He spoke about his own fear during the coup, especially after his arrest with its interrogations, unannounced transfer among jails and incarceration in a small solitary isolation cell with abrasive walls. In those terrible years, the coup in Brazil was followed by others in Bolivia, Argentina and Chile. Social justice could be won only at a price.

GTT   Thank you. This has been a very good explanation and your experience is really very important, thank you for sharing. So, carrying on, I would like to go on with a Freirean approach to education, especially in today's climate of anti-democratic education: like praxis, dialogue, problem-posing education and critical consciousness. We all study those and keep reading and trying to empower ourselves and our students in our classrooms. I would like to ask, how can you conceptualize these concepts to understand the present day's problems of education?

Ira Shor   Yes, for over forty years now, neoliberal policies in school and society have created global austerity and authoritarianism. These are hard times to earn a living but also hard times to practice critical pedagogy in classrooms. The space for questioning the status quo has been narrowing despite some heroic episodes of resistance (like the international Occupy movements of 2011, including the Arab Spring and the Black Lives Matter rebellion in 2020).

When Paulo Freire started developing his literacy methods, the space for critical pedagogy and for mass opposition was growing, if uneven, in Brazil but especially large enough in the rebellious Northeast. There, mass movements were gaining ground from the bottom-up. Peasant leagues and labour unions were emerging, while a bloc of liberal nationalists held some power in government and commerce, desiring to drive Brazil from backwardness to modernity with industrialization, urbanization and education. As I mentioned, at that time, about 20 million adult illiterates in Brazil were not only impoverished but also constitutionally disqualified from voting. Conditions were ripe for change. Freire emerged from the liberal Catholic activism of the 1940s to lead for ten years a social service programme in the Northeast, offering programmes on family life, civic participation and literacy. By 1963, as popular insurgency expanded, Freire was at the University of Recife when President Goulart appointed him director of a national literacy campaign to teach reading and writing to 5 million working-class adults in time for the national elections in 1965. Their literacy would give them the right to vote, and through the vote, the bottom of society might vote out the conservative oligarchy dominating the nation. But, the coup launched March 30, 1964 destroyed that promising path ahead.

Later in life, back in Brazil after a long exile, Freire eventually became Education Secretary for the 643 public schools of Sao Paulo when the Workers' Party won the mayoralty there in 1989. Turning a traditional mass-education system into a critical and democratic programme was a very different political task than his earlier work in adult basic literacy. Freire's literacy circles using his problem-posing, generative theme and dialogic methods were not like the state-regulated mass education in traditional schools. Over the decades, Freire's pedagogy has migrated into mass education despite official opposition to the many social justice teachers experimenting with critical-democratic practices. This 50-year migration of radical practice from non-institutional adult education to institutional mass education was more than matched by a 50-year resurgence of authoritarian control following the democratic movements of the 1960s–1970s. What Freire called 'the banking method' of teaching, that is, teachers transmitting prescribed information for students to memorize and be tested on, has been reasserted as a formidable firewall against radical teaching.

Today, mass education is over-regulated and underfunded. This obliges teachers to work under surveillance and mandates from above. Teachers are under more risk and greater stress. Our work is an experiment in how far our work can go, to test how much space there is for critical deviations from the standard programme. The discovery of open space to teach against the status quo, is a situated project, situated locally in the power relations of the school and the community. A global neoliberal age favouring authoritarian control and standardization is distributed widely but unevenly. In some nations and in some locales, in some school subjects and departments, everyday classroom work is more heavily policed than in others. Discovering the uneven profile of power relations in a specific time and place involves researching what Freire called 'the archaeology of power' at the site of our practice. Official restriction against critical teaching and learning was named by Freire a 'limit-situation', against which we invent and test 'limit-acts'.

Critical teachers who continue experimenting despite austerity should find local allies for support and should try to publish reports on their classroom work. Allies make each individual less vulnerable to punishment because it is much easier for authorities to discipline an isolated oppositional teacher than it is to silence a group. The circulation of reports on practice will encourage other embattled teachers to persist in their own situations, and will give them potential tools to test in their classrooms. In the USA, critical educators have produced an awesome library of critical practice despite this being the worst of times for oppositional pedagogy. One of the most creative and critical projects questioning the status quo has been the Rethinking Schools group founded in Milwaukee, Wisconsin, in 1985. Rethinking Schools prints a widely read journal with reports on K-12 practice from teachers working in diverse subjects and locales. The group publishes books on teaching about special topics like Black Lives Matter, global warming, gender equality, teacher unionism and education for the many non-native children in US classrooms. Started by a group of elementary teachers in the kitchen of founder Bob Peterson, they have tenaciously shown what can be accomplished even in the worst of times.

Formal mass education has never been organized democratically. When mass movements from below compel authorities to retreat, schools also experience democratic openings. This happened in the USA in the 1960s. In between democratic insurgencies, official power reconquers control, like now, far less democratic space for experimental, oppositional practice than when I began teaching fifty years ago, when I first started experimenting with critical pedagogy. Freire proposes that all education is politics and all politics is educational, while all politics comprises a local practice situated in the community and in the dominant forces of an age. 'Situated pedagogy' means that classroom practice is multiply conditioned by converging social contexts: the intentions of the teacher, the culture and conditions of the students, the profile of authority exercised in the local school and outside. All human experience – education, work, family life – emerges from this complex of converging situations.

For teaching practice, Paulo Freire offered a foundational starting point based in the social relations of power in the classroom. He wrote early in chapter 2 of *Pedagogy of the Oppressed* that the first problem of education is solving the teacher–student contradiction. At the heart of this contradiction is the unilateral authority of the teacher, based first in the teacher's position as an officer of the institution, second in the teacher's formal certification from an accredited programme, and third in the middle-class identity conveyed on and by the teacher due to position, salary, knowledge, dress, race and speech habits which distinguish the teacher from the working-class majority of students in mass education. Representing the institution and a privileged class fraction of the status quo, the teacher's possession of some elevated privilege depends on authority approval of her credentials, demeanor and practice. Teachers are produced by state-regulated institutions and then invested with authority so far as they perform as agents of the status quo (what Foucault called 'relays' or human delivery systems for knowledge and behaviors do not question authority). Students are positioned as passive receivers of teacher-talk ('narration sickness'). This great problem of teacher–student alienation identified by Freire as the power conundrum for critical educators to transform by dialectically using their authority to democratize authority, by animating passive students into active co-developers of knowledge and the learning process. To expel the banking method, critical teachers invite students to participate in constituting the terms and conditions for mutual knowledge-making. The goal here is to end the student experience of schooling as something being done to them but rather to initiate learning as something they undertake with their peers and their teacher in a mutual project of self- and social development.

Of course, this is a difficult undertaking. In the last forty years, stagnant wages, rising costs of living and increased tuition and prices for books and commuting, have made education much more difficult for my working-class students. There is far more stress among students than when I started fifty years ago. The vocational promises of education matter now more than ever. Students are paying too much for a lesser education which is not certain to lead to a better-paying occupation. To adjust to their declining economic conditions and their rising occupational anxieties, I moved the syllabus closer to working-life themes. I began experimenting with databases and charts related to earning a living. I brought in more media reports on the job market, including statistics which I see as graphic or pictorial texts (diagrams, charts, tables), along with prose texts (stories written in sentences, paragraphs, chapters). The thematic contents of both related to student themes – unemployment and wage levels, college majors, occupations vis-à-vis salaries, racial and gender distributions in various professions, family wages across racial divides, demographics of marriage, longevity, homelessness, incarceration, etc. Generative themes from student life were represented both in the media stories and in the data charts. The data graphically and quantitatively retold stories about working and living, and differences based on social class, gender and race. These materials questioned the status quo because their contents reported subordination of women, folks of colour and working-class families.

My students were all post-literate, able to read and write, which allowed me to pose problems using printed texts of all kinds. In contrast, Freire developed his literacy method for adults who could neither read nor write, so he had to use pictorial representations from everyday life to elicit verbal responses for discussions leading up to the introduction of printed words and writing. (Freire did plan a post-literacy phase of adult education but was prevented by the coup of 1964.) In my classes, after I pose a problem, students alternate verbally discussing the theme and writing brief compositions (called 'low-stakes writing'). My role is to draw out student cognition in speech and writing in successively deepening inquiry. As the teacher leading the process, I use the 'interrogative' voice, which refrains from uttering conclusions, generalizations, speculations or comments in my 'declarative voice'. This interrogative stance is what I call 'the democratic discipline of the teacher's voice'. If I start with declarative comments on the problem at hand, verbally analysing it in my academic voice, I risk pre-empting student expression by narrating what things mean and what is important, which can displace their own act of cognition, which should precede the teacher's. This interrogative posture by the teacher privileges student expression first so as to reposition students from passive receivers of official knowledge to active makers of knowledge in their own idiom. By restraining my academic idiom so foreign to the students, I create linguistic space for student utterances and also earn the right to elevate my declarative voice, my voice of commentary, judgement and generalization, once students have engaged in these cognitive activities. I must provoke a student-centred discussion of the subject matter to reach a moment in the dialogue where my own educated idiom can join the flow without driving students into withdrawal. Their prolonged verbal and written responses teach me how to speak into the knowledge they are making so that my teacher's voice integrate[s] into an ongoing student-based inquiry to accelerate and deepen it.

GTT   Yes, very relevant, Ira, thank you so much. It's really very stimulating. Eda and I want to leave our prepared questions aside. We want to pose you the questions from our participants here. The first question from our participants is from Norway. It is from Mr Ali and the question actually is really related to what you have offered so far. How to work with critical theory when fake news is becoming so powerful that it is difficult to distinguish between fact and fiction?

Ira Shor   Yes, this is a problem, fake news, students captured by the toxic myths of the Trump era. I taught for over forty years in a very conservative area of New York City, Staten Island, which Donald Trump won by twice large margins in 2016 and 2020. This locale has many conservative Police and Fire Department families as well as organized crime families living there. Racism and homophobia are rampant. When I first moved there in 1971, a black family nearby had their house firebombed. Five years later, a white mob with baseball bats attacked black students bussed in from the North Side of the island to the white South Shore. My primary 'limit-situation' as a teacher has been the deep conservative politics brought to class by many white students. Many distrusted the mainstream media even before Donald Trump proclaimed 'fake news' and declared the news media to be 'enemies of the people'. As it happens, my students rarely watch TV news, listen to radio news stations or even read newspapers. Some are devoted to right-wing network and cable news channels on TV; others check in with online sites. Most pick up their conservative tilt on society and world events from talk in their homes and neighbourhood. Their exposure to political discourse is from a very narrow right-wing part of the spectrum. My task as a critical teacher is to expand their contact with a broader slice of the political spectrum.

To introduce themes, materials and alternative points of view, dialogic problem-posing and the interrogative voice are helpful assets for the teacher. So is grounding problems and texts in themes familiar to them without lecturing them on what is good and what things mean, which would invite defensive withdrawal. Posing legible, meaningful problems for writing and discussion. The sooner and the longer my teacherly voice operates in class discussion, the sooner the students will peg me as a liberal outsider, there to disapprove and correct how they think and live. So, I must be careful how I speak in class, not only because the students are predominantly conservative, but also because they are urban working-class; my college-educated voices identify me with elites and authorities who look down on them.

Posing theme-based questions rather than lecturing cedes the floor to student voices, helping me navigate the teacher–student alienation here. Also, I invite students to suggest the themes and reading materials we should study and write about in this college composition class, so the syllabus I initially hand out on the first day is brief and minimal, without a long agenda of preselected topics and readings. This keeps the class schedule open for pursuing themes, issues and texts offered by the students or emerging out of our dialogues. Thus, the subjects for critical inquiry emerge from my suggestions as well as from students' own remarks and writings. Further, to ease their suspicions that the teacher will reward students who copy the teacher's words most, I announce explicitly in class that a grade of 'A' is not awarded for 'A'greeing with the teacher. In addition, simply refraining from lecturing them, by back-loading my own commentaries after the dialogue has front-loaded their thoughts, I provide fewer words of mine for them to copy. In addition, I hand out drafts of grading contracts for us to negotiate in class. These drafts propose requirements for A, B and C grades. I invite them to amend, replace, refine, rewrite or reject any of the items. Each change a student proposes is stated as a motion for debate, requiring a second and then a majority vote from the whole class. In my book, *When Students Have Power*, I report at length how this process worked in a sample class, including my objections to some student amendments proposed.

In another class, when I invited students to suggest themes and readings for the semester, a strong majority voted for a student-nominated topic, 'kids cursing'. They maintained that children are too vulgar and speak too many curses. Their dislike for such a feature in their everyday lives was an education for me. I agreed to this theme, and began by asking them to compose in class a rough draft ('low-stakes writing'), commenting on kids cursing. As it happened, when they read drafts aloud, many blamed the mass media for encouraging children to curse. This perception also surprised me because I doubted it. However, I did not immediately comment on or dismiss their perception. To keep student thought and expression primary in this process, I proposed testing their claim: I asked them to watch TV and listen to as much radio as possible for the week until our next class, and record every curse word, logging the day, time and media source. At that time, HBO and streaming services with their frequent cursing and female nudity were not yet online; cursing was rare on cable TV and almost nonexistent on network TV because of federal regulations. (I knew this in advance but wanted the students to discover it through observation.) A week later, the students reported very little cursing on network or cable TV or on radio. So, why do they indict the mainstream media as the prime villain encouraging kids to curse? We began research and writing, and ended by writing a booklet called, *Kids Cursing*, which we published and distributed to other teachers, students and family members. The critical pedagogy here re-presented student 'claims' as questions to be investigated.

Regarding their claim about 'fake news', I did the same, making it into a syllabus item, a problem to investigate. Another method to approach a widespread social issue like 'fake news' is called 'teaching the conflicts', named by Gerald Graff in a book with that title. The method presents arguments from contending sides regarding a social condition or conflict: Should abortion be legal? Do women have the same freedom and opportunity in society as do men? Have people of colour become equal to white people in the last fifty years? I collect material on different sides of the issue for students to study and debate, and invite students to bring in materials also. The 'teach the conflicts' approach is one way to present controversial issues in a repressive teaching environment which severely polices the teacher; it helps deflect charges of propagandizing because multiple sources from various political sides are put on the table for discussion. Especially in a time or site of austere surveillance, this approach can be useful.

When a meme like 'fake news' achieves a toxic spread through society, I emphasize in class that we all are entitled to make claims but that we also need to back up our claims with evidence and argument to be convincing. So, when students utter claims, my practice is to invite them to bring in evidence backing up their point of view and present it to the class. Many students will take their claim quietly off the table rather than having to do the intellectual work of actually defending it; however, some will take up the challenge, and because most claims raised by one student are also held by others, the debate going forward is a cognitive challenge to more than the single student willing to take it on.

When I hear claims such as 'fake news', I cannot scowl, snicker or ridicule the students uttering them. No matter how provoked I am, I must maintain a level demeanour because institutional authority demands such professional behavior from teachers and because dirty looks or sarcastic tones will only fortify toxic beliefs instead of unpacking them from the social body. What matters most is keeping critical inquiry focused on student understandings and not fall into the trap of changing the subject from unproven claims to unprofessional behavior by the teacher. Critical teachers invite students to externalize their ways of seeing. It takes teacherly discipline to maintain an open demeanour when hearing racist or sexist or homophobic comments. If I hope to start a useful class inquiry into such beliefs, I must use my authority to open extended debate and study.

GTT   Yes, this is really very interesting and very stimulating to listen to you. But I'm afraid we are over time and our time. Our participants are sending so many questions, very interesting questions, and comments all positive. What should we do, I don't know. What's your timing, if you're able to stay?

Ira Shor   I can stay longer if you like.

GTT   Let's take one more question from Guy Senese, if you don't mind. Right?

Ira Shor   Okay. Yes, I'm happy to have another question.

GTT Thank you, okay, one more question, maybe, okay. When we talk about Freire, we inevitably talk about language, and you have just offered some amazing techniques. So, as offered by Guy Senese, here is a question, a challenging question, really. In social cultures where students expect a declarative lecture style, and your critical pedagogy takes an interrogative style, does problem-posing lessen the teacher's authority? What would you like to say about that?

Ira Shor Yes, I understand the problem. Paulo Freire famously criticized the 'banking model' of pedagogy which dominates traditional classrooms. In banking classrooms, teacher-talk transfers official content for memorization. Students are positioned as passive absorbers of authoritative information. Freire said this produces 'narration sickness' because the transfer of content through the teacher's voice silences students into passive learners. Freire strongly objected to identifying this model as rigorous learning; he also objected to considering problem-posing dialogue as lacking rigour and content. To Freire, dialogue is not permissive and directionless (not 'say whatever you want whenever you want to'), not without method and not content-free. Problem-posing dialogue is a disciplined mutual inquiry, driven by student expression and teacher-direction into topics of consequence. The critical teacher leads a participatory dialogue, not an undirected conversation.

The cognitive failure of banking pedagogy is apparent in the many classrooms where teachers struggle to motivate student interest against a wall of passive faces. In my classes, students arrive expecting another semester of 'narration sickness'. This is their predominant experience of mass schooling, year after year, noted by John Dewey some fifty years before Freire wrote, *Pedagogy of the Oppressed*. Dewey lamented in *Democracy and Education* (1916) how talkative 5-year-olds start school with boundless curiosity, only to become sullen teenagers, whose high-school teachers try everything to stimulate interest in the curriculum. In my classes, native students as well as non-native immigrants both expect me to narrate from the front of the room, uttering rules, advice, assignments, warnings and instructional discourses on what subjects mean and what to believe. While non-native students tend to be more traditionally respectful of the teacher than are the native-born, they all expect me to wield unilateral authority over the syllabus as well as over the learning process. Foreign students often come from traditional societies, so they tend to be more respectful of authority than those raised in raucous American mass culture. American-born students in my classes are more self-assertive and less intimidated by teacher authority than the foreign-born. So, while immigrant students show their respect for authority by speaking little in class, native-born students feel more authorized to speak but are generally disinclined to do so because schooling is largely a repetitive and routine bore to them. They pay the least attention needed to get by with a grade.

All in all, then, foreign and native students are both mostly passive, waiting for the teacher to tell them what things mean, what is good and bad, and what they are required to do. This passive withdrawal is not easy to transform into critical participation; neither is it easy to transform the respectful withdrawal of traditional foreign students. If we critical educators are serious about developing civically oriented, animated, knowledge-making adults, we have no choice but to design a participatory classroom based in posing meaningful problems, which they work on with peers and the teacher in classrooms organized as activity systems. The more cognitively active you are in any setting, the more you learn. This is why it's extremely important for pedagogy to be participatory, challenging and interactive. If this learning process gradually invites and involves more students in dialogue and inquiry, then I am able as the teacher to raise the level of my declarative interventions, commenting more in my own evaluative voice because my interventions join student interventions underway, thus not pre-empting or silencing their thought and speech. But, I, too, have had classes with native and foreign-born students who refuse all invitations to participate. When such refusing students form a critical mass in any class, they compel me to become a traditional teacher who talks first and most. I feel compelled to teach traditionally because the students demand it, and Paulo Freire joked that, of course, 'We cannot kill the students,' if they refuse dialogue.

I understand the difficulties of teaching traditional students raised to be quietly respectful around elders, authorities and teachers. When I am confronted by a critical mass who reject the dialogic process, the most I can do is try to ease reluctant students into participation by posing familiar problems in understandable language, then asking students to write brief, unthreatening texts. Five-minute compositions are modest expectations which initiate cognitive activity. I circulate in class during low-stakes writing and sometimes stop to read what a student writes, encouraging them to write a few more sentences. Because many students will be reluctant to read their written thoughts aloud, especially non-native students whose various accents make them defensive in front of native teachers and peers, I ease them into public reporting by starting in small groups. I ask them to read in groups of three. Small-group sharing is less intimidating than reading aloud to the whole class, so the peer group habituates students into small-scale participation. I next ask if any short compositions agreed with each other. Almost always, some do, and I invite that group to read their work to the whole class, one by one; peer-group support makes it easier for students to deal with shyness or fear. As they and others subsequently read, I give positive feedback while also posing questions to draw out further their thoughts. In my mind, I am thinking of next questions to pose which go deeper into the problem, step by step. This gradual process of initiating participation through posing problems legible to students from which they do low-stakes writing followed by peer-group reporting leading to whol-class reading aloud and discussion is my pedagogy for gradually changing the learned passivity and instilled fear which many students typically bring to class in mass education.

GTT   Ira, your answer is very relevant to teacher education classes, too. Some scholars, some colleagues in this meeting, you know, are teaching in teacher education and I myself should say that I learned a practical technique for not necessarily learning activities but consciousness activities. Okay, as for the questions, we are having so many again. We want to say to our participants that we will be sending all questions and your comments to Ira Shor and then we will keep the dialogue. Actually, I want to say, this is a start, Ira. what do you think?

Ira Shor   Yes. Sure. I'm happy to meet with you again.

GTT   Yes, very important for us, you know, to keep communication, to keep solidarity and thank you so much. I'm really very grateful and I'm honoured to have you here and, as I said before, this is a start. We will continue in maybe different forms, different platforms, maybe in a book, in publishing book articles and we will be reading you. Great, thank you, very good, just let me know [if] I can be of help. Thank you so much. Take care.

Ira Shor   Bye everybody.

Part II

FROM GEOGRAPHICAL PEDAGOGIES TO UNIVERSAL
MOMENTS: THE UNITED STATES, MEXICO, TURKEY,
GERMANY AND NORWAY IN THE PANDEMIC

Chapter 8

RACE, PLAGUE AND RESISTANCE

Guy Senese

Preface: Dewey's dream

I was honoured to be invited to speak at the Global Thursday Talks series, regarding the George Floyd protests which are continuing and have spread around the world, in the context of Global viral plague. This is an 'Extra Edition', an update of the story I wrote to read on 18 June. I came into public schooling trained in 'Social Studies' education, a leftover from a time when everything seemed possible in The Movement, including hopes, and democratic commitments that Dewey would crystalize in the demand, that school and society would treat every child with the same care and concern as the 'best and wisest parent' would treat their own.

Dewey is part of a world community of writers and thinkers who were also engaged in the politics of their homelands and spoke also on a world-historical stage. Incidentally, Dewey can spark a debate, and a fierce one, in any 'café' or media platform in Turkey, any place educators meet to work, study and 'organize'. His critical 'gaze' begins with his invited visit, in the year following the 1923 revolutionary moment in Turkey, and later his reports and public comments, all regard the development of Turkish public schooling, the struggle toward a 'language of freedom' is a struggle for conditions for free dialogue. It is necessarily, a changing language. So, what the 'best' parent wants provokes a debate about 'moral meaning of democracy'. I wrote these remarks with a camera in my hand and in my head.

My friend, film-maker Müberra Mızıkacı, encouraged me to recall the early critics and writers who used their self-conscious distance and their cameras, to begin nineteenth-century critiques of the impact of capitalism on everyday life. The writer-photographer must 'include' themselves as a subject, to be self-consciously aware of their own observational position. My use of camera photos as a kind of 'flaneur' requires that I must exercise extreme self-consciousness, to maintain whatever true solidarity I hope for. Thus, my hopes are built in part by what I would want, not only for my own children, but for all children. For that is the ideal of a truly democratic public, exquisitely sensitive to the responsibility to *those most nearly touched* by a social or political condition. For me, I must acknowledge the way my professional life as a servant of *public* education, afforded and right now, affords me 'relative' leisure to engage with an audience in thinking about how these crises, the George Floyd 'movement' amid global suffering from both police violence and the grind of this plague, affect communities who don't have the privileges I enjoy.

Dewey has us imagining that we include in schooling, 'what the best and wisest parent' wants for their children. With this, does he ask anything of the elites who have us work in what Richard Brosio called our 'Janus-faced' world? Does he ask them to work harder to imagine the suffering, the servitude, the deep alienation and poverty of some parent, wanting, wanting, wanting, for that condition in their countries where it is not simply *cynical* for Dewey, or for me now, to write a sentence like that. For in too many places, and those include places were education itself is impossible, *at all*.

The *wisdom* I must use as a guide to how we should construct our 'hopes' must work hard to feel, to imagine the very earned and '*warranted* desperation' of so many who, under current conditions, are themselves cynical to the point of hopelessness, not because they lack desire, or will, but have, in fact, lost hope in an enlightened order, a new social order, at all, for all, and forever after. As a writer here, I will be okay hearing about my mistakes in what follows. I will speculate about how this critical moment is embedded in a dream of democracy, a desire, a hope. I share responsibility in this community of dreamers and activists. It is a world community, in time and space. And with this responsibility comes possibility, of guilt.

I have a nightmare. In it, I am losing my humanity. I have become a hypocrite for suggesting that others, teachers, parents, fight battles to create the conditions where desires, where hopes, for education can be meaningfully realized. Here I hope to avoid that particular nightmare, in the service of that one far better.[1]

Unlike almost a quarter of the people living in the richest country in world history, I have a decent living, enough money to eat, and write, on a public teacher's pension, in an empty restaurant. I am not the best witness or critic; there is already an oversupply of middle-class white academics writing about the black lives struggle, and the socioeconomic impact of this colossal, paradigm shifting pandemic. Systemic inequality has expanded dramatically, has had a multiplying

---

1. John Dewey, 'The school and social progress', *School and Society* (Chicago, IL: University of Chicago Press, 1907), 6–29. See also, Walter Benjamin, *Charles Baudelaire: A Lyric Poet in the Era of High Capitalism*, trans. Harry Zohn (London: Verso Books, 1983); Richard A. Brosio, *A Radical Critique of Capitalist Education* (New York: Peter Lang, 1994); Turan Selhattin, 'John Dewey's Report of 1924 and his Recommendation on the Turkish educational system', available at: https://files.eric.ed.gov/fulltext/ED416159.pdf (accessed 25 May 2021). I am indebted also to Gerald Wood, who pointed me to Ariella Azoulay's brilliant, *Civil Imagination: A Political Ontology of Photography* (London: Verso, 2014). Also see, David Michael Levin (ed.), *Modernity and the Hegemony of Vision* (Berkeley, CA: University of California Press, 1993).

devastating impact on a class or caste in which I am not encased. I cannot possibly *really* imagine the way a nervous mother or father, or child, in these expanding impoverished groups, would want me to use these privileges to help them in their desperation.

Introduction

I came to the Ankara University College of Education Sciences as a William Fulbright Research and Teaching Fellow. Two years ago, I returned to Ankara, to Middle East Technical University (METU). I know that this seven-year period has been the most dear, valuable and enduring of my working life. I want to thank you all for being here. And to my friends Fatma Mızıkacı and Eda Ata, who organized this so expertly, *çok teşekkürler ederim*. It is gratifying to see you organizing, building communities and agitating with Global Thursday Talks.

I started writing this in a Burger King restaurant on the east side of Tucson, Arizona, USA, where I live. But just a note on the 'approach' I have chosen for this paper. I am acutely aware that my efforts to share ideas with this audience are 'entangled'. By that, I mean my impressions of, and opinions about the events of the pandemic and the George Floyd movement are suspended in a mind, mine, that is self-conscious. I am self-conscious about my personal journey and my country's national journey with Turkey. Critical pedagogy is an activist and communal project at its best. Communities in solidarity are not housed well in mere abstract structures, but in communes where efforts are shared, personally and socially, shared struggles involving ethical, moral, emotional relationship. Arguments emerging from data, and the data included, are scientific efforts to be sure, but it is the *science* embedded in the word 'conscience', (con)science, that matters most. I report here as a storyteller mostly, hoping that approach makes a healthier contribution here. I have become acutely aware that media, social, news, phone, internet, is as important in telling my own story of Covid-19 and George Floyd.

Mobile phones are a revolutionary device and the only reason I am talking to you today in this way. For it was on such a device that the murders of black men, more than twenty of them in the past seven years, were caught on camera. I was going to write this in the Pima County Library branch, but it was closed. It is like most of the restaurants here, and where you are, closed, except for 'take out'. I walked across the street and found the restaurant open for sit-down eating. Exactly right for the spirit of Global Thursday Talks, Burger King burgers are global, served in almost 12,000 restaurants in over 100 countries every day, Thursday included.[2]

The workers in there were all people of colour. Mostly Latinx cooks, and one African American man, a general manager. I was the only sit-down customer. As they walked around or served me coffee, I talked to people through my little mask.

2. Available at: https://en.wikipedia.org/wiki/Burger_King (accessed 20 May 2021).

My glasses kept steaming up. The general manager makes about $32,000 per year. On Google, I investigated wages there. I mentioned that to him. He smiled and said, 'That's high.' He wore a blue tie with a little gold crown on it. But he is not a king here. Without looking it up, I know that every time he is driving and sees the lights of a police car behind him, his heart jumps into his throat. The other workers make less than $10 dollars per hour. They can barely make their rent, bills, car payments and childcare. Some of them are immigrants with no citizenship. I hear them gossiping in the kitchen in Spanish. When they are driving to work, and they see the lights of a police car, their hearts jump into their throats, too. Deportations threaten. They are all the type of service workers whose children populate our schools, whose teachers in training populate your classrooms and now, your workrooms where you hide the laundry or the guest bed, pointing your webcam as you teach, with a few books behind you, like I do, to make it look more 'professional'.

These service employees and their counterparts in health and elder care, childcare, include teachers, who can barely make ends meet, are facing mass eviction or mortgage foreclosure. Many are hungry and their children do not have enough to eat. Our government's response to the Covid-19 crisis has caused a catastrophe for these people.

In 2014, while teaching at Ankara University, I was invited to give a talk to a student club from the Middle East Technical University (METU; [in Turkish, Orta Doğu Teknik Üniversitesi, or ODTU]), about an event that affected teachers. Particularly Teacher Education students, half a world away, but not far from where I live, in Tucson, near the Mexican border. It was a talk about 'The 43', as they are called. Living in a poor rural area called Ayotzinapa, they were progressive students, and they were going to a big rally in Mexico to an annual celebration of their comrades, who, a generation before them, had been killed by the Mexican military police protesting injustice. Many had been teachers. Like Floyd, the police stopped them, too. And they were never heard from again.

I discovered that 'The 43', like tens, hundreds of thousands of citizens, activists, knowledge workers, were murdered, disappeared.[3]

Those police work for the ruling classes mainly, who, supported by the US Central Intelligence Agency, worked hard to jail or kill anyone who threatened American and American-allied business interests. What I show here is a digital photo which was sent to me six years ago in Ankara. It is a photo of me reading from [a] paper, and an overhead picture on a screen of, well … photos. Both of those photos, I took for this 'slide' I took from photos that were on the internet. I only say this because everything about the story you read here is so distorted by multiple copies, copies upon copies, that how we think now is potentially more unstable from the point of view of the lives of the martyrs themselves and the struggles they represent. I first read Marxist critical theorist Guy Debord's, *Society of the Spectacle*, twenty-five years ago, where among many other startling

3. Dragana Temelkov, 'The mystery behind the disappearance of the 43 Ayotzinapa students: What's left?', *International Journal of Educational Policies*, 14 (1) (2020): 59–68.

Figure 8.1 Guy Senese lecturing at METU, Ankara, Turkey. *Source*: Guy Senese, personal file.

predictions, he warned that eventually the world would include nothing but copies. Then, I thought he was exaggerating. Now, I am listening.[4]

The other image in the photo, as Figure 8.1 shows, is that of Michael Brown, as a High School graduate, who was murdered by police in much the same way as George Floyd. His was one of the early killings that saw the light of day due to the existence of the mobile digital photograph. Since then, hundreds of other photos made public have initiated crime investigations, not of the victims, but of the police murdering victims under suspicion or in custody. The victims were black, and it just goes on and on. Two days ago, another black man was killed, shot twice in the back while fleeing.

It is hard to tell which virus is spreading faster, COVID-19 or hate, because they are now on stage together.

This proliferation of digital alarms mushroomed after the murder of George Floyd. The anger and fear reached a critical mass. I can speculate with the best, so I think the existential threat of the combined force of Covid-19 and the darkening sky of right-wing terror and the cancer of authoritarianism in state after state – that was the nuclear trigger.

The world press overflows with reports of solidarity in the George Floyd protests, all while facing the harsh reality of Covid-19.

This is just one example from one of dozens of press outlets, the whole world was . . . relating:

4. Guy Debord, *The Society of the Spectacle* (Black and Red Books, 1970 [1967]).

- Campaigners across the Balkans and in Central Europe have held a series of rallies in recent days to show solidarity with ongoing protests in the United States against racism and police brutality.
- Anti-racism demonstrations have been held in several Balkan cities ... On Tuesday evening, activists led by the Initiative against Police Violence and Racism held a protest in Zagreb to ... support vulnerable groups that suffer discrimination in Croatia such as refugees or the Roma minority.
- Dozens of people took part in a protest march in the Montenegrin capital Podgorica on Monday evening. 'There is no doubt that racists are also hiding among all our local Balkan fascists. That's why Floyd is also "ours",' said a statement announcing the protest.
- Several hundred young people joined a protest in Sofia the same day, not only against racism around the world but also in Bulgaria, where discrimination is often targeted on Roma people.[5]

This passion for justice comes in countries like so many everywhere, where moralities were gradually transformed by revolution, evolution and by enlightened modernity, from the natural slavery extending from empire and generations of servitude to kings, sultans, and oligarchs. Note the way activists imagine the relation between these events and local reality, groups of currently and historically marginalized in their own regions, in this case, Middle Eastern refugees, and the Roma. There is an ominous rise of 'race' hate, directed at immigrants, migrants and the Roma. The Balkans emerge from millenia of layered empire. They struggle with new oligarchs and their ties to regional and global corporate exploiters who immiserate their populations for profit, misdirecting fear, resentment and insecurity. This is a misdirection away from their own responsibility; directed instead to scapegoats, immigrants, socialists, not toward these elites who create the illusion.

The *Atlantic Magazine* has an article showing protests in 36 countries.[6] And the networked press intersectionality is demonstrated by the following, for it is a report about a *US* incident, the reaction in *Turkey*, reported on the global net, from an outlet in *China*.[7] The digital headline: 'Turks Protest in Istanbul against Police Killing of Unarmed U.S. Black Man':

ISTANBUL, June 5 (Xinhua) – Turkish people on Friday staged a protest in Istanbul against the killing of an unarmed black man in the United States last week.

---

5. Alan Taylor, 'Images from a worldwide protest movement', *The Atlantic Magazine*, 8 June 2020, available at: https://www.theatlantic.com/photo/2020/06/images-worldwide-protest-movement/612811/ (accessed 22 May 2021).

6. Temelkov (2020).

7. Xinhua   English.news.cn (xinhuanet.com), 'Turks protest in Istanbul against police killing of unarmed U.S. black man', 6 June 2020 (accessed 10 May 2021).

The crowd gathered in front of the Trump Towers in the Sisli district of the European side of the largest Turkish city . . .

Protesters carried banners, which read: 'Long live international solidarity,' 'Black lives matter,' and 'Justice for George Floyd.'

Several protesters wrote Floyd's last words 'I can't breathe' over their facial masks.

We saw this support last summer. For, in our own country, we saw this, and the support was appreciated. The power of unrestrained militarize police was unleashed on protesters throughout the summer and early fall. The Marshall Project blog warned that:

Federal military might be called again, as it did this summer to band with local police for protestor arrest, intimidation, beatings and in one case, kidnapping. A contributing factor to excessive use of force by police is the increasing militarization of many police departments ... Over the years, many police departments have explored options for crowd control during protests, weapons that have been labeled 'nonlethal' like bean bags and pepper balls, though they can inflict grievous harm.[8]

Writing or organizing?

This webinar is part of a democratic justice project. It is communication and community, and communal. It is a project that 'organizes'. And we may have in mind the socialist activists in the early American labor movement, at the turn of the last century, notably the Industrial Workers of the World or IWW – the 'Wobblies'. They were idealists, and romantics possibly but their organizations were the most bias-free of any. And beyond idealism only they suffered the most in these early labour struggles, partly for their anti-racism. Blacks, women, all 'others' were welcome in the *One Big Union*. The Wobbly writer, artist, singer, and organizer Joe Hill is remembered worldwide for his martyrdom. He was shot by a Utah firing squad on a trumped-up charge, similarly to others famous and not so famous in this period. Sacco and Vanzetti come to mind. On his last day, before being shot by that firing squad, he told his weeping followers, 'Don't waste time mourning me, boys. Organize.' And, 'Don't mourn, organize!' has energized activists in many parts of my country and the world, in difficult times.

Steinbeck's *Grapes of Wrath* was written in that generation. And Tom Joad, is transformed from a cynical criminal hurt by poverty and homelessness and jail during the Great Depression and is transformed. By living shoulder to shoulder with workers, by seeing their families hurt, including his own, he is changed.

---

8. Available at: https://www.themarshallproject.org/2020/06/03/from-michael-brown-to-george-floyd-what-we-ve-learned-about-policing (accessed 20 May 2021).

When he is finally leaving the only family he knows, his mother asks, 'Where'ya going Tom? Am I ever gonna' see you again?' He says, 'Aw ma, you'll be able to find me. I'll be where there's people fightin' so's kids can eat. Where people are eatin' the food, they raise. I'll be there. And where a guy's gettin' beat by a cop, I'll be there, too.' And he is.

African American socialist intellectual and activist Angela Davis has said the George Floyd global protests were the most heartening of her lifetime. And they may well be. As I write, they continue in thousands of cities worldwide. Turkish audiences can be forgiven if they might not have Davis's hope. What stemmed from the Gezi protests which shook Turkey and the world, was derailed, and placed back on that long arc that bends toward justice. It seems endless. I am sitting at my desk and it is getting late. I am looking at a photo I have behind me. It was a gift from a student in Ankara, six years ago. I will not forget him and think about all the young people around the world it represents. It is a photo of a skinny kid alone on a street, and you may have seen it; armed only with a guitar, he faces a water cannon.

Today, I looked back on my data including the many blogs and social media posts I collected in the hot moment when the world was united aflame in this anti-racist moment. That moment is cooled by the ravages of pandemic certainly, and the election crisis. And like this boy, I think of the thousands who have risked their freedom and their lives, who never make it to a famous photo. I am concerned and following the analysis of Turkish-American media scholar and public intellectual Zeynep Tüfekci, who writes in, *Twitter and Tear Gas*, a brilliant cautionary tale about relatively recent events like the Arab Spring, the Gezi Uprising, events in India and Africa and elsewhere. She warns that the explosive, intersecting expansion of digital tools used to spark protest, suffer from weaknesses stemming from the same qualities that make it powerful.[9]

The movement successes in the national and global labour, civil rights and social just organizing generally, were conducted under pressure for sure, but the relationships that were formed had a resilience born of shared spaces and shared history, and comradeship forged in real time on more solid ground. Alongside the universe of progressive discourse today, we have a neofascist president, who daily, hourly, for four years, steered and shaped hate and division and he had a friend in Twitter. Here is President Donald Trump's: @RealDonaldTrump. And here is hers: @zeynep.

Refuge

Last year, thousands of migrants came from Guatemala and Honduras, fleeing the terror of neoliberal induced poverty and the gangs that filled the void, who

---

9. Zeynep Tüfekci, *Twitter and Tear Gas: The Power and Fragility of Networked Protest* (New Haven, CT: Yale University Press, 2017).

demanded service or promised death. There was a Catholic monastery in Tucson that was housing them as they applied for asylum. My wife worked with them daily, as a trained social worker. I went there, too, and without skills, just picked up trash. We saw the kids just like any kids, horsing around, having fun. We saw the worried parents, who had left everything behind. As I write this, many are incarcerated in camps near the border of Mexico. Hundreds of children were separated from parents and will never see them again. This is the face of libertarian cruelty that has stripped away any pretence that American conservatism has or ever had the 'compassion' it once claimed. They are victims of our nation's broken promise to help the refugee, and especially the political asylum seeker. These people came as families threatened with death by gangs which have filled the political-economic void left by twenty-five years of neoliberal market policy. Despite the US that requires immigration services to conduct orderly investigations when foreign asylum seekers arrive at our borders, these families were met with summary rejection and ordered deported or to one of the dozens of camps that dot both sides of the US Mexican border.

Both racism and Covid-19 feature in this. Figure 8.2 is a photo of children pictures that staff put up. One of a hundred of little pictures showing a home the child may never see again. I know that spending time with them, and doing a little work with them, improved my eyesight, my line of vision. I have a better imagination of what it is like for them. And thus, for any child who might be there in a classroom, from a world alien to me. Protests and social media exploded over the visceral images of children held in filthy cages, torn from mother's arms and put into police wagons. This crime against humanity was also initiated from within the sick soul of the Trump administration. Its evil face was that of Stephen Miller, who orchestrated it. Many thought the protests would shame the nation, and end

Figure 8.2 Kids' drawing home. *Source*: Guy Senese, personal file.

this. But, at this writing, the asylum-seekers' kidnapping crisis remains. It seems to have dissipated as fast as it expanded. I hear it referred to infrequently, as journalists wonder timidly, 'how high', the Biden administration might 'feature' this crime on its long social agenda. Its outlines seem to flicker, appearing as they do with photos of the dead and dying refugees and prisoners left helpless as Covid-19 spreads in their cold, close quarters.

Empowered and encouraged by Trump, the reactionaries are starting here already. They are making critique of police brutality a crime against the nation. Armed militias have been empowered and deployed in our nation's capital. Yes, the statues honouring racist, Civil War traitors, are coming down, but the apologists for inhumanity, for slavery and for radical exclusion, even today, are showing their hand.

Trump is the avatar of a class that has no linkage to the tissue of justice that supports civil rights. He earns for himself and his class, who would bend light itself away from a fact, if it interfered in their right to take profit. They would bend light itself, toward a lie, if it would help the cause of their own power. Their threats to destabilize any attempt to reconcile his political 'brand' of racist tyranny, with reality, empower reactionary terrorists.

They have blocked the bill to deliver modest relief to Covid-19 economic refugees, because that bill came attached to an unrelated proposal that military bases named for Civil War traitors, be renamed. During the Covid-19 response period, fearing the impact on the wealth of his class, Trump ignored the 69-page fact-based pandemic playbook that was available. Testing was made nearly impossible to get because it was hard evidence of a pandemic, he wanted workers and employers to ignore so the stock markets would not fall. He has punished state governors who locked down and helped any of them who ignored the precautions for suppressing the pandemic. The burden fell hard on the medical workers at all levels, including the service medical providers, many black and brown, who often earn less than these employees at Burger King and are fighting for both their economic and bodily lives.

We have witnessed the right-wing resistance and a culture war that is blending the twin crises, pandemic and race. Trump sent the message that to even wear a mask is unpatriotic, for patriotism is to follow a mindless lead, and be a warrior for the economy. Rallies in such places as Charlottesville, Virginia, ended in the murder of activists protesting the celebration of slavers and murderers, who the president referred to as 'some very good people'. Reacting to the states whose governors had citizens 'shelter in place', he called for citizens to 'liberate' their state houses. Armed militias then showed up at these state houses in several states. Dozens of public officials, carrying out the procedures for election conduct, administration and certification, now live with armed guards.

Murdoch's Fox

The militarization of police has continued, where the idea that the federal military, and not just the citizen police force, will be used against the people. This military, now fully obedient to the ruling classes, poised to wage war within the nation. Soldiers began showing up at rallies for George Floyd, wearing only service clothing, but with no identification. They came as volunteers in service to Trump's call for 'liberation'. The consolidation and privatization of the television news has accelerated ideological distortion and polarization. Trump's allies on Fox News have been successful, calling the coronavirus a 'Democrat hoax'. Forty percent of the US electorate believes this, and a large group within that believe the virus was invented to discredit Trump and worsen his chances for re-election. I am not making this up.

The press which Trump has called the 'enemy of the people', was separated by him and his servants, into the 'mainstream' and Fox. He is known to frequently consult with their right-wing newscasters for their opinions on world trends. For about seven weeks, Trump gave a daily news conference on the virus. Reporters who raised questions there were mocked or called 'bad reporters'. He repeated one lie after another, faithfully reported as truth by Fox News. He called Hydroxychloroquine a 'great' treatment for the virus symptoms. It led to the deaths of many gullible listeners. Trump tweeted more madness. He suggested chlorine bleach injections.

All this was to create the illusion that people would not, could not, miss work, miss shopping, miss keeping up the value of stocks, which were inflated by years of deficit spending. This behaviour was mirrored by the despots who floated to the top in the libertarian reactionary neoliberal hegemonic, including such nations as Brazil, the Philippines, Hungary, India and others. Fox has an imprint in every country.

Trump and his ministers have refused to wear masks, and your patriotism can be questioned in the wrong place if you wear one. Obedient governors, like my own in Arizona, urged people to go out, shop and work in their service and warehouse jobs. The death rate in Arizona is still skyrocketing. Incidentally, this movement and Fox also distort the light on global warming, creating an industry of denial 'research' that is harming the effort to organize a resistance to this.

For the teacher

For the critical educator, here again is the question . . . What is to be done? I think it starts with hope . . . and organization and community. But first, it has to do with empathy, compassion with identification. With imagination and storytelling skilful enough to show students a reality that can be *felt*, not just known by them.

Teachers must feel their students fear and feel for their pain and anxieties. And pictures are important, whether they are on paper, canvas or in their minds drawn by you. We used the one on the cover of the 2017 book we colleagues collaborated on. I borrowed it from a photo of that book cover, which I showed students I taught at METU in 2019, to form a lesson. I was working to build imagination and empathy.

Using this picture, which is imbedded here in the photo (Figure 8.3) used to advertise my Global Thursdays Talk today. It may be girl or boy, with a crown or a

Figure 8.3 Global Thursday Talks poster. *Source*: Global Thursday Talks official file.

nest or a . . . *what* on her head? Then they would write what the artwork represents to them, with the idea of *education* in mind.

　　As per METU/ODTU student policy, they communicated ideas in English. The replies they gave (below) I distributed, and we discussed how their ideas compared. They had in common the vulnerability of children, and many of them had just left childhood themselves. They highlighted the responsibility of their teachers. It was a good conversation.

　　I include their collective work here as shown in Figure 8.4. Ideas developed individually. Then we went around the sharing ideas. This small sheet of paper tells

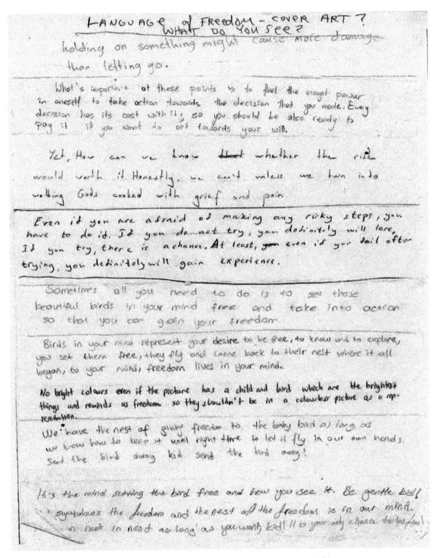

Figure 8.4 Students' collective work. *Source*: Guy Senese, personal file.

a story itself and reflects their developing consciousness. The dreams of these young students feature heavily. The ink has faded but I remember the writing, and that day, as yesterday. The potential for human connection, and humane dialogue, is most needed when there is shared suffering. These connections sustain us, and their loss during pandemic conditions, where this plague cheapens the deep value of community work that is the classroom.

I am reminded that the friendships formed when critical pedagogy is also a pedagogy of love, curiosity and generosity, both academic and personal.

Simit

I took the photo in Figure 8.5 in October 2014, on the way to my class in Room 5, at Ankara University College of Education Sciences.

At that time, I just thought how impressive it was that a man could walk with that kind of load on his head. I did not know then that those things are delicious.

Figure 8.5 The *simitje* is walking away. *Source*: Guy Senese, personal file.

Simit. Then, it just looked exceptional to me. In six years, based on what I learned in Ankara, I think now that I would think of this man, and the advertisement and the post bill on the advertisement and how they relate, and I might invite it all into my class.[10] The *simitje* is walking away, maybe into history, when artisans were at the heart of Turkish and world economies. I think of that world of proto-capitalist production and distribution, embodied here by an old and very loved food, often for millions, a 'fast food' taken on the run. And I can run but I can't hide. There was a Burger King waiting for me in Ankara, not far from the neighbourhood, Batikent, where our hosts lived. I wrote there, too, sometimes, drinking coffee and dining on a familiar burger. Maybe I'm dreaming because I do think there was a burger that can be ordered on simit. The capitalist political-economic transformation implied with fast-food observation isn't a joke, however. It represents one that is playing out everywhere, with paradigm-shifting results.

Fittingly, here the simit seller is walking away, while the loan officer with the white collar in the ad is looking right at us. And there is the woman with bright-red pants, walking somewhere. We know them, but who is she, who might she be?

So, the man with 200 simit breads on his head. Is he religious, is he Turkish, is he a recent immigrant? Is he from a family with lots of property? Is he Kurdish? Is he an 'Arab'? What are his politics, his voting pattern? Because, when he or anybody in is family goes to apply for work or a school or goes to hospital or to buy a car with a bank loan, they go under identity surveillance, just like you and me.

I do not know the banker in the billboard the same way you do. Indeed, he is 'known' to every person who sees that billboard. Now I will ask Turkish readers to kindly consider the same question. Who are these people? They live in *your* teacher's conscience in a way I could never understand. Tell me three things about them. It would be an estimate, but I will bet you would be close. The *simit-seller is: _____. The white-collar guy is: _____. The woman walking away is: _____. You know a lot about their families. Are they your neighbours? Each of them?

These are the people whose kids are in the classrooms of the teachers you are training. We must know them, and they must also know us. They are the workers and their kids. The managers. Who ARE they? And why should you be able to relate to them?

Be safe

Hungry now, I mask up and go up to the counter and order. Latino guy gave me my chicken nuggets. They are on the 'value menu'. Cost is $1 plus 9 cents in sales tax. With his mask on, he said, 'Thanks.' And then said, 'Be safe.' I am struck by the irony. His salary is $10 per hour. He is an at-will employee. This means, he has no job security and can be asked to leave the premises at any time. He is exposed to

10. Available at: https://www.196flavors.com/turkey-simit (accessed 20 May 2021).

people who come in to order without a mask. He is a frontline worker. I am a pensioner, a privileged relic of a time when the social contract included retirement wages for retirees who worked full time. I and my generation have been replaced at my university by part-time workers with no pension hopes, the 'contingent' faculty. The virus has unleashed a greedy board of university directors that protects compliant administrators and cuts wages by 20 percent and faculty by the hundreds. These are PhDs and teacher-workers who were forced for a time, along with students, into face-to-face classrooms. Only a new faculty union we organized was able to agitate, protest and embarrass the administration, controlled by our right-wing governor, to end this practice.

Now, with enrolment in fact growing, the crisis is still being exploited by administration. Faculty are being cut, and those who remain have four, five, maybe six classes to conduct, online, and many works for more than one school. Same salary. I think readers here can relate, and we can all value further Naomi Klein's piercing argument about that tool of social manipulation – existential shock.[11]

Reading The Reading Girl

The photos in Figure 8.6 and Figure 8.7 are pictures of a door at the Kütüphane Library at ODTU, Middle East Technical University again, where I was invited to teach two years ago. It demonstrates a lively political atmosphere, full of posters for justice debates. I do not know what those doors look like today.

One day, I went to study, and I was sitting just inside that entrance, where there is another door, a revolving door, young people coming and going as the door spins. The revolving door of the library, where there is always another 'revolution'. That is how the word in English works. It involves a turning and invokes a circle and a return.

In walking the distance from that door is a word as big as a cruise ship. It is written on an athletic field in the grandstands (Figure 8.8): DEVRİM (Revolution).

The first revolving door I saw in my life was maybe like yours. I was aged 7. Both Chicago and Ankara were modernizing in 1959. These doors were great! They kept the cold out. And even better, for the department store managers in this new form of retail capitalism, they slowed down the shoplifters. Maybe you are old enough like me and were playing going round and round in some department store, and your mother was embarrassed like mine, ready to drag you out, because it was '*not funny!*' Today, the Amazon and Walmart monopolies have absorbed all this commercial retail activity. Every department store from that era is dea or bankrupt.

And with the death of 'retail' as we knew it, the millions of modestly but steadily paid employees, exchanged a middle-class life with the immiseration of work at

---

11. Naomi Klein, *The Shock Doctrine: The Rise of Disaster Capitalism* (London and New York: Picador Publishers, 2007).

Figure 8.6 METU Library, Ankara, Turkey, entrance window. *Source*: Guy Senese, personal file.

Figure 8.7 METU Library, Ankara, Turkey. *Source*: Guy Senese, personal file.

Figure 8.8 DEVRİM (Revolution) at METU, Ankara, Turkey. *Source*: Guy Senese, personal file.

these giants, living precariously, impersonally and poorly, paid at poverty levels. It is beyond the full scope of this paper but the proletarianization of hundreds of millions is important for educators to study, and the fascistic dynamics we discuss here in this work, are a symptom of this new world and new worlds of political-economic exploitation.

In the hall just inside the doors, are chairs and the sculpture, *Reading Girl*, located in the METU Library (Figure 8.9).

I recall what I thought, sitting there, as students revolved in and out on a bright, chilly Ankara afternoon. In my mind, the girl in the sculpture was reading the book, but I realized that she is not reading, but she is talking on her cell phone, with her finger in her free ear. And the book is starting to fall out of her lap. This is *that* mediated world, in art, that I am talking about here. I also connect her to how the sculptor might be hinting that she is *not* the same reading girl as the famous one in *Kızılay*, Ankara. But she is also, is she not, the same?

And I think now of that lady in revolutionary-red pants, near the campus, walking away in that earlier photo. Is she a student? We are near Ankara University, after all, not far from the 'Political Science Café', Mülkiyeliler, where I got a lot of my own education, in Kızılay, the 'Red Crescent' district. Or is she a 'shop girl' rushing to work? Or both a student *and* a 'shop girl'. Rushing to work from a day at university, trying to make ends meet, on a shrinking salary as services are privatized, as expenses go up? What is her situation? Single? Kids? Is she the woman in your class? Is she the mom or sister of a kid in your class? What do you know about her, beyond that she might show up there, in your class, coming to you for life chances, in these times?

In a thought experiment, let us imagine she just got off the bus from Istanbul, where she and her friends were in a rally in solidarity with George Floyd. She will

Figure 8.9 Sculpture in the METU Library, Ankara, Turkey. *Source*: Guy Senese, personal file.

tell her Ankara friends about it, on Facebook. What can she say? '*The whole world is watching*'? Who in Turkey stands in for George Floyd? Who is standing for Floyd and why, in all the countries? Where does the solidarity come from? Why does this happen? It happened because it was organized that way.

By the time you read this, you and I will both know the story, and how it ended. Indeed, this is an artefact, part of a group of talks that are seeking to reflect the education crises around the Covid-19 pandemic. As such, this paper and all of them are a little like the snapshots I collect here. A moment in a time that is evolving daily. It is the view from one day in the gathering storm.

I must also note something, for a part of my story here is the hall of mirrors that is today's universe of distorted, copied, political reality. Not simple Right/Left polarization; rather, this madhouse of mirrors is a digital multiverse that can shape-shift with one click. In fact, I'll do that right now.

Postscript: You can't live without hope

The explosive events surrounding the presidential inauguration challenge the imagination. But reading this again, I can see what played out in the country and at the Capitol Building, and with the last criminal days of the Donald Trump presidency. The role played by the information universe of citizens and their level of democratic illiteracy has been in full display. This is a democratic challenge in a radically monopolized world, where we order food and ideas à la carte, and don't eat OR talk together. We eat, and read, mostly alone. We teach, alone. The following is verbatim, what I wrote in my last draft from 6 January, and it follows below. It is just another 'snapshot', of a moment writing, while listening from my writing desk, the news from that day:

> As this country awaits January 6, the certification of presidential votes, the largest other audience, is not watching our liberal news. It is not hearing Ali Velshi, warning of the possibility of dangerous violence, and what could follow. No, they are watch Sean Hannity on Rupert Murdoch's fascistic Fox News. He is by turns, silent or supportive, of this the most dangerous presidential moment since the end of our Civil War. Listening to him, maybe from another room like me, some blogger is writing, just like me helping organize something for a quite different audience, at this very moment.
>
> Over six years ago, just weeks after I presented the talk shown in the Ayotzinapa/Michael Brown slide that opened this paper, fourteen-year-old Tamir Rice shot dead, while playing in a park fooling around with a toy gun. Phone camera footage showed him as he was shot multiple times by police. His family and all stood for these six years and three months, waiting for justice to be done, got *this* news a few days ago. It is almost cinematic in a most tragic form, and I see it like the old-time movies showing 'newsies' running to the street with an 'Extra' edition of the city paper.

Those kids in their newsboy caps and short pants, are shouting in black and white:

EXTRA! EXTRA! READ ALL ABOUT IT.
TAMIR RICE KILLER COPS GO FREE.
EXTRA! EXTRA!

Yes, that *Extra* happened 29 December 2020. And, yes, Tamir Rice's police killers were freed from further prosecution. It was just coincidentally on the same moral level with news, one day later. Trump, after being voted out of office, but with that vote the vote to be 'certified' by Congress in six days, did this. By that relic of feudal power, the presidential (king's) power, he pardoned, simply freed from jail and life sentences, the privatized mercenary Blackwater guards employed by the military, who murdered Iraqi mothers and children. One by one, they freed from them from any future accountability as well. And he called this . . . 'justice'.

Last night, as I was working at my desk, I heard anchorman Ali Velshi ('sitting in for Rachel Maddow') announcing that the sitting president and his collaborators in our Senate, threaten to simply deny our presidential election results. And I heard Trump's call for far-right gangs to mobilize in Washington on 6 January, a week from this day, . . . to mobilize for treason.

And I know that the *other half* of the news audience is watching Fox and Tucker Carlson, either avoiding this subject entirely, keeping their viewers in the dark or encouraging his dangerous call to support this mobilization as Trump's party stooges step up to call for our certifying officer, Vice-President Mike Pence, to hand the election in battleground states, to his boss. By the time you read this, we will both know what happened.

Our Constitution, like so many, operates too often in service to the ruling classes and the way they have commandeered our police. Politics, liberal politics, fights to be hopeful, even relevant, are deeply frustrated. It seems hopeless at times like this. For his act levels the hearts of these families, even if they were on only slightly lifted by the jail sentences our military courts gave to these murderers. It says to everyone, them, and those of us in my country who are sickened and shamed by this man, 'Yes, this happened, and not only would I authorize it again, not only do I know the evidence of murder is clear, not only that . . . but I would do it again.'

This brave new world of orchestrated and celebrated cruelty, this monster is looking for a mind to rent or buy, a soul, humanity itself . . . in a country near any reader of this. Yes, the beloved, are murdered, twice. And a Plague is among us. You can Google it. Over the years, poets have held us up when it gets dark. And my time in Turkey taught me the writing of Nazım Hikmet,[12] who wrote so clearly, so often and in such desperate straits. In his 'The Great Humanity', he talks of the masses, and conditioned by jail and felt injustice, reminded us by saying bluntly, about life itself and hope, that they are wedded. The living humanity and the departed, are singing, writing, saying together, for Tamir, with George, in one big tired fragmented union. It is a long seven years to live without hope, to do nothing. What *would* Tamir say or George or their families or those Iraqi families, about hope. Would they say, '*Don't mourn me. Organize*'? I want hope, I want to end with hope. But with all these children looking at me right now, I can't find a photo for that.

---

12. Nazım Hikmet, *Poems of Nazım Hikmet*, trans. Randy Blasing and Mutlu Konuk Blasing, revd and expanded edn (New York: Persea Books, 1994), 1,677.

Acknowledgements

I so much appreciate the careful eye and wise editorial help of Sharon Gorman. Great thanks to my dear friend, Dr Corrine Glesne, for her careful attention and terrific suggestions and help in shaping this work. Certainly without Yasemin Tezgiden-Cakcak and her support enabling my chance to teach again in Ankara, and the opportunity to co-teach with Zeynep Alica, that great group of students, our class whose thoughts and ideas help illuminate the paper. To them and the generations they represent, I am grateful. And again to Zeynep, for her comments, insight and encouragement, *teşekkürler bir milyon*.

Chapter 9

LIV MJELDE IN CONVERSATION WITH FATMA MIZIKACI AND EDA ATA

A PEDAGOGY OF QUESTIONING: VOCATIONAL LEARNING

THE ART OF REFLECTIVE CURIOSITY

Liv Mjelde

Global Thursday Talks (GTT)   As a critical educator with a background and praxis in vocational schools, would you like to comment on learning in workshops versus learning in classrooms? In other words, what should we understand about 'the social division of knowledge'?

Liv Mjelde   My own praxis: for many years, I was privileged to work as a counsellor in a large craft and industry trade school in Oslo. I also initiated research projects and did research myself in relation to my experiences in the school while I was working as counsellor. The school had 3,500 students per year – in 50 different trades. There were huge variations in how the 50 trades were organized. Some apprentices had contracts with businesses in the printing industry attending three-month courses in vocational and general theory in the school, whereas others might be one-year students engaged in a trade in preparation for entering an apprenticeship for two years, such as hairdressers, cooks and waiters. Some received their full training in the school such as radio technicians, photographers and tailors; others came for additional adult education courses to upgrade their professional standing. This vocational school was the largest in Scandinavia. The Labour Minister of Education, himself a tailor, said when the foundation stone was laid down: '*Practical schools must be brought into public consciousness and placed where they belong, side by side with general academic schools.*' This was the way of thinking in 1952.

The gender division was highly visible. In the expansion of vocational training in secondary schools which followed World War II, we found a traditional division of labour by gender, which corresponded to the gender-role patterns of the manual labour market, featuring the traditional view of women in the family sphere and men as breadwinners in that period in history. This social organization of masculinity and femininity in relation to work is especially conspicuous in vocational education. It stands out as part of 'the natural order', to use an expression from Antonio Gramsci. The boys populated the 'hard fields' such as the mechanical, electrical and the building trades. Some fields had a mixed recruitment, such as tailors, photographers, cooks and waiters as well as dental technicians. Most girls, however, entered fields having long been traditional for women such as home economics and handicrafts. Often, these fields involved shorter courses in home economics, health and social services as well as aesthetic subjects. The 'women in male occupations' have increased during the recent decades, but most young girls enter the health and social service and aesthetic courses also today. One thing the vocational courses had in common was learning in workshops.

Hands-on learning has been at the centre of learning in vocational schools. In addition, there are vocational theory and general theory. Vocational theory could be technical drawing, knowledge of materials, applied mathematics and physics in the male classes, and human biology and psychology in women-oriented classes. These subjects could be taught in both workshops and classrooms. General theory, such as Norwegian language, mathematics, physics and chemistry, took place in separate classrooms in separate buildings. I have illustrated the different learning arenas as shown in Figure 9.1.

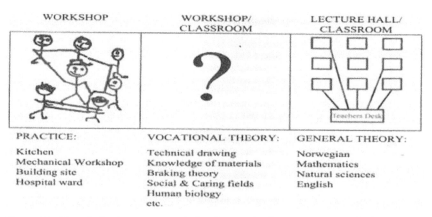

Figure 9.1 The relation between practical and general subjects in vocational education.

The difference between ways of organizing learning is highly visible, the workshop with hands-on activities and the passive rows in the lecture hall/ classrooms. The teachers have different experiences on their way to becoming teachers in upper-secondary vocational streams. Vocational teachers have a double-praxis background. They have been trained in vocational/technical schools and in apprenticeships on the manual labour market. In addition, they have been trained part-time to become teachers in vocational pedagogy in a university college. The academic teachers are mainly trained in their subjects in universities, and they often receive their teacher certificates in their universities. Traditionally, there has been no connections between the two spheres; between the *praxis* workshops/*vocational theory* and the *general subject* classrooms.

One of the main findings in my research in the vocational sector over the past decades is that students and apprentices in the vocational trades prospered and learned when they were in activity in the workshops in the vocational schools or as apprentices in the workplaces, while they found no meaning or relevance to the many hours spent in classrooms for general education. They showed up in the workshops, but often they failed to show up for the academic classes.

The education system has faced a lot of changes during recent decades. Today, young people are expected to complete thirteen years of formal schooling before entering the labour market and/or institutions of higher education. Of the cohort, 50 per cent enter various academic fields and 50 per cent technical/ vocational fields. This has been part of a global trend which, among other things, is built upon a belief that the expansion of equal access and rights to higher education would solve class contradictions in society. 'Equality through Education' and lately 'Social Justice' have been slogans used in this connection (Mjelde 1987, 207).

The reality of the aim for social change reveals the complexities of these issues. The education system might be the most important factor reproducing class society today. Norway's upper-secondary schooling is also marked by a decrease in workshop instruction and an increase in the more abstract general curriculum during the past decades. Learning difficulties and drop-out rates have been substantial both in lower and upper-secondary schools and in higher education (Mjelde 2017; Johannesen 2019). We find similar developments in Sweden and Denmark (Albæk et al. 2019; Gottlieb 2018).

The contradictions between hands-on learning and academic learning traditions are fierce and persistent in the current school reforms in vocational and adult education as well as in higher education in Norway today. During recent decades, approximately 30 per cent of students in upper-secondary vocational education drop out. Hedwig Skonhoft Johannesen (2019, 278), based on recent OECD [Organisation for Economic Co-operation and Development] reports, points out that only 38 per cent of the students in the vocational trades get through on time, that is, after two years in vocational trades in upper-secondary school, followed up by two years of apprenticeship in a workplace. She points out that 6 per cent used more time and obtained their craft certificates. But 32 per cent did not complete their education.

In my research project among apprentices in 1982, I interviewed 1,617 apprentices in five different cities in Norway. I interviewed them in classrooms when they were in schools for vocational theory. Of the youngsters, 89 per cent preferred to learn in workplaces. I also did fieldwork in a mechanical engineering factory among seventeen boys, 16 years of age. I worked together with them in the school workshop and in the factory. I was also a participant observer in workshops and classrooms, together with apprentices in a graphics class, eight boys and one girl. The apprentices in both fields preferred to learn in workplaces. The emphasis on *practical work*, on *doing something real*, on *being paid for it* and *good workmates* were the expressions used by apprentices about their contrasting experiences at work and school. In the words of a graphic apprentice: '*School gives you no insight into the actual reality of work and how things develop. By and large, school grinds you down with all its theoretical subjects.*' A mechanic: '*The school just doesn't cut the mustard – neither for the craftsman nor for the academic.*' Another point the apprentices made was that schools lag behind what was happening in '*real working life*'.

To sum up, the expansion of schooling has created new challenges and a continuing need for developing revolutionary ideas and praxis in our everyday lives as teachers and mentors for coming generations. The question is how to make learning meaningful for all young people intent upon leading fulfilling lives in whatever profession they are entering. This is at the core of discussions not only across Europe, but also elsewhere in the world.

The social division of knowledge

My experiences in the vocational sector and empirical data from my research projects made me pose new questions about the social organization of knowledge in the expanding educational system. It made me also pose questions about the nature of my own abstract 'learning' in the Sociology of Education. I started to understand more of the contradictions between vocational and general streams in education when I started to study the texts of political economists. Adam Smith and Karl Marx and Friedrich Engels treated the social division of knowledge in their major works. They were concerned about the education of the new working classes in the industrial world. Alfred Sohn-Rethel (1978, 18) made me understand the longevity and fundamental nature of these divisions within our abstractions. He states: '*One must take into consideration that the philosophical tradition in itself is a product of the division between intellectual and manual labour and that since its inception, starting with Pythagoras, Herodotus and Parmenides, it has been safeguarded by intellectuals for intellectuals, inaccessible to manual labourers.*'

The Greek/French professor of law at La Sorbonne, Paris, Nicos Poulantzas (1975) inspired me with his writings on the division between mental and manual labour and the development of class society during the past hundred years. Pierre Bourdieu and Jean Claude Passeron (1977) discussed in their work *Reproduction in Education*, how the school system reproduced the established order, with its distinctive class divisions. The divisions, directly visible in vocational education, are described empirically in Claude Grignon's book, *L'Ordre des choses* [1971]. Craft and industry teachers in their blue work-clothes were teaching in the workshops and often in vocational theory, whereas academically trained teachers in their suits were teaching academic subjects in their separate classrooms. There was no formal interaction between the vocational and academic teachers, nor between the subjects they teach. The dress code might have changed, but the social division of knowledge is the same whether you are in Rio de Janeiro, Nagoya, Paris or Oslo. And there is no connection between general knowledge and real work and the real world of vocational students and apprentices. This is visible in the history of the development of the educational system, where there is such a social division of knowledge that it alienates the working class from the search for knowledge. General theory is presented as though it were not connected to the materiality of their everyday lives. These divisions create learning and teaching problems in upper-secondary education. The prevailing organization of conceptual learning kills the learners' curiosity whenever praxis is separated from their own earlier-acquired stored knowledge. Curiosity is the most important driving force of learning (Skonhoft Johannesen 2019).

This social division of knowledge is challenged in our times. The development of information technology has brought revolutionary changes to the work of the hand and the mind in all practical professions as well as raising challenges to scientific work and the art of teaching. The expansion of education in formal institutions after World War II has reinforced fundamental questions about learning and teaching in society. Today, the labour market demands new ways of solving these contradictions.

In Europe, the attention has been drawn to the advantages of education regarding economic growth in a globalized economy. The Lisbon Strategy, also known as the Lisbon Agenda or Lisbon Process, was an action and development plan devised in 2000 for the economy of the European Union between 2000 and 2010. Its aim was to make the European Union the most competitive and knowledge-based economy in the world, capable of sustainable economic growth, with more and better jobs and greater social cohesion. Key concepts used in these documents were: '*The Knowledge Society*' and '*The Learning Economy*'. Innovation should be the motor of social change. Economic crisis has shown that these goals are far from fulfilled. Part of the Lisbon Strategy was to reduce the drop-out rates in education. Research in Scandinavia and elsewhere shows that reducing the drop-out in vocational and further education is a challenge to the actual ways we practice our teaching. Mentoring has become a new central concept in this regard (Mjelde 2020a and 2020b).

GTT It is striking that this division has roots back to history and fed by even philosophical tradition. Would you like to elaborate on 'Hand and Mind and Learning' and your understanding of the social division of knowledge, especially in these times of the Covid-19 pandemic?

Liv Mjelde Thank you for the question. My first published work on this matter had the title: 'From Hand to Mind'. It appeared in a publication called, *Critical Pedagogy and Cultural Power*, in 1987. The foreword was written by Paulo Freire and Henry Giroux. I was then a visiting professor at the Ontario Institute for Studies in Education (OISE) in Toronto, Canada, working with some excellent scholars, among them the editor of *Critical Pedagogy and Cultural Power*, David Livingstone. The book met with good reviews, and I received a letter from the University of Malta. Professor Ronald Sultana wrote, 'What you are saying gives indications towards the education of the future.' He addressed his letter to me: 'DEAR SIR'! I wrote him a thank you letter saying, 'I am not a sir. I am a woman.'

The Department of Sociology of Education at OISE in Toronto was also a centre for interrogation of the development of the social division of knowledge from a woman's point of view. I was inspired and started to grasp the scope of the complex contradictions between vocational and academic education, the issues surrounding the questions of: 'Whose Knowledge, Whose Science?' Women have entered the scientific world in recent decades, having posed new fundamental questions to the traditional social organization of knowledge. Women have entered as participants into academic positions, and they have presented theories critical of the prevalent ways of thinking in both the social and natural sciences. Within my own field, sociology, the Canadian sociologist Dorothy Smith's (2005) critique of the development of Western science has had a widespread influence during the past decades. She shows how the central feature of ruling and managing in Western societies is the role of 'objectified knowledges' or 'textually mediated discourses', far away from people's everyday life. These textually mediated discourses rule our lives in what she calls 'the relations of ruling' and are, of course, central in the educational system as elsewhere. Women's voices have put new questions on the agenda which are important in our research and education of the future. New concepts and new practices will develop. Vocational pedagogy, vocational didactics and pedagogy of professions are central in relation to the complexities around learning and labour in the production and the reproduction sphere today. In these pandemic times, we have experienced both how important professional workers and cooperation are in our global world and how our continuing success as a species requires fewer social barriers and more cooperation.

GTT   Most of education, especially higher education worldwide, has been moved to online platforms. How do you think that has affected students and educators? What are your own reflections on virtual classes and workshops?

Liv Mjelde   This is a complex question. I do think it is possible to organize workshops on the internet. Global Thursday Talks are doing it right now. I remember sitting in Oslo, sharing my knowledge with students at the University of Tampere, Finland, many years ago. I had to go to a television studio and work from there. Today, I sit in my own home using Zoom, and I am learning new possibilities of research and interaction. But I think that digital processes can never replace face-to-face communication in learning and teaching processes. Workshops need meeting with our whole selves. But the digital world has given new opportunities and we have to reflect and discuss our experiences and possibilities.

Here, I would like to draw your attention to how the pandemic has created serious complications in the practical world of vocational students and apprentices and students in professional studies in higher education, whether these are apprentices on a building site, in a kindergarten or in a hospital. Most youngsters today are advanced users of the ICT [information and communications technologies] world, at least those who have access to ICT equipment. Young apprentices are also schooled in using the internet in relation to their trades and professions. Virtual learning has been in place, for example, in building sites in recent decades. ICT is used every day and teach learners, often with simulations, the complexities of factors involved in working on sites, among them cooperation between skilled workers and apprentices in different trades. But vocational students cannot learn their trade to be a hairdresser or a plumber virtually. ICT is a tool used in the work process. The learners also need hands-on learning *in situ*, fellow workers and good mentors in most professions. Salient features of this Covid-19 epidemic are also lockdown and bankruptcies. Apprentices connected to these workplaces may lose their practical jobsites of learning, as well as their apprenticeship contracts and incomes. The same is true for students in medicine who are apprenticing in operation rooms. Hospital wards are locked down to meet the needs of the Covid-19 patients. Students in nursing and teaching would in more normal times pass practical exams in hospitals and classrooms. Covid-19 hinders this praxis. Currently, learners must take oral exams via Zoom instead of being evaluated when they are in practice. The showing of their hands-on work, for example, their communications with patients in a hospital or fellow craftsmen and apprentices on a building site, are not being evaluated (*Dagsavisen* 2021, 8).

On the other hand, I have also been encouraging group-learning using ICT in my practical experience of preparing Master's students in vocational pedagogy to write their theses. The students come from all over Norway, and they are part-time students, over four years. They continue to work as teachers in the schools and come to the university six times a year. Groups are formed; members of these groups work together in their interim periods and they cooperate and meet their mentors and each other through internet connections. The pandemic creates challenges, but it might also create new questions on how to combine virtual learning and cooperation between students in many fields. You can practice workshop learning on the net.

GTT   How should we see this separation for the adult learners? Typically, adult vocational learners can be pictured as retired or 'houseworker' middle-aged women, who join vocational courses with a motivation to learn for the 'joy of learning' and to 'do something' and 'broaden their horizon', who feel lonely and tired and want to make friends and meet new people. It was [deduced] that the main motivation for the participants for vocational courses was *not* work-oriented or for professional advancement. What do you think about this? I know that in Norway, laws on educational matters are ratified by the Parliament. Schools and universities are mostly public and free of charge. Could you make a comparison regarding adult learner's participation to vocational courses in the Scandinavian context?

Liv Mjelde   I assume you refer to adult education centres as they have developed across most of the industrialized world since World War II. I have argued in my earlier work that vocational education and adult education are two sides of the same coin (Mjelde 2006; Antikainen 2005). Adult education courses in Norway have often been tied to unemployment. Unemployed workers have been offered adult education courses when they have lost their jobs (Lien 1984). Research shows, however, that men prefer a job rather than adult education courses, whereas women might have been more open to such education possibilities. The policies in Scandinavia during the past fifty years have been women's right to work and to support themselves. Today, this is taken for granted. These changes have also created the need for new labour power in the public health care and the social service sectors. Adult education courses have opened possibilities in new labour markets for working-class women in these sectors during the past decades.

Adult education has not been given much attention in the research world in Norway during recent years. But reskilling of workers is part of adult education and royal commissions and proposals in Parliament on skills and competence have addressed this problem, again and again. The last proposal, 'Lifetime Learning', was passed in Parliament in 2020. It was a competence reform, with the goal that no one should be left behind due to lack of competence in relation to finding a job. It is geared towards both new immigrants and Norwegian born who lack competence in relation to demands of the job market. The OECD report from 2017, *Education at a Glance*, reported that 400,000 youngsters had been through ten years of schooling in Norway without acquiring a grasp of elementary abilities in reading, writing and mathematics (Norway's population: 5 million). I think that adult education is also tied to upgrading a lot of the youngsters who have dropped out of school, particularly from vocational education. But the complexities between hands-on learning and classroom learning are very much present in adult education with the same contradictions as you can observe in vocational education. The situation is ripe for change.

GTT   You argue that vocational pedagogy and vocational didactics are essential in today's world. What do these terms and practices have in common with the learning processes found in the Dewey, Freire and Montessori traditions?

Liv Mjelde   There is a deep crisis in the educational system in these times of neoliberalism. Crises enforce change. The absurdity of New Public Management with its marketization of educational systems faces considerable criticism. The new concepts of vocational pedagogy and vocational didactics and the pedagogy of professions related to higher education are concepts growing out of the need for fundamentally rethinking the art of teaching. There is a need for critical thinking and critical pedagogy. The newsletter, *Khrono*, of Oslo Metropolitan University, documented in 2020 that medical students were protesting against the remoteness from practical hands-on activities they experienced. They demanded other ways of learning. They criticized the lecturing traditions of their professors. These contradictions demand change and new understanding in educational science, whether you train to be a carpenter, a medical doctor or a laboratory technician. Drop-out rates and the rate of exam failure are considerable also in higher education in Norway (*Khrono* 2021).

These contradictions are old in the world of education. They stem from the scientific perceptions which evolved in Western Europe and separated hand, mind and heart during the rise of industrial society. Friedrich Engels (1949) in, 'The Part

Played by Labour in the Transition from Ape to Man', written in 1876 and published posthumously in the journal, *Neue Zeit*, in 1896, addresses these questions. Engels develops the idea that hands-on labour is the source of all wealth as the political economists of his time also asserted. He states: '*that it is the prime basic condition for all human existence, in this to an extent that in a sense, we have to say that labour created man himself.*

The development of hand and mind through the development of tools and communication lays the foundation for an understanding of how human beings learn through labour and cooperation. Friedrich Engels also gives optimistic criticisms of the division of knowledge and the separation of man from nature as it has developed under the Era of Industrial Capitalism, saying:

> that the more our understanding progresses the more will men (German: Mensch- gender neutral) not only feel but also know their oneness with nature, and the more impossible will become the senseless and unnatural idea of a contrast between mind and matter, man and nature, soul and body, such as arose after the decline of classical antiquity in Europe and obtained its highest elaboration *in Christianity (1949, 13).*

The cathedral schools of the Middle Ages developed this division of knowledge separating hand and mind. Louis Althusser (1971) argues that the education system has taken over the role of the Church during capitalism. He argues that the reproduction of the conditions of production is secured through the 'ideological state apparatus'. He says that through the school system, students receive the ideology which corresponds to the role they are going to fill in class society. This role that the exploited are required to assume is accompanied by highly moral and apolitical consciousness (Mjelde 1987, 213; Ural and Aysun 2020, 223). Today, this mantra is contested terrain.

To sum up, the education system has been cast in two traditions, which both arise from the way the instruction of the young was organized during the Middle Ages, on the one hand the *Schola* traditions coming out of the cathedral schools and on the other hand the master/apprentice craft traditions with hands-on learning growing out of the guild system. The contradictions that can be observed between these different learning traditions are part of the social division of knowledge in today's capitalist society. They are the same contradictions that the great thinkers, John Dewey, Paulo Freire and Maria Montessori, addressed. They have in common a pedagogical model based on the belief that learning takes place in people's actual activity in their everyday life. PRAXIS is central to their thinking. 'Learning by doing' is a well-known concept from John Dewey's laboratory schools. He proclaims: '*There is a form of fruitless theory that stands opposed to practice. Real scientific theory is located within the bounds of practice and functions as the impetus for expansion; it provides direction toward new possibilities.*' In his writings, Dewey promoted workshop learning – learning through hands-on labour and cooperation. He broke with all the usual formalism in the organization of teaching. He broke with the system of school classes, school lessons and school subjects. He stressed interdisciplinary approaches, especially through experimentation. By means of hands-on experiments, the students would deny or confirm the hypotheses they put forward. They acquired knowledge and competence through praxis and curiosity about former knowledge in the field they were exploring. To a considerable degree, theory became linked to practice. John Dewey was well known in Scandinavia, and he influenced ways of thinking about learning and teaching for decades.

Critical pedagogy, from its development in the 1920s, was forgotten during the Cold War in Norway, but came up again in the 1970s. In the late 1960s, young students started to question the content and the organization of learning and teaching in the old 'gymnasiums' (high schools) in Oslo. They claimed that the teaching methods and curriculum were antiquities. They demanded to have influence in their everyday life in the school system. These youngsters wanted democracy rather than the old authoritarian 'Prussian' school system, as it was called, *Forsøksgymnaset*. The *Experimental Gymnasium* was started in Oslo in 1968. It was an experimental gymnasium based on democratic principles in the sense that the school's highest authority was the *allmannamøtet* (the students' and teachers' 'everybody' meeting), based on the principle of 'one man, one vote'. Students took part in choosing the content in the curriculum, and they were free to attend the courses they desired. But there was a limit to their freedom. They had to conform to the public exams of the state. A critical periodical called *Praxis* was also started in Oslo in 1970, a periodical that called for revolutionary changes in the *Schola* traditions of the times. New critical education journals also appeared in Denmark and Sweden.

Denmark had more liberal social democratic traditions than Sweden and Norway in this period. Private schools were more accepted in Denmark than in social democratic Norway and Sweden. The integration of the different school systems, the secondary modern and the grammar school, the old gymnasiums and vocational schools under common laws came later to Denmark compared to Norway and Sweden. A provision in the Danish constitution allowed any group to form a school and receive government funding. This fact opened experimental opportunities. The private school sector and a variation of pedagogical approaches in elementary schools were more developed in Denmark compared to Norway and Sweden in the 1970s. One of these schools had a big influence in Norway. The Tvind Schools were started in Jutland in Denmark in 1970 by a group of teachers headed by Mogens Amdy Petersen. They wanted to build a school system for the future, a school based on production. These schools cooperated with the labour unions in the Jutland region. They established ecological gardens and farms. A wind turbine, which they called Tvindkraft, was built to fight the expansion of nuclear plants in Scandinavia. The system was also based on teacher/student cooperation. The students were often leading the 'All Man/Everybody Meeting' and were part of decision-making. The Tvind consortium established numerous private, alternative schools, in their spirit across Denmark. Their influence expanded to Norway and Sweden in the coming decades. I have visited the Tvind schools in Denmark over the years. (See also, Wikipedia, 'Tvind International School Centre'.) The pedagogical ideas were inspired by the writings of Anton Makarenko and the revolutionary practices among orphans in the Soviet Union in the 1920s. The Tvind schools developed into a successful 'empire', with a teacher training college called 'The Necessary Teacher Training College', where the students' admission depended on the applicants' praxis in industrial production or farm work. They also conducted 'The Travelling Folk High School', where students travelled to Africa and Latin America to learn about and participate in the material conditions on other continents. They also lent their hands to building new schools in the so-called developing countries they visited.

Paulo Freire, with his book, *Pedagogy of the Oppressed* (1970), was another inspiration in this period. He put basic questions on the agenda in Europe again as well as in other parts of the world. His book had a big influence in Scandinavia in the 1970s. Praxis is the central concept which Freire adopts to capture the dialectical relationship between consciousness and the world. He was inspired by the works of Antonio Gramsci, Friedrich Engels and Karl Marx (Mayo 2016).

The concept of praxis in this context has its origin in the ancient Greek tradition. Freire's writings, echoing Marx, generally refer to the process of consciousness, whereby people reflect on their world of action, of everyday life, to examine its various aspects and generated assumptions about it. Paulo Freire believed education could not be divorced from politics: the act of teaching and learning are considered political acts, in and of themselves. He defined this connection as the main tenet of critical pedagogy. A central feature in Paulo Freire's work throughout his life was the dialectic between theory and praxis. He claimed that: '*theory without practice would be mere abstract thinking, just as practice without theory will be reduced to naïve action*'. Paulo Freire claimed that the traditional school had '*a banking concept of education*', in which the student was viewed as a savings account, to be filled with information obtained from the teacher – savings which students could withdraw from the bank later. As an alternative, he suggested a Socratic approach: 'A Pedagogy of Questioning' (Freire and Vittoria 2007; Mjelde 2020a and 2020b).

Maria Montessori was a woman pioneer in Italy, both in the medical profession and in revolutionary pedagogy (Befring 2018). She was educated in engineering before she became a medical doctor. She was the first woman to be allowed into the study of medicine in Italy, in 1896. She is world famous as a practitioner and philosopher in educational science. Following her graduation, she became a supervision doctor in psychiatric hospitals. Through this work, she discovered the appalling conditions endured by the children in these hospitals, children considered to be idiots. They were simply hidden away in institutions, without any learning and development possibilities. These grotesque conditions made her upset, and she decided to act and liberate the children from such conditions. She took practical initiatives to give these children play activities and learning possibilities. She developed various help-tools. She discovered that the children had hidden potentials and, with time, they learnt reading, writing and arithmetic. These pathbreaking discoveries showed that children with development disabilities had possibilities for learning if they met engaging and problem-solving activities. The results were impressive. It was called Montessori's first miracle.

Montessori opened her first school in Rome on 6 January 1907. It was a school combined with a day-centre directed towards working-class kids. In Casa dei

Bambini, the child's creative potentials and natural learning desires were central to development. This way of thinking about learning stood in sharp contrast to the cathedral views of learning where children should absorb knowledge through blackboard education. She built on experiences which demonstrated that children had huge potential for self-discipline and self-learning. The students could work undisturbed with their learning assignments; self-tuition and engagement were the rule. The teacher's role was to strengthen the child's motivation and self-reliance through giving encouraging and generous responses. The results in the Casa dei Bambini were so impressive that it was called Montessori's second miracle. She often received admiring questions as to how this miracle was possible. She went on to ask herself why healthy and normal children often did not progress in traditional schools and why they quickly forgot what they learned. Her answer was that the school robbed children of the motivation for learning by the endless repetition of abstract knowledge and lack of practical and useful learning. The traditional school had a misconception of children, underestimating their possibilities for learning and self-learning. The key to ignite a curiosity to learn was by encouraging the child's self-activity – using both hands and minds.

Montessori's devotion to research and practice has spread its influence far beyond Italy. There are Montessori-inspired kindergartens and schools in many parts of the world, in Scandinavia, as well as in Latin America and Africa. She became an inspiration and a mentor for many educational scientists in the previous century. To sum up: Montesorri had a strong belief in everybody's ability to learn and was deeply concerned about the teacher's ability to adjust and redeem the inherent abilities in all human beings. A teacher, she argued, should be a guide and a mentor.

These great scientists have been an inspiration to my own praxis and writing. You can talk of a workshop model of learning based on praxis and cooperation like the one you find in vocational and apprenticeship traditions.

GTT   Apprenticeship is one of the key elements in your works. How would you define apprenticeship in today's digital context, where we are mostly sitting in front of a computer? How can our hands, mind and heart in cooperation with other learners communicate and cooperate nowadays?

Liv Mjelde   I think both the concept of workshop learning and apprenticeship became central to me when I was working on my dissertation. My experience consists of interviewing apprentices all over Norway and being an apprentice myself with other apprentices in a mechanical-engineering factory as well as being with printing apprentices in workshops and in theory classrooms where they were enduring general education subjects. Nearly all of them preferred to learn as apprentices in real activity. They had not enjoyed the *Schola* traditions, neither in the nine-year compulsory school nor in the vocational schools. When I was doing my fieldwork, I had not yet grasped the contradictions between the work of hand and the mind in class society as it had developed in the vocational education systems in the industrial era.

I started to understand these contradictions when I began to look upon the historical traditions of production and the need for skills in industrial production (Charlot and Figeat 1985). Apprenticeship as an educational model originated in the guild system which developed in feudal Europe (Corbon 1859). Craftsmen in the Middle Ages joined guilds to protect their craft-wide interests. The guilds were organized in three ranks: masters, journeymen and apprentices. They worked side by side in workshops, often under tyrannical conditions, but that is a matter I will not discuss here. A positive side of the guild system was the craftsman's relationship to the product of his labour. The apprentice invested sweat and workmanship in cooperation with other labourers. He was constantly developing his skills by being guided by his master, journeymen and other apprentices. Hand and mind worked together. The product had direct utilitarian value, often testifying to the creativity and knowledge of the maker (Marx 1970; Mjelde 1993, 54). The workshop was the key learning site in the development of vocational/ technical schools in the transition from feudalism to industrial capitalism. That system is the root of this combination between learning in schools and apprenticeship in craft shops and industry as we also see it today. The root of the word *apprenticeship* originated in the French word *prendre*, to take, and *apprendre*, to learn, we can say *to grip and grasp*. You grip with your hand and grasp with your mind. The first known use of the word *apprentice* in English is from 1362, about apprenticing in a pharmacy (*The Compact English Oxford Dictionary*). The Norwegian concepts, *mester, svenn, lærling*, have their roots in the German language.

I have lately worked with the concept and praxis of mentoring and the Ancient Greeks. Mentoring as a concept in educational theory in the European tradition is connected to what has been called the *Socratic Method*. The role of the teacher is to be an interlocutor, a person of experience with whom young people can converse. The mentor questions the learner's current understanding such that the questions and reflections should help to develop young peoples' curiosity and engagement in their search for new knowledge. The Socratic questioner disturbs the unexamined assumptions of the learner. This approach to knowledge and learning through questioning and discussion corresponds with an apprenticeship model of learning where hands-on activity, both individual and cooperative, is the basis for learning. In vocational traditions, the concept of apprentices and journeymen learning from the master is central.

GTT   As a scholar who has been influenced by Lev Vygotsky and John Dewey and Activity Theory, would you like to discuss how your work is related to critical pedagogy and Paulo Freire in the time of industrialization, especially during a pandemic?

Liv Mjelde   Lev Vygotsky's scientific work was not well known in the Western world during the early decades after World War II. His work and the work of the Cultural-Historical School of Moscow and Activity Theory were not translated into English until the beginning of the 1960s (Mjelde 2006, 2017). The writings of

John Dewey were well known in Norway in the interwar period. Both John Dewey and Maria Montessori visited Norway after WW II. Dewey became an honorary professor at the University of Oslo in 1946. His concepts, *learning by doing* and *the work method is the curriculum*, put its stamp on educational development in the early post-war period.

Lev Vygotsky's work came late to Norway. I started to grasp his work and what it meant to the understanding of the contradictions in educational development in the 1980s. He laid the groundwork for a scientific understanding of how human beings learn through activity and cooperation. The Cultural-Historical School of Moscow provided a historical and material analysis of the development of higher mental function of the human beings: we learn from the social to the individual. Human beings develop their mental activity through interaction with one another by means of speech and communication. Lev Vygotsky also criticized traditional teaching for having an atomistic view of learning. Among other things, he felt that both the individualizing of the learners, the splitting up of school subjects and the parcelling-out of teaching content into individual subjects contributed to the elimination of the meaningfulness of the individual subjects. Knowledge, he argued, cannot be taken out of its natural context and passed on in isolation; it can only yield its richness, its wealth of meaning and create motivation if it is taken up as part of a whole. Human beings learn through activity and social relations. As Vygotsky said, inspired by Francis Bacon: '*Neither the mind nor the hand can do much alone. The deed is brought to fruition through activity and cooperation*' (Mjelde 2020a, 237). This quotation mirrors the work of John Dewey and Paulo Freire. Freire attacked the false dualism of the seventeenth century in the following way:

> I write with my head, but actually I write with my whole body. I do not think with my mind, I rather think with my whole body, with all my emotions, my feelings, my intuitions . . . I think with my common-sense experiences, with the lived facts, that although rarely perceived, are still present in my life, and I think with my reflexive consciousness as well. (Freire and Vittoria 2007: 110)

Maria Montessori said: '*Hands are the instruments of human intelligence.*' The division of hand, mind and heart is a social construction of knowledge which has its different hegemonic ways of manifesting itself in different epochs of history. This epoch of industrialization has divided work of hands and mind and developed our present education system and class society. Present-day industrial production has brought new questions to light. The tools and human knowledge develop all the time and demand new solutions in the social division of education. The vocational/general divide is ripe for change. The education system is lagging behind the technology and the labour processes.

GTT You built up a Master's Programme of Vocational Pedagogy/Vocational Didactics at Kyambogo University in Kampala, Uganda. How was your experience there?

Liv Mjelde   My work and learning experiences, together with colleagues and students from South Sudan and Uganda, were rich. We practised 'Learning by doing,' where we developed the project together with our African colleagues from the very beginning. The Master's programme was based at Kyambogo University (KYO) in Kampala. Formal education in Uganda has its roots in British traditions. Vocational/ technical education was first based on the needs for training labour power that the British needed when they were ruling Uganda as a protectorate of the British Empire; in particular, the colonial protectors needed house maids and builders, mechanics and electricians. We were concerned about how best to plant the Master's Programme of Vocational Pedagogy in African soil, rather than being a continuation of the Colonial Master from the North (Mjelde 2015). We wrote the applications for money, and we built the programme together with students and colleagues from Uganda, day by day. But a point of departure for developing the Master's programme in Kampala was the experience with work-based learning approaches that Oslo Metropolitan University (OsloMet) has developed in vocational pedagogy and vocational didactics over the years. The aim was to practice a workshop model, to create conditions for students to share and cooperate in their research and writing from Day One and all the way to the completion of their theses. Mentoring from the master and mentoring each other are the central aspects of this process, the motto being: '*All for one and, nobody left behind.*'

KYO is the only university in Uganda that has a fully fledged Faculty of Vocational Studies that offers Bachelor's degrees in food-processing technology, art and industrial design, human nutrition and dietetics, agriculture, business management, mechanics, the electro fields, construction as well as information and communication technology. Both our colleagues and students had a double-praxis background. They were foresters, carpenters, electricians, home economic teachers and artists teaching in art and design, many trained in their fields at Kyambogo. These Bachelor programmes are part of the country's vocational teacher education. Both KYO and OsloMet have years of experience in training vocational teachers at the Bachelor level. But KYO had no experience of training at the Master's level. Part of Uganda's 'Poverty Eradication Action Plan' emphasized the need for strengthening vocational education in relation to the economy's need for skill. OsloMet has been developing and delivering a Master's Programme in Vocational Pedagogy for several decades. This programme has created new knowledge of the complex field of vocational education, education related to the ebbs and flows of the manual labour market, and hence the specific educational requirements needed to meet the challenges of changing labour conditions and demands and the need for new skills in the workforce. Master's and doctoral dissertations are often at the cutting edge of knowledge in this field.

We started with 21 students from South Sudan and Uganda. They came from different trades or disciplines and different tribal, religious and geographical backgrounds. Experiential learning is a key-concepts in the learning process, and gender balance is at the core of the programme. We built a house on campus with group rooms, naming the rooms, Juba, Kampala and Oslo. The students had scholarships from Norway, and the programme was a two-year full-time project. We divided the 21 students into groups of seven, and they had a group room each as their workplace. Each group had a mentor who worked together with the group. The students followed a trajectory similar to a conventional apprentice. Students work together in workshops and through hands-on learning, that will say in this regard to write a Master's thesis. Activity in the groups and cooperation are at the centre for learning. Research activities are at the core of the learning process.

From the beginning of the project, we started to go on 'mini' research expeditions to production sites. The students prepared research methodologies to use on research expeditions in the groups, and the students started to work on gathering data in different workplaces, be it in a biscuit factory or an agricultural college. Groups could go to different workplaces, and the members could also be criss-crossed on occasions. The data they gathered were analysed in smaller groups, and the results were presented in plenary sessions with discussions on research methodology. The students enter a new field, that of social research. When they begin, they are neophytes and peripheral actors. When they finish, they are no longer in the periphery in social research. They have become more central, and are ready to be journeymen and to defend a Master's degree. This programme laid the groundwork for vocational pedagogy in Uganda and even South Sudan. Some students have finished their PhDs, and they are practising new ways of teaching. Mentoring is a new central concept in educational debates there as here (Nabaggala 2020).

GTT   Okay. Professor Mjelde, unfortunately we are approaching the end of this interview. My last question will be about classrooms (now screens) that [are] our living milieu. As educators-teachers, how can we help our students learn through praxis? Is praxis possible in an online education context? How can educators adopt the idea and principles of praxis into online teaching?

Liv Mjelde   Maybe I should say by encouraging 'Praxis and Cooperation' or 'Learning by doing', because developing new understanding and practices is central to dealing with the crisis in education today.

I became the first professor in vocational pedagogy in Norway in 1990. The Institute of Vocational Pedagogy hired at the same time their first professor in vocational didactics, Lennart Nilsson from Sweden. The professorships in vocational pedagogy and vocational didactics were new in the academic world and had grown out of the need for more research in vocational education and to get new knowledge about the everyday life of vocational students and teachers. The concepts, as well as mentoring, were new in educational debates at that time. We were developing both our own and the vocational schoolteachers' understanding of these fields. The point of departure was experience-based learning. We practiced a form of activity pedagogy: working in groups with student cooperation was central throughout the four-year part-time Master's programme followed by the students. We started to develop online mentoring with the development of ICT in between the workshop gatherings at the university. We continued to develop these experiences together in Uganda and South Sudan and the projects are alive and being developed further at KYO today.

To conclude: there is a variation of challenges to praxis in the art of teaching on different levels in the education system. But ways of developing learning through activities and cooperation are necessary at all levels of schooling, whether in a time of a pandemic or not. The historian, Herbert Applebaum, sums up core features of praxis learning when he writes (1992, 272): '*Learning through practice and experience, by trying and failing and through action is the basis for true knowledge. Even in the realm of "pure ideas"; whether it be through the activity of writing or of teaching, one learns best when one is in activity.*' Educators currently focusing on online teaching and learning can encourage group cooperation even in this time of pandemic. Online interaction between learners, and a spirit of cooperation between students can enliven this process, as well as taking initiatives, trying them out, and assessing successes and failures. Professors can well create a group-learning fellowship and mentoring processes online. I will end with the words of a Master student in Vocational Pedagogy in Norway who summed up his experience this way: '*The experiences I myself have had in connection to learning during vocational training are relevant to this programme because the activity itself is central. You learn using your hands, mind and heart in cooperation with others.*' The work method is the curriculum.

GTT   Thank you so much for this stimulating conversation, Professor Mjelde.

References

Albæk, Karsten, Rita Esplund, Erling Barth, Lena Lindahl, Marte Strøm and Pekka Vanhala (2019) 'Better late than never? How late completion affects the early careers of dropouts', *IZA Discussion Paper*, no. 12560, 1–39.

Althusser, Louis (1971) *Lenin and Philosophy and Other Essays* (New York: Monthly Review Press).

Antikainen, Ari (2005) 'Between empowerment and control: A state intervention into participation in adult education in Finland', *European Education*, 37 (2): 21–31.

Applebaum, Herbert (1992) *The Concept of Work: Ancient, Medieval and Modern* (New York: State University of New York Press).

Befring, Edvard (2018) *De pedagogiske kvalitetene: løfterike muligheter for barn og unge* (Oslo: Universitetsforlaget).

Bourdieu, Pierre and Jean-Claude Passeron (1970) *La Reproduction* (Paris: Les Édtions de Minuit).

Bourdieu, Pierre and Jean-Claude Passeron (1977) *Reproduction in Education, Society and Culture* (London: Sage).

Charlot, Bernard and Madeleine Figeat (1985) *Histoire de la Formation des Ouvriers en France 1789–1984* (Paris: Éditions Minerve).

Corbon, C.A. (1859) *De L'Enseignement professionel* (Paris: Imprëmerie Debuisson).

Dagsavisen, daily newspaper, Oslo, 8 January 2021, 8.

Dewey, John and Evelyn Dewey (1962) *Schools of Tomorrow* (New York: E. P. Dutton & Co.).

Engels, Frederick (1949) *The Part Played by Labour in the Transition from Ape to Man* (Moscow: Progress Publishers).

Freire, Paulo (1970) *Pedagogy of the Oppressed* (New York: Herder and Herder).

Freire, Paulo (1982) *De undertryktes Pædagogik* (Copenhagen: Christian Ejlers Forlag).

Freire, Ana Maria Araujo and Paolo Vittoria (2007) 'Dialogue on Paulo Freire', *Interamerican Journal of Education for Democracy*, 1 (1): 96–117.

Gottlieb, Susanne (2018) 'How Denmark try to solve the problem of dropout in vocational education', *New Journal*, 17: 48–57.

Grignon, Claude (1971) *L'Ordre des choses: Les Fonctions sociales de l'enseignement technique* (Paris: Les Édition de Minuit).

Johannesen, Hedvig Skonhoft (2019) 'Miskjennelse av yrkesfaglig kulturell kapital i skolen', *Norsk Pedagogisk Tidsskrift*, 103 (4): 277–87.

Khrono (2021) Digital Newspaper for Higher Education, Oslo Metropolitan Unversity (OsloMet).

Lien, T. (1984) *Kvalifisering til arbeid. En analyse av teori og praksis på to arbeidsmarkedskurs* (Trondheim: Norsk voksenpedagogisk institutt).

Marx, Karl (1970) *Verker i utvalg. Bind 2, Skrifter om den materialistiske historieoppfatning* (Oslo: Pax).

Mayo, Peter (2016) 'Praxis', in M. A. Peters (ed.), *Encyclopaedia of Educational Philosophy and Theory* (New York: Springer).

Mjelde, Liv (1987) 'From hand to mind', in D. W. Livingstone (eds.), *Critical Pedagogy and Cultural Power* (South Hadley, MA: Bergin & Garvey), 205–21.

Mjelde, Liv (1993) *Apprenticeship: From Practice to Theory and Back Again* (Joensuu: University of Joensuu Press).

Mjelde, Liv (2006) *The Magical Properties of Workshop Learning* (Bern: Peter Lang).

Mjelde, Liv (2015) 'Mentoring vocational self-reliance: Lessons from Uganda', in Gabriele Molzberger and Manfred Wahle (eds), *Shaping the Futures of (Vocational) Education and Work* (Bern: Peter Lang), 101–24.

Mjelde, Liv (2017) 'Learning through praxis and cooperation: Lev Vygotsky and vocational pedagogy', in F. Marhuenda-Fluixa (ed.), *Vocational education beyond skill formation* (Bern: Peter Lang), 263–83.

Mjelde, Liv (2020a) 'Expêriencia e significado de mentoria: da abordagem Socratica à novo ciência da aprendizagem', *Zenac*, 46 (2): 24–39.

Mjelde, Liv (2020b) 'Mentoring experience and meaning', in Dennis V. Cokkinos, Niki Agnantis, Katerina Gardikas and Constantin R. Soldatos (eds), *The Capital of Knowledge* (Athens: Society for the Propagation of Useful Books).

Nabaggala, J. (2020) 'Sustainable partnership in action research: The role of mentorship in the world of work', *Africa Journal of Tehnical & Vocational Education and Training*, 5 (1): 66–74.

Organisation for Economic Co-operation and Development (OECD) (2017) *Education at a Glance: OECD Indicators* (Paris: OECD Publishing).

Poulantzas, Nicos (1975) *Classes in Contemporary Society* (New York: New Left Books).

Smith, Dorothy E. (2005) *Institutional Ethnography: A Sociology for People* (Lanham, MD, and New York: AltaMira Press).

Sohn-Rethel, Alfred (1978) *Intellectual and Manual Labour: A Critique of Epistemology* (London: Macmillan).

Ural Ayhan and Öztürk Aysun (2020) 'A transformative experience: The influence of critical pedagogy studies on teachers', *Journal of Critical Pedagogy Studies*, 18 (2): 159–95.

Chapter 10

BETWEEN *BILDUNG* AND *ERZIEHUNG*: MASS EDUCATION DURING THE PANDEMIC

Arnd-Michael Nohl

Introduction

Liberal democracies sometimes hesitantly try to influence the attitudes of their adult citizens by educational means. They usually prefer what is called *Bildung* in German: adults are offered a whole range of information on a specific topic, including the possible, but contradictory, political positions on it. The adults are subsequently encouraged to make up their own minds and form their own orientations. However, even liberal democracies sometimes refer to what is known in German as *Erziehung*: the directive education in favour of specific norms and orientations that borders on inculcation and imposition. The Covid-19 pandemic was such a moment when many governments seemed to have no choice but to resort to directive education, even for their adult citizens. At least this was the case in Germany, the country to which my reflections in this chapter refer.

When the Covid-19 pandemic started to attract public and political attention in March 2020, the political authorities in Germany decided against strict curfews and in favour of a lockdown of restaurants, recreation facilities and nonessential shops. This lockdown was accompanied by an urgent appeal to the population to maintain physical distance, observe rules of hygiene and, later on, to wear masks. This appeal and its accompanying processes can be interpreted as directive education in the sense of *Erziehung*. A second phase of directive mass education by the political authorities that I analyse in this paper started when, after the summer and its low infection rates, the pandemic gained momentum in some counties, which were subsequently declared as risk areas. This encouraged the public-blaming of so-called 'superspreaders', accompanied by collective sanctions and what I propose to call 'co-education'. The authoritarian character of this second phase and mode of directive mass education then overshadowed the third phase of directive mass education that followed in autumn 2020, the Chancellor's attempts, given her political powerlessness, to appeal directly to the population via podcasts and insistent speeches in the *Bundestag* and persuade them to physically distance themselves and wear masks.

Before I embark on the empirical analysis of these three successive phases of directive mass education and the specific modes it took, I would like to elaborate theoretically on the suggested difference between *Erziehung* and *Bildung* and to show how *Bildung* historically became the dominant educational process in the democratic discourse of Germany. This will also allow me to point out in the empirical analysis those points where directive education (*Erziehung*) was accompanied or underpinned by non-directive education (*Bildung*) and, at the end of this chapter, to critically reflect on the phases and modes of mass education analysed in this chapter.[1]

Erziehung *versus* Bildung

The analytic distinction between *Erziehung* and *Bildung* is not only helpful for the inquiry into mass education during the Covid-19 pandemic. This distinction, like its conceptually less clear-cut equivalents in other languages, has also shaped many educational discussions in Germany and elsewhere. One area in which this distinction can be particularly well explained – and which has many references to the topic of this chapter – is civic education.

One of the most prominent controversies in civic education relates to the question of whether schools should provide a 'thick, ethically dense education that trains young boys and girls to become citizens of a certain (good) kind' (Fernández and Sundström 2011: 369) or whether the 'state should, as far as possible, be a neutral enabler that refrains from promoting certain life projects over others', but 'should encourage citizens to choose those projects themselves and of their own accord, rather than having them impressed by the church, the state or any other authority' (ibid., 376).

Erziehung

The first option, *Erziehung*, implies that civic education has to 'foster virtuous democratic citizens that will perpetuate and improve their society' (ibid., 374) and that its 'method must be pedagogy that is far more rhetorical than rational' (Galston, quoted in Brighouse 1998, 724). Here, civic education becomes a process 'through which "newcomers" become part and are inserted into the existing social and political order' (Biesta 2011, 149).

1. For important comments on (parts of) this chapter and for inspiring discussions on its topic, I thank Anne-Katrin Helms, Philip Schelling, Steffen Amling, Carola Groppe, Burkhard Schäffer, Denise Klinge, Sarah Thomsen, Martin Hunold, Fabian Kessl, Hannah Hassinger, Erhan Bağcı, Fatma Mızıkacı, Eda Ata and the participants of the Global Thursday Talks.

This first option, irrespective of whether it pertains to children or adults, resembles the definition of *Erziehung*. Wolfgang Brezinka, for example, defined *Erziehung* 'as those actions through which human beings attempt to produce lasting improvements in the structure of the psychic dispositions of other people, to retain components they consider positive or to prevent the formation of dispositions they regard as negative' (1992, 40–1). Looking less at the intentions of the educators than at the interaction that takes place between them and the persons to be educated, I understand *Erziehung* as the sustained imposition of orientations. Such directive education begins where people do not develop new orientations by themselves. They experience the new orientation expected from them (at first) as quite contrary to their own current interests and sensitivities. At the same time, directive education (*Erziehung*) also implies that the educator is convinced that the person being educated is, in principle, capable of adopting the orientation expected of him or her. Here, the concept of orientation refers less to a conscious opinion or conviction than to a way of acting and living that is to become a habit. This imposition of orientation is emphasized by the fact that it can be sanctioned, both by positive and negative sanctions, which are initially only threatened. It becomes sustainable when the results of the attempts to educate the person are checked through communication; that is, when there is someone who pays attention to whether the imposed orientation has been appropriated (Nohl 2020 and 2022).

Bildung

By contrast, the second option, *Bildung*, necessarily includes 'autonomy-facilitating education' (Brighouse 1998, 726), in which, for example, 'methods for evaluating the truth and falsehood, or relative probability, of various claims about the world' are taught and students are exposed to divergent life projects and ideologies, together with their respective critique, 'such that the students can develop the facility to grasp and think through new ideologies as they uncover them' (ibid., 736). One important feature of such education is the space it gives to controversies:

> To teach something as controversial is to present it as a matter on which different views are or could be held and to expound those different views as impartially as possible. It is to acknowledge and explore various possible answers to a question without endorsing any of them. The intended outcome of such teaching is, at least, that students should understand a range of views on a topic and the arguments in their support, and, at most, that they should hold and be able to defend considered views of their own; it is emphatically not that they should come to share the view favored by the teacher.
>
> Hand 2008, 213

If this 'multiperspectivity' (Sander 2004, 9) goes so far as to allow 'the "coming into presence" . . . of a way of being that had no place and no part in the existing order of things', it may lead to a process of political 'subjectivation' (Biesta 2011, 150); that is, a process that has some similarities with what is usually understood as *Bildung*. In this sense, *Bildung* refers to the process in which those world- and self-relations that have previously been handed down by parents and other socialization agents are transformed, based on the person's own judgements and practices (Nohl 2009; Koller 2011). In the American educational discourse, this is often referred to as 'transformative learning' (Mezirow 1978).

Political Bildung *in (West) Germany*

In the field of civic education in Germany, this second option, which I propose to call 'non-directive education', gained momentum in the 1970s. As is well known, civic education has played an important role in the history of twentieth-century Germany. The Third Reich era saw an indoctrinating political education by the ruling NSDAP, its youth organizations as well as by the public schools. After Germany's defeat and the occupation, the Allied Forces, both in East and West Germany, tried to 're-educate' the German people to turn it into a non-fascist society. Since the 1950s, the local authorities took back control over civic education. However, this did not imply that education in general and civic education, in particular, were structured homogeneously. In Germany, it is not the central federal government that is responsible for education but the Länder, the federal states. Despite a coordinating body among the federal states, each state has been autonomous in regulating its education policies. This has caused rivalry and competition between federal states. Another point of contention that emerged after the 1968 cultural and political uprising was the conflict between conservative and leftist activists and scholars of civic education.

In 1976, within this atmosphere of fierce discussions between leftists and conservatives as well as between the different federal states, run by leftist or conservative governments, core activists and scholars of civic education came together in a south-west German village called Beutelsbach. Apparently, the participants again had heated discussions. After the meeting, however, an assistant to the meeting's organizer, who was in charge of writing the minutes of the meeting, wrote down some memorable sentences. Admitting that his ideas were subjective and that the meeting did not serve to find a consensus on civic education, Hans-Georg Wehling outlined the most important points of a possible consensus beyond the discrepant 'political, scientific and pedagogical positions' of the participants. He wrote: 'Seemingly uncontradicted are three basic principles of political education':

> 1. Prohibition against overwhelming the pupil:
> It is not permissible to catch pupils unprepared or unaware – by whatever means – for the sake of imparting desirable opinions and to hinder them from 'forming an independent judgement'. It is precisely at this point that the dividing line runs between political education and indoctrination. [...]

2. Treating controversial subjects as controversial:
Matters which are controversial in intellectual and political affairs must also be taught as controversial in educational instruction. This demand is very closely linked with the first point above, for if differing points of view are lost sight of, options suppressed, and alternatives remain undiscussed, then the path to indoctrination is being trodden. [...]

3. Giving weight to the personal interests of pupils:
Pupils must be put in a position to analyze a political situation and to assess how their own personal interests are affected as well as to seek means and ways to influence the political situation they have identified according to their personal interests.

Wehling 2016, 24[2]

Although these three basic principles were not actually agreed upon in the meeting mentioned above, during the 1980s this so-called Beutelsbach Consensus became a milestone in German civic education. Its basic principles have since been almost synonymous with the concept of political *Bildung*. Indeed, the three basic principles and the respective concept of political *Bildung* have become so popular in West Germany, and later in the reunited Germany, that scholars and politicians tend to think that the German democracy refers only to political *Bildung*. In contrast, directive political education, in the sense of political *Erziehung*, turned into a concept that has only been used to describe political education in dictatorships and totalitarian regimes (such as the Nazi era or the German Democratic Republic), in which 'an existing socio-political state [...] is legitimized by political education in the interest of the power groups benefiting from it' (Sander 2005, 15). In such political education, 'youth is seen as an object' (Hafenegger 2010, 863). However, this is anything but correct. Even though the three basic principles structure a large part of civic education in Germany, there have always been phenomena that can be described as *Erziehung* (Nohl 2022). One of them is the directive mass education during the corona pandemic.

Mass education, Phase I: A means against the pandemic

In many of the countries severely affected by the Covid-19 pandemic, the authorities imposed curfews. In Northern Italy, from 8 March to 3 May 2020, no one was allowed to leave their homes without a valid reason. In Spain, a curfew was imposed from 13 March until 2 May 2020. In Turkey, on 22 March, all citizens under 20 or over 65 years of age were forbidden from entering the streets until further notice, and complete curfews were imposed repeatedly for the most populous provinces, which, for economic reasons, were limited to (long) weekends.

2. Translated by R. L. Cope, available at: https://www.lpb-bw.de/beutelsbacher-konsens (accessed 10 December 2020).

Anyone who wanted or had to leave their house needed written permission from the authorities, as was the case, for example, in Northern Italy.

In Germany, however, when the state governments responsible for disease control in that country's federal system, under the coordination of the federal chancellor, decided against a curfew and in favour of a ban on contact, they set the course for a concerted version of directive mass education, which started, as will be shown with a first phase. A curfew, as in the other states, could have been enforced to a large extent by the police, regardless of whether the people concerned are reasonable or not. However, the ban on physical proximity could hardly be enforced by punishment and threats alone.

Contact ban and mass education

Rather, the Länder governments were dependent on the people themselves being willing to keep their distance from each other. The political decisions, appeals and measures in the following weeks showed that Germany's then Chancellor Angela Merkel and the states' prime ministers did not leave this to chance or to the spontaneous insight of individuals. They relied on the 'mass education', in which the members of a society were 'pedagogically treated' (Prange and Strobel-Eisele 2015, 201), because – and this is the credo of every educator – willingness to act that does not come about of its own accord must be brought about actively. So, even though leaders may not have understood their actions as education themselves, their actions undoubtedly had educational features.

At the centre of the mass education efforts was the speech by Chancellor Angela Merkel on 18 March 2020. Its sole purpose was not only to oblige the country's citizens to keep physical distance, but to convince them that it was 'THEIR task' (capitalized in Merkel's speech manuscript) and in the citizens' own power to curb the speed at which the virus spreads. In this way, the citizens were not only expected to trust the expertise of virology and to massively restrict social life, but were also expected to have the courage to cope with the crisis themselves, because, as Merkel said, 'everyone counts':

> Let me talk now about what I believe is most urgent today. All measures taken by the state would come to nothing if we were to fail to use the most effective means for preventing the virus from spreading too rapidly – and that is we ourselves. As indiscriminately as each one of us can be affected by the virus, each and every one of us must help. First and foremost, by taking seriously what matters today. Not panicking, but also not thinking for a single moment that he or she doesn't matter after all. No one is expendable. Everyone counts, and we need a collective effort.[3]

3. Available at: https://www.bundesregierung.de/resource/blob/975232/1732182/d4af 29ba76f62f61f1320c32d39a7383/fernsehansprache-von-bundeskanzlerin-angela-merkel-data.pdf?download=1 (accessed 28 April 2020).

By appealing to insight, the chancellor's attempt at education was based on a specific conception of the human person, who is sovereign (that is, in principle, free to act), thinks rationally and is able to see the facts, and can act in solidarity. A video speech given two days earlier by Federal President Steinmeier reads very similarly, although it received less attention.[4] Unusually for education, both Steinmeier and Merkel refrained completely from threats of sanctions, but such threats were probably no longer necessary. The media had already made it clear to everyone how strict curfews (for example, in China) can be applied and how terrible it is when the epidemic (as in Italy, where the military transported the dead in trucks) is not stopped in time. Against the background of these deterrent scenarios, the ban on contact and the educational demands associated with it inevitably seemed to be the most bearable alternative.

Most of the time, educators try to convince individuals that it is in their own best interest to obey: to be careful at school, not to fight, or to eat less sweets. During the Covid-19 crisis, this only worked to a limited extent. A large part of the population, being young and healthy, hardly needed to fear the virus. These people were not supposed to act for their own benefit, but, according to Merkel, to act 'in a spirit of solidarity'. It was precisely this 'action in the spirit of solidarity', and not how to best protect oneself, that the educational efforts implied in this and other political speeches were aimed at.

Educational sanctions

Initially, Merkel relied on insight and probably convinced many people. However, as is always the case with education, not everyone is willing. Subsequently, the prime ministers of the federal states threatened punishment. Such punishment, and even its announcement, has an 'educational effect in the sense of general prevention', as Prange and Strobel-Eisele (2015, 208) emphasized. It is unknown

---

4. It says:

Sometimes reason requires drastic action. That is now the case. We must now change our everyday lives. Each and every one of us! Together we must ensure that the virus spreads as slowly as possible. So, wherever possible: stay at home! Avoid close contact. Look for and use other ways to communicate, to work, to be helpful to each other! And: Be understanding for all restrictive measures. They are necessary – please stick to them! Do not say: 'I am young and strong, I am not affected by this!' Say: 'Yes, I take responsibility! For my family, for parents and grandparents, for the old and weak. For my village and my city. For my country, I assure you: Your self-restraint today will save lives tomorrow'

Available at: https://www.bundesregierung.de/resource/blob/975954/1735780/7d585de 53fd7dd22df8e4e4f339c239c/39-1-bpr-coronakrise-data.pdf?download=1 (accessed 1 May 2020).

which intentions lead, in the following days, the press to report constantly about police controls and imposed fines. By doing so, however, they strengthened the threats of sanctions and helped in such a way that everyone took seriously and adopted the orientation the chancellor expected them to take.

The extent to which the media became a resonating space for mass education can be illustrated by two press articles. The German daily *Frankfurter Allgemeine Zeitung* of 27 April 2020, reported in detail about the funeral of an old woman. Funerals during Covid-19 times were difficult anyway, as only a few mourners were allowed to attend. However, the deceased was the mother of a man who was considered the patriarch of an 'extended family', notorious as an Arab 'clan' in Berlin. The fact that its members not only gathered by the hundreds immediately after the old lady's death and also at her funeral, but also did not observe the rules of distance, was mentioned by the newspaper in the same breath as the criminal offences of which these people were accused in general.[5] In this way, the disregard for the ban on contact was directly placed in the context of gang crime. Again, without insinuating a specific intention on part of the newspaper, this 'appeal to insight' was here 'underpinned by drastic descriptions of the misconduct' (Prange and Strobel-Eisele 2015, 208).

The preventive orientations imposed by these mass education efforts were also directly contoured against the background of (fictitious) counter-models. In the Berlin daily, *Tagesspiegel*, of 7 April 2020, a guest article appeared whose author argued that everyone should wear a mask and download a Covid-19 app to their smartphone. He also demanded that the leisure and professional activities of anyone who did not wish to submit to this commandment be further restricted, as they represented a 'special danger'. The newspaper subsequently headlined the article: 'Lockdown Yes – but Only for Dangerous Persons', and in this way moved all fellow mask- and app-averse fellow citizens into the proximity of Islamist terrorists, for whom the word 'dangerous persons – Gefährder' had been reserved until then.[6]

Non-directive education

The containment of the pandemic did not rely only on the lockdown and imposition of orientations. There were also several media formats within which the population was informed in understandable language about the scientific results, ongoing research, and advice from proven virologists and epidemiologists. For example, the public broadcaster, Norddeutscher Rundfunk, issued a regular podcast in which the head of the virology department at Berlin's university

5. See at: https://www.faz.net/2.1844/wie-ein-clan-in-corona-zeiten-eine-beerdigung-abhaelt-16744179.html (accessed 28 April 2020).

6. Available at: https://www.tagesspiegel.de/politik/menschen-mit-maske-und-app-sollten-raus-duerfen-lockdown-ja-aber-nur-fuer-gefaehrder/25719078.html (accessed 28 April 2020).

hospital, Charité, Christian Drosten, answered questions from a science journalist; this podcast made the professor a celebrity, but also gave the population important insights into how science was dealing with pandemic issues.

Numerous newspaper articles, interviews, television programmes and other media formats provided information on the pandemic. Some of these media services may have been imbued with orientation impositions; that is, *Erziehung*, but most also enabled interested recipients to form their own opinions about what was happening with the pandemic. To the extent that this took place, therefore, these instances of non-directive education offered opportunities for *Bildung* in the sense discussed above.

Educators' disagreement

However, the success of mass education is not only dependent on accompanying information (non-directive teaching or education) and threats of sanctions. It is also important that the educators themselves do not contradict each other. This is well known from 'Mum' and 'Dad', who sometimes let themselves be played off against each other when they revealed their own disagreement to the children. A similar situation emerged among the states' prime ministers. At the beginning of the Covid-19 crisis, there was a small competition among the prime ministers to see who could introduce the strictest bans the quickest. When the ban on contact then took effect, but increasingly caused problems for people and the economy, some prime ministers of the federal states tried to outdo each other in relaxation proposals. When Angela Merkel then warned against 'relaxation discussion orgies' – actually behind the closed doors of her Christian Democrat Union party's executive board, like an exclusive talk between parents – this may have had something to do with a TINA attitude of which she is sometimes accused.[7] Beyond this political dimension, however, this warning can be understood as an appeal to the unity of the educators. For as soon as the pupils – in this case, the entire population – sense that the educators are not (no longer) sure of their own cause, they not only look for further gaps – they also lose confidence in the educators and the orientation they are expected to follow.

The fatal success of pandemic containment

Despite some disagreement among the prime ministers of the German states and Chancellor Merkel, the lockdown and the accompanying directive mass education efforts turned out to be – at least temporarily – successful. Infection rates dropped and the hospitals that had previously cleared their wards for Covid-19 patients

7. TINA, 'There is no alternative', originally a 'bon mot' by Margaret Thatcher.

began to complain about empty beds. In their repeatedly convened video conferences, officials agreed to ease the measures starting in May 2020, with schools and daycare centres as well as retail stores set to reopen and restaurants and hotels to follow. The usual precautions – wearing masks, maintaining social distance, and hygiene rules – continued to apply, and were especially enforced in all enclosed areas open to the public (such as restaurants, governmental buildings and shops).

Because infection rates varied considerably from area to area, and because the states had actual control over pandemic measures anyway, it was agreed that a mechanism would be in place to provide a differentiated response to new Corona outbreaks: wherever more than 50 new cases per 100,000 population occurred in a county or city within seven days, local authorities were required to tighten pandemic measures.[8] As will be discussed below, this regionalization of pandemic control would turn out to be significant for mass education efforts as well.

However, the preliminary success of pandemic measures had a fatal consequence in that some people started to think that the pandemic was not as severe as expected. Moreover, many people began to question the previous lockdown as they saw the drop in infection rates caused by the increasing temperatures and the upcoming summer. As a result, individuals started to take the pandemic lightly and infection numbers increased again towards the end of the summer.

Mass education, Phase II: Authoritarian relationship, risk areas and collective sanctions

After the summer of 2020, some counties started to experience infection rates that exceeded 50 cases per 100,000 inhabitants per week. It was within these circumstances that a new, phase of mass education began, Phase II, which was more authoritarian and more connoted by negative sanctions and took a new mode. An incident in the Bavarian Alpine town of Garmisch-Partenkirchen exemplifies this new mode. On 11 September 2020, the Health Department of Garmisch-Partenkirchen attributed the increased number of Covid-19 cases to 'visits by highly infected persons to several bars'.[9] The district's press spokesman added that the bulk of the infections had been caused by a 26-year-old American woman, who,

---

8. This ratio was seen as the limit for both intensive care units and for the health departments' ability to trace each Corona infection. See the press conference by Angela Merkel on 6 May 2020, available at: [https://www.bundesregierung.de/breg-de/aktuelles/pressekonferenzen/pressekonferenz-von-bundeskanzlerin-merkel-ministerpraesident-soeder-und-dem-ersten-buergermeister-tschentscher-im-anschluss-an-das-gespraech-mit-den-regierungschefinnen-und-regierungschefs-der-laender-1751050 (accessed 11 December 2020).

9. Press communique of the county Garmisch-Partenkirchen of 11 September 2020.

despite having symptoms, had not adhered to the quarantine order after a vacation in Greece, and had enjoyed the German nightlife. Newspapers nationwide promptly ran the headline, 'Super-Spreader on Pub Crawl', almost in unison.[10]

A wave of outrage followed. Throughout Germany, the media reported for several days on the tightening of the Covid-19 measures in Garmisch-Partenkirchen and the cancellation of trips to this vacation region. Bavarian politicians also called for harsh punishment for the young woman. Bavaria's Prime Minister Markus Söder spoke of a 'model case for unreasonableness' and added: 'This recklessness must also have consequences,' and 'heavy fines' should be imposed.[11] The Munich public prosecutor's office immediately started investigations on suspicion of negligent bodily injury.

How did the health department and the press come to put the young woman, whose workplace, age, and nationality were made public, through the hell of public outrage? Among several other plausible explanatory factors, one cause is certainly politicians' use of directive mass education as a tool to keep the effects of the pandemic at bay. As shown in the previous section, the chancellor's 18 March 2020 speech can be interpreted as the launching event for this education campaign. In the crisis, it was imperative that everyone, no matter how strong their risk of falling ill, 'act in solidarity'. Angela Merkel urged citizens to trust the expertise of virologists and to massively restrict their social life. The important thing was that, as Merkel put it, 'everyone counts'.[12]

Superspreader

The fact that 'everyone counts' – that is, that everyone should act responsibly, keep their distance, wash their hands, and wear masks, took on a special meaning when the virologists introduced the term 'superspreaders' into the public discourse. They had discovered that not all infected persons were equally responsible for the spread of the virus, but that individuals could be particularly infectious. It was not

---

10. See at: https://www.sueddeutsche.de/bayern/garmisch-partenkirchen-corona-test-ergebnis-1.5032571 (accessed 30 November 2021); https://www.bild.de/news/inland/news-inland/garmisch-partenkirchen-corona-superspreaderin-legt-nachtleben-lahm-72867842.bild.html (accessed 30 November 2021); and https://www.faz.net/aktuell/gesellschaft/gesundheit/coronavirus/corona-infizierte-in-garmisch-partenkirchen-machen-nachtleben-unsicher-16949970.html (accessed 30 November 2021).

11. According to the German daily, *Süddeutsche Zeitung*, available at: https://www.sueddeutsche.de/politik/kabinett-garmisch-partenkirchen-soeder-leichtsinn-in-garmisch-muss-konsequenzen-haben-dpa.urn-newsml-dpa-com-20090101-200914-99-558366 (accessed 11 December 2020).

12. Available at: https://www.bundesregierung.de/resource/blob/975232/1732182/d4af29ba76f62f61f1320c32d39a7383/fernsehansprache-von-bundeskanzlerin-angela-merkel-data.pdf?download=1 (accessed 28 April 2020).

the masses that made the difference – the more people who complied with the rules, the fewer infections there were – but a single breach of the rules could have massive consequences. For example, anyone who disregarded the quarantine requirements, as a tightening of the distance requirement, could infect many people. Matthias Köpf, who commented on the situation in Garmisch-Partenkirchen in the South German daily, *Süddeutsche Zeitung*, referred to this as follows:

> It didn't take much for a region that had previously been fairly inconspicuous in the Corona pandemic to become a new hotspot overnight, as it were: a single person, who was apparently indifferent to the requirements of the Garmisch health department including a personal quarantine order, seems to have spread the virus among at least three dozen colleagues and revelers. Garmisch-Partenkirchen is therefore neither the second nor the twentieth Ischgl. And yet the case shows how quickly the virus can catch up with everyone and how important it is then to test as much as possible and deliver results quickly. Above all, however, the case shows that pandemic containment still depends on every individual.[13]

The last sentence of this quote subtly modified Merkel's statement that 'everyone counts' and emphasized the responsibility of the individual, who was then not only expected to comply with the rules, but also made personally responsible. This imposition of orientation, which obliged everyone to comply with the pandemic rules and to observe any quarantine imposed, was not only sanctioned by the fines threatened by the Bavarian prime minister. It was much more serious that an example was made of a single person with the media-staged outrage, in which the quality papers and public media also took part. From then on, anyone who violated the Covid-19 rules and, in particular, did not observe the quarantine requirements, should have to fear being publicly pilloried. The *Bild-Zeitung* even had no shame in mentioning the first name of the young American woman, who was described as a 'potential killer'[14] in a video report of this newspaper.[15]

The public outrage that was staged here, however, fell apart when, after a short time, several hundred people, mainly young people, in Garmisch-Partenkirchen had been tested, but only three cases of corona had been discovered, moreover not

13. Available at: https://www.sueddeutsche.de/bayern/garmisch-corona-kommentar-1.5030364 (accessed 12 December 2020). Ischgl is a small Alpine town in Austria, where many skiers became infected in the winter of 2020 and subsequently, upon their return home, spread the Covid-19 virus throughout Germany.

14. Available at: https://www.youtube.com/watch?v=S_gzCN9ImT8 (accessed 30 November 2021).

15. Available at: https://www.bild.de/bild-plus/regional/muenchen/muenchen-aktuell/corona-in-garmisch-us-army-ermittelt-gegen-superspreaderin-72934552,view=conversionToLogin.bild.html (accessed 30 November 2021).

even attributable to the young woman. However, the fact that citizens were now not only expected to comply with the Corona rules but would also be publicly reprimanded if they failed to do so, became engraved in the collective memory. Directive mass education took on an authoritarian character, which was also associated with the negative touch of harsh sanctions. For example, on 24 August 2020, Bavarian Prime Minister Markus Söder said, 'We must tighten the reins again, not loosen them,' referring to increased penalties for violating the mask requirement.[16] This choice of words, indicating an authoritarian relationship between politics and the population, was then frequently adopted by the media when they reported on the tightening of the Covid-19 measures.

Risk areas and collective sanctions

The sanctions that were threatened or exercised when people refused to comply with Corona rules did not apply only to individuals. Since the general lockdown was lifted in May 2020, a dynamic had developed that led to collective punishments. One can understand the end of the lockdown as a reward to all those who had previously allowed themselves to be educated to physical distancing. However, this directive education did not stop there; it only changed shape and took a new mode in this second phase. Most importantly, the agreement reached between the federal states on 6 May 2020, was relevant here (see above). If more than 50 new infections per 100,000 inhabitants were reported in a county or city within a week, measures to contain the pandemic should be taken locally again. Furthermore, similar to distant countries with high infection rates or ailing healthcare systems, these administrative districts were also declared 'risk areas' or, as the media referred to them, 'hotspots'.

The dynamics that unfolded with the designation of risk areas became clear when, in mid-June, the infection figures at the Tönnies meat products factory in the small town of Rheda-Wiedenbrück rose to such an extent that the agreed limit was exceeded in the county surrounding it. The factory, and with it the county, became known in the media as a 'hotspot'. Schools and daycare centers were closed and travellers from the county had to fear that they would no longer be able to find accommodation in hotels elsewhere. Those affected gave vent to their anger at Tönnies.

In terms of mass education to comply with the Covid-19 rules, the introduction of the 'risk areas' created a serious difference. Previously, individuals had been asked to practice physical distancing and had to fear falling ill if they did not comply. However, the collective consequences remained quite abstract and were hidden behind ratios such as 'R-values' and 'active cases'. Even if the appeal had

16. See at: https://www.donaukurier.de/nachrichten/bayern/Soeder-will-in-Coronakrise-Zuegel-anziehen;art155371,4668734 (accessed 14 December 2020).

continued to address individuals since 6 May, the consequences of possible misconduct since then had neither been only individual nor only abstract. For, wherever a 'superspreader' infected others in his or her vicinity, everyone living in that circle had to endure the consequences: daycare and school closures, restrictions on freedom of assembly or shortened opening hours of restaurants.

A similar mechanism was also found on a smaller scale: if a Covid-19 case occurred in a school class or daycare group, perhaps because someone had been careless and had not adhered to the Covid-19 rules, the whole group had to suffer. A period of quarantine was in store, which also had negative consequences for parents and families, not to mention the risks of contracting the disease. But the individual who was said to have 'caused' this was shamed.

The emergence of co-educators

The fact that not only the individual but the whole group (or even all inhabitants of a county) experienced disadvantages because individuals did not adhere to the Covid-19 rules made all fellow human beings potential co-educators.[17] This concept requires some explanation. Initially, only the politicians required the population to adopt certain orientations (Covid-19 rules). Very early on, however, it could be observed that the mass media reinforced these orientational impositions (and threats of sanctions) through their reporting (see above); that is, they became co-educators, even if they probably did not see themselves that way. At that time, however, these (co-)educators, as mass media outlets, remained abstract. One could ignore them and was not exposed to their gaze.

However, at the moment when it was in the immediate interest of all that everyone adhered to the Covid-19 rules, each person got into the position of the one who could legitimately educate the other. It was not an abstract rule that had to be observed, but the concern about being able to send one's child to school the following week or to keep one's job at a hotel, that motivated and legitimized people to demand that others observe the rules. Thus, it came about that the individual, as a member of a sanctionable collective (county, school class) and therefore out of self-interest, did the work that previously only politicians had done. Whether intentionally or not, the quarantine rules (such as for school classes) and the 50-case rule for counties somewhat closed the large gap that existed between the educating politicians and the more or less educable population. However, the question is whether this was a positive development, especially since mass education in this second phase had acquired a more authoritarian character and the connotation of negative sanctions.

17. For the term, 'co-educator', see Nohl and Pusch (2017).

Mass education, Phase III: The end of Erziehung?

When the number of cases rose even higher in October 2020 (for example, 4,000 new infections were recorded throughout Germany on 7 October 2020), the prime ministers of the states met again with the chancellor to decide on further measures. Although an agreement was reached on a slight tightening of the measures, Angela Merkel was dissatisfied with the compromise as she, unusually, had it launched in public. It may have played a role in the prime ministers' hesitation that their states, as well as individual counties, were very differently affected by the pandemic; in some places, the incidence had risen above the 50-cases mark, while in others there were almost no cases. Be that as it may, the chancellor felt compelled to address the population directly in view of the hesitancy of the heads of the federal states. On 17 October 2020, she released a video message calling on people to make greater efforts to combat the pandemic. At the beginning of the video, she informed her viewers about the skyrocketing number of cases and the danger of the pandemic getting out of control. But then she directed her appeal to the entire population:

> So what can each and every one of us do to help bring the numbers back down? A great deal, most of it simply by ensuring that every one of us consistently keeps the minimum distance, wears mouth and nose protection, and adheres to hygiene rules. But we must now go even further: Science tells us clearly: the spread of the virus is directly linked to the number of contacts, of encounters, that each of us has. If each of us now significantly reduces our encounters outside our own family for a while, we can succeed in stopping and reversing the trend toward more and more infections. That is precisely my appeal to you today: meet significantly fewer people, whether outside or at home.[18]

These words echoed the most important calls for action that had already been made by politicians to the population since the beginning of the Covid-19 pandemic, not least by Merkel herself, for example, in her televised address on 18 March 2020. As if this were not enough, the chancellor had the same clip repeated a week later for her next Saturday video message. On the one hand, this again made it evident that the imposition of orientation contained in the chancellor's words – reduce contact, wear a mask, keep your distance – was not only uttered once but was sustainable. On the other hand, the renewed broadcast of the video showed that the political actors did not modify their appeals to the public, but constantly repeated the same imposition of orientation. With this repetition, however, directive mass education changed its significance and again took a new mode, because an appeal gains a new meaning when it is voiced several times to the same public. If everyone already knew what the Covid-19 rules were, then

18. See at: https://www.bundeskanzlerin.de/resource/blob/822020/1799280/5f77200169 a30cbe36a3d582da61382d/2020-10-17-video-podcast-download-pdf-data.pdf   (accessed 19 October 10.2020).

their repetition could only have the purpose of reacting to the insubordination of the population. Hence, the appeal to the public turned from a friendly invitation to an angry rebuke.

However, the effect of this third phase and mode of mass education remained limited from the outset. Far from reducing the number of infections, Merkel's appeal could not even limit their increase. One can only speculate about the reasons for the lack of effectiveness of this educational effort. First, there was confusion about each state's corona policy and situation. Although the coronavirus had spread throughout the population, some states still had relatively low numbers of cases, as well as those in which several counties had been declared risk areas at once. Accordingly, the heads of the states appeared as Covid-19 hardliners or as politicians with an ear for the concerns of the business community and the common man. Second, a relatively small but vocal protest movement had formed over the summer, which, under the title of 'Querdenker' ('lateral thinkers'), not only condemned the Covid-19 measures taken by political leaders (and those leaders themselves along with them), but also downplayed the danger of the coronavirus or made it the subject of conspiracy narratives.[19] Third, it is possible that the simple repetition of educational messages, especially in the face of rising pandemic fatigue, not only led to their ineffectiveness, but also provoked reluctance and protest. I will return to this point.

As the number of new infections grew exponentially, on 28 October 2020 – a day when 16,000 new infections were reported in Germany – state premiers were finally ready to agree to at least a partial lockdown, closing restaurants, bars and overnight accommodations again. Those who hoped that this would break the second wave of the pandemic were soon disappointed. Although the increase in the number of infections slowed, it could not be stopped. Not only had control over the pandemic (such as tracking chains of infection) been completely lost, but hospitals were on the verge of collapse. In this situation, it was decided on 13 December 2020 to impose a strict lockdown from 16 December 2020 until at least 10 January 2021. This lockdown implied not only the closure of schools and daycare centers and all non-essential retail businesses, but also imposed an absolute ban on the consumption of alcohol in public as well as curfews in some cases. These developments can be interpreted in two ways. On the one hand, one could argue that politicians no longer trusted directive mass education and instead relied on coercive measures when they replaced educational prompts with legal regulations. According to this interpretation, the mass education that had been set in motion by political actors since the beginning of the Covid-19 pandemic would have come to an end. On the other hand, the restrictive measures taken can be seen as an intensified form of negative sanctions. According to this interpretation, the failure of education would not have been caused by the appeal (the imposition of orientation) itself, but by the insufficient threat that had consequently to be

19. This protest movement was able to network and publish its ideas on social media. In general, social media played an important role during the Covid-19 pandemic, a point that I cannot inquire into here.

intensified. As this chapter was written at the end of December 2020, it remains unclear which of these two interpretations will prove to be most appropriate.

Some critical reflections on mass education in the corona pandemic

Although the Covid-19 pandemic has not yet ended, I wish to reflect critically on the three successive phases and modes of directive mass education outlined in this chapter. Of course, it is impossible to determine whether mass education in the Corona pandemic was successful or not. First, there are no clear criteria for such an evaluation (what percentage of the population would have to have internalized the imposed orientations to promise success?). Second, there are no empirical data to measure the extent to which these criteria were met. However, mass education can be critically discussed in other respects. In doing so, I would like to progress from an immanent critique to the question of whether it is legitimate to rely on directive mass education in a democracy at all.

The appeals of the political leaders had an educational quality, but they were not pedagogically reflected, and the politicians may not even have defined their doings as education. A pedagogical reflection of mass education might have made it possible to avoid the dead ends into which the politicians obviously fell, as elaborated in this chapter. It could also have helped to enter into a differentiated pedagogical communication with the population. Dead ends of the present mass education and possible alternatives become apparent at least in five points.[20]

First, the regionalization of pandemic response, the declaration of risk areas, and the threat of collective sanctions in the second phase of mass education led to the interposition of other actors who acted as co-educators between the government and the population. However, these co-educators (including the mass media) acted primarily with admonitions and shaming, which only reinforced the sanctions component of mass education. Instead, it might have been a good idea to involve local civil society actors (NGOs) in the pandemic response and to use their creativity, not only to make compliance with the Covid-19 rules palatable to the population, but also to facilitate it in everyday life.

Second, some politicians tended to blame the population for failures in pandemic control.[21] Even though they may have been correct in their theses (no

20. Important for this critique and the implied development of alternatives, are several ad hoc reports that, while not specifically addressing educational issues, generate ideas on how to create greater acceptance of Covid-19 containment beyond current strategies. See, among others, WHO-EURO (2020) and Schrappe et al. (2020).

21. A prominent example of this is the prime minister of Saxony, who spoke in a nationally televised interview about the need to 'counter the stultification in this country', although he himself had repeatedly downplayed the danger and need for drastic measures; available at: https://www.zdf.de/nachrichten/politik/corona-interview-michael-kretschmer-heute-journal-100.html (accessed 14 December 2020).

judgement will be made here), this put the population in the situation of being considered badly educated or uneducable. In this way, the entire political communication on Covid-19 took on a negative touch, so that even successful attempts to connote compliance with Covid-19 rules positively[22] were overshadowed by this.

Third, more could have been done to stage the orientation impositions associated with directive mass education in a way that is specific to the respective target group. Even if the imposed orientations were largely the same, they could be formulated and visually staged in a language specific to the respective target group (young people vs adults, students vs families, seniors vs children).[23]

Fourth, during the Corona pandemic, and especially in the third phase of mass education, politicians tended to repeat their messages, including their appeals to the people that they changed their behavior. For the communication of political ideas and opinions, this might be a good strategy, but in educational matters this is not necessarily the case. The same words that were addressed to the population at the beginning of a pandemic took on a completely different meaning in the second wave. If it was, at the beginning, still an invitation to do the right thing, the repetition became a reminder or even an implicit rebuke.

Fifth, although directive education, including mass education, is always based on an asymmetrical relationship between the educators and the educated, it seems necessary to avoid letting this asymmetry turn into an authoritarian relationship, especially with regard to adults. This is important precisely because an imposition of orientation ultimately threatens to curtail the autonomy of adults. In the Covid-19 pandemic, however, phrases such as 'tighten the reins' were sometimes used that could easily be interpreted as an outgrowth of an authoritarian attitude.

The fact that politicians, through directive mass education, adopted an authoritarian attitude toward the population leads me to a more examinant criticism. The question is whether directive (mass) education is a suitable means for democracy to bring about the willingness to act in the population. As I have suggested above, it may be tempting for politicians to become authoritarian in the course of directive mass education, even though they operate in a democracy. In some circumstances, directive education itself, without the participants explicitly

22. For example, slogans such as, 'We keep our distance together,' or, 'The good news: Solidarity is contagious, too,' that were published by the Berlin city government were intended to use irony and puns to help people avoid viewing the rule of distance and the wearing of masks as an imposition, but as part of a positive, relaxed lifestyle. See at: https://www.berlin.de/rbmskzl/aktuelles/pressemitteilungen/pressemitteilung.919242.php (accessed 1 May 2020).

23. One, albeit very isolated, attempt by the Federal Press Office to reach young people was to publish irony-soaked video spots, in which older people in the year 2070 look back on the 'dangerous times' of their youth, in which they had become 'heroes' by doing only one thing: 'nothing' except sitting around at home. See at: https://www.youtube.com/watch?v=EJvPEUSp6cc (accessed 14 December 2020).

wanting it, has this tendency toward authoritarianism. It is precisely for this reason that it is so important that a democracy not only prefers to *describe* itself in terms of *Bildung*, but actually fosters the practice of *Bildung* (see above). *Bildung* that emphasizes the controversial always undermines any authoritarianism.

A first step towards getting out of the momentum of directive mass education could be to publicly discuss its limits and necessity. Such a discussion can become the starting signal for political *Bildung* because political *Bildung*, and democracy in general, thrives on the controversy of opinions, including on how to deal with the coronavirus crisis. Not only having different political views but discussing these differences of opinion controversially and publicly creates opportunities for all people to develop their own attitude to the question of how we want to live together with and after corona. In this sense, political *Bildung* encourages the independent development and change of political orientations on the basis of the controversial exchange about different political options. Directive education in the sense of *Erziehung* may sometimes be a necessary and exceptional evil in extraordinary times, but political *Bildung* is and should be the normality of democratic societies.

References

Biesta, Gert (2011) 'The ignorant citizen: Mouffe, Rancière, and the subject of democratic education', *Studies in Philosophy and Education*, 30 (2): 141–53.

Brezinka, Wolfgang (1992) *Philosophy of Educational Knowledge* (Dordrecht: Kluwer).

Brighouse, Harry (1998) 'Civic education and liberal legitimacy', *Ethics*, 108 (4): 719–45.

Fernández, Christian and Mikael Sundström (2011) 'Citizenship education and liberalism: A state of the debate analysis 1990–2010', *Studies in the Philosophy of Education*, 30: 363–84.

Hafenegger, Benno (2010) 'Politische Bildung', in R. Tippelt and B. Schmidt (eds), *Handbuch Bildungsforschung* (Wiesbaden: VS Verlag), 861–79.

Hand, Michael (2008) 'What should we teach as controversial? A defence of the epistemic criterion', *Educational Theory*, 58 (2): 213–28.

Koller, Hans-Cristof (2011) 'The research of transformational education processes: Exemplary considerations on the relation of the philosophy of education and educational research', *European Educational Research Journal*, 10 (3): 375–82.

Mezirow, Jack (1978) 'Perspective transformation', *Adult Education Quarterly*, 28 (2): 100–10.

Nohl, Arnd-Michael (2009) 'Spontaneous action and transformative learning – Empirical investigations and pragmatist reflections', *Educational Philosophy and Theory*, 41 (3): 287–306.

Nohl, Arnd-Michael (2020) 'Politische Erziehung – Ein blinder Fleck der Diskussion zur politischen Bildung', in I. van Ackeren, H. Bremer, F. Kessl, H.-C. Koller, N. Pfaff, C. Rotter, D. Klein and U. Salaschek (eds), *Bewegungen. Beiträge zum 26. Kongress der DGfE* (Opladen: Budrich) 161–71.

Nohl, Arnd-Michael (2022) 'Orientierungszumutungen für Erwachsene (Wiesbaden: Springer VS).

Nohl, Arnd-Michael and B. Pusch (2017) '"Wir schaffen das": Politische Erziehung im Zuge der CDU-Flüchtlingswende 2015', *Vierteljahresschrift für wissenschaftliche Pädagogik*, 93 (3): 324–44.

Prange, Klaus and Gabriele Strobel-Eisele (2015) *Die Formen des pädagogischen Handelns* (Stuttgart: Kohlhammer).

Sander, Wolfgang (2004) 'Incitement to freedom: Competencies of political education in a world of difference', *Development Education Journal*, 11 (1): 9–11.

Sander, Wolfgang (2005) 'Theorie der politischen Bildung: Geschichte-Didaktische Konzeptionen – Aktuelle Tendenzen und Probleme', in W. Sander (ed.), *Handbuch politische Bildung* (Schwalbach: Wochenschau Verlag), 13–47.

Schrappe, M., H. François-Kettner, M. Gruhl, D. Hart, H. Knieps, P. Manow, H. Pfaff, K. Püschel and G. Glaeske (2020) 'Thesenpapier 4.1 zur Pandemie durch SARS-CoV-2/ Covid-19: Der Übergang zur chronischen Phase', *Monitor Versorgungsforschung*, 05/20: 35–68. DOI: http://doi.org/10.24945/MVF.05.20.1866-0533.2253.

Wehling, Hans-Georg (2016) 'Konsens à la Beutelsbach? Nachlese zu einem Expertengespräch', in B. Widmaier and P. Zorn (eds), *Brauchen wir den Beutelsbacher Konsens? Eine Debatte der politischen Bildung* (Bonn: BPB), 19–27.

World Health Organization – Regional Office for Europe (WHO-EURO) (2020) *Pandemic Fatigue: Reinvigorating the Public to Prevent COVID-19* (Copenhagen: WHO Regional Office for Europe).

Chapter 11

THE AGENDA OF CRITICAL PEDAGOGY DURING THE COVID-19 PANDEMIC IN TURKEY

Fevziye Sayılan and Zeynep Alica

The economic crisis, environmental-climate crisis, political crises are merging with the pandemic crisis and getting deeper. This brings about a fundamental change in the social, political and educational world to which we have become accustomed. When we look at the last thirty years under the full hegemonic domination of neoliberal globalization, the dystopian, discordant opera of capitalism (natural disasters, destructions, war, riots, military interventions) has expanded its repertory even more.[1] Misery, poverty, unemployment, war and climate migrations, all sorts of evils were on the stage with garish new costumes. Hence, the pandemic gave a new meaning to the idea of 'disaster capitalism'.[2] The pandemic brought the darkness in the heart of capitalism to the surface. The profound inequalities it has created have become visible, we are witnessing the rapidly expanding circle of desperate people, simply not able to meet their families' basic needs. In this chapter, we are going to analyse how, in Turkey, the public education service, which has already been weakened by neoliberal education policies for long years, has slid into a deep crisis due to the Covid-19 pandemic.

The humanitarian crisis is intensified by privatization in basic public services (such as education, health, housing) and how the call to 'stay at home' works within class grounds and class division, unequally and unfairly. For 'the stay at

1. Immanuel Wallerstein, *Bildiğimiz Dünyanın Sonu: Yirmi Birinci Yüzyılın Sosyal Bilimi*, Çev. Tuncay Birkan (Istanbul: Metis Yayınları, 2016), 9; ibid., *The End of the World as We Know It: Social Science for the Twenty-First Century* (Minneapolis, MN: University of Minnesota Press).

2. Nancy Fraser, 'Taking care of each other is essential work', 2020, available at: https://www.vice.com/en/article/jge39g/taking-care-of-each-other-is-essential-work (accessed 12 September 2020). Within this talk, there is a reference to the 'disaster capitalism' idea, which has been developed by Naomi Klein. See Klein, *The Shock Doctrine: The Rise of Disaster Capitalism* (New York: Metropolitan Books, 2007).

home' comfort of some, the ruling classes sacrifice labourers' lives which should be sacrificed in their service and in service to the virus. Governments use this epidemic situation for their own interest and to maintain the hegemony of capital, to whom the resources are lavished. The class consequences of these economic measures that function to keep capital alive have all become clear during this period. All the measures taken against the pandemic opt for the death of the citizen without regard and for the profiteers, capital on a global scale. Not only in employment, but finance capitalists continue press the rentier class, demanding loan payments, forgoing rent forgiveness toward and forclosure and homelessness. Employers are threatened by big financiers, placing workers in industrialized sectors and small business markets on a collision course, effectively ending working- and middle-class dreams.

States, schools and rising authoritarianism

With these conditions of multiple and interwoven crises, Western-style democracy is itself in crisis as well. State after state has fallen to radical rightist, neofascist totalitarian rule, and no nation is exempt from the rising power of neo-fascist parties and fascistic influences bending the will of established parties. Capitalist democracy is an oxymoron in any case, but the expected redress and critique which bring about change are too often met by outright rejection if not negotiation, by force. Fundamental rights and freedoms are being curtailed. Customary means of protest in country after country are being limited by decree, not due process of law. Authoritarian processes feed off increasing political polarisation, and are deepening those fascistic measures which are on the agenda to shock, terrify and to misdirect the masses, who despite the expansion of communication technologies, fall prey to even more confusion, constantly fearful, even paranoid, and increasingly suspicious.

As it has done in previous crises, capitalism seems again to have a 'mind' of its own, planning and managing the production system with the support of technology. Used to prop up present and future profits, capitalists compete to exploit. Driving down their wage bill, automation gains momentum used with packages like Industry 4, and more smart factories without workers are on the agenda, indeed, here in reality, with market transfer centres that cover square kilometres, some operating with less than fifty workers. Robotics extend into every level of production and distribution. Trucks without drivers will soon be turning onto a road near you. Training and learning packages adapted to this production system are needed. Tele-working is presented as a great thing for professional jobs and new jobs in the IT sector. In other words, education and training systems are going to be adapted to the change in labour processes and the organization of work in the upcoming period. Rising antidemocratic and authoritarian tendencies reinforce control, blunting critique and intimidating critics.

It seems the system no longer needs nor desires the mass education ideal that was shaped during the modern age, where liberal education, inspired by

Enlightenment principles, has played such a role raising citizens and empowering the wisdom needed for useful democratic citizenship. Under the lifelong learning strategy in developed capitalist countries, school/education and training systems have undergone a significant transformation. The commercialization of education, knowledge and learning and increasingly the individualization of learning has become the norm. The primary function of education and training systems has been reduced to offering modular 'skill sets' appropriate for the individual's role in production and reproduction processes. Thus, the separation of academic and practical knowledge from each other was realized. As such, the learning cosmos is organized by algorithms and based on preprogrammed protocols. It is both run and designed 'on the run', by artificial intelligence without students and teachers, or with students and teachers playing only supporting roles. It is a learning world, where the teacher and the learner are robotized, and this dystopian vision is no longer in the future.

Thus, the ruling classes, who took advantage of the pandemic, took a significant stride toward individualizing learning through distance education. This situation has played an important role in reducing education spending, which is seen as a great burden, through diploma/certification that bypasses school systems via distant education.

Education in the distance

The subject of distance education has been heated by debate and kept alive throughout the neoliberal era. The ground has been laid for the transition to teaching from home in order to 'bring learning closer to learners' and 'individualize learning'. In Turkey, the 'New Conservatives', especially, have kept on the agenda, the question of how the possibilities offered by technology provide a financial incentive for popularizing education from home. Raising conservative, docile and merely 'skilled' children and youth turned against liberation opportunities and the socialization and liberalization offered by school.

Thus, the public education service, weakened by the neoliberal education policies implemented for forty years, has been dragged into a severe crisis, along with the pandemic. Despite recent privatization and commercialization of schooling, basic and secondary education in Turkey are still mainly presented as public service broadly, with the overall growth and development of all citizens, toward a free and fair access to that schooling process leading to all walks of life as scholars, medical, technical and businesspersons, civil servants, etc. Underpinning this is the constitutional ideal of fairness of opportunity, despite family circumstances. While this ideal has always been a goal worth reaching, now the distance education system (EBA), tragically, as organized by Ministry of National Education (MoNe) has excluded the children most in need of education. Too often, they and their families simply do not have the appropriate technology infrastructure to participate in the system. Astoundingly, approximately 40 percent of children and young people cannot make use of the system today.

In Turkey, where poverty and unemployment are serious and extensive, many families do not have adequate equipment, computer-server access, adequate computers, adaptable televisions and smartphones to even reach online teaching facilities, much less reach them flexibly and adequately. The state MoNe initiative to open local technology tries to compensate for this, but is not working successfully and cannot reach entire age cohorts of students.[3] Therefore, the already chronic education inequalities are deepened in this failed process. We are also seeing that female students are disproportionately affected, and are simply abandoning the education system in large numbers.

Just like the developed world in general, political power in Turkey (AKP) interlocked with university managements everywhere and are all too enthusiastic about moving education to online platforms. Dividing the curriculum into 'modules' and making it functionally inseparable from market demands was a substantial line item on the neoliberal agenda, and the pandemic provided the opportunity to implement this. In many universities, there is feverish excitement from managerial quarters about continuing education online from now on, and this is especially true in, of all places, the field of Social Sciences, where the education profession itself is developed.

Of course, in a society free from exploitation and alienation, teaching from home could have a function as one of the types of learning. But we are very far away from this. Unfortunately, not everyone has the opportunity to learn from home, and recent United Nations Children's Fund (UNICEF) data shows that thousands of children and young people around the world are excluded from the system during the distance education process, because millions of children on earth live without basic education and social services.[4]

Critical educator itself was developed as a response to the anti-democratic manifestations of mass compulsory education. We know that reinforcing the competitive environment in schooling is essential to capitalist ideology and has always been a part of the structural foundation of public education. Even in this crisis, its relentless hegemonic processes must not be interrupted, not even to accommodate this sudden critical global crisis. The poor certainly, and many of the struggling working classes with marginal incomes and/or living in marginalized areas, are sacrificed. No thought that would slow or delay the requirements for school-grade success can be considered. For this would shed light on other ways that capitalist competition, might be inconveniently interrupted – by humanity.

3. EĞİTİM SEN (Education and Science Workers Union), 2017, 'Salgın Günlerinde Uzaktan Eğitim Raporu', (Distance Education Report during Pandemic in Turkey), September 2020, available at: https://egitimsen.org.tr/egitim-sen-uzaktan-egitim-calistayi-sonuc-raporu/ (accessed 23 August 2021).

4. UNICEF, 'How many children and youth have internet access at home?', 2020, available at: https://www.unicef.org/press-releases/two-thirds-worlds-school-age-children-have-no-internet-access-home-new-unicef-itu (accessed December 2020).

Monopoly capitalists in the lead

High-tech teaching is marketed by tech monopolies such as telephone companies and online platform providers, which have interlocked their business models. The transition to distance education has been thus accelerated as a competitive profit leader, through the intensified commercialization and marketization of 'digitized' education. The learning and knowing processes of the technology monopolies in the communication and information sector have gained new positions of influence and their control has increased. Their influence in capitalist political-economic linkages is not new, only new in the sense that, without effective critics, or with critics effectively silenced in the upcoming period, the consolidation and dependence of education services on this monopoly capitalist control, can only increase.

There are not a large number of competitors, for this is how monopoly capitalists deal with competition. They eliminate it not by defeating but by absorbing competitors. This process of consolidation has led to gargantuan information companies with platforms that touch every aspect of human communication and operate in thousands of nations. McGraw-Hill Global has offices in 53 countries, but the largest, Pearson Education, operates in more than 80 countries, including Turkey. With 40,000 global employees, it is a leader in prepackaged, technologically mediated education. On their Pearson Türkiye website, you can: '*Meet Pearson Kariyer Akademisi, Turkey's new career preparation platform! Get your students the skills they need in business early with Pearson Career Academy!*'[5]

In order to expand power and influence, politicians are getting into the education market. Political power is setting new agendas, especially at the higher education level. The recent draft on restructuring of universities includes on the agenda, a 'board of trustees' model that allows the inclusion of non-university actors in university administrations. We know that behind this model is the drive to turn the university into a mere commercial enterprise, evidenced by the trend toward making representatives of the business world, not just advisors, but actual full members of university management. Similarly, the MoNe-authored, *Secondary Education Reform Draft*, prepared in 2019, aims to regulate the transition from certification to its system. According to this draft, the student will be able to complete some of his/her courses by obtaining a certificate from private institutions, not from the school they attend. The longer the impact of the pandemic, the more likely this draft will be put into practice.

Public education: Religionized

Another problem that comes to the fore within pandemic conditions is related to the gradually expanding 'religionization' of education (Islamization). In approved

---

5. Kariyer Akademisi Pearson Türkiye, 2020, available at: www.mheducation.com (accessed 18 October 2020).

educational materials and textbooks and course content, at the level of basic and secondary education, and extracurricular education, propaganda derived from religious knowledge and religious figures, feature greatly. The distance-education process has largely limited the initiative of teachers on the course contents and made the lessons open to central intervention. Thus, academic freedom, such as it has existed, if in modulated forms, deteriorates further.

At the same time, public adult education and public education are being used for the Islamization process. Presidency of Religious Affairs (PRA), especially, and the ministries of family, youth and culture are working hard to rearrange the reference frame of the society, religionized where, for example, under the pandemic, the Ministry of Youth organized 24,000 religious workshops.[6] These workshops created an environment for the spread of attitudes empowering fallacy and superstition to diminish the importance of scientific, medically advised protections, needed to slow the pandemic in Turkey.

The way forward

In such times, where should we critical educators begin? First, we can start by defining the crisis within its concrete context. The second step should be related to the production and circulation of empowering knowledge. We are facing a crisis situation, where knowledge, skills and habits that we have known and have been using until now, are being radically endangered. For years now, at least since the early 1980s, we have been analysing how education, pedagogy and the modern school system fell under the spell of neoliberal philosophy, and the 'commonwealth' ideal of public education, which emphasized access, and public interest, was replaced by a philosophy of social Darwinist cruelty, where freedom was redefined as expanded freedom to exploit the public fund to line the pockets of those already privileged. Now the crisis of pedagogy and school policy is deformed further. Now, because of this epidemic, we see that the world we used to know is rapidly changing its shape and entering a new phase. It seems now that capitalism will continue on the route embodied in, and conditioned by, pandemic conditions, and education and school systems are adapting to this huge change. It is being restructured in ways that turn young dreamers into accident victims.

The tight link between the needs of capitalism and the school system is being restructured during this period. This is a route with exploitation, not enlightenment, nor human emancipation, at its heart. Education and training systems that have

---

6. Presidency of Religious Affairs (PRA, Diyanet) has its own budget, which covers formal religious affairs within the country. According to the budget organization for the year 2021, the Diyanet is going to get 12 billion, 977 million Turkish liras, which exceeds the budget of seven other ministries, including the Ministry of Foreign Affairs and Ministry of Internal Affairs; available at: https://www.birgun.net/haber/diyanet-in-2020-butcesi-sekiz-bakanligi-geride-birakti-273683 (accessed 10 September 2020).

been restructured, step by step, during the long neoliberal period, are opening up and exploiting these more radical changes.

An educator should be able to recognize the social, political and pedagogical character of such crises, evaluate the crisis in its socioeconomic and historical context, and proceed by accepting that everything that is social is the subject of pedagogy. Therefore, the teacher that has been reduced to the technician needs to be reoriented with social sensitivity and perspective. We have to evaluate all the possibilities (including lectures and courses) of critical educators to share and circulate/increase the knowledge of reality. We have to use the means and possibilities we have in order to grasp the anatomy of this crisis correctly, to see how humanity itself is endangered by this changing structural crisis of capitalism. Both the environment-climate crisis and pandemic crisis interlock and possibilities emerge for educators to teach, communicate, counsel and write to create collective awareness on these issues.

Left unmediated by humane and principled educators and public officials, the managers of education systems and programmes have always preferred to remain indifferent to life and death, crisis and social problems, as if these were not the role of education. The human task of Critical Pedagogy is to help redirect minds to comprehend, feel and fight indifference. The neoliberal education curriculum generally excluded social and natural disaster and crises from education programmes. The will and means to incorporate such inclusion are not easy to find, but find them we must, for the sake of the youth and the future. Unfortunately understanding and coping with the crises are not among the twenty-first-century skills of the OECD. In line with the demands of the market, skills for training semi-qualified workers and entrepreneurial citizens come to the fore. Technology adaptation, communication and entrepreneurship, language skills and skills are for the survival of the 'conservative family'.

Therefore, as teachers and educators, we have to create discourses and content that will enable all learners, children, young adults, to see the dark side of this form of life in capitalism. We need to reflect and encourage new skills and new energy dedicated to this critical viewpoint. In order to realize this, we need to start by accepting that spreading the correct knowledge of reality is empowering information for everyone. There is a need for information about all that will strengthen all of us, including all the oppressed. It is necessary to decipher how religious discourses are used to cover up the system's inadequacy; cruelly requiring pledges of piety in exchange for basic services. We need to demonstrate how such discourses are used to justify people living in bad conditions, passively accepting life and death as fate, undermining science-based policy which supports the protection and survival from this world pandemic. Accurate and real information is vital in this regard.

Education must proceed from a line that supports life. We have to defend life against discourses where 'destiny', 'fate', 'will of God' explain away suffering, and that lead society to submission when scientific principles and policies offer not just hope but successfully attack the biological causes of disease, and the social causes and effects of increasing inequality. At the same time, most of the publications by the cultural industry and the official media intend to steer society, offering a 'secular' diversion, saying, 'this is an occasional situation', to hide from scrutiny how unfair and brutal the capitalist consumerist civilization we live in is. The fact that destruction and poverty are systemic problems, and global, and such mass epidemics will go on spreading within these problems, is being hidden. It is essential to grow critical knowledge around this, critical knowledge of the world and of what is happening all around us, without evasions.

Another significant point is that the political Islamist AKP does not claim responsibility for the pandemic crisis. He pushes the pandemic crisis, deepened by poverty and unemployment, to the area of personal responsibility. If you get sick or die, they say, 'You are responsible, you do not stay at home, you do not wear a mask, you have no idea about distance.' Yet, another discourse works to hide the government's own inadequacy by directing mass discontent, anger and wrath toward the senior citizen, under the pretext of protecting the elderly. The current government hopes to calm the reaction of the masses by providing incomplete and incorrect information about the pandemic. Therefore, empowering knowledge should start with making visible and sharing the knowledge of this reality. That is the knowledge of the whole universal content. It is also vital to create practical agendas about what we will do to survive accordingly. We imagine a horror thriller on a planetary scale, yet children, youth and the wider society can overcome this situation with the help of real knowledge. Thus, in order to overcome fear, anxiety and alienation, community consciousness and solidarity are needed to sustain the sense of reality.

The pandemic may appear to offer opportunities to totalitarian regimes and those who want to herd the masses. Within the conjuncture we are in, when it seems this crisis is over, another one will take place. However, it is not correct to think that the crisis gives a new opportunity only to the rulers. Such eras open the door to massive transformative experiences such as opening minds, seeing the unseen and seeing things from a different perspective. That is the work of critical educators.

During this intensified crisis moment, the struggle for life (survival) and democracy are interwoven in many parts of the world. Critical education is a significant part of this struggle. Critical pedagogy can direct this situation towards liberation rather than merely striving for the system to return to an inadequate normal out of this crisis vortex. The social problems and consequences of this pandemic crisis may be a sudden, unexpected opportunity for critical educators, creating from the anxiety, favourable conditions for questioning the basic assumptions of capitalism within education and learning context. Proceeding from this point, we can spread questioning to work against the habit of submission; develop a common perspective on what is happening around us and all around the world. We can circulate an optimism and hope, strengthened by the commitment: 'We can intervene and we can effect change. It is possible.'

Part III

CRITICAL REFLECTIONS AND MOBILIZATION:
CONSTRUCTING DIGITAL COMMUNITIES

Chapter 12

TRANSFORMATIVE POWER OF DIGITAL COMMUNITIES: A CRITICAL EDUCATOR'S PERSPECTIVE

Eda Ata

If it were not for the Covid-19 pandemic and the global lockdown, would you have imagined online platforms as a safe, inclusive space, where ideas can thrive? What is an educator seeking dialogue to do when all the learners 'mute' and are all signified by a black screen? What about a confined activist with a burning desire to be out on the streets during national and/or global quarantine state? These are not theming of a streaming platform's drama sci-fi exploring a twisted futuristic universe; these were items on the agenda for a considerable number of social groups worldwide during the Covid-19 pandemic. However, I challenge the reader here to reflect and ask if these were emerging concerns regarding the pandemic. As an educator and activist, who has been a part of transformative online communities that fight against matters which can be defined as limiting for some groups. I am going to reflect on my experience on the questions posed above.

Critical student becoming critical educator: Digital spaces before and during the pandemic

As an undergraduate student in Linguistics in 2006, I remember being amazed by the prospects of studying Language on online platforms. As a fresh Linguistics student, keen on Sociolinguistics (thanks to phenomenal Derya Duman, who made me realize I could be more than just an angry student interested in language), I found the interactive nature of the emerging social media platforms and the potential they hold fascinating and curious. As undergraduate students back then, we were aware of the challenges in access to internet and relevant software. We were experiencing those issues. In the capital city of Turkey, Ankara, in a prestigious state university, we used to wait in long lines to access the 'internet'. Libraries and computer labs were free of charge for us to access free internet and extremely cheap print options. From where I stand now, as a lecturer at a prestigious private university in Ankara, I cannot imagine education during the pandemic without the platforms and means which were not there for me during my undergraduate studies. However, the world changed quickly, Language evolved accordingly at a very fast pace and, within a few years, the computer technology was an indispensable part of higher education.

Apart from the neoliberal policies surrounding the time I was hired, when I first entered my classroom as a lecturer, it was impossible for me not to observe the 'class' and power relation within the physical space we called 'school'. Actually, until that point, I had lots of tutoring experience and had interacted with various students from diverse socioeconomic backgrounds of differing ages; however, I remember being really alienated when I first started teaching at a university. I had amazing students and the students are still the most motivating aspect of education for me to stay in the game and fight against the inequalities in education.

A critical student interested in critical theory, semiotics, communication, existentialism, freedom and philosophy of education; I became involved in Critical Pedagogy when I started teaching in 2010. I was imagining a safe, participatory, egalitarian, motivating learning space for all. I was a part-time lecturer, and I was suffering as a part of the newly graduate precariat. I was lucky as I had social support from family; however, I was constantly looking for a safe space for my fundamental needs as well. I also remember being invisible as a young part-timer and I was not sure if I was receiving a satisfactory in-service training, given the fact that most of my 'full-time' colleagues did not even know my name. That was also when I met the concept of the professional development units bombarding us with all the mainstream roles and rules and regulations to equip us, new teachers, with ways to reproduce all the pre-existing methods to socialize us into the status quo and dishearten teachers and thus students in a way to serve to standardized tests. I cannot blame all the fellow colleagues who were just doing their jobs to make sure the quality standards are met and some forms are filled and some paid and unpaid hours were allocated to make sure the teachers were 'enough'.

As part-time teachers, we were asking each other during coffee breaks, though. What was a teacher to do if they were constantly questioned about their 'teaching' skills and they were always asked to 'upgrade' and 'up-skill'? With those questions in mind, I started to pursue a Master's degree in Lifelong Learning and Adult Education.

After taking classes from amazing critical educators such as Niyazi Altunya, Hayat Boz, Meral Uysal, Ahmet Yıldız, Fevziye Sayılan, Guy Senese, Cevat Geray and Ş. Erhan Bağcı and exploring the works and ideas by Paulo Freire, Henry Giroux, Antonia Darder, Peter Mayo, Michael Apple and Peter McLaren and meeting amazing international critical and feminist pedagogues and activist through conferences, I felt critical education could be my refuge amidst the alienation and harsh conditions I was experiencing as a teacher and a student in the academic world.

It was thanks to Senese and his classes at Ankara University and at Middle East Technical University (METU) that I also could be a part of one big union where I met Fatma Mızıkacı, Yasemin Tezgiden-Cakcak, Zeynep Alica, Pelin Taşkın, Fahriye Hayırsever, Zeynep Taşdemir Üstün, Cansu Taşdemir, Naciye Aksoy, Hasan Hüseyin Aksoy, Ayhan Ural, Birol Algan and many more scholars and fellow learners. I was lucky enough to have the space where we could exchange ideas and, organize and do our best to be hopeful and resilient.

However, for me, there came a point where it was all too much. So, I had to take a break and pause my PhD studies only to take them up later on and to be expelled due to bureaucracy shortly afterwards. It was when I was away from the 'academic bubble' that I could go on and dive deep into the mental health, awareness and activism part of my journey in a more serene and meaningful way, away from the performative nature of even the most critical and egalitarian academic bodies.

I may now talk about when I first started teaching languages and designing curriculum and in-class teaching material to refugees through online platforms. Critical Theory encourages educators to self-critique and question their ways of teaching. Giroux (2009) explains that personal criticism constitutes a significant aspect of Critical Theory. Viewing pedagogy from a critical perspective leads educators to question practices they never doubted before. As a result, educators implement strategies that promote a holistic view of education in consideration of the effects of race, culture, class, gender and language on student learning experience. However, sometimes as teachers in institutions, we are not the decision-makers. As the education in formal institutions is highly standardized and testing-oriented, a teacher might easily feel they are losing their 'power' and also 'will' to change the world. That was a moment like that for me when I first decided to try volunteering as an educator and citizen. I had tried volunteering for art galleries, for literature magazines, for TV shows and they all went well; I mean, I learned a lot and it was meaningful for me. So, I asked myself why I would try volunteering as a teacher this time. I am not that good with young learners and my expertise is Adult Education. And back then, in 2016, I was really concerned about a global issue, refugees. A colleague I met in Japan in a foreign language education meeting I informally joined during my vacation told me about Paper Airplanes. The NGO was to reach out to those who were affected by the conflict. They were looking for volunteers to teach English. That was a perfect opportunity for me to use my free time as an individual who teaches English to help make the world a better place. They also had some other programmes such as journalism, and women in tech. I got accepted and I went through a training on trauma, how to communicate with 'marginal students' and how to myself, as a teacher take care of my mental wellbeing when working with tough students.

I must admit, though, during the training before the courses begin, as a critical educator, at first I thought it was uncanny because 'we' generally critiqued technology in education and argued it to foster inequalities between the rich and the poor. If you do not have access to technology just because you cannot afford it, generally you miss the tools and the opportunity to reach education, and to reach out to the world to share your voice. Right? But I soon realized it was not always the case.

I started to dig deeper on this and I came to realize that smartphones were used by refugees as a survival tool. 'Water, phone, food,' in that order as stated by Gillespie, a sociology professor at the Open University in the United Kingdom. These are now the three most important items refugees take with them when they are unexpectedly forced to leave their homes. I also could verify that today's refugees have replaced their suitcases with smartphones as they pursue their migratory journeys throughout the region (Kaplan 2018).

Smartphones were used for communication, yes, and for translation and representation. I was challenged, and I could really see how my Syrian student, a computer engineer at my age, who had to leave his home behind was using his phone to communicate, and get informed. Another one was using technology to finish his Master's and to pass the English Language Test for Study (IELTS) to prove his competence. As we had English as the only medium of communication sometimes, we got lost and asked Artificial Intelligence tools and machine translation to help us. Later, I could explore more use of machine translation in the classroom (Ata 2019).

As a volunteer tutor 'in love with the act of teaching', as Freire puts it (1997), exploring online education to empower some disadvantaged groups, I noticed some advantages of technology, actually, and I was challenged as I was in a school of 'critical education', where technology resonated with advertising, globalization and inequalities, I realized I could reach students who otherwise might not have access to Foreign Language Education (FLE), for example women who have family obligations at home, or people with work obligations who don't have the flexibility in their schedule to attend classes. It was also time-saving and flexible as it was not an education offered via a formal institution. More importantly, we could form a dialogue and exchange our stories, songs, concerns and dreams as the tutors and the learners. Without a doubt, the fact that we could connect and help each other grow and thrive through online medium and forming a community of other fellow tutors around the world was deeply meaningful and it was beyond words that can be described in our common language.

As an educator, I noticed volunteering in an educational context helped me use the technology I could afford to volunteer for people who are motivated but are not able to participate to formal schooling. As the NGO was also creating a 'diverse, inclusive, accepting, welcoming safe space' for everyone, I can also say it was impressive! It was also robust training for me to practice ways to create a 'diverse, inclusive, accepting, welcoming safe space' for everyone in my classes as well. It was beyond any mandatory teacher development activity imposed by any institution.

Volunteering also let me meet amazing people, hear their stories and share mine, and I went on looking for more activism in the field, this time with a specific focus on creating gender safe spaces. That was how I found out about Sabancı University Gender and Women's Studies Center of Excellence (SU Gender) and the Purple Certificate Program. This inspiring programme aims to contribute to the elimination of gender-based discrimination by raising teachers' awareness on gender equality. I joined a team preparing educational materials led by amazing

Emirhan Deniz Çelebi. Within the scope of this programme, Purple Folders were developed to provide gender-inclusive teaching materials and I joined one. As we were in different cities, we started to meet via the Zoom platform (yes, as teachers we were offered the famous Zoom platform before it was cool). Even before the pandemic, as teachers who are well aware of the inequalities posed by the society and the policies, we were doing our best to keep the solidarity and make use of technology for a better world.

Right before the pandemic, I was also a part of national and international spaces for democratic, free and inclusive education. I knew I was lucky to have access to the internet and the necessary equipment. As a burned-out PhD student away from school, I found the 'praxis' I was looking for outside academia and I was feeling empowered through online communities. It was not the usual discourse I was used to as a student in education. I remember when I mentioned my positive experience with online tools as an activist to Jamie Senese. An inspiring social worker and an activist with refugees herself, Jamie was really encouraging, and we also had the chance to discuss how we can mobilize by these tools, after all, we were technological beings using smartphones, apps and the like.

As the coronavirus swept through our cities, streets and schools in March 2020, I was lucky to have the chance to work from home with all the necessary gadgets and social, economic and institutional support. Moreover, I felt luckier as I had the 'skills' for being online as an educator and I have been hopeful for the power of online media to help us come together and feel empowered.

Feeling empowered to work towards a better society and a better world by fighting challenging aspects of inequalities feels natural to some people. However, it is also common to overlook the fact that being overwhelmed is also natural and humane in this process. As I have experienced myself, burn-out and exhaustion might lead to alienation and isolation. After joining the Transformative Activism programme by SU Gender right before the pandemic, I realized I can raise my awareness on societal transformation through art and awareness. I had the chance to meet inspirational fellow activists around Turkey and had the chance to attend workshops mainly by Ayşe Gül Altınay, Tuğçe Tuna, Ebru Nihan Celkan and Tarık Tekman.

Thanks to my experience as a volunteer and critical education background, new digital spaces and a refreshed awareness of body and soul, I found the courage and power to stand up and hang on as a woman living alone, teacher struggling to be hopeful and as a global citizen concerned with a sustainable and equal future under a conservative, neoliberal government that does not acknowledge the existence of fragile and marginalized groups. When the pandemic became the 'new normal' as some people like to call it, and sometimes became unbearable as we could not meet the beloved family members and interact with colleagues and dear students, I had full confidence in my community, which can only be available through the online platforms.

So, when dearest Fatma Mızıkacı *hocam* (teacher), an inspirational role model for me in many parts of life since 2012, offered we organize a talk with international scholars and create an online public space, I had the full motivation, resilience and power to work towards it. When we organized and held our first talk as Global Thursday Talks, I was extremely excited to see this new type of solidarity led by two women: a critical online community where ideas on certain issues on education could be shared with a group of scholars, educators, students, activists both instantly and also over social media channels to make it more accessible during uncertain and dangerous times. We were doing our best to deal with all the challenges of Covid-19 to create a sanctuary for our international and national community (via online tools) for a form of being we longed for and have been non-violently fighting for: *hope* (Mızıkacı and Ata 2020).

As the moderator and organization team member at Global Thursday Talks (GTT), I was feeling safer when we discussed issues such as racism, social justice, education and hope. I decided to complete my PhD studies as I felt the need to create and proliferate academically as well, I applied to my PhD programme again and got accepted and it also made me experience being a student during pandemic as well. I must say, I have never felt more motivated to make an effort in studying my courses and then focusing on the problems faced by the older people, especially those who get involved in activism concerned with issues of ageing and social inclusion through the lens of an adult educator.

Thanks to our digital and ever-growing community via GTT, I was interacting and meeting the critical educators who gave me hope since I first started my transformation. Exploring the social movements, teachers' role, cultural Marxism and hybrid classes with McLaren in Global Thursday Talks with a large group of international participants made me feel less alone in my own lockdown. When we explored more on pandemic and critical education with a reference to higher education with Peter Mayo in GTT, I had the 'guilt' of having the access to basics during pandemic. I had students fighting problems that disabled them to learn or participate; however, I did not yield to despair, thanks to the solidarity with my precious friends, sisters and colleagues, Nurcan Saltoğlu Özleyen and Sinem Günbay, both of whom also shared their valuable experience and insight with GTT community later on. We worked hard to find ways to include and engage our students during online education terms. We had long meetings almost every day, having heated discussions, reading and learning as much as we can, and we modified our practices in order to create a more inclusive and engaging curriculum and evaluation practice during the pandemic.

As Guy Senese and Michael W. Apple were covering the topics such as gender roles, teachers' roles and isolation of teachers during the pandemic and were covering the loss of momentum and social movement. We were actually finding new modes of praxis as teachers and students in order to stay strong and resilient. My students and I started reading clubs, fellow teachers around Turkey in our volunteer roles came together in an intellectual and human perspective. I had deep conversations in roundtable online meetings which inspired me to come up with interactive and student-empowering 'online meeting' techniques. Although the students in our classes were sometimes not really responding, we found novel and engaging ways to do our best and as good as it gets. I remember listening to Antonia Darder and noticing how the poverty was marked in our bodies and how it can also be observed in the 'windows' in online classes. Also, after Darder's talk, I was aware of the 'heteronormative', abled bodies and how bodies are a map of power and identity. In our interview with Henry A. Giroux, as we revisited the idea of teachers as cultural producers and how critical pedagogy is about unlearning, I felt more informed, heard and hopeful. Another inspiring and indispensable critical educator, E. Wayne Ross, helped us explore education and education technologies to commodify education around the end of the ill-famed year of 2020. By exchanging emails after her talk at Global Thursday Talks, Liv Mjelde offered us insight into adult education, praxis and principles and practices in Norway and Turkey. Listening to Arnd-Michael Nohl on *Bildung* and political education, I was happy to read his work in Turkish and even join some other online conferences where I can explore his views on mass education and 'risk areas'. After horrible news on women's rights in Turkey's withdrawal form and Istanbul Convention, a legal instrument to tackle violence against women, we mourned and organized together in Fevziye Sayılan's talk. In conclusion, as an ever-growing organic community, Global Thursday Talks has given room for critical educators to convene, evaluate the current issues faced globally, pursue new forms of culture and knowledge, share their vision for a just world and help teachers and students to become reflective, organic, resilient, transformative intellectuals by redefining the praxis in the time of the Covid-19 pandemic in a new form of solidarity.

Hope as a sustainable asset: Where to from here?

Exploring the education in a world different from 'the world as we knew it', Global Thursday, Purple Folder and Transformative Activism groups became safe digital spaces for me to mobilize, create and stay resilient.

I wish to think more and thrive as a critical educator and seek an answer to this question: Can we make the positive aspects of digital communities sustainable and accessible for all?

I believe the following insights I have gained during my experience with online communities before and during the pandemic might work for educators and learners around the world to connect even after the pandemic:

- Praxis can be redefined by making use of technological devices and basic access to the internet should be provided free by the governments for all.
- The disadvantaged groups can be empowered through volunteer programmes now that more and more NGOs and social groups are aware of the use of technology.
- Interest groups can mobilize and meet in a safe and instant way.
- Sources can be sponsored by the funding institutions to be made available to public good.
- Artists can work closely with educators and students from different parts of the campus and even around the world.

- International scholars and students can join and visit different institutions, thus creating a flat hierarchy.
- By saving trees and spending less on air travel, future classes and gatherings can be made eco-friendlier, thus saving resources for the future.
- Lessons learned during the pandemic might pave the way to promote mental health awareness among the overall public.
- We can create safer spaces for the fragile groups in the society thanks to free, inclusive digital support groups.
- Teachers can promote awareness on ageism and sexism by referring to the poor practices which the young and the elderly faced during the pandemic.
- Digital communities worldwide can merge and become 'neighbours', thus exchanging valuable good practices easily.

Although being confined to online platforms to come together and let the ideas thrive has been challenging for the intellectuals, activists and social groups and building communities online sounds negative, it comes with benefits. As an educator and learner, I am more resilient than ever to combat the inequalities and I know that I have friends, comrades, sisters and brothers all around the world and also at home who can and will assist me in my path to a more just education whether the medium is online or not. I suppose I know how to reach out to fellow colleagues and learners around the world to seek solidarity. Most importantly, I know that I can feel the heated argumentation and emancipatory dances and gatherings on any street and square around the world with that burning desire we share: freedom, equality and hope for all.

References

Ata, Murat (2019) 'Elephant in the classroom: English learners and instructors' perceptions, attitudes, and beliefs regarding the use of online machine translation tools' (Master's thesis, European University of Lefke).

Freire, Paulo (1997) *Pedagogy of the Heart* (London and New York: Bloomsbury).

Giroux, Henry (2009) 'Critical theory and educational practice', in Antonia Darder, Rodolfo D. Torres and Marta P. Baltodano (eds), *The Critical Pedagogy Reader* (New York and London: Routlege), 27–52.

Kaplan, Ivy (2018) 'How smartphones and social media have revolutionized refugee migration', UNHCR Blog, 26 October 2018. Available at: https://www.unhcr.org/blogs/smartphones-revolutionized-refugee-migration/ (accessed 5 January 2021).

Mızıkacı, Fatma and Ata, Eda (2020) 'Global Thursday Talks: How critical educators united locally and globally during pandemic', *International Journal of Educational Policies*, 14 (2): 131–7.

Chapter 13

GROUNDING CRITICAL EDUCATORS' LIVES ON SOLIDARITY, COMMUNITY AND FRIENDSHIP

Zeynep Alica and Yasemin Tezgiden-Cakcak

Coming from an academic space characterized by alienating individualism, hostile competition and cold distance, I (Yasemin) found my 'intellectual/academic home' at a critical education conference in 2013, when I was a PhD student. My first encounter with the conference was in Ankara, Turkey. I could not afford to follow the entire conference in my busy teaching schedule. Yet, in a few sessions I attended I thought the discourse and the critical tone of the conference were surreal. Plenary speakers were talking about solidarity and the first keynote, Dave Hill, was addressing the community as 'comrades/*yoldaşlar*'. I saw that this was more than 'an academic conference', it was a gathering of critical scholars from around the world. I decided to be a part of this community and attended the conference in Thessaloniki, Greece, the following year, which was a turning point in my scholarly work. Waiting for the conference to start, I was startled by the excitement of scholars meeting each other in the halls of the university. When the first session was over, I knew I was in the right place. Each talk broadened and deepened my intellectual horizons and gave me food for further inquiry for my dissertation. More importantly, after each session, I found myself among a group of friendly scholars discussing the educational and political atmosphere in their countries and exchanging ideas. I had never seen such a welcoming, supporting academic crowd before. Bothered by the ingenuity of networking interactions during coffee breaks of academic conferences, I had often felt disconnected. Yet, here I was experiencing a sincere interest in what other scholars had to say. The spirit of trust, friendship and solidarity marked the conference.

Navigating my way to the room to present my paper, I met colleagues trying to find the same place. Those people would later become influential in my academic and personal life: Zeynep Alica, my co-author in this chapter, Guy Senese my mentor, and his wife, Jamie Senese a close friend. Zeynep and I were presenting in the same session that day. While we were preparing for our talks, I remember Guy was jumping around to help us set the place, closing window blinds. I felt like I was thrown onto a different planet. During my talk on the empowering potential of critical reading on non-native English teacher candidates, I vividly remember how Guy listened to me – with full attention, taking notes. After the talk, he gave me feedback and was genuinely interested in my paper. Later on, I met them again among the group of Turkish scholars, who had travelled to Thessaloniki in a bus arranged by their professor, Hasan Hüseyin Aksoy. Soon I learnt Guy would visit Ankara University the following semester and I offered help with the translation at this Turkish-medium university.

Zeynep and I became friends quickly perhaps because we were 'speaking the same language' in many respects. I remember us telling stories about the situation in Turkey to 'comrades' we met during the conference. We shared the agonizing pain of our lives and reconsidered our lives with the questions and comments of international critical educators. Our friendship with Zeynep got deeper when Guy and Jamie came to Turkey. We met during and after Guy's classes at Ankara University. We worked together on translations on critical education.

Guy's classes in Room Five rebuilt and strengthened the spirit of the conference for me and probably for other colleagues. Along with graduate students registered for the course, there were many other guests like me. I met Fatma Mızıkacı and Eda Ata, editors of this book in that class. It was the first critical education class I had ever attended and was mind-opening for me. I was both struggling to understand the ideas and trying to translate them into Turkish for those who did not speak English. Guy's attitude and enthusiasm in learning *from* and *with* the members of class and the desire for the course attendees to connect and learn from each other built a new community of scholars, which Guy calls 'One Big Union' – naming it after the historical concept of trade unionists.

The first accomplishment of this union was our book project, *A Language of Freedom and Teachers' Authority*, edited by Fatma Mızıkacı and Guy Senese, for which scholars from Turkey and the USA wrote their educational experiences.[1] Our work together for the book project brought us together in person and in the virtual space several times. We did not only share our academic expertise but also shared difficult times together in solidarity. When Turkish academics started to be fired, our fellow co-authors in the book sent video messages of solidarity to us, softening our hearts.

The second reunion of the group took place when Guy came to my institution, Middle East Technical University (METU), as a visiting Erasmus scholar. Guy, Zeynep and I co-taught an undergraduate class in the Department of Foreign Language Education in the spring of 2018. Teaching teacher candidates together helped us discuss critical issues further. Our joint work was also welcomed well by the students, some of whom also became interested in critical education. We also arranged a group of critical education seminars offered by Guy; old and new members of the One Big Union convened again at METU. Guy also inspired our

---

1. Fatma Mızıkacı and Guy Senese (eds), *A Language of Freedom and Teacher's Authority Case Comparisons from Turkey and the United States* (Lanham, MD: Lexington Books, 2017).

student collective called *Maske*, and we organized a poetry slam in the front yard of the College of Education, writing and reciting poetry.

The following semester, I was in Arizona, as a visiting scholar at the Northern Arizona University, working with Guy and fellow members of our union in the USA. Not only did I learn with them, I was also welcomed in their personal space, residing in their homes. It was an amazing academic year, full of discovery, exchange of ideas and writing, which further expanded my understanding of the world, education and academia.

The third major work inspired by this group I believe is the Global Thursday Talks. One day, during the first wave of shock and desperation of the pandemic, I received an email from Eda Ata. She had a suggestion to reconvene the group in these dark times to help each other out and was asking for my opinion. I thought it was an excellent idea and Eda arranged our first meeting over Zoom. She was asking that crucial question we had discussed earlier in Guy's seminars to overcome alienation and isolation: 'How are you?' That question, along with our cyber meetings, eased our worries and helped us overcome our isolation. We had long-recurring meetings for several weeks, sharing our feelings and discussing the political, social and educational issues our countries faced. Those meetings went on for weeks because they were healing to us. As far as I know, during or after one such meeting, Fatma and Eda came up with the idea to organize the Global Thursday Talks and they successfully managed to bring us together with leading educators in the field. That has probably enlarged our union on a global scale, with more educationalists joining and contributing to the series of talks.

Most often, we organize such events believing in the 'possibility' of inspiring ourselves along with others interested. But we never know if these efforts to reach out, and to build solidarity ever inspire others. During the question-and-answer session of one Global Thursday Talk, I saw that our attempts paid off. After Guy's talk, one research assistant from METU spoke out and said she followed this group since she met the group by chance at METU. Neither was I aware of the identity of this colleague nor had I any idea about the impact of our gatherings. She said she had heard music playing in the front yard of the College of Education one day and learnt about our group. We were having a poetry slam that day, when Guy played music while students sang songs. She told us she started to follow our activities from then on. Hearing this anecdote refreshed my faith in our actions. That 'possibility' had turned out to be real and we were learning that three years after the event. It was a pleasant surprise.

This nice anecdote came at a time when we were locked down because of the pandemic and I felt totally detached from the rest of the world, leading a solitary life at home. I was pregnant back then and was invaded by excitement along with worrisome thoughts. I was beginning to be thrown into the trap of the 'possessive individualism' Michael Apple talked about.[2] Yet, the talk series reconnected me to

2. Michael Apple, 'Critical analysis and discussion of the Covid-19 crisis', Global Thursday Talks, Michael Apple, 9 July 2020.

the world of critical education, reminding me of what I strongly believed in. I felt energized after attending each session and I had an exciting event on my calendar each week to look forward to. Those critical educators whose works I had read became real persons speaking before us, which gave us a chance to dialogue with them in real time. Ironically, the social distance we had to observe due to Covid-19 was providing us with a chance to bridge the distances we formerly had. I realized I had not even thought of reaching out to these keynote speakers before. Thus, Global Thursday Talks did not only make those scholars accessible for us, but also the series helped me realize my flawed thinking about the 'distance' we had with the community of critical educators.

I vividly remember that day when Guy gave his Global Thursday Talk. Listening to Guy, I remembered 'who I was', identifying myself as a critical educator. I felt honoured to hear him talk about our joint actions and his impressions from METU. Hearing his talk, I noticed again what we had achieved as 'one big union' over the years. We had taught classes, organized talks and meetings, released publications and, most importantly, built lasting relationships and a spirit of true solidarity, which brought us back to our feet when we had hard times. Knowing that you have a community of colleagues to turn to is invaluable and as Guy would say, a perfect cure for alienation. During critical moments in your professional and personal life, it makes a great difference to feel the support of understanding colleagues/friends around you. I do not think it is possible to survive wild capitalist academic life without having such a democratic community – at least for those of us who want to keep their sanity when indulged in building counter-hegemonic spaces. Otherwise, it would not be possible to learn, to teach, to research, to struggle or to resist.

As Michael W. Apple put it in his dialogue with Guy Senese in the talk series, 'winning back space starts with small actions'.[3] Rather than 'mourning' what we lost with the physical educational/academic space, Global Thursday Talks helped us 'organize' a digital solidarity network to face problems together. As a transformative mobilizing action taken against the desperation which the pandemic created along with the gloomy political-economic climate, these talks reconnected us, lifted our spirits and paved the way for further critical reflection and action.

The fourth accomplishment of One Big Union I believe is the very act of writing for this book. It gives us a chance to explore and exchange ideas collaboratively. It is also a gesture of solidarity, especially for me, when I am trying to get back to scholarly work after becoming a mother six months ago. Engaged in full-time mothering, it felt unimaginable for me to bring myself together to sit down, to think and to write. Without Zeynep's encouragement, I would easily give up on this endeavour. I feel writing for this book is bringing me back to the intellectual

3. Michael W. Apple, 'A talk with Michael Apple on critical issues in education', Global Thursday Talks, Michael Apple and Guy Senese, 6 August 2020.

field I adore and fills me with the fuel to produce. This community is now taking me out of my cave to the light.

Yasemin recalled so many meaningful and inspiring moments intersecting within our stories. The salon on the roof of the university building facing all Thessaloniki was covered with protective and at the same time respectful style of Guy and Jamie. This teaching and learning form keeps on helping us view the world as a place in which friends exist against kilometres and moments of despair. This dialogue among us continues whenever we are left with many different questions about life. When I get the chance of teaching in university, these are the people I call first to share all the excitement and questions. We ease each other's lives at crisis moments. How far from the atmosphere academia provides as Yasemin described well at the beginning. How precious it is to share anxiety, despair and joy of friendship. Here again comes a question, we often ask together and separately. And I will try to go on in dialogue with Michael Apple's talk and Guy Senese's words while writing about reflections in my daily experiences as a teacher to answer our good old question: What is the meaning of 'being a teacher' (during the pandemic)?

I (Zeynep) am an English teacher in a state high school. This is my twentieth teaching year. I have been working in this high school for six years. The school is settled in a neighbourhood that used to be a slum area. It is an urban-transformation area now. In other words, when I started teaching here, the school was surrounded by shanty houses. During the last six years, all those houses were destroyed and now there are 20-storey huge apartments, instead. Most of our students came from closer streets; they did not have high academic profiles. So, most of the time, teachers complain about the students' weak relationship with learning. As this is an academic high school, the final aim of the students is entering a university. But most of the time their social capital does not support this aim. They have a limited number of books at home, the majority of their parents have graduated from primary schools or secondary schools. But during the previous two years, we had a different experience. As an English teacher, the last two years have been really special for me because of a language class who struggled a lot to open their specific field. They tried to gather enough petitions to open a language field in the school. In our regular academic high schools, students choose their field at the end of 10th grade. Their options are generally either mathematics and science fields for entering engineering, medicine, etc. departments at university and Social Sciences and Literature fields for Social Sciences. For entering the Law Department at university, they have to choose a mixture of these two fields. Every year, a minor group tries to choose mainly English or language lessons to enter university exams for language departments. And most of the time, because of the lack of enough classrooms, students are not able to open this path for their future. But, for the first time in the history of the school, a determined group of students managed to open this field. And during their last term, the pandemic started. It was an exclusive experience for me as a language teacher and for them because they really pushed hard and created a public space of their own in school. These resistant dreamers welcomed Guy Senese in our school as well. And they were preparing a play,

Sherlock Holmes. They performed their rehearsals in front of Guy and Jamie once and then in another visit they performed in front of two teacher-candidate student visitors from the course we have conducted together with Yasemin and Guy at METU. So, it seems there is a form of knitting both in our friendships and work sites that nourishes each side on multilevels.

Whenever I felt locked, squeezed at school because of the limitations you can imagine within a state school order, curriculum and sometimes usual school hierarchy, etc., I remembered *hocam* Guy Senese's words. He describes school as a public arena, a public place in which we as teachers can spread the word of peace, democracy and equality, no matter what. In other words, this bit of knowledge has worked as a hope pill for me most of the time. And when the Global Thursday Talks started, it was great to meet, this time globally, to feed minds and to defeat the feelings of isolation. Moreover, again the idea of public space, no matter what became real. Although these meetings have been visual and distant, it was great to meet with the educators who deal with all the issues about education.

The meaning of being a teacher, however, seems to be changing during these Covid days. At almost each online lesson, as a teacher, I find myself asking questions about this change. Maybe I need to start from the beginning: the schools in Turkey were closed in the middle of March (13 March 2020). We were not ready for anything like this. We were so much used to going to school, doing all the schoolwork under any kind of conditions, we could not imagine being locked at home without schools. So, realizing what was going on took some serious amount of time for us teachers as well as students. Days went by, some of us discovered Zoom, and met with our students through it. Actually, private schools were really quick to catch up with the new conditions. And this was an extra disillusionment for public school teachers. Because we knew that our students already lagged, and we now were witnessing this gap between opportunities widening. So, during these times, a teacher started to mean someone who has to be aware of both students' and their families' conditions, like a social worker. We were calling each of our students, asking about their health conditions and life conditions. If there were students who were experiencing problems due to Covid, we would talk to them and their parents. Sometimes, some of the students fell into the void of meaninglessness, and we tried to be there to listen (although we felt that huge void held our hand, too). When we could not reach the student via phone, we reached their families. These connections made both sides glad. Because we all need to feel we are not alone.

Trying to keep up with the needs of 12th graders who were struggling to get ready for the university exams was another big issue. The language class I mentioned at the beginning was getting ready for the university exam and this was an extra feeling of responsibility. These students would be in a race with students who were generally more advantaged for coming from either private colleges or higher standardized schools. They needed published material to study and this age group were not allowed to go out. We (my colleague and I) piled the textual resources, grouped them at school and distributed them, contacting the parents. We tried hard to keep these students' connection to their aims alive via online lessons, held extra meetings for motivation, put aside our right to disconnect and stayed in contact till late hours. Still, we were far behind the conditions of private schools and courses.

We knew who these students were. As their main field teacher, I have spent a lot of hours with these students and I have learnt a lot from the deep connections we have built together. Each student was a world on their own. These students were wanderers, the more I learnt about their world, the more I felt responsible for each of them. During his talk in Global Thursday Talks, Michael Apple reminds us of the importance of constantly asking 'who these students are' to continue the act of providing a transformative learning and teaching area both for the teachers and students.[4] Who are these young people? What are their conditions like? What are their dreams? These are real questions, when teachers wish and work to create living, lively classrooms. While trying to create classroom atmospheres during distance education, these questions find little space. Because we find ourselves running most of the time alone with our questions related to the topic we are trying to teach. We are teaching like runners; we have to be fast and to communicate what we have in our plans within a limited time without discussing or thinking enough about the topics we are dealing with. This new type of teaching includes minor dialogue. Even if we want dialogue, students are either not behind the black screen or their voice system is not working. When these two conditions are okay, students may be reluctant to speak. Most of the time, if you want to create a classroom as in the old days, a dialogic classroom is kind of a nostalgia during the pandemic.

How much I miss the discussions we had in the language class born out of texts we were dealing with when we were studying grammar or vocabulary. As they were in a special field, we were given the chance to study whichever textbook we liked. That means we were able to read about so many different topics. And, generally, those topics included contemporary issues about gender, literature, etc. We would discuss, listen to each other and laugh a lot.

Different from the previous term in which we were able to use extra materials in schools, during this pandemic, the sources we are to use are prepared by the Ministry. And it is so disappointing to see the rising dose of religionation and nationalism within textbooks through which we are trying to teach English. It seems we have to teach English by reteaching Turkish and Ottoman history and cultural features of Muslim countries mostly. And if we teach about historical heroes (I do not know why we have to), we teach the success of men in general. The texts are difficult to follow and at the same time ideologically overloaded. Because of the pressure of standardized exam possibility, we focus on these textbooks and it is not possible to use extra materials. Apple addresses this issue very clearly with the term 'conservative modernisation'.[5] Within textbooks by international writers,

---

4. Michael Apple, 'Critical analysis and discussion of the Covid-19 crisis', Global Thursday Talks, Michael Apple, 9 July 2020.
    5. Ibid.

Western culture was being taught. As Apple says but now with the effect of neoconservatism which describes the problems in education 'are caused because too many minoritized people, too many women, too many progressives have taken over the curriculum. We must restore what it means to be Turkish or American as the core element of a curriculum.'[6] And to do this, the decision-makers have reshaped the English textbooks with Turk–Islam stories, with 'our culture'. So, within this context, the English language is being 'taught' without the culture within which it was shaped, as if this is something possible.

Starting from the new educational year, we continued our lessons via Eba (the online system of Ministry of Education). As we are being recorded, the feeling of 'Big Brother is watching you' never disappeared. Normally, as a teacher, I always thought classrooms are special areas. When we close the door and start the lesson, it is always possible to lead dreamlike lessons, filled with dialogue. It is great to see students sharing their ideas and dreams. It is maybe the best part of being a teacher, you see the flourishing of young seeds. But now I understand that school and the classroom in which we keep on humanly face-to-face interaction is the place of this type of experiences. Online teaching gives the feeling of an artificially controlled experiment room. You have to load the student with given information just as described in the Freirean banking system of education. And whenever a moment of criticism occurs, you feel the camera. That tiny light coming to your face directly from the computer uneases relationships and shapes the words you use.

So, trying to teach English through mostly Turk–Islam synthesis books without criticism can be a big tension exam for the critical teacher. Whenever we teach in class, another big question to answer was: 'Did we produce a meaningful encounter during our interaction in the classroom?' During these chaotic distance education days, with these teaching experiences, the question keeps on being on the agenda. Unfortunately, the answer includes too much silence. Reasons for this silence are plenty. In each class, regular attendants of the lessons are limited. The best rate is 20 out of 30 students. But there are classes in which regular attendants are 4 or 5 out of 35 class members. Why can't students join the lessons? Well, we can imagine several answers but we do not know the answers in detail yet. When they join, they do not turn on the camera. So, we are unable to understand if they are really following the lesson. And the ones who are following, try to understand what is going on in these English texts. As I said earlier, the textbooks are really difficult to follow. So, students spend most of their time to understand the texts and there is not enough time for them to practice speaking skills. But they need time to practice to learn this language. And there is neither the time nor are there the conditions for this to happen. So, to be honest, I feel like I am floating in a meaningless (but I always wish and work to make it meaningful) medium during the lessons. Although Guy Senese keeps reminding us about the power of narrative, the power

6. Ibid.

of sharing stories to achieve a fulfilling teaching experience, distance education limits opportunities of sharing stories of each other. The voice which is so central in empowerment is getting lost on the student's side. And it is hard to create a voice heard atmosphere in this virtual classroom. But, as Guy Senese reminded us in our chats, reaching out to one student, one life at a time is crucial. As a teacher, I am in search of meaning in life and in these confusing times, trying to be available to my students provides the core of that meaning.

In his talk in the Global Thursday Talks, Michael Apple talks about the dangerous rise of the tendency towards home-schooling due to several reasons among parents from different political perspectives and social backgrounds. And he says that 'through home-schooling a new neoliberal identity will be formed. That is possessive individualism. The home and the family are the limit of my social consciousness.'[7] We are witnessing the realization of this identity; it is a forced identity for the young students. Especially the ones who passed the university exam, dreamed of leaving home and forming a new identity by this new huge step. We have students who have the worst conditions at home, who are suffering because of their strict fathers and other related patriarchal limitations. Some of these students, especially girls, studied so hard to go beyond the limits. They dreamt of being the first generation who completed high school and even became the first ones in their families to attend university. Although they tried to force the limits, they have to go on with the limit of the social consciousness of the family and home. The family describes the role of being female according to family orders and patriarchal values. And because of Covid, they could not open up a new path for their personal freedom by attending university. As young people, they need space, they need new encounters to form a new identity that will most probably be nourished from the emancipatory knowledge sources within university circles. But these forms of transformations do not seem possible during the Covid days. Lockdown has a different dimension for these young people, they are locked down from transformative encounters.

Working in a teacher education context in the university setting, my observations are similar to Zeynep's: exhausted students under the heavy personal, emotional and academic workload, puzzled academics having to conduct dual labour, unresolved access problems, and communication breaks between students and teachers. In my Zoom meetings with students, I (Yasemin) always ask how they are and how distance education is going. After taking deep breaths and hesitating to speak for a while, they start talking about their increased labour at home, non-existence of physical or psychological space for study, never-ending irrelevant assignments and non-responding teachers. I try to encourage them to speak up and communicate their demands. They say it does not work even if they dare to speak. Hearing students' silenced scream, my heart breaks. I feel paralyzed as my attempts to share student complaints with my colleagues meet either with complete silence or aggressive defence.

7. Ibid.

Not being able to satisfy their basic survival needs, rarely do students talk about their social isolation or missed opportunities at the university campus. They tell me they are on the verge of losing their mental health. I feel pain in my chest. I can only say, 'I wish I could do something to ease your suffering.' Seeing my despair, they add that having a listening ear and being able to express themselves feel like therapy. Later I learn that that simple question inquiring about their wellbeing makes them feel they are valuable. Thanks to the relatively more democratic space university classes provide, I do not have to worry too much about 'being watched' and I enjoy the luxury to converse with my students and organize my course content independently. Following Michael Apple, I believe critical pedagogy starts with building caring relationships. It begins with exchanging feelings, hopes, fears, dreams and experience. When you achieve to establish that genuine bond with your students, it is easy to discover the world of ideas with them. The 'epistemological fog' becomes thinner in a relationship of trust because you challenge the roots of injustice and dehumanization together.

Global Thursday Talks achieved what we aspire to do within our classrooms in a global setting: (re)building community and challenging the mystifying gloom of our times. Despite witnessing many forms of despair during the times we followed Global Thursday Talks, continuing a live virtual dialogue with 'good teachers' and 'organic intellectuals', 'friends with whom we conducted dialogue whenever possible' provided good feelings and were our sessions of emotional and intellectual therapy. These meetings helped to overcome feelings of incurability and isolation. With each inspirational meeting, we refreshed our beliefs in the transformation of life and left with thankfulness to the human beings' creativity in building up alternative ways of meeting, discussing and solidarity – just as in the words of Leonard Cohen: 'There is a crack in everything, that's how the light gets in!'

Chapter 14

COMING TO TERMS WITH THE COVID-19 PANDEMIC: PERCEPTIONS OF A LANGUAGE TEACHER

Murat Ata

Due to Covid-19 pandemic, there has been an ongoing paradigm shift in how the shareholders of education engage in educational activities. Experiencing the rapidly evolving nature of teaching practices, I, as a language teacher, have found myself questioning how the pedagogy I am supposed to follow is informed by the changing social structures and psychological development of learners and educators. The new normal initiated by the pandemic has introduced countless inequalities among students, highlighted the digital divide, caused psychological issues, limited social interactions, minimized mobilization and weakened the oppressed. However, we are an industrious breed, famous for determination and collective brilliance. I, for one, am a hopeful person, and I find it fitting to ask the following question: Can the pandemic also open doors to more democratic education, inclusive curricula, accessible technologies and critical world citizens?

One of the most widely used phrases since the beginning of the Covid-19 pandemic is *social distancing*. It has been used by scholars, institutions and government representatives. Even the World Health Organization mentions the phrase in some of its guides and briefs (WHO 2020). It became a catchphrase, uttered automatically while referring to what individuals can and should do to prevent the spread of the virus. In the early havoc created by the sudden change in our lifestyles, I did not brood over this emerging term much. However, as time went by, it started to bother me. In his Global Thursday Talk, Michael Apple asserted that, with the pandemic, 'there has been a loss of momentum and loss of mobilization', much needed in such times of uncertainty and despair. In this atmosphere, what we need is definitely not distancing socially. Actually, it has always been the opposite: we should be socially united. Physically distant? Sure. Socially distant? Definitely not! Before long, I came across a new and much more sensible catchphrase: *Physical distancing, social solidarity!* That is what we needed then and definitely need now. Global Thursday Talks has been an excellent means to achieve this goal.

In his Global Thursday Talk, Henry Giroux pointed out that critical pedagogy 'keeps us aware of the questions that we need to ask'. Then he went on and asked: 'How do we talk about pedagogy as an ongoing struggle over relations of power and the preconditions that absolutely have to be present for creating informed and critical citizens who can act on the world?' My answer might be: *By preserving our social solidarity*. When our pedagogy is informed by the hardships and tragedies we experience and at the same time reflect our solidarity, it becomes a strong message to the oppressors who are always seeking ways to render us disconnected, helpless and lacking agency. The power of agency is attained and retained through collective actions. When our pedagogy reflects the issues that the oppressed are going through, when our unions find ways to create action plans, when our social distance is minimized despite the indoctrination for the contrary, we can create more of those Henry Giroux's *informed and critical citizens who can act on the world*.

I assume it is fair to continue my reflection with some self-criticism. As an English instructor teaching young adults for more than fifteen years, I spent most of my career following the curriculum I was presented, to the letter. I tried my best to cover all the topics included in the programme. How to cover so much in so little time was the number one issue among my day-to-day professional worries. How my students would do in the exams was also an ever-present source of apprehension. Teaching for me had a lot to do with how much I taught my students between exams. Like many in Turkey, I went through my entire school life, preparing for one *ultimate* exam after another. That was what education meant for me as a student, and I had no doubt that my students were on the same path. The best thing I could do was to help them pass those endless number of *ultimate* exams. And the guaranteed way to do this was to follow the curriculum which was created by the wise and the learned.

At one point, however, as I became more senior and got more involved with beyond the in-class teaching aspects of my job, I realized that those people were not that wise. I could tell because I was one of them. We were mostly concerned with what we would include in the tests during and at the end of the term. We were designing the curriculum to cover the topics that we were, for some reason, too eager to test. While deciding on the curriculum, we were building linguistic prison cells for our students and teachers alike. Whether reading materials promoted critical thinking and had an inclusive language was important but secondary. We cared more about how to standardize speaking assessments than whether the discussion topics would allow students to express their opinions freely and without being judged. We were more concerned with how much of the grammar we taught our students was reflected in their writing and in the variety of vocabulary they used in their spoken and written performances. I am not implying that these are to be ignored altogether. However, we were missing a valuable opportunity to guide brilliant individuals into being critical world citizens because we were simply not raised to be those, and we were consumed by the irrational tradition of teaching to test. Fortunately, I later came across the works of the real wise and learned people like Freire, Giroux, Shor, Apple and many others, and pedagogy for me is much more than tests now.

Covid-19 has come without warning and it led to the closure of my school as well as most schools around the world. It forced us to stop whatever we were doing. We had to stop travelling, coming together and doing our jobs. At first, there was widespread confusion among everyone involved in education. That was hardly surprising because the confusion was extending to the administrations of countries. When we, the educators, realized that the closure would continue for more than a few weeks, we set out to consider what we could do with what we already had at hand. No matter how proficient we are in using technology, we set about transforming our teaching materials into digital copies. With these materials, we started asynchronous education. Students were supposed to access online platforms where they would find materials prepared and digitalized by their teachers and do the tasks within the given time frame. At this point, administrations had not conducted comprehensive surveys to find out how capable the teachers were in teaching in this fashion, mentally, physically and professionally. Some teachers lacked the technical means to do these tasks. They simply did not have a capable computer that can carry out the expected duties. Some lacked the technological know-how; some lacked the peace of mind to go on while they were watching the world they knew come to a halt. We went on, though. The ones with extra computers shared them, the tech-savvy ones guided the less technologically proficient ones, and many teachers assumed the role of a psychological counsellor for the distressed ones. Solidarity was naturally born, and it kept the teachers going.

In one episode of the famous podcast, 'This American Life', there was a bittersweet story of a college professor who got stuck in an elevator with his kids and still managed to deliver his online lesson in the elevator while tending to his kids and waiting to be rescued. This reminded me of the time I had to start my lesson on my mobile when my computer refused to start. Teachers are adaptable and quick to improvise solutions. However, I keep reminding myself that I should not be carried away by how adaptable I am in my current, privileged state. It is easy to improvise solutions to technical problems when you have access to two computers (one at home, one at the office), a capable smartphone and broadband internet. As Giroux mentioned in his Global Thursday Talk, some tenured professors tend to forget the struggles of others without a tenure. I never want to be the privileged teacher who is oblivious to the struggles of the students who have to share a single computer with their siblings and join the online lesson via their neighbour's internet.

While we were carrying out asynchronous education, the students were freer to do their tasks at a time of their choosing. They were not totally free, but they were at least able to allocate themselves a time slot to use a computer when others in their family did not need the device. This was a definite advantage. The disadvantage, on the other hand, was the feeling of the lack of face-to-face guidance. At least this was the result of the student surveys carried out to figure out which mode of teaching the students preferred in my institution. The results showed that a big proportion of the students in my institution opted for synchronous online education. It is quite understandable because these young people want to feel connections at different levels. They want the community feeling of a classroom, no matter how virtual it is. Some want to have more and regular contact hours with their professors. Some simply want to share the experiences and miseries of being a university student. After all, even misery loves company. That is how we moved to synchronous distance education. This, however, naturally brought us the issues of privilege and digital divide. Systemic inequalities surfaced immediately since the living conditions of many students had totally been transformed compared to their previous lives. In their current state, for many students, it was and still is impossible to adhere to the schedule they had when they were on campus. Digital divide has become more pronounced when privileged students use state-of-the-art computers, huge screens and fast broadband connections to access synchronous courses without a moment's loss. On the other hand, less privileged ones struggle to have access to the basic means. Some have to work to support their crisis-stricken family, while some have to take care of their younger siblings, who happen to be expected to attend their own synchronous online classes at the exact same time frame. The dilemma is still at large, and it will be here to stay until and unless we achieve Freire's pedagogy of liberation.

It is really disturbing that the pandemic is discriminating. As Jerome Ravetz (2020) puts it, 'microscopic viral predators cull our populations, as ever, but with a selection that is not natural but social and political'. Of course, it is not really the pandemic that discriminates. It is the neoliberal, capitalist world order that renders the weak weaker and more passive. The poor have very limited or no access to proper healthcare. They are also the first ones to lose their job security due to lockdowns. Unfortunately, the education sector is no exception in being harsh to the less privileged. The neoliberal model wants the victims of the pandemic to keep striving to survive, too preoccupied to initiate an overhaul of this predatory system. Students from low-income families were left alone in their struggle for their basic and universal right to have access to knowledge.

Emergency distance education has no doubt had a huge impact on students and their families. Distance education is not a new concept, and many universities offer courses through the distance education system. However, a great majority of the students in higher education had not opted for this way of education prior to the pandemic. They simply had not signed up for online distance education. Most of my students were from other countries, and before the borders were closed, they all returned to their countries and their family homes. In the confusion of the first couple of weeks, when we had no regular contact hours with students, I kept sending them emails and regularly posted on our Moodle page. It was a relief to learn that almost all were doing fine with their families. One of my students, however, never replied to my emails. None of his classmates had any contact with him either. I asked the student affairs to contact the student through other means, but their efforts failed, too.

When Covid-19 lockdowns happened, most of the students were given no alternatives but to totally redesign their lives. The first shock was when the school buildings, classrooms, conference halls, and libraries were closed down. These premises were the only venues where students could study comfortably. Many students share crowded dormitory rooms or rented apartments, which are hard to compare with libraries and study halls, where they can find quieter, more comfortable, and warmer conditions to study. When they were denied of these conveniences, seemingly lucky ones packed and went back to their family homes before the travel restrictions were introduced. Many were hesitant to move due to financial issues, the uncertainty of the future, or simply being optimistic that the lockdown would last just a couple of weeks at most. As time went by, and it became clear that we would carry out emergency distance education, the students were expected to have a working, capable computer to have access to this new mode of education. If they hadn't had one, tough luck! Although some private universities provide their students with free laptops or tablets computers, a great majority of students are on their own in finding a device to carry out the activities they are expected to follow. But, is it enough to have a working, capable device to be a student during the pandemic? Of course not! The students are also supposed to have an internet connection that should be strong enough to support videoconferencing and stable enough to keep a healthy and uninterrupted connection during examinations. Again, some universities provided free internet for their students for a limited time, but the effort was too feeble to cover the majority of the students. Some GSM operators and internet service providers offered reduced fares or free internet for students for a period of time, but I suspect that was rather a public relations move than real support. Who in their right mind expects a profit-seeking company to offer free services for customers during a time ripe for increased profits?

The material necessities expected of the students is just one side of the coin. Students face myriad of psychological issues directly or indirectly stemming from the pandemic and emergency distance education. According to research on student wellbeing during the pandemic, students reported experiencing depression, anxiety, disappointment, sadness, isolation and loneliness as well as financial setbacks (Active Minds 2020; Super and van Disseldorp 2020; Van de Velde et al. 2021). The main cause of anxiety is reported to be the possibility of having a family member get infected. Students are also anxious about the continuity and quality of their education. They rate the quality of the emergency distance education poorly, and they feel downtrodden due to many additional requirements of online education. Having to share their family home, often with multiple siblings causes a considerable amount of stress and helplessness and, as a result, depression. When students are away from school, as far as administrations are concerned, they become somebody else's problem. During our online sessions, two students of mine can only speak when they are asked a question, and they speak for merely a few seconds before muting their microphones again. It is impossible to blame them for this because the moment they unmute their microphones, the voices of their younger siblings are heard, who are also trying to do their primary school lessons online in the same room. Because the parents are away at work during the day, these students are also responsible for taking care of their younger siblings. These are junior university students, and they need time on campus to feel the connection with a diverse group of other university students.

They need to learn the beauty and power of acting together and making changes collectively. The pandemic is denying them these fundamental opportunities. When one listens to the problems they are going through, it becomes apparent that they face so many different issues, and go through all kinds of distresses. Another student of mine joined my online office hour once and explained her frustration and stress due to a possible return back to normal. She had to give up her rented accommodation when she had to go back to her family home. Now she was very concerned that if the administrations decided to start face-to-face education for the spring term, she had nowhere to stay. Feeling the distress of having no fixed accommodation, coupled with the worsening financial condition of her family, she was deeply worried.

I would like to think of myself as a person who has an open mindset towards the conveniences of technology. Moreover, as a fan of the science-fiction genre, I am always curious about what prospects await us in the future. As an optimistic and hopeful person, I believe technology will bring us more good than evil. I am inclined to see new educational technologies in this light. That was one reason why I did my Master's thesis on the use of machine translation in foreign-language learning. While I was teaching face to face, I used to test new and free software to enhance my lessons. I also paid utmost attention to my students' feedback regarding the practical uses of those tools. As long as we were free to explore new ways of connecting with the world and each other via these tools, I was content. When the pandemic restrictions and school closures hit, some software has become indispensable rather than experimental. This is a conundrum for me because I am not at liberty to abandon crucial software as before when they are no more convenient.

Our communication with students is reliant on online collaboration tools such as Zoom, Webex and Microsoft Teams. With the rapid deployment of emergency distance education around the world due to the Covid-19 pandemic, these tools have suddenly become mandatory parts of our day-to-day educational activities. Despite some privacy and abuse issues in the first months, these tools, especially Zoom, have managed to penetrate into the lives of all teachers and school administrators, and naturally students. The company became so integral in Covid-19 communications that it became a generic term for online teleconferencing. The first entry in the Cambridge online dictionary for the word *zoom* is the description of this company at the moment. And these collaboration tools are just a window between the teachers and students. There are many more specialized in other tasks. The likes of Pearson and Cambridge learning management systems offer their course materials online.

For language classes, these platforms offer one-size-fits-all course solutions, complete with reading, listening and writing materials with tests. The packages are also polished with interactive video and audio supplements. I am not saying these are low-quality products, on the contrary. However, they come at a price well beyond the purchasing power of many in a country like Turkey. Almost all the educational technologies companies bombarded the institutions and teachers with their discounted or free-to-try solutions in the first couple of months of the pandemic. To be honest, it was a good opportunity to try out new and innovative technologies as long as they lasted. But, one by one, as it became apparent that the pandemic measures are here to stay for much longer, the free subscriptions expired, leaving a bittersweet taste of how things can be done in better ways in a shorter time using those tools. This was the infamous charm of the bourgeoisie, the insidious invasion of the neoliberalism. Then, when the new academic year started, few of these tools stayed free, some of them were subsidized by the schools which were able to do so, and some of them replaced coursebooks finding their way into the to-buy lists of the students. We may have been naively optimistic about the continuation of these services with subsidies from our institutions. How can we be sure that these tools will offer us free or low-cost education and communication solutions for long? How can we tell our privacy is safe? I am not trying to demonize some of the most useful tools for us during the pandemic, just hypothesizing some possibilities. Having been born and lived in Third World countries, I have a tendency to expect things to get worse.

With Covid-19, the nature of in-class or in-school communication has been totally transformed. Now, we depend on different profit-seeking platforms to be able to come together with our students for a class, to assign them homework, to grade their assignments. In order to administer a test, my institution requires students to download extra software. Since we started the extended emergency distance education in the 2020-1 academic year, we have been using a paid online platform for grammar teaching, another one for writing feedback, another one for reading and vocabulary tasks. These platforms provide considerable discounts and they are subsidized by the institution as of this year. On the other hand, it is not hard to guess that their discounts will not last forever, and the school administration may decide it is a good idea to dissolve these costs in student tuitions. According to Winslow, 'neoliberalism has always relied on chaos, crisis, and upheaval to achieve its political and economic prescriptions' (2017, 586). The Covid-19 pandemic has created the perfect conditions for neoliberalism to prowl around schools. In an era of decreased funding for higher education, it is not hard to imagine a future with private educational software companies tightening an economic grip on schools, where they provide the only possible means for education to take place. As Schwartzman (2020, 509) puts it, emerging expenses of teaching and learning can be an inevitable eventuality as long as the governments see education as a cost. The accessibility to these profit-ridden companies will remain as one of the main issues that will harm the less privileged students. As Giroux explains in his Global Thursday Talk: 'the accessibility of these technologies … has to be framed within the question of inequality who has access, whose privilege, and who doesn't. Inequality is central to fascism, to say the very least.' Predatory companies, some of which dominate the publications market, are expanding their impact area and penetrating and monetizing the simplest communications between a teacher and their students.

Even under these circumstances, I tend to consider the unfolding crisis due to coronavirus as a chance to transform the current pedagogy into one that centres around the learner and reflects ideas that create informed and critical citizens. I hold the belief that today is the day that our pedagogy paves the way for freely and easily accessible curriculum and embraces learners with limited or no means to take part in education. It is today that the *new normal* in education is being defined. As an educator, it is time for me to ponder about how to reach all my students, how to empower them, and how to engage them productively in the new and unexpected era of online synchronous and asynchronous education. In his Global Thursday Talk, Ira Shor emphasized the interrogative mode of teaching, which encourages problem-posing and question-asking students. And the pandemic-induced new normal could be the best time to start to minimize the declarative side of our pedagogy and support the future critical world citizens. Times of great distress are usually followed by new beginnings. As always, capitalist profit-seekers will try to monetize the opportunities that arise. This time it can be different. This time, we can shape the post-pandemic pedagogy with what we have learnt while we are physically distant but socially united. We can redesign our curricula now that we have clearly seen how digital divide cripples education opportunities for some of our students. We can work together to develop free and democratic technologies to support education even in times of crisis. We can connect with each other in novel ways now that we have learnt myriads of new communication possibilities. Post-pandemic pedagogy is waiting for us to shape it.

References

Active Minds (2020) 'COVID-19 impact on college student mental health', *activeminds.org.*

Ravetz, Jerome (2020) 'Science for a proper recovery: Post-normal, not new normal', *Issues in Science and Technology*. Available at: https://issues.org/post-normal-science-for-pandemic-recovery/ (accessed 18 December 2020).

Schwartzman, Roy (2020) 'Performing pandemic pedagogy', *Communication Education*, 69 (4): 502–17.

Super, S. and Lieke van Disseldorp (2020) 'Covid-19 International Student Well-being Study (C19 ISWS): Data from Wageningen University & Research', Wageningen University.

Van de Velde, Sarah, Veerle Buffel, Piet Bracke, Guido Van Hal, Nikolett M. Somogyi, Barbara Willems, Edwin Wouters and C19 ISWS consortium# (2021) 'The COVID-19 International Student Well-Being Study', *Scandinavian Journal of Public Health*, 49 (1): 114–22.

Winslow, Luke (2017) 'Rhetorical matriphagy and the online commodification of higher education', *Western Journal of Communication*, 81 (5): 582–600.

World Health Organization (WHO) (2020) 'A guide to WHO's guidance on COVID-19'. Available at: https://www.who.int/news-room/feature-stories/detail/a-guide-to-who-s-guidance (accessed 18 December 2020).

Chapter 15

RETHINKING SOCIAL TRANSFORMATION FROM INFORMAL LEARNING TO POLITICAL LEARNING IN THE COVID-19 PANDEMIC

Ali Tansu Balcı

Introduction

We are going through a process in which the world population has grown more than ever throughout human history and man dominates the rest of the world as never before. Although this process of growth and domination is known and of great concern, it is often ignored. However, in some cases, the problem can become something that cannot be ignored. The Covid-19 pandemic process, which affects the whole world, is an example of this. Although there is not enough emphasis on mainstream information production centres, practices that disregard human health lie at the basis of the epidemic. The emergence of the pandemic in China and oversimplifying the problem to just eating bats in China serves to somehow hide the truth.

The industrialization movements that have gained momentum since the industrial revolution and the accompanying industrial production processes have reached a dimension that has shaped the whole world under the name of globalization, especially with the developments in technology since the 1980s. The wave of globalization, whose theoretical and practical infrastructure has been created by the United Nations, World Bank, OECD and similar international organizations, brings many problems with it. The problems that are persistently ignored by the organizations are becoming a major threat to human health and the planet beyond (O'Neill 1998).

Globalization shaped over the concept of neoliberalism, which came into our lives with the transformation in economic-political practices and thoughts in the 1970s, basically suggests a global level of trade and capital movements. For this, it is expected that the state will withdraw from many areas in the market and take steps to create a market for capitalists (Boratav 1999; Harvey 2007). Here, there is a mutual consent, not a competition between capitalists and states. Because it is the states themselves that consent to the circulation of the capitalists at the global level. In this sense, states do not see any problem in the transfer of public services to capital, on the contrary, they do it themselves consciously and willingly. Because the globalizing world requires this! However, there are serious contradictions between the requirement in question and the reason for the existence of states.

Roughly, shaped through the criticism of the cumbersome and repressive structure of states, this movement, in essence, is presented as a non-governmental and individual-oriented libertarian approach. However, in practice, its equivalent is reflected in the free movement of capital from the social state to the capital state (Gorz 1999); this libertarian approach plays the role of a 'mask'.

While criticisms of liberal approaches (ibid. 1988; O'Neill 1998) drop this mask a lot, this study deals with the role of neoliberal policies and globalization in the Covid-19 process. The impact of the globalizing world on the emergence and spread of the Covid-19 outbreak cannot be denied. In addition, crisis situations that affect the whole world not only in the field of health but also in many other areas, especially in the economy, are observed at certain periods. However, neoliberal policies, which are the main source of epidemic or crises, are expected to produce solutions to the epidemic and crisis, and this vicious circle continues.

Health, education and work are among the areas where the damage caused by the globalization policies shaped within the framework of the neoliberal approach with the Covid-19 outbreak is seen. This study focuses on the damage seen in these areas and the learnings created by it. Learning processes are considered as informal and political learning in the context of the contradictions caused by the crisis and the reasons for the crisis to occur. Each crisis contains certain contradictions, and no crisis occurs without a reason. Revealing these contradictions strengthens political learning and includes social transformation practices.

Informal learning in the Covid-19 outbreak

Informal learning, with its best-known definition in the literature, is a spontaneous learning process based on life experiences (Livingstone 2001). Schugurensky (2000) stated that informal learning is an extremely broad concept and classified it under three headings, according to two variables (intention and awareness): 1. self-directed, 2. incidental, 3. socialization. In self-directed learning, the individual enters a process to learn something and becomes aware of what he or she learned at the end of the process. For example, a 55-year-old woman with breast cancer can learn about her disease as much as a specialist by constantly researching and reading. There is an intention at the beginning of this learning, and it is known that there will be an awareness at the end of the learning. In incidental learning, while there is no intention at the beginning of the learning process, awareness arises at the end of the process. An example of random learning is when a young child learns that this is not a good thing because of touching the iron. There was no intention at the beginning of the process, but awareness was created at the end of the process. Socialization is the internalization of attitudes, behaviours, skills and values that emerge during an individual's daily life. In socialization, there is neither an intention at the beginning of the learning process, nor an awareness at the end of the process. There is neither intention nor awareness in this socialization of a child who is born in a racist family and develops bad attitudes towards different beliefs. According to Livingstone (2001), what distinguishes intentional informal learning from other socialization and daily perceptions is that people consciously define this activity as a significant learning. Therefore, consciousness is an important feature in informal learning.

Accordingly, the epidemic process has added new learning to people's life experiences and the spontaneous learning process has accelerated more than ever. According to Schugurensky's (2000) classification, the Covid-19 epidemic particularly affected self-directed and incidental learning. Throughout the epidemic, people have self-directed access to information and gained awareness from online sources, health organizations, research reports, media and many other areas, either implicitly or consciously. Although this awareness has different reflections in each individual, the attitude that emerges about masks and cleaning is one of the most important learning. In addition, it is thought that this and similar learning that takes place under extraordinary conditions will be permanent for the rest of people's lives. Even if the epidemic ends, it can be predicted that people will continue to use masks in their future lives. Therefore, informal learning that occurs during crisis periods such as epidemics has a direct impact on human life.

Another informal learning brought about by the epidemic process is seen in incidental learning. Throughout the epidemic, people have made many incidental learning in their daily life practices (Watkins and Marsick 2020a). While there was no intention at the beginning of these learning, it is seen that an awareness was created in the process. For example, many of the anti-virus measures were initially realized through random learning. Interactions and experience sharing in public or private spaces are the places where incidental learning is most common. These learnings turned into awareness over time and became permanent.

In addition, the informal learning caused by the epidemic can be classified according to education, health, and work fields. For example, people did not know until now that hand-washing can be so important; The experiences of teachers and students regarding the provision of education outside of school were largely lacking; or many occupational groups did not have the experience that jobs could be continued without working in the workplace at certain time intervals. Examples can be increased, but all these learnings are informal learning that people learn because of their own life experiences and social practices, and from now on they will turn into permanent learning (ibid. 2020b). As has been stated a lot, it is possible to see some changes in education, health, and work areas in the period after the epidemic. However, it can be said that these learnings bring about radical changes in many areas and therefore have the essence that will provide a total social transformation. For this, it should be considered that the informal learning acquired during the epidemic has a potential that includes political learning. Therefore, revealing this potential constitutes the basic dynamics of social transformation.

Political learning in the Covid-19 outbreak

In addition to the informal learning that emerged in the epidemic, political learning, in which the reasons causing the epidemic are questioned, constitute another important learning topic. These learnings improved people's political learning. Globalization can cause global crises; the liberal economy is not as liberal as mentioned; and the public policies have vital importance, are just a few examples of these political learnings. However, as it is known, these issues have been discussed for a long time in the field of critical education and reflect many different perspectives. These include Peter McLaren's critical pedagogical interpretation; Henry A. Giroux's interpretation of educators and public pedagogy as transformative intellectuals; Michael W. Apple's official notion of information; Paulo Freire's pedagogy and critical literacy studies of the oppressed; Antonio Gramsci's conceptualization of hegemony; Marxist approaches of Frank Youngman, Paula Allman and John Holst; Globalization criticism by Shirley Walters, Ove Korsgaard, Michael Welton and Judith Marshall; Zygmunt Bauman's critical lifelong learning perspective; Myles Horton's critical citizenship interpretation; Griff Foley's learning studies in the social action have an important place (Mayo 2009). During the epidemic process, these discussions become more crucial and generate new learning. Especially Foley's (1999) approach to learning in social action evaluates social movements as important learning areas and the effects of these learning on economic, social and cultural transformation are emphasized.

Informal learnings that occur during the epidemic are important, but they will not be sufficient for learning in social action alone. Informal learning can turn into political learning within its context. For example, while learning to wash hands to protect against bacteria during the epidemic process is an informal learning, questioning the reasons behind the transformation of the bacteria as a threatening factor will bring political learning with it. At this point, consciousness (Freire 2005) and hegemony (Gramsci 2011) that will transform informal learning into political learning should be created. From another perspective, these and similar periods of crisis are important periods that reveal the basic contradictions and dissolution of capitalism (Marx 1990). Hence, periods of crisis are border situations, where reality emerges more than ever before and directly affects large masses of people (Freire 2005). According to Freire (ibid.), border situations can be overcome by border actions. Border situations are likely to be met with a challenge and border action, when considered as oppressive or impeding the emancipation of people. It is thought that such actions will be aimed at denying and transcending what is given rather than accepting it passively. Border situations are a problem with historical, social and dialectical dimensions in front of people and they contain the possibility of overcoming this problem with critical consciousness (Hayden 2016). When the Covid-19 epidemic period is considered as a crisis period and border situation, the potential for implementing border actions becomes important.

To define border actions correctly, it is necessary to analyse the current border situation first. The pandemic process, which can be defined as a crisis caused by the globalization process, which is basically shaped through neoliberal policies, appears in the field of health, but its effects are seen in all areas of life. However, neoliberalism violates one of the most fundamental human rights – the right to health – for the sake of capital's interest. Two dimensions of the violation of the right to health can be mentioned. The first of these is the privatization policies in the field of health; the second is the ignoring the practices of practices that threaten human health.

Privatization policies implemented in the field of health can be summarized as leaving human health to the interests of capital and not benefiting from health services sufficiently by those who do not have sufficient capital. However, one of the most important political learning created by the pandemic period is seen at this point. The health status of the society directly affects the individual well-being for each. The manipulation of 'being on the same ship' often emphasized by the sovereigns essentially expresses this concern. However, to be on the same boat that the dominant ideology is persistently manipulating, one must have the same fundamental rights. However, in a system where even the most basic human rights are made to be bought and sold, only individuals who have the capacity to buy it as a commodity can benefit from the right to health. As the health of public cannot be provided totally, the public health problems that threaten human health arise, (Rosen 2015), and, unfortunately, as long as policies that prioritize the interests of capital continue, similar health problems are likely to be seen (Yıldırım 2021).

Another violation of the right to health is the ignoring of practices that threaten human health for the sake of capital's interests. For example, with industrial food production, access to healthy and reliable food has become almost impossible. With the neoliberal policies applied in agriculture, the elimination of agricultural production at the local level, and the encouragement of industrial agricultural production, agricultural and animal products are produced by unnatural methods in large factories, not in agricultural areas and pastures, against the law of nature (Boratav 2004; Bernstein 2010). As such, foods that disregard human health are produced in these factories for the sake of more profit and people are condemned to these foods. However, from the liberal point of view, there is no problem in this case. Because, in free market conditions, people are free to buy the products they want. If people want to have access to healthy food, they can get it by paying for it. After all, people have the freedom to choose!

The future in which the neoliberal approach, briefly summarized above, drags humanity is not seen as bright. Crisis processes, such as epidemics that affect all of humanity, also shape the future of humanity. One of the possible and permanent changes in human behaviour will undoubtedly be seen in the health field. The health policies summarized above and ongoing are expected to direct policy makers to different alternatives in the upcoming period. However, it is also important to increase a social demand for this. On one hand, changes in the preference of people to access healthy food are also possible in daily life. For example, turning towards local agricultural products instead of industrial foods, increasing demand for local producers, gaining importance of local policies in the agricultural field is the main dynamics of change. Moreover, a change in this direction is also reflected in the policies of the United Nations, and, for example, in the context of supporting local producers, 2012 is declared as the International Year of Cooperatives with the theme, 'Cooperative enterprises build a better world' (UN 2012). Similarly, the emphasis on localization, which has been in European Union policies for a long time, indicates a perspective transformation in general.

On the other hand, the policies followed around the world since the 1970s have been based on reducing the rural population and reducing agricultural employment. Especially in the IMF and the European Union, corporatization in agriculture came to the fore and the liquidation of small producers was aimed. This process, in which consumption is encouraged instead of production, was dealt with mostly through 'urban' discourses, and ultimately, neoliberal globalization brought along agricultural transformation (Bernstein 2010). For example, it said policies in Turkey caused a decline in the labour force in the agricultural sector and the share of agriculture in gross domestic product (GDP) has dropped.

While in 1985, the labour force was in the agricultural sector at a rate of 47 per cent, in 2019 this rate decreased to 19.6 per cent. While the share of agriculture in GDP was 26 per cent in 1980, it decreased to 7.5 per cent in 2011 and 6.4 per cent in 2019 (OECD 2008). In addition, as of 2005, the rural population growth rate in Turkey, since 1990, has turned negative for the first time. The rural population ratio, which was 35.10 per cent in 2000, decreased to 7.2 per cent as of 2019 (TURKSTAT 2020). The number of farmers in Turkey in the field of agriculture decreased from year to year, and as of 2020 the number of farmers only last 12 years decrease 48 per cent; agricultural areas decreased by 12.3 per cent (Euronews 2020). Similar changes are happening in the rest of the world.

At this point, one can talk about the bankruptcy of the globalization policies implemented so far. However, this bankruptcy has had severe consequences for humanity and is not a situation that can only be explained by wrong policies followed. Because the policies that have continued until this period reflect a conscious choice, which, as explained above, prioritizes the free-market economy and in any case protects the interests of capital, and ultimately imposed on the society as what should be by using all ideological tools to work. In other words, it is not a spontaneous and ought-to-be phenomenon, but a product of a will that is conscious of its own goals (Gramsci 2011). Adherents of this mentality correspond to a large segment of people who have an influence in education, media, companies, government agencies and international organizations (Harvey 2007). This will, which tries to be legitimized as a hegemonic discourse with fancy phrases such as 'globalizing world order', '21st century world', 'technological developments' – as seen in the pandemic process, now poses a threat to humanity the planet as virus. Therefore, the will in question cannot be expected to produce a permanent solution to any problem. Although international organizations (especially the EU, UN, OECD, World Bank) and governments, which were primarily responsible for the policies carried out in the past, show different political orientations as a way out of the crisis, in essence, they contradict with their ideological backgrounds. To explain with an example, it would not be realistic for a political line that prioritizes globalization to put localization on its agenda as the opposite direction. Moreover, when the globalization emphasized here is the global circulation of capital; localization will continue as capital dominates local resources. While the place where industrial agriculture brings humanity is a public health problem, the solution to this is not the kind that can be solved by turning to local production. Because turning to local production alone will result in the industrialization of the local. From the Gramscian point of view, the problem can be solved by the transformation of hegemonic thought.

Conclusion

Although the Covid-19 outbreak is a health problem, it refers to a social crisis that occurs because of wrong policies carried out, especially in the field of health. Therefore, to define the epidemic correctly, it is necessary to make inferences not only in the field of health but also in many other areas. Education, health and working life are at the top of these areas, which directly affect human life. These are the areas where the effects of the Covid-19 outbreak are most intense.

The most fundamental learning emerging in the field of education is access to education. Education systems used as a means of reproduction of inequalities (Bourdieu and Passeron 1977) made inequalities more visible and deepened with the pandemic. At the same time, the educational practices of students and teachers have changed, and the importance of the school has emerged once again. As critical educators advocate, although the school is the production area of current ideologies, it always contains the potential for resistance (McLaren 2003). As a result, the importance of inequalities in education and the transformative potential of the school constitutes vital areas. For this reason, in the period after the pandemic, it will be important to bring up policies that eliminate inequalities and reveal the transformative potential of the school.

The most basic learning emerging in the field of health is seen in public health (public health services) and access to healthy and safe food. The public health risks of health privatization steps implemented in line with neoliberal policies have once again become clear with the epidemic. Health is too vital to be condemned to the interests of capital. For this reason, in health, public policies should be prioritized for the benefit of human, not capital. In addition, people's access to healthy and safe food is considered important in terms of preventive health services. Policies should be implemented to ensure that every individual has access to healthy and safe food. Policies based on local production should be implemented instead of industrial agriculture policies under the control of big capitalists. In the words of Yıldırım (2021), it is not enough to examine whether the foods are healthy or not, if not, to make them healthy. The conditions that make foods unhealthy should be eliminated. Therefore, resolving the pandemic is not enough, the conditions that created it should be eliminated.

The most basic learning that emerges in the field of study is that more flexible working practices can be applied, especially working hours, and working place.

Considering that employees who are left at the mercy of the capital are employed even under epidemic conditions, steps must be taken to ensure the rights of employees. Because stopping working life is equivalent to stopping human life. As seen once again during the epidemic process, the working class, especially, has a position that creates life in all areas of life. In addition, while the rate of deaths in all occupational groups during the epidemic process is 31.4 per 100,000, this rate is 143.2 per 100,000 for factory workers (*Handelsblatt* 2021).

With the collapse of the Soviet Union, capitalism is on the rise more than ever in a unipolar world order, and if it is necessary to issue a bill at the end of this process, it will be the policy practitioners of first-degree capitalism responsible. The political line in question is the neoliberal thought that can be described as the expansionist market economy shaped in the axis of liberal thought and the global circulation of capital. However, at the point reached, the reasons for the emergence of the Covid-19 epidemic and the policies followed throughout the epidemic once again revealed that capitalism is harmful to human health. In such a situation, it is obvious that this political line is now 'out of date' in the twenty-first century, and even a mindset that needs to be changed as soon as possible.

As Marx (1990) stated, capitalism contains certain periods of crisis. Although these crisis periods have painful consequences for humanity, they are expressed as critical periods in questioning capitalism and emerging new quests. Therefore, although the Covid-19 epidemic process has painful consequences for humanity, it will become important to discuss a new world order. For this, cultural hegemony must be ensured (Gramsci 2011) and broad masses of people must become common in a more humane world order. Today, we can say that even international capitalists agree that globalization is on the brink of bankruptcy. However, for the sake of the capital they hold, they are not expected to return from this mistake. Instead, localization moves that will breathe globalization policies are preferred. These localization moves are shaped by the opening of local resources to the market and the exploitation of the local, under a non-governmental mask. The understanding of multicultural society, supporting local production, opening local products to the market and cooperatives are just a few of them. However, it should not be forgotten that no understanding that does not prioritize the public interest will provide the solution of the problems.

In this period, when the importance of public policies in all areas of life, especially in education, health, and work, emerges once again, what needs to be done is to implement policies that protect human interests instead of capital interests. For this, the political needs to be made more pedagogical (Giroux 2004). The correctness of the words of critical educators who have been working in this field for many years and emphasizing the currency of the critical education approach during the pandemic period has once again been demonstrated at Global Thursday Talks meetings. In the next process, areas should be created to ensure that these words reach more people. Because humanity is looking for a way out.

References

Bernstein, Henri (2010) *Class Dynamics of Agrarian Change* (Halifax: Fernwood Publishing).

Boratav, Korkut (1999) 'Bir Küreselleşme Eleştirisi', *Türk İş Yıllığı*, 29–38.

Boratav, Korkut (2004) *Tarımsal Yapılar ve Kapitalizm*. (Ankara: İmge Kitabevi).

Bourdieu, Pierre and Jean-Claude Passeron (1977) *Reproduction in Education, Society and Culture*, trans. Richard Nice (London: Sage Publications).

Euronews (2020) 'Türkiye'de son 12 yılda çiftçi sayısı yüzde 48 düştü', 14 May 2020. Available at: https://tr.euronews.com/2020/05/14/turkiye-de-ciftci-sayisi-yuzde-38-dustu-tarim-alani-yuzde-12-azaldi (accessed 28 November 2020).

Foley, Griff (1999) *Learning in Social Action: A Contribution to Understanding Informal Education* (London: Zed Books).

Freire, Paulo (2005) *Pedagogy of the Oppressed*, trans. Myra Bergman Ramos (New York and London: Continuum).

Giroux, Henry A. (2004) 'Public pedagogy and the politics of neo-liberalism: Making the political more pedagogical', *Policy Future in Education*, 2 (3–4): 494–503.

Gorz, Andre (1988) *Critique of Economic Reason*, trans. Gillian Handyside and Chris Turner (London and New York: Verso).

Gorz, Andre (1999) *Reclaiming Work: Beyond the Wage-Based Society*, trans. Chris Turner (Cambridge: Polity Press).

Gramsci, Antonio (2011) *Prison Notebooks Vol. II*, ed. and trans. Joseph Anthony Buttigieg (New York: Columbia University Press).

Handelsblatt (2021) 'Britische Behörde: Arbeiter sterben am häufigsten an Covid-19', 25 January 2021. Available at: https://www.handelsblatt.com/dpa/wirtschaft-handel-und-finanzen-britische-behoerde-arbeiter-sterben-am-haeufigsten-an-covid-19/26850384.html?ticket=ST-11711684-pS10GwWFNMyT1KIY3Jt6-ap1 (accessed 22 February 2021).

Harvey, David (2007) 'Neoliberalism as creative destruction', *Annals of the American Academy of Political and Social Science*, 610: 22–44.

Hayden, Patrick (2016) *Camus and the Challenge of Political Thought/Between Despair and Hope* (Houndmills: Palgrave Macmillan).

Livingstone, David Walker (2001) *Adults' Informal Learning: Definitions, Findings, Gaps and Future Research* (Toronto: NALL, New Approaches to Lifelong Learning).

Marx, Karl (1990) *Capital: A Critique of Political Economy*, vol. 2, trans. Ben Fowkes (London: Penguin Books).

Mayo, Peter (2009) 'Flying below the radar? Critical approaches to adult education', in Michael Apple, Wayne Au and Luis Armando Gandin (eds), *The Routledge International Handbook of Critical Education* (London and New York: Routledge), 269–80.

McLaren, Peter (2003) *Life in Schools: An Introduction to Critical Pedagogy in the Foundations of Education* (New York: Longman).

O'Neill, John (1998) *The Market/Ethics, Knowledge and Politics* (London and New York: Routledge).

Organisation for Economic Development and Co-operation (OECD) (2008) *Environmental Performance of Agriculture in OECD Countries since 1990* (OECD).

Rosen, George (2015) *A History of Public Health* (Baltimore, MD: Johns Hopkins University Press).

Schugurensky, Daniel (2000) 'The forms of informal learning: Towards a conceptualization of the field', *NALL Working Paper*, 19: 1–8.

TURKSTAT (2020) 'İstihdam Edilenlerin Yıllara Göre İktisadi Faaliyet Kolları ve Dağılımı', Available at: https://tuikweb.tuik.gov.tr/PreIstatistikTablo.do?istab_id=2263 (accessed 15 May 2020).

United Nations (UN) (2012) International Year of Cooperatives. Available at: https://www.un.org/en/events/coopsyear/ (accessed 15 May 2020).

Watkins, Karen E. and Victoria J. Marsick (2020a) 'Informal and incidental learning in the time of COVID with Drs. Karen Watkins and Victoria Marsick', *Academy of Human Resource Development*, Webinar. Available at: https://vimeo.com/458639997/b53ece0e8d (accessed 22 February 2021).

Watkins, Karen E. and Victoria J. Marsick (2020b) 'Informal and incidental learning in the time of COVID-19', *Advances in Developing Human Resources*, 23 (1): 88–96.

Yıldırım, Mihriban (2021) 'Toplumsal Tıbbın İzinde Sağlık Hakkı', *sendika.org*, 25 January 2021. Available at: https://sendika.org/2021/01/toplumsal-tibbin-izinde-saglik-hakki-606581/ (accessed 21 February 2021).

Chapter 16

CRITICAL PEDAGOGY CONFRONTS TECHNOLOGY:
RESPONSES TO THE CHALLENGES OF THE NEW
EDUCATION REALITY DURING THE PANDEMIC

Kemal İnal

Introduction

Technology that characterizes the machine age and a totality of instruments, devices and contrivances, is also a way of organizing and maintaining (or changing) social relations, a manifestation of prevailing patterns of thought and behaviour, and a means of control and domination (Marcuse 1998, 41). It on its own could provide freedom as well as authoritarianism (ibid., 41). Technology is not only a matter of rationality in terms of technique, production and efficiency but a problem of power that also has political implications. Lewis Mumford argued that the main motive behind the mechanical discipline and many inventions was not technical efficiency but a matter of power over business or people (1934, 364). For Marcuse, during technological development, a new rationality and new standards of individuality spread throughout the society, which are not the direct or indirect effects of the machines on its users or the consumers of mass production, but rather the determining factors in the development of machines and mass production. In order to understand the full impact of these changes, it is necessary to examine the traditional standards of rationality and individuality dissolved in the current machine-age stage.

Accordingly, in this new stage, individuality did not disappear, but evolved towards the object of large-scale organization and coordination, and individual achievement was also transformed into standardized efficiency. The performance of the individual is motivated, guided and measured by standards external to him/her, namely standards related to predetermined tasks and functions. The efficient individual is one who makes his/her performance according to the objective requirements of the apparatus. His/her freedom is limited by the choice of the most appropriate means of achieving an end that (s)he has not determined. While individual achievement is consumed in the work itself, regardless of acceptance/ recognition, productivity is rewarded performance and is consumed only within the value of the device itself (ibid., 44–5). In other words, for Marcuse, in terms of the new rationality conditioned by technology, the individual can only find a ground and a movement area according to the logic in which performance is measured in an efficiency controlled by devices. The new rationality is now a social force. For Marcuse, how did we get here and what's missing? He says: the principle of individuality, that is, the pursuit of self-interest, was conditioned according to the premise that self-interest is rational, that is, it constantly emerged from the guiding and controlling of autonomous thinking. It was assumed that there should be an appropriate social and economic order (stage) in order to implement this rationality. In this order, social performance was something of the individuals themselves. Liberal society was organized as a suitable order (stage) for individualist rationality. In the field of free competition, the concrete achievements of the individual, whose products and performance are shaped according to the needs of the society, were the signs of his/her individuality.

In sum, individual rationality was transformed into technological rationality under the influence of this apparatus, which expresses institutions, devices and industrial organizations. This new situation or change is not limited to the subjects and objects of large-scale enterprises, but also characterizes the common way of thinking and even various forms of protest and uprising. This rationality sets judgement standards and supports attitudes ready to accept and even encourage the orders of the apparatus (ibid., 44).

Marcuse's thesis that the liberal society suffers during the transition from individual rationality to technological rationality, is very important. The pandemic has largely eliminated the relative, illusory or limited subject or subjectivization. On the one hand, the oppression of political systems, on the other hand, the digital technological world shaped according to the rationality of the market, increasingly penetrates our lives more and more. Political control, along with the pandemic, developed and used all kinds of surveillance tools, while also putting technical control into effect to ensure a so-called healthy life. But 'we will now have to learn to live a much more fragile life full of constant threats lurking in a corner' (Žižek 2020).

Critical pedagogy on technology

In a highly globalized world, we switched to the distance education based on digital technology. In fact, the proposal for a more primitive and varied version of this educational model came from a critical thinker, Illich (2018), who proposed a 'deschooling society', where individuals can freely exchange their relevant knowledge and skills through a peer-matching system based on informal learning networks. This model predicts the World Wide Web (Hart 2001, 72). Illich's proposal later turned into a new private sphere-based school practice and educational institution open to exploitation in the market, or, as Habermas put it, market reality 'colonized the world of life' (Morrow and Torres 2002, 68). Deleuze (1987) assumed that the control society we entered into was very different from the Foucauldian disciplinary society. For him, instead of being closed to institutions such as schools, in this new form of society the activities of jobs, and services, studies would be drawn to the homes and education will be carried out over computer networks instead of going to school. We all the more live in this kind of education system in a great crisis and age of uncertainty, predicted by Deleuze, in which, as noted by Schwartzman (2020, 502), the two crisis areas came to the fore: 1. digital gaps and divisions based on inequalities in access, skills and features to technology; and 2. the fact of which the educational neoliberal approach was re-emphasized.

Accordingly, a new pedagogical context predominantly created through digital technology has led to the review, definition and regulation of teaching conditions. The advantages and disadvantages of using advanced technology in education have already been discussed by many (Armstrong 2013; Gautam 2020; Omidina, Masrom and Selamat 2013; Duma and Monda 2013). But these sorts of discussions before the pandemic were generally made in a very technical language and that the philosophical, social and political aspects of the problem were not critically addressed, resulting in narrowing and dichotomizing the problem within the framework of the benefits and harms of technology (Hamidi, Meshkat, Rezaee and Jafari 2011; Göksel and Bozkurt 2019; Lase 2019). However, while some are seeking solutions to the problems in the new education reality, some philosophers like Slavoj Žižek and Byung-Chul Han, arguing that a new repressive regime tradition (e.g. digital surveillance-based dictatorship, oppression-based digital biopolitical regime, etc.) originating from technology is being built, formulated a technology-centric political critique (Han 2020; Kurianowicz 2020). In the field of education, it is possible to say that there is very little critical work, considering the new education reality. The compliments and criticisms of online education are squeezed into technical fields and terms, leading to the inability to provide the necessary social and public response based on citizen rights to the challenges posed by the new era. At this point, critical pedagogy must respond to the challenges of the new education reality by neither rejecting technology nor accepting it as it is.

Critical pedagogy has long been struggling with the challenges posed to the oppressed in education by neoliberal capitalism based on economic marketist logic and neoconservatism with a sociocultural dimension (Aronowitz and Giroux 1987; McLaren 1995; Apple 2012). A new challenge has been added in recent years. With the use of advanced technology in teaching, this new context, which started with the mass use of computers in schools in the USA in the early 1980s (Apple 2012) took the form of distance or online education during the pandemic based on the assumption that it would solve the problems of quality and access in education.

The locomotive of these three challenges appears to be technologized education and shapes the new education reality today. The new education reality suggests that the goals such as quality, efficiency, effectiveness and success in education can only be achieved if education is designed according to the logic and tools of high technology. The new education reality appears to be a new context for challenging critical pedagogy today, as it is based on a highly individualistic, marketist and technical logic. This new education reality either pushes to the background or trivializes or even deactivates the pedagogical tools such as dialogue, participation, agency/subject, critical consciousness, interaction and solidarity that critical pedagogy uses in the context of face-to-face education in the school environment. However, critical pedagogy should propose a new approach, in which technology is shaped according to the logic of the public approach, rather than opposing the use of advanced (computer-aided, online, digital, virtual, etc.) educational technologies in teaching. This new approach should be able to develop a new critical pedagogical language to counter the challenges that arise in the new education reality. Nevertheless, new approaches trying to establish this critical language began to be formulated and proposed during the pandemic. For example, Henry Giroux, who treats the coronavirus plague as not only a medical crisis, but also a crisis of politics, ethics, education and democracy, argues that 'Pandemic Pedagogy' as the new version of critical pedagogy is ready for an anti-fascist praxis (Giroux 2021). As another example, Sharon Ravitch (2020) stated that 'flux pedagogy' is a humanizing pedagogy that transforms teaching and learning in the coronavirus era and is the solution in moments of uncertainty.

The new education reality

The new education reality today based extensively on the advanced technology, relies entirely on complex digital tools. The old moment started with the idea of using high technology as an auxiliary, supportive and compensatory tool for efficiency and effectiveness in teaching, then evolved in the comprehensive technologicalization of education. It reached its final point with the conditions that dictated the withdrawal of education to the backup of technology. The new education reality points to a context in which the market and conservative logic of capitalism is intertwined with advanced educational technology and radical changes in education begin to occur, as exemplified in 'Education 4.0'.

'Education 4.0' and expectations

After the Soviet Union sent a satellite to space in 1957, the USA, looking for reasons of staying behind its rival in space technology, decided to reform the education system, and enacted laws and made reforms to improve its military defence (Tröhler 2016). The high competition in the markets, triggered by the technological developments of education and between ideological blocs and countries, put pressure on the need for a continuous innovation in the educational institution. Until the 1980s, technology in education was based on the use of some traditional mass-based communication tools such as newspapers, radio and TV in a position to support education in schools. Computer use in classrooms was mentioned for the first time in the USA. 'When computers first appeared in school mathematics classes in the 1970s the emphasis was, rightly, on how they might be used to improve student learning' (Clark-Wilson, Robutti and Thomas 2020). However, from the 1980s on, the emergence of neoliberal capitalism intensified competition in the world of economy, leading to some effects on education. The need for a workforce that can withstand high competition in the markets led to the questioning of the content and training systems of education, resulted in the idea that schools should be reformed over curricula, teaching materials and technological tools. Thus, the technologicalization of education started with the intensive use of computers in education in the 1980s. During the 2000s, the phenomenon of technologicalization of education has become well established. However, this points to a completely different context. Although it is claimed that online learning does not replace education, but only completes the deficiencies of education and supports individual teaching and makes education effective/ efficient (Duma and Monda 2013, 48).

Digital-based distance or online education is presented as a projection of the 'Industrial Revolution 4.0'. Here the point is what components of education are affected by this revolution and how should education respond to these implications (Lase 2019; Gray 2016; Aziz Hussin 2018). For Schwab (2016), 'Industrial Revolution 4.0' would fundamentally change the way we live, work and relate to each other. The fourth-generation industrial era is characterized by increasing connectivity, interaction, development of digital systems, artificial intelligence and virtuality (Lase 2019). What needs to be done is to adapt to the conditions, requirements and logic of this new era. This can only be possible by improving the quality of human resources through education. Accordingly, students and teachers should be equipped with new competencies, skills, knowledge and data literacy for a graduate quality. The curricula should be oriented and shaped to meet the requirements of the Industrial Revolution period, referring to the reorientation of curricula, ICT-based learning, the internet of things, big data and computerization, as well as entrepreneurship and internship (ibid.). It is assumed that 'Education 4.0' must first address to the production of a creative, innovative and flexible workforce by intertwining human, machine and technology. It is claimed that 'Education 4.0' emerged as a result or combination of nine different trends: 1. instruction can be done at any time and place; 2. learning can be personalized according to the special situation of individual students; 3. students have the right and opportunity to determine how they want to learn; 4. students are oriented towards project-based learning; 5. Students are forced to learn hands-on with field experiences such as internship, mentoring and collaborative projects; 6. students are prompted to apply their theoretical knowledge to numbers and interpret data that they are expected to use their reasoning skills to make logical and trend-based inferences from the available data sets; 7. students will be evaluated differently; 8. students' views are taken into account in designing and updating the curriculum; and 9. students become more independent in their learning, which forces teachers to take on the role of facilitator to guide students. Therefore, teachers should support this new process (ibid.).

Some expectations for this moment in education have been grounded on the assumptions for more easily learning and access to ICT tools, increasing efficiency, effective flow of information and content creation, a high sense of community and cooperation among students, elimination of inequality, less environmental pollution, high motivation to perform better (Duma and Monda 2013; Kim 2011 quoted in Duma and Monda 2013; Ferrer, Belví and Pamìes 2011; Moberg, Johansson, Finnveden and Jonsson 2010). It is hoped that technology will help to achieve international compromise, mutual understanding, peace and brotherhood. This is seen as a factor in strengthening independence and the development of democratic ideas, even as a liberating factor in Third World countries (Hamidi et al. 2011, 370). In this new education reality, one of the skills suggested for the twenty-first century is 'critical thinking and problem solving' (Hauer 2017). However, it is unclear how, why and for what the information obtained will be criticized. This skill is considered for the demands and requirements in the market with a very technical logic; that is, it does not address a social and political context.

To sum up, technology in the new education reality is presented as a new saviour or emancipatory agent, replacing class forces, political will and social movements. So, how can critical pedagogy put forward a new perspective to these challenges without opposing the use of advanced technology in education?

Critical pedagogy: Responses to the challenge

'What role do the new information technologies play in critical education?' (McLaren and Jandrić 2015, 201). Do new information technologies increase the mystification and control of the dominant Western culture and its ruling factions or provide an opportunity to create a new kind of society (socialist society)? Such questions have been not adequately addressed by critical educators so far (ibid., 202). Even though critical educators stressed on the role of advanced technology in reproduction of capitalism, they did not investigate the potential of education technology in playing a role in subjectivating or liberating educators and students. As is very well known, the digital technologies played an alternative communication and educational tool role in social movements such as the Arab Spring, Occupy Wall Street (OWS), Indignados, Syntagma and Gezi (İnal 2013; Gezgin, İnal and Hill 2014). Faced with the consequences of precarization and the economic crisis, young people who created and organized these social movements were more educated and skilled than their past generations. However, they also had the communication skills to make their discontent clearer than in the past and '[were] in a position to create networks of struggle and solidarity, thus making themselves more than instrumental for the creation of new public spaces, both real and virtual' (Sotiris 2014, 320). All these show us that digital technologies could also be used for the interests of the public good and play a role in subjectivating and raising awareness. Thus, critical pedagogues did not have a satisfying explanation on how these technologies were able to be used practically in educational settings for emancipation.

However, there are some quests that speak from within critical pedagogy. Maboloc (2020) argued that technology would facilitate personal relationships by providing meaningful experiences between teachers and students. Modern tools are 'necessary to self-discovery and critical for more freedom'. Claiming that critical pedagogy is possible under the 'new normal', said Maboloc: 'The new normal must now emphasize the role of education as a source of inner strength that can empower to live well reinforcing values based on a social consciousness' (Maboloc 2020). Morris also speaks of transformative 'critical digital pedagogy', based on equality, agency and critical consciousness. According to him, this pedagogy provides the opportunity to humanize the relationships between teacher and student (Morris 2020). But our main question remains unanswered: How can the school and all its agents put digital technology into the service of culture, emancipation, democratization? How is it possible to build a collective partnership and respond to the challenge of the future of the world, and relationships, interactions, and learning? (Forum Ecole Alternumérique 2020).

Critical pedagogy's perspective on the use of technology in education

Technology in critical pedagogy was primarily seen as a form and practices of 'control' and 'deskilling' of dominant power ([Apple 2012, 151–72; Darder 2012; Giroux 1981). Technology does not replace the teacher but causes significant formation, management and transmission problems for the teachers. In every new technological development, even if the teacher does not compete with the technology, which (s)he sees as functional and indispensable for teaching, (s)he can respond to a possible objectification attempt by a technology by further subjecting herself/himself to the technology by comparing his qualifications with the capacity of the technology. The main point is that teachers approach technology as a totally 'autonomous process', as said by Apple (2012, 151). 'It is seen by teachers as if technology has a life of its own independent of social intention, power and privilege' (İnal 2019, 473). Apple argues that in the early 1980s, when the computer started to be used in education in America, technology was seen as a 'saviour' (Apple 2012, 152) both economically and pedagogically. According to Apple, the language built in this framework is defined under qualifications determined by market forces such as effectiveness, efficiency, standards, cost-benefit, professional skills, work discipline and imposed on the state/public education system. According to him, there should be concern about this language in education. Because this language in education pushes aside issues such as democratic curriculum, teacher autonomy and class/sexual/racial equality. If new technologies are not subjected to criticism, teachers will face 'deskilling' and 'impotence' (Apple 2012, 153–62, cited in İnal 2019, 474). Teachers are reduced to the position of technicians, not producers, planners and evaluators of the plans, procedures and evaluation mechanisms prepared by out-of-school experts with the developing technology. This involves the danger of passivation for both teacher and student. Therefore, Apple points out that in the long term, the use of advanced and intensive technology in schools can have negative consequences for the teachers: loss of old important skills and dispositions, inability to plan their own curriculum, blindness in areas such as individual assessment, etc.

'But more importantly, the industrialization of the school (opening up school education to the value, demands and appraisal of the industry) opens classrooms to mass-produced commodities and turns education into a market. In this case, teachers will have little choice but to purchase these ready-made materials. Thus, important educational materials will not be produced locally, but will be bought and consumed from commercial resources whose main purpose is not to improve education but to make a profit. In this context, the knowledge transferred in the school will be a part of the technical-administrative 'cultural capital' of the new middle classes. Computer skills and 'literacy' are a partial strategy for maintaining middle-class promotion/mobility patterns. On the other hand, as new technologies transform the class within its own structure, the more a technical logic will replace critical political and ethical understanding. Thus, while the dominant discourses in the classrooms are more centralized on technique and less emphasis will be placed on the substance (Apple 2012, 162–71, cited in İnal, 2019, 475).

This technology-weighted conservative educational discourse, which is deeply secured within the positivist ideology, by emphasizing technological knowledge, creates an empirical analytical research method that combines the notion of objective observation with countless objective facts (Darder 2012, 52, cited in İnal 2019, 475). 'The belief that information can be transferred to students objectively, impartially and independently of the knowing subject by using technology in the form of an amorphous force may lead to a process in which technology objectifies students' (İnal 2019, 475). Therefore, the approach to the use of technology in education for critical pedagogy includes a critical stance on its use and its negative effects in accordance with the economic interests of the ruling power and the practices of science making, rather than rejecting it. Critical pedagogues, who do not deny that technology in education leads to richness in productivity, creativity and learning, emphasized more on teachers' relationship with technology than students, and saw technology as a means of controlling and deskilling of labour. Consequently, they claimed that the curriculum and teaching materials produced in the markets bypassed the teachers' conception skills and reduced the teacher to a simple practitioner, namely 'information technician' (de Certeau 2009, 278). What should then be the responses of critical pedagogy to the challenges of the technologicalization of education in the new education reality?

Increasing knowledge by technicalization

Critical pedagogy should rethink the ways in which subjects produce, use and disseminate knowledge in education. Instead of relying solely on digital sources, information can be obtained in hybrid forms, for example, by using verbal sources as well as the internet to study history, by checking the accuracy of information from different sources and by encouraging students to produce information themselves. For the 'counter-knowledge' (McLaren and Jandrić 2015, 208), which takes into account the self-reflexivity and recursive interactions between nature and technology, which will include qualities that will foster critical consciousness and produce information in favour of the oppressed, a new approach should be adopted. Freire (2000) formulated such a new approach by saying that the teacher should create opportunities for the production and construction of knowledge rather than transmitting information. A critical approach should take into consideration the production and transfer of knowledge to critically filter the information whose number, variety and source is increasing in the new education reality. In bourgeois educational formations, the formation of students as human capital to withstand intercompany competition in the markets transforms them into commodity producers seeking individual interest rather than working for the public good. To prevent this, one must consider how information will be produced for the public good through digital technologies.

Four pandemic-originated challenges

These challenges can be listed in four points: first, the concept of pandemic education has given rise to a new 'technological inequality' in various contexts, including class, racial and ethnic, in terms of access to online education, ownership of tablet computers and obtaining adequate internet quota. Most of low-income countries have not been able to reopen their schools. It is predicted that there will be a decrease in the education budgets of low-income countries due to the economic crisis. In low-income countries, student development cannot be fully controlled by teachers. The pandemic has negatively affected 1.5 billion students and 63 million teachers worldwide. Again, in Kaymak's appropriate statement: 'Distance education, which is carried out over technologies that are not based on pedagogical principles, deepened the inequalities in reaching the already existing quality education' (2020, 10).

Marc Pensky (2001) expressed this inequality in two laconic terms: world populations are divided into two separate categories in terms of digital technology: 'Digital natives' (northern countries) born in the world of information and communication technologies and able to use technologies as their mother tongue and 'digital immigrants' (southern countries) who encounter these technologies late in their lives and are not as competent with them as the first group. Second, with online education, the disappearance of the classical school opportunity as an educational manifestation of the public sphere has started to prevent students from acquiring even the simplest 'awareness of citizenship'. At school, students do not only gain knowledge, skills and abilities. At the same time, they experience the first example of a civic philosophy by socializing, acquiring identity, learning norms, internalizing values, adopting role models, learning the opposite sex, and assuming various roles and duties at school. This awareness of citizenship is not something that can be given at home by the parent who is not self-educative, has no authority in knowledge and does not have the ability to give civic values in a planned-programmed manner. Third, the fact that the various duties of the teacher in the school cannot be fulfilled by the parents at home has revealed how important the missing 'teacher authority' is. Fourth, the problems caused by the inability to socialize, namely the absence of dialogue, interaction and solidarity resulting from home-centred education life, hinder both teachers and students from having 'critical awareness'. Critical pedagogy unable to withstand these four challenges cannot provide praxis, the synthesis between critical consciousness and transformative practice, in the new pandemic conditions. Critical pedagogy must therefore defend the thesis that consciousness can only be practically experienced in the concrete school space for the public use of reason in this new educational reality.

Conclusion

In conclusion, critical pedagogy should develop an approach that critically addresses and promotes digital technology without opposing it. It is just time to critically examine the transition to the digital revolution and consider how critical pedagogy can adapt to it in ways that promote democracy. In this context, we should see digital technology not as a set of high-tech tools, but as a true ecosystem that profoundly changes the way we think, socialize and work. We need digital technology, focused lens, which is the key feature of schools and school education all over the world (Selwyn 2011, ix). However, the use of technology in education rarely attracts sustained critical attention and thought. We need a non-technologically perspective to look at the technology issue objectively.

Marx saw technology as a means of continuation, exploitation and alienation of the limbs of the workforce within the capitalist system (Hernandez, Prysner and Ford 2019). Heidegger argued that even though we passionately defend technology or deny it, we are deprived of freedom and chained everywhere, so that we must master it (Heidegger 1977, 4–5). However, today digital technology has become an extension or even an integrated part of our thoughts, feelings and behaviours by going beyond our limbs. Technology has brought us to the point of breaking away from some practices of social life. It even shapes our thinking and logic. So much so, that a life without technology has become unthinkable. In this context, we are experiencing the technologicalization of our lives. Technologicalization of education also transformed the teacher/student and technology relationship. In the new education reality that emerged as a result of these transformations, education with digital tools is now faced with many new problems, tensions and contradictions. Therefore, in order for critical pedagogy to respond to the challenges in this new education reality, it must develop a new critical pedagogical approach and language of digital technology.

It is also possible to say that critical pedagogues work with heart and soul in this way. Giroux's conceptualizations such as 'pandemic pedagogy' and Ravitch's 'flux pedagogy' seem to be meaningful examples of how a new perspective can be formulated through technology in an extraordinary period like the pandemic. Public intellectuals and critical educators' digital communities, dialogue, solidarity, and praxis for a post-digital age seem to be formed under the need of creating a new critical language of technology. In an extraordinary context such as the Covid-19 pandemic, this has a triple stage: to create a new approach by gathering in the digital field; to announce this approach to the public in a printed publication; and to realize praxis by bringing the intellectuals and the public together. The leading worldwide pedagogues and intellectuals, Peter McLaren, Henry A. Giroux, Michael W. Apple, Antonia Darder, Peter Mayo, Guy Senese, Arnd-Michael Nohl, Ira Shor and E. Wayne Ross, who gathered in this collection as the fruit of the digital community, Global Thursday Talks, held by Fatma Mızıkacı and Eda Ata from Turkey, emphasized some common points in their presentations: 1. critical education cannot remain unanswered to the classical problems as racism, poverty, inequality, discrimination, and exploitation created by capitalism; and 2. digital education, proposed as a remedy for Covid-19, for which capitalism has difficulty in finding solutions, has produced more problems than solutions. Although education with digital tools makes it difficult to represent and analyse social problems in education, advanced technology should be used effectively and criticized by public intellectual and critical pedagogues in order to create a widespread awareness about social problems on digital platforms.

The meetings at Global Thursday Talks have been an example of theoretical praxis via creating a critical digital community for solidarity based on dialogue, interaction, and exchange of ideas. As assumed by the editors of this volume, 'in the hard times of Covid-19 pandemic', even though critical pedagogies 'are shut down home and out of schools, classrooms, and campuses', this volume became a practical example of connecting 'the community in a documented form that will remain as an example of solidarity in the times of crisis'. As stated in the title of this volume, for *Keeping Communities Together in the Times of Crisis*, critical pedagogues should play the public intellectual role by using digital tools more intensively as a means of creating consciousness. For this, as stated in this volume, we need 'hopeful discussions' (McLaren), 'critical analysis' (Apple), 'Resistance' (Senese), '*Bildung* on mass education' (Nohl), 'revolutionary praxis of body' (Darder), 'Pandemic Pedagogy' (Giroux) and 'analysis of curriculum in relation to pandemic/online education' (Ross). In this volume, to which many critical pedagogues from Turkey have contributed, the transformative power of being a digital community can open new horizons to critical pedagogy as a form of pedagogical resistance during the pandemic. As Marcuse said, the replacement of individual rationality by technological rationality in the 'machine age' was a major problem. This problem has become widespread nowadays. Only by strengthening individual rationality for public philosophy can we counteract the solution to this problem.

References

Apple, Michael W. (2012) *Education and Power*, 2nd edn (New York: Routledge).

Armstrong, Stephen (2013) 'What are the advantages and disadvantages of online learning?', *eLearning Industry*, 5 April 2013. Available at: https://elearningindustry.com/advantages-and-disadvantages-of-online-learning (accessed 3 May 2021).

Aronowitz, Stanley and Henry Giroux (1987) *Education under Siege: The Conservative, Liberal and Radical Debate over Schooling* (New York: Routledge).

Aziz Hussin, A. (2018) 'Education 4.0 made simple: Ideas for teaching', *International Journal of Education and Literacy Studies*, 6 (3): 92–8. Available at: https://doi. org/10.7575/aiac.ijels.v.6n.3p.92 (accessed 8 May 2021).

Clark-Wilson, Alison, Ornella Robutti and Michael O. J. Thomas (2020) 'Teaching with digital technology', *ZDM Mathematics Education*, 52: 1223––1242. Available at: https:// doi.org/10.1007/s11858-020-01196-0 (accessed 9 May 2021).

Darder, Antonio (2012) *Culture and Power in the Classroom: Educational Foundations for the Schooling of Bicultural Students* (Boulder, CO, and London: Paradigm Publishers).

de Certeau, Michel (2009) *Gündelik Hayatın Keşfi-I. Eylem, Uygulama, Üretim Sanatları*, Cilt I, çev. Ç. Eroğlu (Ankara: Dost).

Deleuze, Gilles. Filmed in 1987. Available at: https://twitter.com/oguzhan_duru/status/136 6844655015501832?s=08&fbclid=IwAR2kUD9lSx67NnPlm6wBNp4lcQuHOnljB6UY 2Q8YS_sLQxCwWh8-C_iSn2k (accessed 1 May 2021).

Duma, Lazslo and Ester Monda (2013) 'Impact of ICT based education on the Information Society', *Journal of Futures Studies*, 18 (1): 41–62.

Ferrer, Ferran, Esther Belví and Jordi Pamìes (2011) 'Tablet PCs, academic results and educational inequalities', *Computers & Education*, 56 (1): 280–8.

Forum Ecole Alternumérique (2020) 'Manifeste pour une école démocratique dans une société numérique', 4 November 2020. Available at: https://www.facebook.com/collectif ForumEcoleAlternumerique/?view_public_for=114827640420739 (accessed 1 May 2021).

Freire, Paulo (2000) *Pedagogy of the Oppressed*, trans. Myra Bergman Ramos with an Introduction by Donaldo Macedo (New York and London: Continuum).

Gautam, Priyanka (2020) 'Advantages and disadvantages of online learning', *eLearning Industry*, 10 October 2020. Available at: https://elearningindustry.com/advantages-and-disadvantages-online-learning (accessed 2 May 2021).

Gezgin, Ulaş Başar, Kemal İnal and Dave Hill (eds) (2014) *The Gezi Revolt. People's Revolutionary Resistance against Neoliberal Capitalism in Turkey* (Brighton: Institute for Education Policy Studies).

Giroux, A. Henry (1981) *Ideology, Culture and the Process of Schooling* (Philadelphia, PA: Temple University Press).

Giroux, A. Henry (2021) *Race, Politics, and Pandemic Pedagogy* (New York: Bloomsbury).

Göksel, Nil and Aras Bozkurt (2019) 'Artificial Intelligence in education: Current insights and future perspectives', in S. Sisman-Ugur and G. Kurubacak (eds), *Handbook of Research on Learning in the Age of Transhumanism*, (Hershey, PA: IGI Global), 224–36.

Gray, Alex (2016) 'The 10 skills you need to thrive in the Fourth Industrial Revolution', *World Economic Forum*, 19 January 2016. Available at: https://www.weforum.org/ agenda/2016/01/the-10-skills-you-need-to-thrive-in-the-fourth-industrial-revolution/ (accessed 3 May 2021).

Hamidi, Farideh, Maryam Meshkat, Maryam Rezaee and Mehdi Jafari (2011) 'Information Technology in education', *Procedia Computer Science*, 3 (2011): 369–73.

Han, Byung-Chul (2020) 'Güney Koreli felsefeci, kültür kuramcısı Byung-Chul Han: Koronavirüs bizi bir 'sağ kalma toplumuna' indirgedi', *A3haber.com*, trans. Ayşen Tekşen, 21 May 2020. Available at: https://www.a3haber.com/2020/05/21/guney-koreli-felsefeci-kultur-kuramcisi-byung-chul-han-koronavirus-bizi-bir-sag-kalma-toplumuna-indirgedi/?fbclid=IwAR3HO6axb4fyMQJbi7nDdMgyxrwax7JvH4mX5J7E IRsPyS1WKHZPqjW3mdc (accessed 7 May 2021).

Hart, Ian (2001) 'Deschooling and the Web: Ivan Illich 30 years on', *Educational Media International*, 38 (2011): 69–76.

Hauer, Thomas (2017) 'Technological determinism and the new media', *International Journal of English, Literature and Social Science*, 2: 1–4.

Heidegger, Martin (1977) *The Question Concerning Technology and Other Essays*, trans. and with an Introduction by William Lovitt (New York and London: Garland Publishing).

Hernandez, Estevan, John Prysner and Derek Ford (2019) 'A Marxist approach to technology', *Liberation School*, 9 December 2019. Available at: https://liberationschool.org/a-marxist-approach-to-technology/ (accessed 12 May 2021).

Illich, Ivan (2018) *Deschooling Society* (Victoria: Camas Books).

İnal, Kemal (2019) *Öğretmen ve İktidar. Öğretmenliğin İnşasında Öznelleşme, Çelişki ve Dönüşüm* (Ankara: Töz Yayıncılık).

İnal, Kemal (ed.) (2013) *Gezi, İsyan, Özgürlük. Sokağın Şenlikli Muhalefeti* (İstanbul: Ayrıntı Yayınları).

Kaymak, Murat (2020) 'Pandemi Koşulları Altında Eğitimdeki Kriz', *Tebeşir*, 8: 10–12.

Kim, Andrew (2011) 'South Korea to convert to digital textbooks by 2015', *Technorati*. Available at: http://technorati.com/technology/article/south-korea-to-convert-to-digital/ (accessed 15 May 2021).

Kincheloe, Joe (2008) *Critical Pedagogy: Primer*, 2nd edn (New York: Peter Lang).

Kurianowicz, Tomasz (2020) 'Slavoj Žižek: "The pandemic is only a test for the real crisis"', *Berliner Zeitung*, 2 December. Available at: https://www.berliner-zeitung.de/en/slavoj-iek-the-pandemic-is-only-a-test-for-the-real-crisis-li.123096 (accessed 16 May 2021).

Lase, Delipiter (2019) 'Education and Industrial Revolution 4.0'. Available at: https://www.researchgate.net/publication/334837153_Education_and_Industrial_Revolution_40 (accessed 18 May 2021).

Maboloc, Christopher Ryan (2020) 'Critical pedagogy in the new normal: Teaching values-based education online', *Voices in Bioethics*, 7 August 2020. Available at: https://journals.library.columbia.edu/index.php/bioethics/article/view/6888 (accessed 19 May 2021).

Marcuse, Herbert (1998) *Technology, War and Fascism: Collected Papers of Herbert Marcuse*, vol. 1, Douglas Kellner (ed.) (London and New York: Routledge).

McLaren, Peter (1995) *Critical Pedagogy and Predatory Culture: Oppositional Politics in a Postmodern Era* (New York: Routledge).

McLaren, Peter and Peter Jandrić (2015) 'The critical challenge of networked learning: Using Information Technologies in the service of humanity', in P. Jandrić and D. Boras (eds), *Critical Learning in Digital Networks* (New York: Springer), 199–226.

Moberg, Asa, Martin Johansson, Göran Finnveden and Alex Jonsson (2010) 'Printed and tablet e-paper newspaper from an environmental perspective – A screening life cycle assessment', *Environmental Impact Assessment Review*, 30 (3):177–91.

Morris, Sean Michael (2020) 'A pedagogy of transformation for times of crisis', *OebInsights*, 17 April 2020. Available at: https://oeb.global/oeb-insights-a-pedagogy-of-transformation-for-times-of-crisis/ (accessed 21 May 2021).

Morrow, Raymond Allen and Carlos Alberto Torres (2002) *Reading Freire and Habermas: Critical Pedagogy and Transformative Social Change* (New York: Teachers College Press).

Mumford, Lewis (1934) *Technics and Civilization* (New York: Harcourt, Brace and Co.).

Omidina, Siavash, Maslin Masrom and Harihoddin Selamat (2013) 'An examination of the concept of Smart School: An innovation to address sustainability', in Gary Lee (ed.),

2nd Proceedings of the 2nd International Conference on Advances in Computer Science and Engineering (Dordrecht and Paris: Atlantis Press), 326–9.

Pensky, Marc (2001) 'Digital natives, digital immigrants', *On the Horizon*, 9 (5): 1–6.

Ravitch, Sharon (2020) 'FLUX pedagogy: Transforming teaching & learning during coronavirus', *MethodSpace*. Available at: https://www.methodspace.com/flux-pedagogy-transforming-teaching-learning-during-coronavirus/ (accessed 20 May 2021).

Schwab, Klaus (2016) 'The Fourth Industrial Revolution: What it means and how to respond', *World Economic Forum*, 14 January 2016. Available at: https://www.weforum.org/agenda/2016/01/the-fourth-industrial-revolutionwhat-it-means-and-how-to-respond/ (accessed 21 May 2021).

Schwartzman, Roy (2020) 'Performing pandemic pedagogy', *Communication Education*, 69 (4): 502–17.

Selywn, Neil (2011) *Schools and Schooling in the Digital Age* (London and New York: Routledge).

Sotiris, Panagiotis (2014) 'Thoughts on the political significance of the Turkish movement', in Gezgin, Ulaş Başar, Kemal İnal and Dave Hill (eds), *The Gezi Revolt: People's Revolutionary Resistance against Neoliberal Capitalism in Turkey* (Brighton: Institute for Education Policy Studies), 315–27.

Tröhler, Daniel (2016) 'Educationalization of social problems and the eucationalization of the modern world', in Michael A. Peters (ed.), *Encyclopaedia of Educational Philosophy and Theory* (Singapore: Springer Science+Business Media Singapore), 1–6.

Žižek, Slavoj (2020) 'Žižek: Koronavirüsü, Kapitalizme "Kill Bill-var" Bir Darbedir, Komünizmin Yeniden İcat Edilmesine Yol Açabilir', *Terrabayt*, trans. Öznur Karakaş and Koray Kırmızısakal, 28 February 2020. Available at: https://terrabayt.com/manset/zizek-koronavirusu-kapitalizme-kill-bill-vari-bir-darbedir-komunizmin-yeniden-icat-edilmesine-yol-acabilir/ (accessed 22 May 2021).

Chapter 17

CULTURAL RESISTANCE OF CRITICAL PEDAGOGY IN THE AGE OF AUTHORITARIAN POPULISM

Gamze Gonca Özyurt

It is known that we have been going through difficult times, has there ever been an easy time in human history, anyway? In these difficult times, with a collective subconscious, people can cover the painful experiences pushed deep by social memory with so-called heroic stories. However, people do not need lies and disinformation to survive from the hard times. A weird concept of neoliberalism, also called social engineering, can easily manipulate the human – which is a sociocultural animal – with the cultural strategies in hard times. This manipulation owes its continuity to authoritarian populism. Subjected to the often distorted information and subjective history dissemination of the dominant ideology, society has almost become a test subject of operant conditioning.

Society must come out of this strange experimental set-up and act like a free human being on this planet. So, how? This may seem like a very political question to some; however, this question concerns pedagogy, which undoubtedly has more influence on social and cultural existence of human than politics. The transformative effect of Global Thursday Talks on me is right here: the cultural resistance of critical pedagogy. This is a strong realization because I felt like an anvil had fallen on my head during Giroux's speech on Global Thursday Talks. I was shocked, shaken and excited. I realized that my chronic despair towards the human condition is a huge obstacle to what we can do. His introductory style with Mızıkacı was like a magnetic wave that drew the centre of critical pedagogy; I recalled our importance in our war against the dark as educators. The 'war against the dark' that I use here is a comprehensive allegory that includes authoritarian populism. Because this is a 'darkness' that closes our eyes, prevents us from seeing or discovering the facts, and tries to turn our organic intelligence into passive and obedient artificial intelligence in a threatening atmosphere. It is dark, because it does not allow to go beyond the variables that set under its authority. It's dark, because it covers up everything that is against its authority. On the other hand, critical pedagogy wants to open up whatever is covered: it wants to question and discuss, to notice and to liberate.

Cultural attitude in critical pedagogy

I have known Henry Giroux as an intellectual, who theorized the different approaches of great thinkers such as John Dewey, Zygmunt Bauman and Paulo Freire in education as a political, moral, and cultural practice area. The first book I read was Giroux's, *Twilight of the Social: Resurgent Politics in the Age of Disposability* (2012), which was translated into Turkish. I think it was very striking to see the transformative potential of my profession in the problems he was referring to. The fact that he conveys so many major social problems in a promising style has encouraged me to take part in both academical and educational field. Maybe that is why I turn to adult education, where the critical approach comes to my life informally. However, education is continuous in human life, and its strength comes from here. It owes this strength to the discovery act in the human's cultural evolution and development.

Giroux's critical pedagogy emphasizes the role of education in creating cultural space. Cultural areas are habitats where democracy comes to life. The close relationship of democratic education with culture helps protect one another from economic, social and political threats. The separation of this togetherness pushes both into a fragile position. Therefore, critical pedagogy should present the promise of democratic education with its cultural infrastructure (Giroux 2011, 8–9). Because humanistic education is faced with an organism that cannot get enough, although eating more and more in this age, where the political and economic interests of the authority are increasingly diversified. Today, with globalization, culture is divided into many subcultures and becomes moribund with neoliberalism's 'divide-and-rule' strategy. The constantly recurring political discourse of identity politics and cultural diversity makes the society move away from the basic culture and education problem; just like overlooking the educational and cultural needs of society. It is not difficult to find the right side in this cultural war, in which fast consumption and instant living are promoted and continuity and renewability are not taken into account. It's a matter of determining the side; in fact, it is as easy as claiming the human right to liberty, the right to live and learn, the right to enjoy and read, the right to love and to be loved, the right to discover and research, the right to speak and raise our voice, and the right to come together and to live in solidarity. How can educators, who are public intellectuals, contribute to cultural resistance in this authoritarian populist age, where people are prevented from knowing their rights, let alone claiming their rights? The answer to this question lies in critical pedagogy.

All the critical educators that Global Thursday Talks reached during this anthropogenic crisis period, which increased with the pandemic and pushed the stress threshold on social psychology, shared the same opinion that this process was actually an educational and cultural crisis. Economics and politics are not at the centre of the crisis; and educators have a lot to do about it. The first is to explore critical pedagogy. As teachers, we should think about content without passing on the curriculum imposed by the authority to our students as it is. As schools are not mass-producing factories, we cannot act like vending machines as teachers. We are cultural workers and critical pedagogy needs culture for education. Giroux's critical pedagogy approach is also structured in a cultural framework that enables Giroux to conceptualize his critical educational approach and capture his transformative political power in a democratic praxis. These concepts have been the source of pioneering studies with the idea of cultural integration. Strengthening the critical education approach with these theories, Giroux has made good use of cultural contexts to ensure that education takes place in a sustainable and accessible platform.

Popular culture, whose introduction in critical pedagogy is a challenge, was also treated as an academic issue in Giroux studies. The pleasure-oriented lifestyles stand for authority and have an intention focused on weakening the culture. This can also be seen as an authoritarian pedagogical agent because power does not hesitate to use education to pump populists. Giroux began to shed light on the analysis of popular education, which is such a critical driver with critical pedagogy. Refusing to merely imitate the emphasis on the popular who conducted cultural research, Giroux refocused on a long-standing concern with cultural radical democracy. At this stage, concepts such as justice, freedom and equality in which radical democracy finds strength, formed a culture-centred domain in Giroux's understanding of education. Using the interdisciplinary tools of cultural studies to turn critical pedagogy into a democratic practice, Giroux has conducted many studies that will reveal the potential of talent in pedagogy as well as reflecting the potential of social change.

There is another problem that Giroux expects us to realize in today's populist culture: The issue of privacy. We live in a period where being constantly observed and watched is tolerated. Many individuals, especially young people, are now escaping privacy and increasingly demanding services with which they can share every personal aspect of their lives. Popular culture devices, which are also encouraged by the governments, become increasingly aggressive with private initiatives, offering young people two options for uploading or watching audio-visual media. Young people serve popular culture by publicly sharing their identities and values as digital commodities. This has almost reached a level of addiction and is one of the most beneficial behaviours for authoritarian populism. Popular culture is also one of the sources that foster wild capitalism's uncontrolled marketing techniques in our transparent lives. While culture has such an impact on authoritarian populism and capitalism, critical pedagogy must be persistent in focusing on the healing, bringing and sustainable features of culture. The authoritarian state, with new generation techniques such as data-mining, applies a more severe manipulation by determining the interests of individuals, political tendencies and even which food they like. This manipulative situation becomes more painful, especially with the indifference of children and young people fed with fear, and teachers who are afraid to do anything about it. Critical pedagogy has a great meaning in preventing the collective indifference of individuals who resist this insidious cultural change in our daily life (Giroux 2016, 17). We need to realize cultural manipulation and the understanding of education used to prepare a suitable environment for it, and abandon these concepts as soon as possible. We need to abandon this understanding for the future of our children as well as for ourselves.

Global Thursday Talks hosted another intellectual who made clear the relationship of critical pedagogy with culture: Michael W. Apple. Underlining that culture is an action, not a noun, Apple said that teachers should pay attention to culture in motion. Apple made a point later in the conversation, while arguing that one of the primary tasks of critical pedagogy is to make culture visible. In response to this manipulation of knowledge, which the authority uses to render existing inequalities invisible – Apple calls it the 'epistemological fog' in his speech – the stance of critical pedagogy is clear. In Apple's speech, I recalled once again that democracy and access to true information are included in the epistemology of critical pedagogy as mutually reinforcing phenomena, and I told myself again, 'Not being a puppet, is actually one of the key words.'

Apple also stated that authoritarian cultural policy creates a moral crisis. Inequality between people, the class problem and the unfair distribution of income can also be associated with the moral crisis in the education system (Apple 1996, 13–19). Critical education stands in the face of this moral crisis at this point. Neoconservatism does not care about individuals' school dropout, poverty or learning needs. What is important for neoconservatives is to think only of yourself in order to stay in power in a Macchiavellist style. Critical pedagogy is therefore the most radical, effective and sustainable solution for cultural politics.

According to Apple's analysis of the formal/informal, culture and knowledge of schools are very important (2017, 14). The profound influence schools have on students can illuminate the relationship of schools with society. This analysis can be possible by taking together the cultural and economic reproduction made for 'dominant culture' in Williams' words. Today, however, culture and economics are still studied from different angles, and an interdisciplinary approach is rarely encountered in research on their reproductions. Cultural education affects economy and politics in many ways. However, education should progressively affect all factors related to human life. Critical education presents the key to progressivism, freedom and humanistic living to the society. It prevents the isolation of culture, economy and politics from each other. Critical pedagogy, on the other hand, is not only concerned with the cultural elements in the curriculum but also with the communication and creation forms of society. Because for critical pedagogy, the school is not just a building. Public intellectuals should take seriously the real daily experiences and objective conditions in which people live. We must develop means of analysing the cultural, political and economic reproductions (or productions) of society in classes. There is already a maturing critical pedagogy approach involving these tools. From my point of view, we don't need to explore *gravity* again, the answers are already in critical pedagogy. The way we can liberate our children and youth from this cultural war is to do cultural analysis critically. For this reason, the relationship between critical pedagogy and culture is extremely practical and solution-oriented.

Education, culture, politics, economy … It is somewhat meaningless to say which of these are priorities. Apple recalls his grandfather's words on this subject:

'*When the left lines up in a firing squad, it lines up in a circle*' (Apple 2012b , 11). In this age, where neoliberal and neoconservative groups shape the dominant culture, it was inevitable for them to use schools for political and cultural transformation. It is no coincidence that schools are becoming neutral, apolitical places and are distracted by popular culture guided by authority. That is why we must believe in the power of education, which unites culture, politics and economy that affects human life. However, while understanding the cultural policy of education in the relations of curriculum, teaching, assessment and evaluation, we should also think about its connection to power. For this, there is a need for educational sociology and critical education studies.

Another inspirational dialogue about the place of culture in critical pedagogy was an interview between Guy Senese and Michael W. Apple at Global Thursday Talks. These two activists and critical educators are my role models to become a public intellectual. One of the concepts they emphasized in their speeches was 'critical literacy'. Critical literacy, one of the most important supporting concepts of the cultural resistance of the educator against hegemony, showed me again the reflection of critical pedagogy in the public sphere. Critically literate individuals relieve education from a shallow rhetoric. These individuals, who begin to look at their environment with critical eyes, can benefit from many sources of inspiration to take action and get rid of trail addiction.

One of the articles on this resistance that impressed me very much is, 'Warnings on Resistance and the Language of Possibility: Gramsci and a Pedagogy from the Surreal' (Senese 1991, 13–22). Senese's argument is still up to date because the 'language of probability' we use as educators has not been consistently studied. Senese gave me an unfamiliar option, with examples from Gramsci's concept of ideological hegemony. He made me realize that Freire's critique of banking education was not alone in the cultural resistance. He enabled me to take into account the cultural struggle of educated intellectuals, taking advantage of the discipline of this field of study, without leaving the tradition of liberal education outside. It is now more possible for me to approach liberal education with a critical point of view rather than looking suspiciously. Because rationality is the basis of traditional intellectual power, and this cultural resistance must be complemented by a broader objectivity than experiential.

In Global Thursday Talks, E. Wayne Ross has given a lot of inspiration for my thoughts, too. Ross stated at every opportunity that teachers are not passive recipients of the schooling culture. Although the authority works to shape the professional role and identity of teachers in cultural and institutional terms, they are actively involved in shaping teachers' educational culture. Teachers should question the main purpose of curriculum development, both theoretically and practically. In this case, the practical effectiveness of the theory in the curriculum may increase. Therefore, teachers should be aware of their actions. At the end of the process of creating a curriculum in which they are not involved, they should react if they are pressured to transfer a curriculum. Critical pedagogy comes into play at this stage. Through critical pedagogy, we can understand and resist the cultural effects of reflective and passive educational practices. If we, as critical pedagogues, cannot develop a reaction, children and young people cannot unconsciously and passively step outside the dominant culture. The power to change this lies largely in the hands of teachers, as long as they can be critical of the imposition that exists (Ross 2012, 13).

So, in what forms do cultural tensions appear in educational programmes? Although Ross answers this in the context of social studies, I think there are the same problems in most of the course disciplines today. Mathematics, science or art cannot stay away from these tensions with a framework-programme approach. Since the authoritarian system finds strength from polarization and majoritarianism, educational programmes are also prepared in a tense and overly deterministic way. Ross highlighted the two prominents of this tension (Ross 2018, 371–89):

1. The dominant culture of society versus critical thinking.
2. Conflicting concepts such as social reconstruction and cultural reproduction.

Ross has also made constructive comments on critical pedagogues and liberal educators. According to him, a *messiah complex* can be found both in mainstream liberal educators, who unconditionally believe in the cultural power and saviourity of education, and in critical pedagogy, which tends to transform teachers into priests who mediate students' daily life. The adoption of a macro approach in the conceptualization of critical pedagogy brought some handicaps with it. Still, I think the most reasonable way for the development of citizens who speak out, know their rights and seek their rights is through critical pedagogy. What Ross describes as a dangerous citizenship to authority is about setting up an agenda dedicated to the creation of education that combats and distorts inequalities and oppression. Here, education presents the possibilities of eliminating exploitation, marginalization, poverty, cultural imperialism and violence in society with a broad understanding and understanding in an action-oriented way. The practice of education thus turns into a practice of democracy, freedom and equality. Beyond those traditional manoeuvres such as practical voting and petition-signing, it strives for the acceptance of a popularly inspired mindset of opposition and resistance. Ross states that this practice is considered dangerous as it perceives it as a threat to the authority's unjust status quo, oppression and rigid hierarchy (ibid.).

A recipe I got from critical pedagogy

As teachers, we have the right to choose and change the educational contents. We also have the right to intervene programs prepared according to the developmental characteristics of children and young people. If policy and decision-makers see us as automats, it's up to us to prevent it. We must be involved in the structuring of the education system, we must push the conditions for inclusion. If all our efforts still do not produce results, we must embrace the schools that the state built with the material and spiritual power of the people. Teachers are not just the transmitters, teachers are the ones who cooperate with students. For this reason, we have to use our opportunities and conditions in favour of 'human'. Ross cited this choice in his talk, with the concept of 'The Wig' (la perruque), which is also mentioned in Michel de Certau's (1984, cited in de Certau 2011) book, *The Practice of Everyday Life*. This concept can be briefly expressed as people using the opportunities in their workplace (companies, schools, shops, etc.) to reveal their potential and talent. So, we educators, like in this example, should be able to control resource use as cultural workers.

Another suggestion I paid attention to Apple's speech was about the use of technology. Especially during the pandemic period, we need to consider the possibility of creating new options in social media and digital platforms, which are one of the most powerful ideological devices of authority, neoliberalism and hegemony. The school is not a building; the school is a cultural set. That's why we are not alone in our struggle. Teachers' support groups should be structured as a democratic mass organization, together with students, parents and local initiatives. We should not expect someone to ask us about our decisions and views on the education system. Teachers are decision-makers, there is no need for someone to offer us this right as an opportunity. Therefore, we should announce our decisions and claim our cultural resistance.

As Senese and Apple said, one important thing that we can do as teachers is restore our memory. So, we can look historically at how education has become a commodity in the hands of postmodern industrialization and how education is exploited in stages in the hands of authoritarian populism. Recognizing the use of education as an ideological device to constrain children and, of course, perceive it historically, is an essential task for critical pedagogues. A critical teacher should not only see what is going on, but also grasp the stages that create the result. Teachers should do this wholeheartedly, because our choices to be a teacher lies in 'volunteering to serve the society'.

Giroux, who places culture at the centre of critical pedagogy, made me see critical pedagogy in a liberating practice as well. As important as ethnographic research to analyse the cultural structure of a community is for education, I think autoethnographic research is also very important. Giroux fuelled this idea a little more because, if cultural relations are the facts that the educator ignores, then the educational process ends when the school-exit bell rings. Of course, I am not talking about a didactic and deterministic role model, it is a prerequisite to be aware of the culture or subculture of children and young people with whom they are in contact, to realize their living conditions economically and politically, and to prepare them for the ideal of an equal and solidaristic future. I think teachers should be persuasive and convincing, first. This sounds Freireien, but if education does not include the cultural pattern, it becomes a commodity that is only bought and sold. Of course, since not everyone has the money to buy this commodity, it will deepen the inequality in the technocracy of the elite. Just as no one cares much about the learning needs of children without technological devices in the pandemic.

Educators are directly concerned with the constant data bombardment of historical, controversial and conspiracy theories in order to strengthen the power of authoritarian populist discourse without distinguishing between right and wrong. Because we are obliged to speak the truth, it is our primary duty to tell the truth. Because teachers have universal ethic rules. These ethic rules are so strong that they cannot be shaken by any ideology or authority. It is like saving lives, so the teacher's principles are nothing short of the Hippocratic Oath. Within the framework of this ethical framework, critical pedagogy also tries to solve the basic moral crisis of society: the free and equal existence of human. This issue of freedom and equality – as in today's authoritarian populist discourse – is not something that can stretch, it is not something that varies from person to person, and it is not something that can be questioned with postmodernism. On the contrary, equality and freedom are positive triggers of human cultural evolution. If humanity is able to sustain its lineage, if it can make the planet more liveable, these can only be done with solidarity, equality and freedom thought.

There are many ways we can speak out and react. One of these ways is to reach our matched counterparts. This is another cultural resistance. In Apple and Senese's talks, being aware of the local and knowing what is going on next to it means resisting the populist disinformation imposed on us. This awareness automatically creates an intellectual solidarity. For us educators, collectivity and collaboration should start with thought, and then we don't have to look for reasons to act together. Therefore, we should support our local. We should notice that our student does not have breakfast in the morning, is losing weight, is tired/sleepless, unhappy, irritable or has tearful eyes. If there are other teachers who do not realize this, we must open their eyes because this child may be too poor to have breakfast, as a child labourer he/she may be exploited, or this child may be a victim of violence. In this case, the school, the curriculum or the educational approaches actually does not matter. The only important thing is to do everything in your power to protect the child from that hell of interests; that is why it is extremely important to get the child to speak first. It is very difficult to direct the Generation Z, who are tried to be raised on a 'mass-production line' and shaped by social engineering to be obedient to the authority, without raising their voices. Fortunately, there are pioneering groups among the new generation. There is a responsible and conscientious fraction that can use technology, organize on digital platforms and – as Ross told us so – easily adapt to digitalization and create the speech space itself. This cut is critical in spreading the truth and reality. As teachers, we should be in this action, because their attitudes are just as they should be. It just needs a little more collectivity. While the authoritarian right sometimes draws support from troll squads to use social media and similar digital platforms, critical pedagogy should draw its power from these sensitive and responsible young people. The young people tend to use their social media accounts as a *Vendetta Mask*, where they manage to stay anonymous to threats. Of course, unlike them, as educators, we should be nominal in digital. Still, we need to embrace young people who strive against authority with constructive contingency.

Critical pedagogy does not overlook the relationship between culture and language. Another thing I paid attention to at the Global Thursday Talks and added to my roadmap, was the use of language. All of the speakers knew how to listen, spoke openly, and managed to explain terminological information to the audience in a simple way. This made me want to reflect on my pedagogical communication skills with children and young people. I wonder how long I listen, how much I talk, how I explain my problem. These are questions that a progressive educator should ask at regular intervals from the moment he/she starts teaching. The first thing that inspired me was to include a concrete example when answering the questions. Of course, this is not a big deal for us who have moved to the steps of abstract thinking (I have concerns about the majority) but if we are not talking about the details of string theory or hilbert space, supporting the cultural reflections of education with concrete examples is a key to understanding.

Another question I ask myself is about how much I talk. This is actually a question that Apple mentioned in his speech and writings, about the fact that there is more talk in critical pedagogy than action. We need to talk about the issue of culture, avoiding the noise crowd. Educators are the labour class that speaks the most because of their profession, but when it comes to cultural resistance, we need to talk about solution and action. Of course, this has a duration; that is the time period where you can keep the interest high. All these speakers talked for over an hour on average in Global Thursday Talks. No one was bored, no one left the meeting – which I often listened to with headphones even while putting my baby to sleep – and no one was left out of the league. This measured speech also balances the rhetoric of critical pedagogy.

As I listened to the speakers, the last and most important question that emerged in my mind was about how I express my problem. The duration of the talk above and the concrete examples in the conversation are a kind of answer to this question. However, the main thing is the style. I think that our energetic and dynamic speech as teachers is much more effective than our static and controlling speech. This is a fact that we all have fixed with experience during our student years. However, speaking both by simplifying it and by adopting a certain style has not lost its rhetorical value for ages. The rhetorical integrity provided by the speaker having moral virtues, being cautious about the discussions he created (ethos), encouraging the listener to ask questions and being drawn to the speech (pathos), integrating and convincing from each other (speaker and listener), understanding differences (logos), are examples of good speech for teachers.

A long prescription indicates that the disease is also complex. However, I do not think that the cultural resistance of education will take place in such a difficult way. The way is clear, the description is clear and the method is clear. For this reason, the recipe I got from these talks includes certain treatment methods, applicable and effective.

Conclusion

All sessions of Global Thursday Talks have a high level of inspiration. I am personally impressed by the promising and hopeful state of the cultural resistance of critical pedagogy in the authoritarian populist chaos we live in. The transformative power of culture and education has created a desire for me to take a step on any platform. While the sudden cultural transformation we have been experiencing during the pandemic period, from our working conditions to our socialization, a periodic repetition of such meetings as these had a clear message: it is possible to unite, no matter where we are. That is why I realized again through education that culture is an extremely cooperative phenomenon.

It is no coincidence that the dominant culture leaks into our privacy through media and communication, while authoritarian populism has driven all its ideological apparatus towards rights and freedom with relentless greed. While children and young people are pushed to showcase their lives, while the organizational field of education is full of inequality and poverty, teachers should not just be automats that do not even replace authority's data transfer. As public intellectuals, we need to see education as more than gains from a reference book. We must go out of school and use our cultural power. Because we are strong. Because teachers do not have a supposed capital that can be commodified. The greatest power in the teacher's hands is culture and knowledge. These are not concepts that can reach the public with oxymoronic (like Orwell told in *1984*) discourses such as 'obey to be free', 'wait if you want to act', 'earn as you consume', that the authority tries to sell to us with marketing tactics. Culture, like a torch carried by the educator, is essential to illuminate this dark path. But, if there is no hand that carries it, such as education, this heavy torch would be doomed.

As educators, we can clearly understand our role in culture and the impact of culture on education through critical pedagogy. Beyond that, there is a 'recipe' effect that awakens in me above. To briefly mention this in order:

1. To use the right and initiative to intervene in educational programmes.
2. To be included in the next generation's organizational sets on digital platforms.
3. To comprehend all stages of education with a critical historical analysis.
4. To follow the culture we live in closely.
5. To ensure that our teaching ethics is not affected by mainstream trends.
6. Balancing rhetoric and action within the framework of a praxis.

I realize, the items above may seem a little bit didactic. As a result, a teacher who likes problems and is familiar with mathematical processing steps may approach the subject like this. This is how I was able to draw the most possible road map for me from these talks. The most lasting impact this road map left on me as a person trying to be a conscious and just teacher, and a mother who sees the bright face of the future in her child, was the hope that critical pedagogy could change the world through culture. Hope brings us together, and this is the same hope which meets us with our students every morning. For this reason, the power of teachers is much more than we think, while faced with authoritarian populist discourses and the tricky moves of the dominant culture. I want to end with reference to an anonymous phrase that I recently saw on the internet: 'Let's make *1984* fiction again!'

References

Apple, Michael W. (1996) *Cultural Politics and Education* (New York: Teachers College Press, Columbia University).

Apple, Michael W. (2012a) *Can Education Change Society?* (New York: Routledge).

Apple, Michael W. (2012b) *Education and Power* (New York: Routledge).

Apple, Michael W. (2017) *Cultural and Economic Reproduction in Education: Essays on Class, Ideology and the State* (New York: Routledge).

de Certau, Michel (2011), *The Practice of Everyday Life*, trans. Steven F. Rendall (Berkeley, and Los Angeles, CA, and London: University of California Press).

Giroux, Henry A. (2011) *On Critical Pedagogy* (New York: Bloomsbury).

Giroux, Henry A. (2012) Giroux's, *Twilight of the Social: Resurgent Politics in the Age of Disposability* (Boulder, CO: Paradigm Publishers).

Giroux, Henry A. (2016) *Dangerous Thinking in the Age of the New Authoritarianism* (New York).

Orwell, George (1949) *Nineteen Eighty-Four* (London: Secker and Warburg).

Ross, E. Wayne (2012) *The Social Studies Curriculum, Purposes, Problems, and Possibilities* (New York: State University of New York).

Ross, E. Wayne (2018) 'Humanizing critical pedagogy: What kind of teachers? What kind of citizenship? What kind of future?', *Review of Education, Pedagogy, and Cultural Studies*, 40 (5): 371–89.

Senese, Guy (1991) 'Warnings on resistance and the language of possibility: Gramsci and a pedagogy from the surreal', *Educational Theory*, 41 (1): 13–22.

Chapter 18

REDISCOVERING TEACHER VOICE IN HIGHER EDUCATION IN THE MIDDLE OF THE COVID-19 PANDEMIC

Nurcan Saltoğlu Özleyen

Despite my eagerness to have a catchy introduction from Charles Dickens saying, 'It was the best of times, it was the worst of times' (1859, 3), I think it would be more appropriate to quote from Orhan Pamuk, who wrote, 'It was the happiest moment of my life, though I didn't know it' (2010, 7), in his renowned book, *The Museum of Innocence*, because, in contrast to the awareness in the first quote, I was totally unaware of the threat ahead and living carelessly in my bubble until the very beginning of 2020. It was not until February that I started to worry a little bit as the virus started to be recorded in Europe and I remember my last trip to Istanbul, where I caught up with a few friends and relatives. Upon my return, the schools were suddenly closed due to the Covid-19 alert. Just like that! On the last official day of the school, many students did not show up and I left a note on the board for those who came to say, 'Goodbye,' inviting them to my office because it was also the end of Spring Term for our university. While I was writing the note, I thought this would only last during the spring break. However, now I can see that it was the last time that I wrote on the board in my class in the sense that I know it. For that reason, I cannot help but think of the aforementioned opening lines of *The Museum of Innocence*. I was too optimistic to realize I was writing the last note of an era.

From that day on, we hit the ground running. We had to finish the term first and organize the final exams. It was such a process that we had not been trained for, or the experience we had did not immediately fit to this new order. However, adapting to the new circumstances was one of our merits due to our institutional culture, the foundation of which was based on teacher performance. Without contemplating the disaster at the door and its implications for both the past and the future, we went into a huge transformation process which was quite revolutionary.

During this process, we had to work on the final exams first. In order to organize them, we had night-long meetings with every single authority at school. Of course, the rules were announced by the administration first and, let's give them some credit here, they were really student-oriented. For the first time in the history of our institution, we focused on performance and creativity rather than the test scores, probably because, in one day, all the tests became meaningless. Then, we came up with procedures in our core curriculum and testing units after long discussions. Next, we presented these to our department and right after the board's approval, the final exams were completed. When I think of those times today, I believe that we worked really hard to be fair and I have no doubt that we did our best to avoid the suffering of students at the beginning of the crisis.

Just after the craze of the finals, the preparations for the new term started. In the meantime, we never had a break. For teachers especially working in private institutions, closing the school never meant actually stopping working. I do not want to be misunderstood here. I am writing this not to complain but to explain the situation we were in. We, as the curriculum designers, test developers and administrators, never had a chance to stop and look around to understand the phase we were going through. There were curfews, even looting, but still we could not understand the criticality of the situation because we were constantly in meetings, planning the next term. We did everything by the book and the books suggested decreasing screen time, so we decreased the class hours along with the length of the courses. Such changes had important implications for the curriculum. As a curriculum designer, I had goals to achieve and units to finish until the end of the term; however, it was not easy and I found the solution in playing with the materials.

Everything, from syllabi to materials, was adapted to the online teaching platform. I took part in seminars to get some help with the materials and I think, at this point, the publishing houses were among the ones who were the first to have a reaction and ease the transformation with their digital interactive books. Although they are the ones we blame most for making profits and dominating especially language education, they were actually more prepared than us. Of course, the change of books was not enough, because this whole system required a new language, so all the teachers and students needed a new type of literacy. As for the teachers, we organized sessions to practice our new medium of teaching: Zoom, which definitely later became the star of the pandemic. We tried different features of the application to deliver our classes as effectively as we can. We had demo lessons where some of us acted like the students and gave feedback to each other. When I was sharing the weekly programme, I added contingency plans and some ideas to increase the interaction in online classes. This hard work inevitably created a sense of solidarity and unity among the teachers in the institution. We were even having very large meetings with professors from other departments, with whom under normal conditions we had no contact, to increase the efficiency of online classes. As for the students, I prepared a 'netiquette' programme, to familiarize them with our new medium and set the standards of our new classes because, in this new order, they had no chance of randomly speaking and sharing their opinions. In addition, they had to see this as an actual class, not a random twitch stream.

Finally, we set the floor and the new programme looked fine on the computer screen. By that time, we were even a little bit proud of ourselves to achieve so much in such a short time. However, being a TESOL-certified English teacher, I was well aware of the fact that there was no place for some of my previous practices in my new classes. In contrast to my classes in New York and in Ankara, this time I was expecting my students to sit still in front of the camera and talk if they raise their hands. This was something that you do not wish to happen in a language class, but there we were, with a well-thought curriculum and materials for a new term. I also remember reading a very inspirational tweet by Peyton Anderson, Coordinator of Professional Learning Chesterfield County Public Schools, quoted fully below:

> School is not closed for the year. The building is. If you listen closely you can hear the hum of hard working teachers, administrators, and support staff preparing to save the day in ways and means never seen before. Yes, we are brokenhearted, but these broken hearts will lead to unconditional resolve in doing what we do best. Teach. Hold on kiddos. Keep watching those videos, practicing your content, and keeping your brain ready. We are coming. Hold on parents and community members. Keep a close eye and an open mind to what you are about to see. We are coming. There are no off days when it comes to all of our kiddos. Game on. Let's do this. Together.
>
> @PBL_Peyton, March 24, 2020

I was so amazed by this tweet that it provided me with the belief that we will survive this and I was fully motivated for this new order. Except that there was a crucial point missing in this picture: the students! When the picture was completed, the conflict began. It was not difficult to recognize that the students were not as ready as we were, both physically and mentally.

As a lecturer in a private institution, my first acquaintance with Global Thursday Talks coincides with my struggles during the first online semester in the Covid-19 pandemic when I was trying to look for ways to make sense of my teaching practices in this new order.

With this unprecedented system, there emerged new rules. In fact, I was one of those who came up with some of them in my classes. These rules were mostly to increase the control over the online classes to maintain a certain level of authority. As stated earlier, some students needed to be reminded of the fact that they were still in a class. So, it was not a good idea to connect when they were still lying on their bed or keeping their cameras off during the whole class without saying a word. As Michael W. Apple suggested in his talk, the pressure now was also on controlling what goes on at home as well as in school and we created this pressure by forcing the students to turn their cameras on during the classes. I was a 'camera police' when I was listening to Apple bringing down the utopia of online education by explaining the impossibility of schooling as the new system assumes that the students have internet connections, computers, cell phones and it also 'has an ideological vision of what the home looks like ... there is a place in an apartment or a home where a student can do school work' (2020). Although I was working with more advantageous students who had computers and internet connections, I realized that I was ignoring their reluctance to show their rooms. I was just assuming that the students can find a small place to attend the class and they can turn on their cameras there. Living in an age where personal privacy has utmost importance, the use of a camera in class felt like a breach of privacy after hearing Apple and it was totally inconsiderate of me to disregard the conditions in which my students were living. Especially at the beginning of online education, more students were unwilling to even turn on their microphones to talk because, when they turned it on, we could hear background noises of other family members talking, siblings screaming, roosters crowing. So, there was a life going on in each house and asking the students to stop life in their homes for a few hours was not realistic.

To be honest, before the pandemic, I was an advocate of online education as I believed it provides a chance for those who cannot travel or has limited time to attend school all day. However, the lurking problem was my assumption of everyone having a computer and a stable internet connection. When Apple shared the statistics of students having computers even in the United States which is known to have higher life standards, it was obvious that the other side of the coin was not really shining. It was clear that the new system was feeding on inequalities, and obviously far from emancipating individuals from ideological or social pressures. In other words, its implications were exactly the opposite of what critical pedagogy aimed for. Therefore, the myth of accessibility through online education collapsed for me when I experienced it. Of course, I cannot deny the fact that it has its own merits for those who are actually ready and eager for it. However, when you try to turn it to a key that fits all locks, it does not work, as the conditions are not equal.

Throughout his enlightening session, Apple also pointed out to the fact that the virus literally made the disadvantaged groups of students invisible as they were now lost in the system as the schools closed. This remark totally overlapped with the news around Turkey at that time. The news was about students who had no connection to online classes in the remote areas of the country or who had to work. Some of them did not have televisions to watch the classes offered by the state. In my experience, even the students who were at home with all their hardware had difficulty because there were other people who were also attending online classes or the internet was shared by other family members, which slowed down the connection and made it difficult for everyone in the house. One of my students told me that his mother was also a teacher and she was teaching in another room, so he had to turn off his camera and microphone to make it possible for his mother to teach. It would not be fair to say these problems started with the pandemic. On the contrary, it was obvious that the problems that became visible after the pandemic have actually been there for a long time. However, this new order just sharpened the edges by deepening the gap universally. It became evident that we shifted into a paradigm where a student from Milwaukee and a student from Şırnak were actually suffering from the same educational drawback. The system was not empowering at all, on the contrary, it made the education available only for the privileged. For now, we do not know how many students will actually continue their education and will have a chance to go back to school and make up for what they have missed when this lockdown is over. So, the reality had just hit me.

Keeping these in mind after this thought-provoking session, I had to humanize the 'camera police' in me. As teachers are not the rule makers in this context, it was mandatory for us to stick to the rules, but I tried the best I could do, which was ensuring that this was a safe environment for everyone where they can feel equal and their presence is appreciated. However, my idea of creating a safe space was actually refuted by Henry Giroux when he stated there is no such thing as a safe digital space. Following this remark, we started reading news about security flaws in some of the online tools used for education. Of course, my idea of a secure place was kind of more abstract and depended on trust whereas the security flaws were actual threats to basic individual rights. But still, I tried reaching out every student via email and arranging office hours to keep in contact because being invisible in a language class also meant losing motivation and purpose. In contrast to the traditional classroom, where we tend to 'silence students', as Antonia Darder suggested in her talk, this time we asked students to talk and be visible as much as they can because this was the only way for ensuring communication, no matter how broken it was.

Another factor that affected my teaching practice came to light after Darder's talk. Although it was liberating to attend a lecture from any part of the world, not being in a class physically led to confusion and alienation, which could also be observed in students' missing the quizzes or the deadlines of assignments even though they were literally bombarded with reminders in class and via emails and online education tools. This talk has also helped me to confront how strict curriculum and standardized testing practices led to the ignorance of the body in classroom, which was one of the ailments of my own classes in pre-Covid days. Therefore, I could not help but to appreciate the importance of physicality in the classroom. Walking around the class for vocabulary-learning galleries, working in pairs or groups, making presentations in front of the class were actually the tools that helped creating classroom dynamics. Now it is hard to imagine if we can go back to those practices as we are so accustomed to the term 'physical distancing'.

Despite the difficulties of virtualized classrooms, I found hope in Henry Giroux's talk when he encouraged teachers to have their own agenda, and this was possible through the materials used in classrooms. It was our responsibility as teachers to help students become more independent of pressures in an age where 'pedagogy becomes a force of enormous oppression that excludes questions of ethics, questions of social responsibility, questions of justice, questions of power, questions of values . . . this is a very oppressive pedagogy' (Giroux 2020). Regardless of the borders, critical pedagogy was the key solution to the problems that I started to recognize with the pandemic through Global Thursday Talks.

As a person new to critical pedagogy, I was really finding relief in seeing many people from different parts of the world had similar concerns and were experiencing exactly the same problems. So, these weekly talks became a platform for me, where I can listen to prominent figures of the field, share my concerns and feel a sense of belonging to a group in these turbulent days.

I preferred to describe the days as turbulent because online teaching was manageable in many ways if you ignore the factors, some of which are discussed above, and at the beginning of the online teaching term we started hearing teachers whose contracts have been cancelled or salaries were halved. Working in an environment of brutal capitalism, we could not help worrying about our jobs and I remember sharing this concern with Guy Senese in one of the talks and I still cannot forget the sincerity of the answer and the effect of it in my life. When Senese answered my question, he also shared an experience when he worked for an institution as an online teacher and how automated his work became. At that point, he also realized that if there is a cheaper worker, he can be replaced. This sense of insecurity was exactly the carbon copy of my feelings. However, I was totally enlightened as Senese continued his speech:

> Welcome to the world of the ordinary worker because that automation that concentration has been a force that has accelerated the exploitation of the workers against machines, putting workers against machines we are now in that world ourselves as teachers. It gives us more empathy and sympathy for those who were threatened by automation, unemployment. Maybe being fired or being replaced. All I can say is it helps our sympathy . . . because they are us now.
>
> 2020

I think this was one of the key moments in my career to assist me in understanding my position in the society. Until this time, I had never felt insecure about my job and I was confident of my skills. However, the pandemic showed me that whatever your skills are, you might be unemployed if there are no students or enough demand for your teaching skills. Therefore, as Senese suggested, I was actually sharing the concerns of a blue-collar worker, which I had never thought of before. Interestingly, with the closing of the schools, a kind of a hatred campaign in Turkey started against teachers, especially for those who worked in state schools. On social media, many people were blaming teachers for not working and being unwilling to go back to school. It would be ridiculous to try defending teachers by listing their workload during the pandemic, but this discussion was really disappointing for people like me, who are trying to reach out to everyone around. They are probably comparing the teacher with an office worker and looking for billable hours for the payment, which is far from the reality of a teacher's life. However, there are some school owners who probably share the same opinion with these people because we hear that some of the K-12 students in private schools are attending six to eight hours of online classes a day. This is not bearable for students at that age. It is even difficult for adults. There is no way of staying on the screen for such long hours. Once again, unfortunately, we see that quality is defeated by the quantity and private institutions try to promote this unbearable system as the 'best' education during the pandemic.

In conclusion, reminiscing about the days before the pandemic, it would be fair to say that we were not living the best of our lives in terms of education. It was already unequal and too much testing-oriented. For decades, education has been the element that can be easily given up in case of crisis. In order to avoid this happening to our students, it is in the teachers' hands again to be the voice of the silent child in the remote area of the country and to be the leader for the one who cannot regularly attend the classes because of poverty. No one can claim that we will totally go back to our normal lives when this is all over. It is clear that we will definitely have a new normal, and as a person who believes in the good in humanity, I think now we have a chance to redesign the education system and make it at least more student-oriented. As I always repeated in our weekly meetings with our colleagues, when these days are over, our students probably will not be talking about the grades they got, but they will remember their teachers' approach to them and how they felt during the classes in the middle of the pandemic. For this reason, let's try to hear them more and be ready for transformation.

References

Anderson, Peyton (@PBL_Peyton) (2020) 'School is not closed for the year. The building is.' Twitter post, 24 March. Available at: https://twitter.com/PBL_Peyton/status/1242236378827706370 (accessed 3 January 2021).

Apple, Michael W. (2020) 'Global Thursday Talks', filmed July 2020, Video, 27:23. Available at: https://www.youtube.com/watch?v=Xv0HhB_3gNQ&t=1228s (accessed 30 July 2020).

Dickens, Charles (2003 [1859]) *A Tale of Two Cities* (New York: Penguin Classics).

Giroux, Henry (2020) 'Global Thursday Talks: Henry Giroux on critical issues in education during pandemic', filmed August 2020, Video, 21:48. Available at: https://www.youtube.com/watch?v=tRA3ZMbPaDc (accessed 24 August 2020).

Pamuk, Orhan (2010) *The Museum of Innocence* (London: Faber and Faber).

Senese, Guy (2020) 'Global Thursday Talks', filmed June 2020, Video, 91:15. Available at: https://www.youtube.com/watch?v=-l6J0S7xtZs (accessed 17 July 2020).

Chapter 19

MOVING FORWARD

Fatma Mızıkacı and Eda Ata

In this volume, the idea of building communities has started with reverence to Paulo Freire and his legacy of critical pedagogy that once more becomes extremely vital to have in the times of Covid-19 pandemic. Nearly two years after we started to gather the community in June 2020, we could foresee that the management of the pandemic did not come to its end without much damage to the human being, to the earth and to the values that made us survive in crisis. The pandemic undoubtedly has not remained as a health issue only but it is once more understood that health is strictly bound with social, economic and racial inequalities generated politically. The moment the pandemic started, thousands of people lost their life as they were under higher risk of the Covid-19 virus because of their ethnicity, socioeconomic status and the geography of where they lived. It is revealed that there is a large scale of deprivation from health services, vaccination and safe food and water in certain groups such as African Americans, immigrants, women, LGBTI+, handicapped, children and adults living in poverty due to socioeconomic inequalities in society.

Where are we now?

There is evidence that deprivation of education is as crucial as of health. The world communities have witnessed that public-schooling has failed; teachers have been inactivated; students of all ages have been deprived of their rights to education; forms of education have been reduced to online courses; and the online forms of education have rendered pedagogy to a simple form of training. The era was soon marked by a global online education market, where one can buy education, teachers, professors, courses, friends, skills, knowledge freely but not free of charge. Building this online education market, using Henry A. Giroux's terms, is a process of 'elimination of public imagination' and 'manufacturing ignorance'. For the interests of online education market suppliers, education has to be presented as an elusive case in relation to everything else *but* education itself, so that it is over and above manageable. This new market is reshaping the context by shaping the public mind. It is now uncontested to think that the widespread closure of schools can be normal; teachers can be sent home if schools are closed; students can 'learn' online; learning can be condensed into staying online; teaching can be transferring knowledge online; and computers can replace teachers, books and educational materials. Schools passed from state to private and eventually to online technology corporates such as Zoom, Google Hangouts and Microsoft Teams. The state has washed its hands of schools. Studies showed that dropout rates increased and enrolment rates decreased at all levels of schooling. Race, ethnicity and gender were influential factors in disenrolment and dropout in 2020 and 2021 (Chatterji and Li 2021; Dee and Murphy 2021; Abedi et. al. 2021). It is as dramatic that during the pandemic, 'In the U.S., a kid drops out of school every 41 seconds' (Paraskeva 2021, 2). The accelerated school closures and transition to online education are the consequence of an ongoing project of commodification of education which could ideally have happened in an immobilized world.

In the final analysis, our efforts to build digital communities require a critical understanding of the digitalized age and its normalization process during the Covid-19 pandemic. Moving further from the first dialogues to the final chapter of this book, we become obligated to pursue dialogue with enlarging communities. Global Thursday Talks was an initiative to move forward. It has become a model for some of our colleagues' courses and activities. Ayhan Ural at Gazi University, Turkey, used the videos of Global Thursday Talks as discussion material in his graduate classes. In addition, local digital communities have been established among critical pedagogy groups, where discussions have been held in Turkish. The Global Thursday Talks initiative published two articles: one in the Turkish journal, *Eleştirel Pedagoji* (Critical Pedagogy), and one in the *International Journal of Educational Policies*. The story of Global Thursday Talks was presented as a conference paper at STAR (Society of Transnational Academic Researchers) online Conference (2021).

The issues we started with two years ago in June 2020, when the pandemic and the confusion accompanying it were at their peak, have now piled up. The global community of Global Thursday Talks had started with the topics of challenges to racism, neoliberalism, neoconservatism, rightist ideology, capitalism, new cultural and social agendas of totalitarian regimes and their influence on education, schooling/home-schooling and its dangers, poverty and education, disembodiment, social gender inequality, and teachers' isolation. Time has shown us that these topics keep their essential position as society is still under the imposition of pandemic education policies. However, the online education market has bankrupted pedagogy in its mission, in its sham educational promises. The pandemic has confirmed that the school, even the worst one, is worth going to; education should take place in schools; teachers and students should be in real classrooms. Online education has failed. It is apparently confirmed in Turkey when the schools fully opened in September 2021, and students, teachers and families have celebrated school. A university professor told me her students confessed that they had been happy with the closure of onsite education in the beginning but now they are the happiest to go back to the campus after a loss of three semesters.

Where are we going?

I am hopeful from your [young] generation; you hear and act about racism, homofobia, rights, etc. That we did not . . . so widely.[1]

—Henry A. Giroux

As Henry inspires us that 'hearing and acting' is the major point in our situation, they are both making way to move forward. What we did not hear and act on before the Covid-19 pandemic is here with us now that there are ways to challenge. Even though with the Covid-19 pandemic, profound problems of inequality, segregation and injustice become visible, it also made the problems widely pronounced and protested against. Now we are moving forward to the inclusion of larger communities and to the larger scope of topics in various contexts. We can call this 'the era of hear and act', that started as a post-pandemic case. Critical pedagogy communities will be empowered as we answer the questions: Hear what? Hear how? Act how?

As the Global Thursday Talks community moves on, the issues of the planet, climate change, eco-pedagogy, empowerment, student protests, academic freedom, women and LGBTI+ rights and ageing are included in its agenda. As an example, Dr Zeynep Akyol Ataman, a scientist in biology, was the speaker in our community to discuss threats on the Earth and humanity in relation to education. As the vaccination among the countries made the inequalities even more visible, we need to discuss large-scale inequalities in relation to school subjects for the legacy of critical consciousness. Among the less promising fields and with the political atmosphere around the world, the question now is: What do the post-pandemic times hold for critical educators? There might be reasons for optimism. With the power of communities (online or face to face), people find it easier to access each other and act together. We are proud to be a part and architect of such a valuable community. We will be empowering the community to maintain the discussions, the projects, dialogues, the work and the hope among the intellectuals and scholars globally. As of October 2021, we will explore ways for post-pandemic revelations in relation to decolonization in education with João M. Paraskeva. Paraskeva was one of the first theorists who questioned the Eurocentric curriculum with reference to decolonization, which became a topic again during the pandemic.

The kinship we longed for and found in the challenging times of pandemic might enlighten new forms of solidarity and mobilization. With the brilliant hope we could create together in Global Thursday Talks, we will not let the opportunity to connect and become more empowered slip away against all the sectarianism and the radicalism surrounding the education after the post-pandemic. We believe that education for liberation contributes to social justice. As Freire states: 'One of the tasks of the progressive educator, through a serious, correct political analysis, is

---

1. From an interview by Julian Casablancas. [AQ: Who is he, date and place of interview.]

to unveil opportunities for hope, no matter what the obstacles may be' (2014, 3). After all, to keep going, there is little we can do without hope in the era of hear and act.

References

Abedi, V., O. Olulana, V. Avula, D. Chaudhary, A. Khan, S. Shahjouei, J. Li and R. Zand (2021) 'Racial, economic, and health inequality and COVID-19 infection in the United States', *Journal of Racial and Ethnic Health Disparities*, 8 (3): 732–42.

Chatterji, P. and Y. Li (2021) 'Effects of COVID-19 on school enrollment', *Economics of Education Review*, 83, 102128.

Dee, T. S. and M. Murphy (2021) 'Patterns in the pandemic decline of public school enrollment', *Educational Researcher*, 0013189X211034481.

Freire, P. (2014) *Pedagogy of Hope* (London: Bloomsbury).

Paraskeva, J. M. (2021) '"Did COVID-19 exist before the scientists?": Towards curriculum theory now', *Educational Philosophy and Theory*, DOI: 10.1080/00131857.2021.1888288.

Society of Transnational Academic Researchers (STAR) (2021) 2021 Global Conference, O.P. Jindal Global University, Sonipat, Haryana, 10–12 December, online.

INDEX